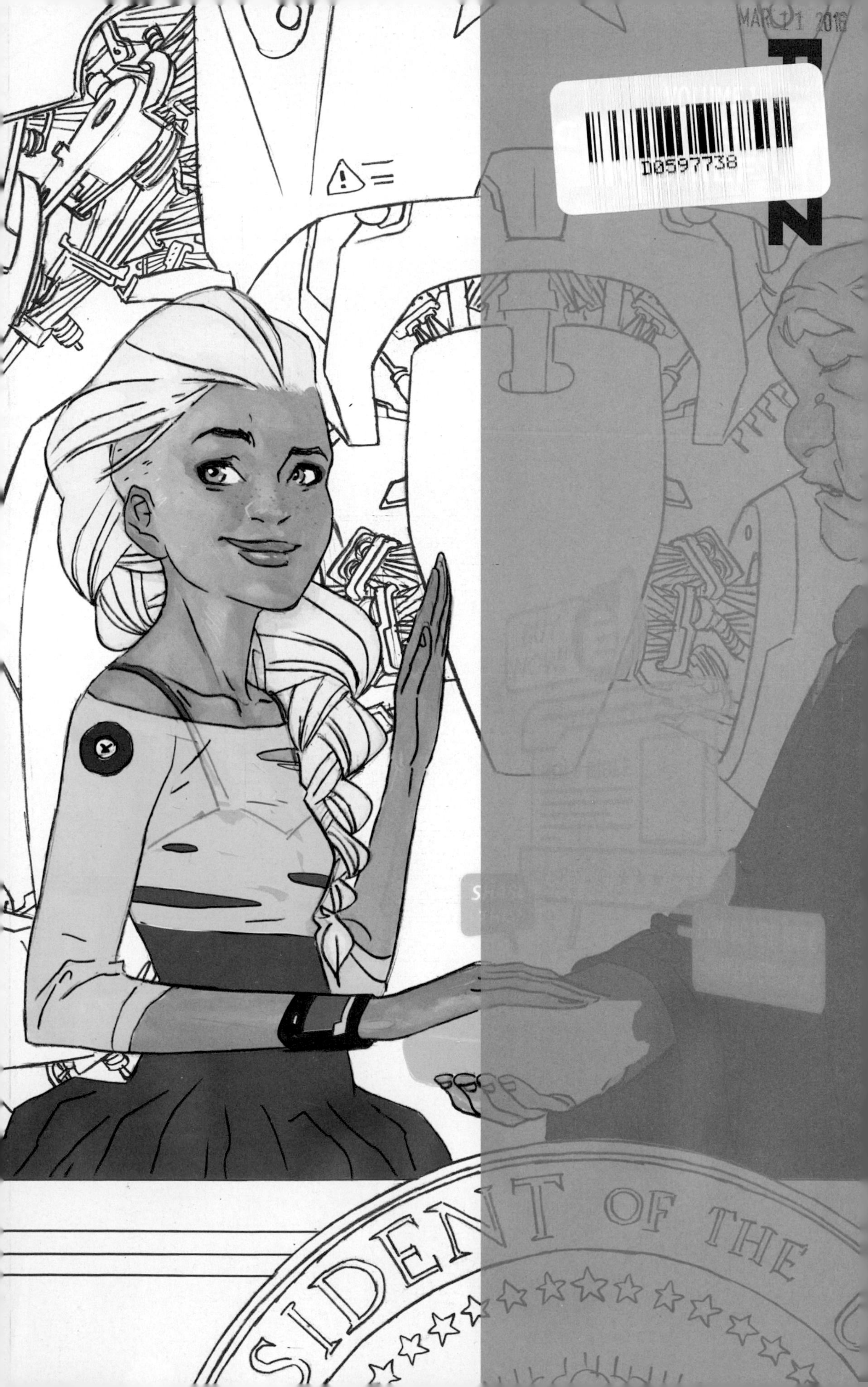
SIDENT OF THE

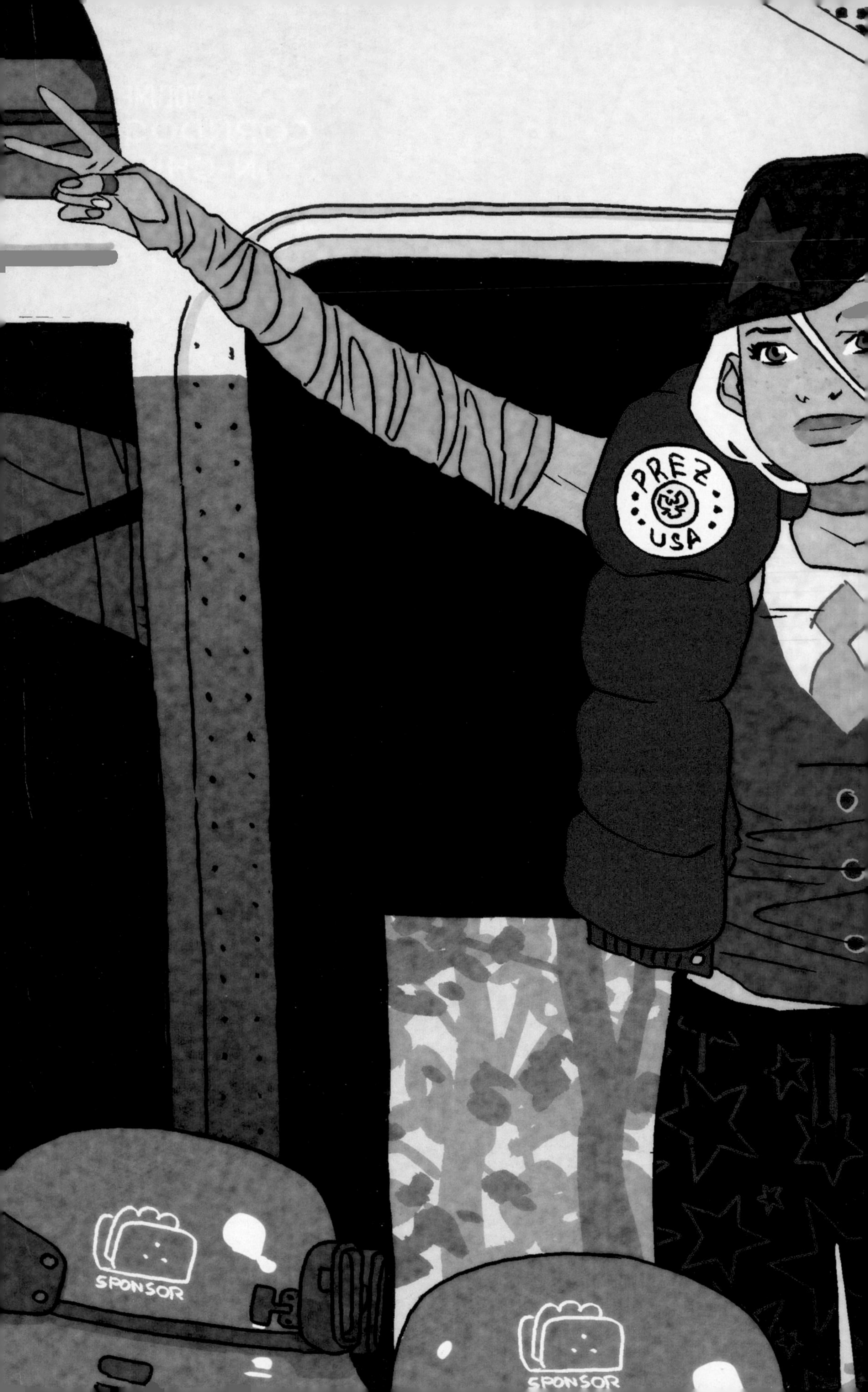
PREZ
USA
SPONSOR
SPONSOR

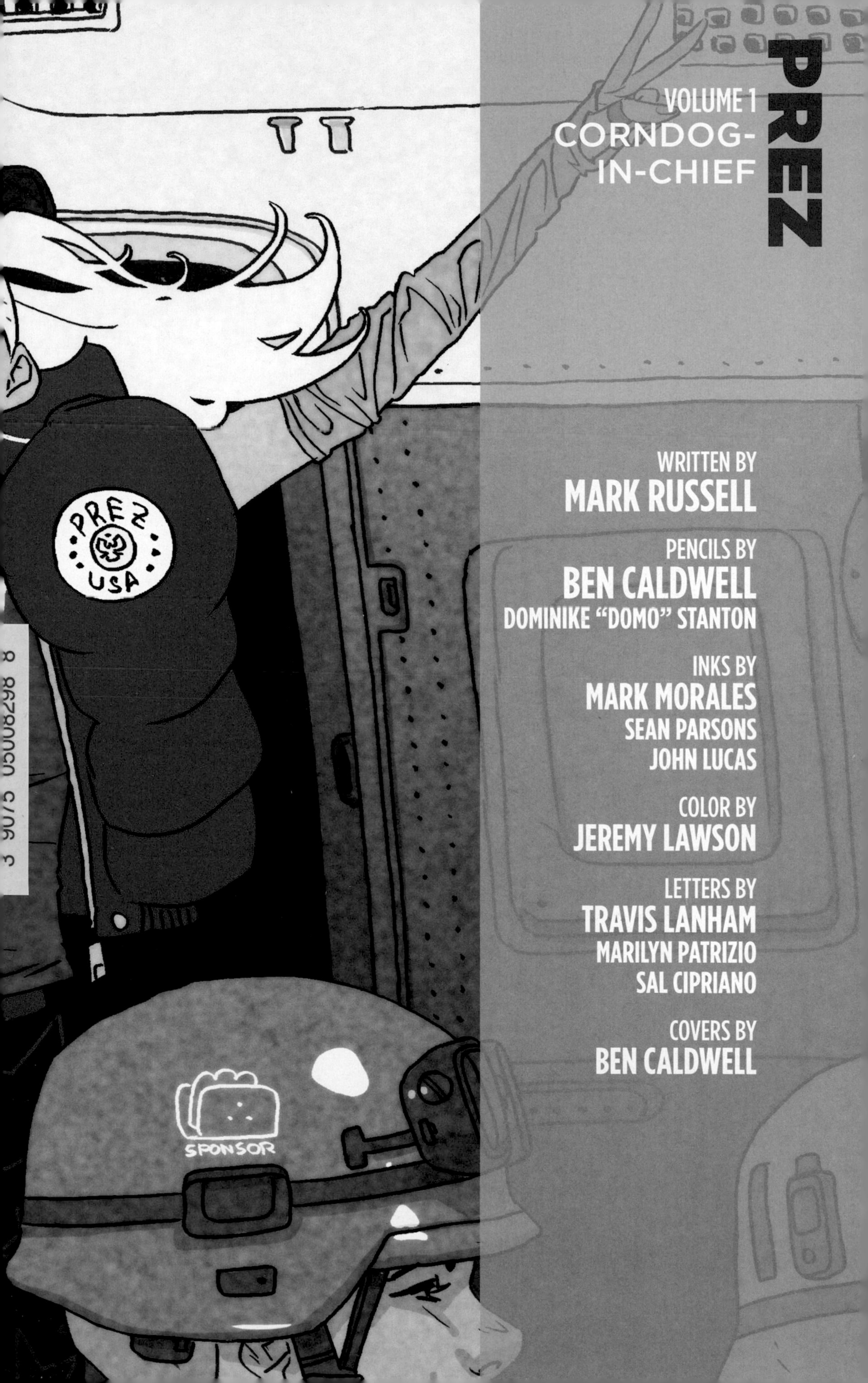
PREZ
USA
SPONSOR

PREZ

VOLUME 1
CORNDOG-IN-CHIEF

WRITTEN BY
MARK RUSSELL

PENCILS BY
BEN CALDWELL
DOMINIKE "DOMO" STANTON

INKS BY
MARK MORALES
SEAN PARSONS
JOHN LUCAS

COLOR BY
JEREMY LAWSON

LETTERS BY
TRAVIS LANHAM
MARILYN PATRIZIO
SAL CIPRIANO

COVERS BY
BEN CALDWELL

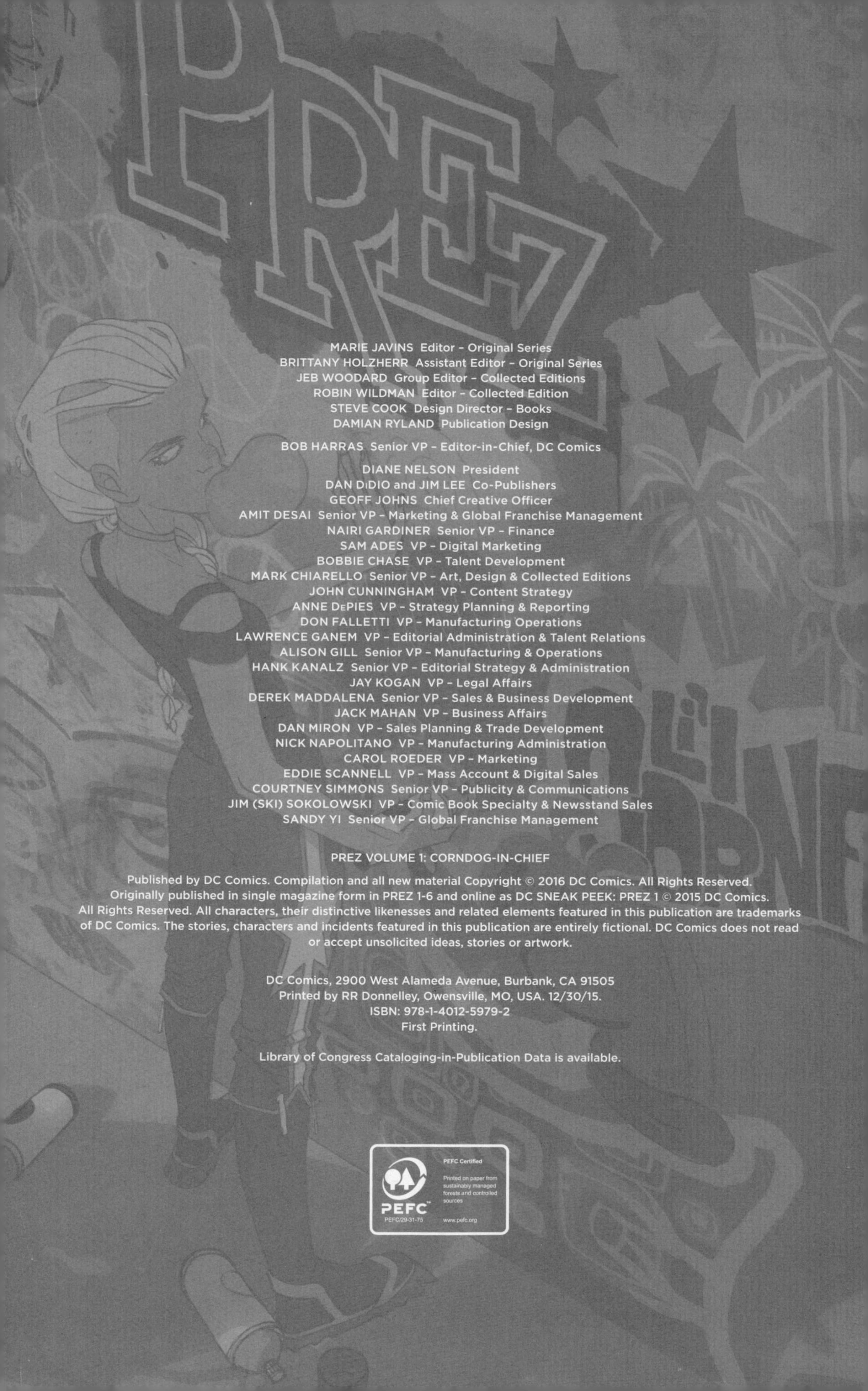

MARIE JAVINS Editor – Original Series
BRITTANY HOLZHERR Assistant Editor – Original Series
JEB WOODARD Group Editor – Collected Editions
ROBIN WILDMAN Editor – Collected Edition
STEVE COOK Design Director – Books
DAMIAN RYLAND Publication Design

BOB HARRAS Senior VP – Editor-in-Chief, DC Comics

DIANE NELSON President
DAN DiDIO and JIM LEE Co-Publishers
GEOFF JOHNS Chief Creative Officer
AMIT DESAI Senior VP – Marketing & Global Franchise Management
NAIRI GARDINER Senior VP – Finance
SAM ADES VP – Digital Marketing
BOBBIE CHASE VP – Talent Development
MARK CHIARELLO Senior VP – Art, Design & Collected Editions
JOHN CUNNINGHAM VP – Content Strategy
ANNE DePIES VP – Strategy Planning & Reporting
DON FALLETTI VP – Manufacturing Operations
LAWRENCE GANEM VP – Editorial Administration & Talent Relations
ALISON GILL Senior VP – Manufacturing & Operations
HANK KANALZ Senior VP – Editorial Strategy & Administration
JAY KOGAN VP – Legal Affairs
DEREK MADDALENA Senior VP – Sales & Business Development
JACK MAHAN VP – Business Affairs
DAN MIRON VP – Sales Planning & Trade Development
NICK NAPOLITANO VP – Manufacturing Administration
CAROL ROEDER VP – Marketing
EDDIE SCANNELL VP – Mass Account & Digital Sales
COURTNEY SIMMONS Senior VP – Publicity & Communications
JIM (SKI) SOKOLOWSKI VP – Comic Book Specialty & Newsstand Sales
SANDY YI Senior VP – Global Franchise Management

PREZ VOLUME 1: CORNDOG-IN-CHIEF

DC Comics, 2900 West Alameda Avenue, Burbank, CA 91505
Printed by RR Donnelley, Owensville, MO, USA. 12/30/15.
ISBN: 978-1-4012-5979-2
First Printing.

Library of Congress Cataloging-in-Publication Data is available.

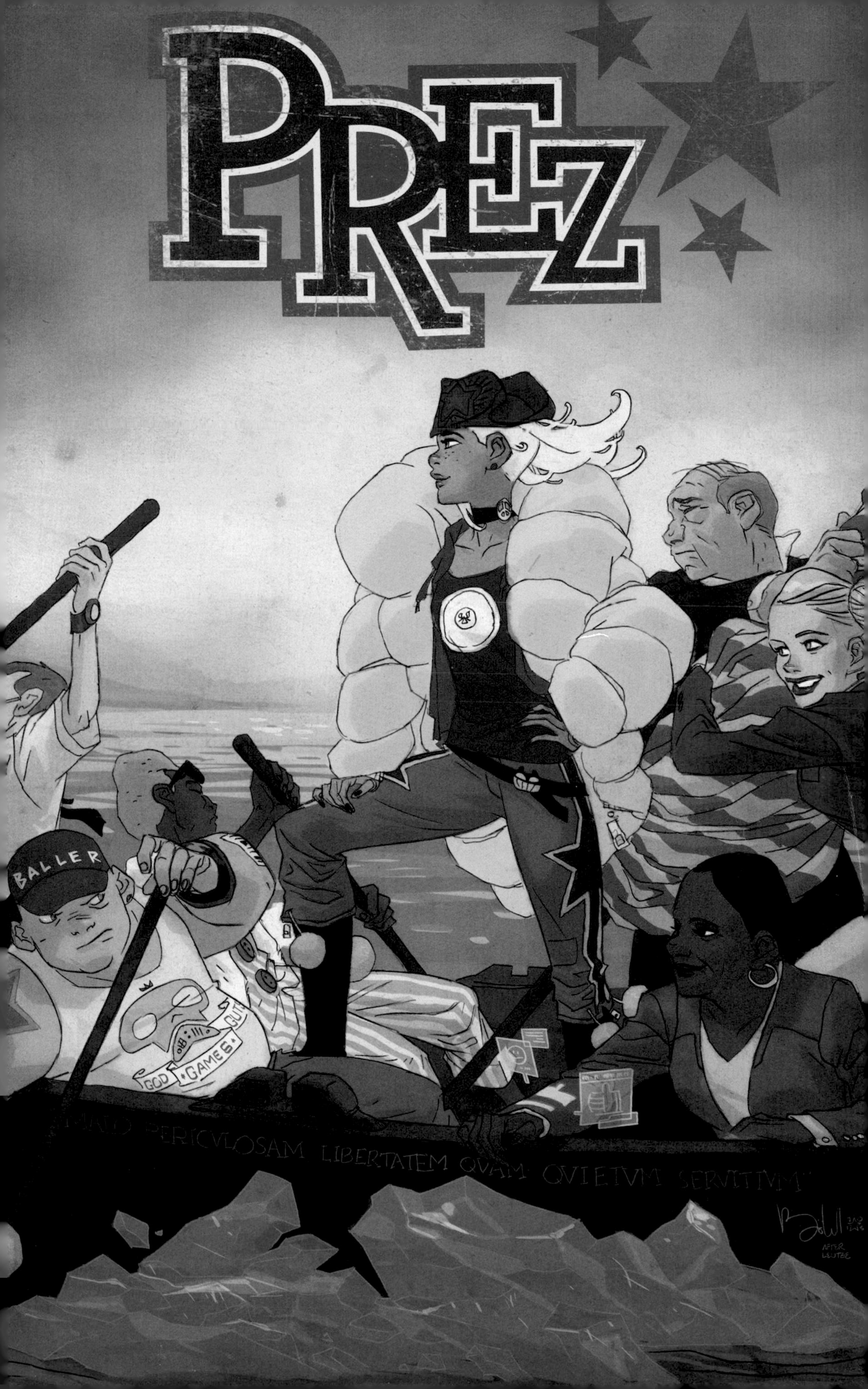
PREZ
BALLER
GOD GAME 6 GUTS
PERICVLOSAM LIBERTATEM QVAM QVIETVM SERVITIVM
AFTER LEUTZE

CORNDOG-IN-CHIEF

MARK RUSSELL writer **BEN CALDWELL** penciller **MARK MORALES** inker **JEREMY LAWSON** colorist

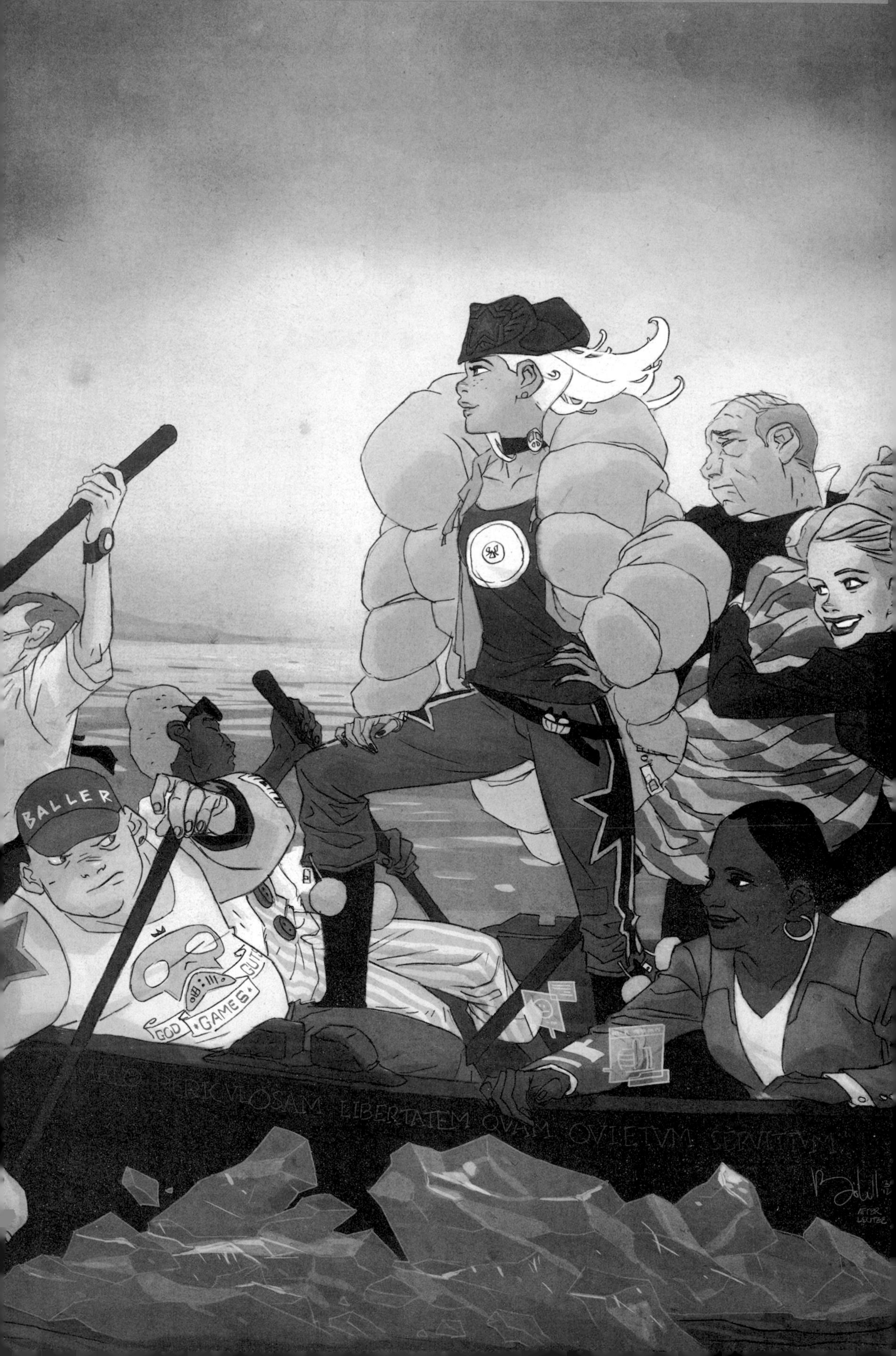
BALLER

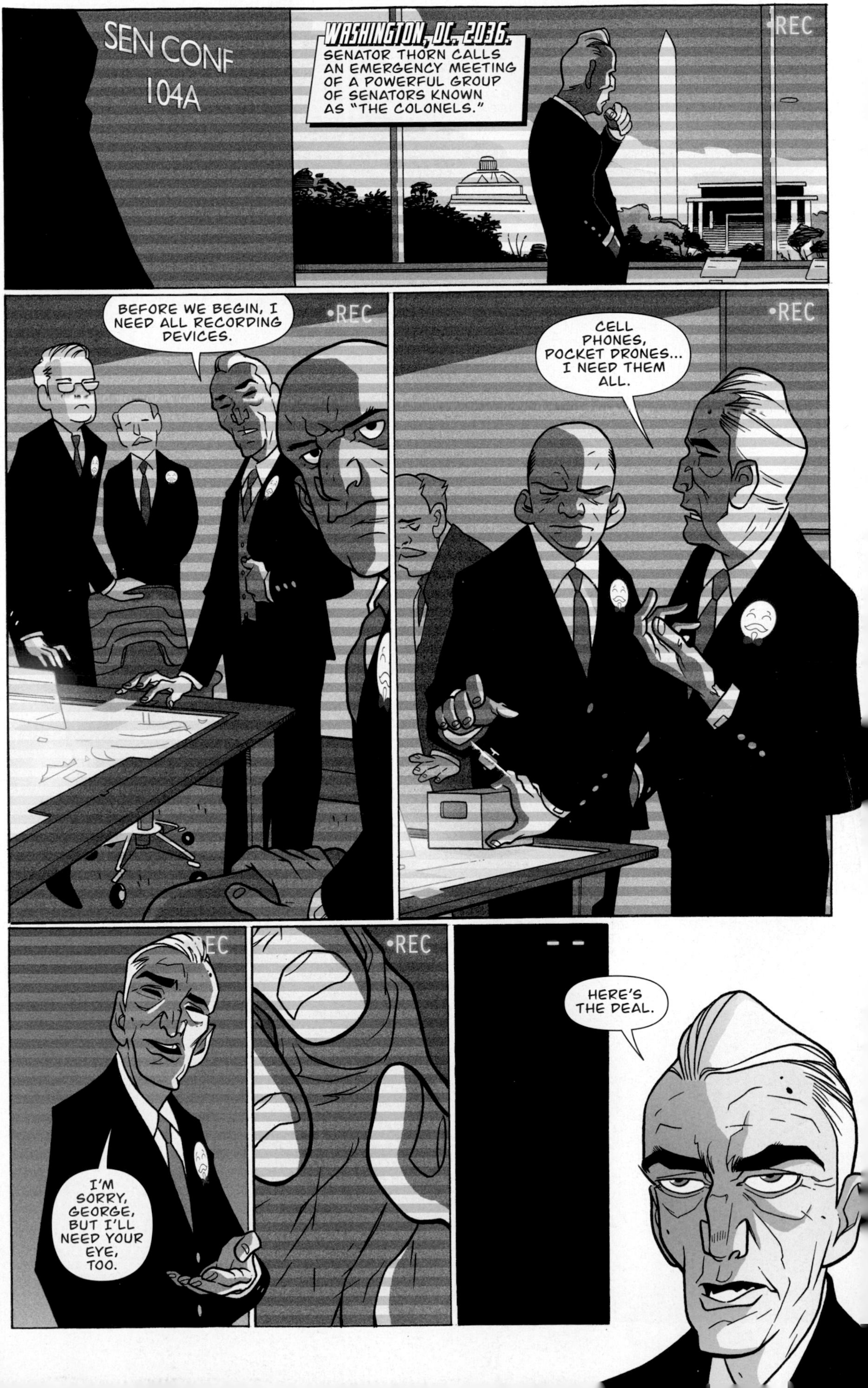
SEN CONF
104A
WASHINGTON, DC, 2036.
SENATOR THORN CALLS AN EMERGENCY MEETING OF A POWERFUL GROUP OF SENATORS KNOWN AS "THE COLONELS."
•REC
BEFORE WE BEGIN, I NEED ALL RECORDING DEVICES.
•REC
CELL PHONES, POCKET DRONES... I NEED THEM ALL.
•REC
I'M SORRY, GEORGE, BUT I'LL NEED YOUR EYE, TOO.
•REC
HERE'S THE DEAL.

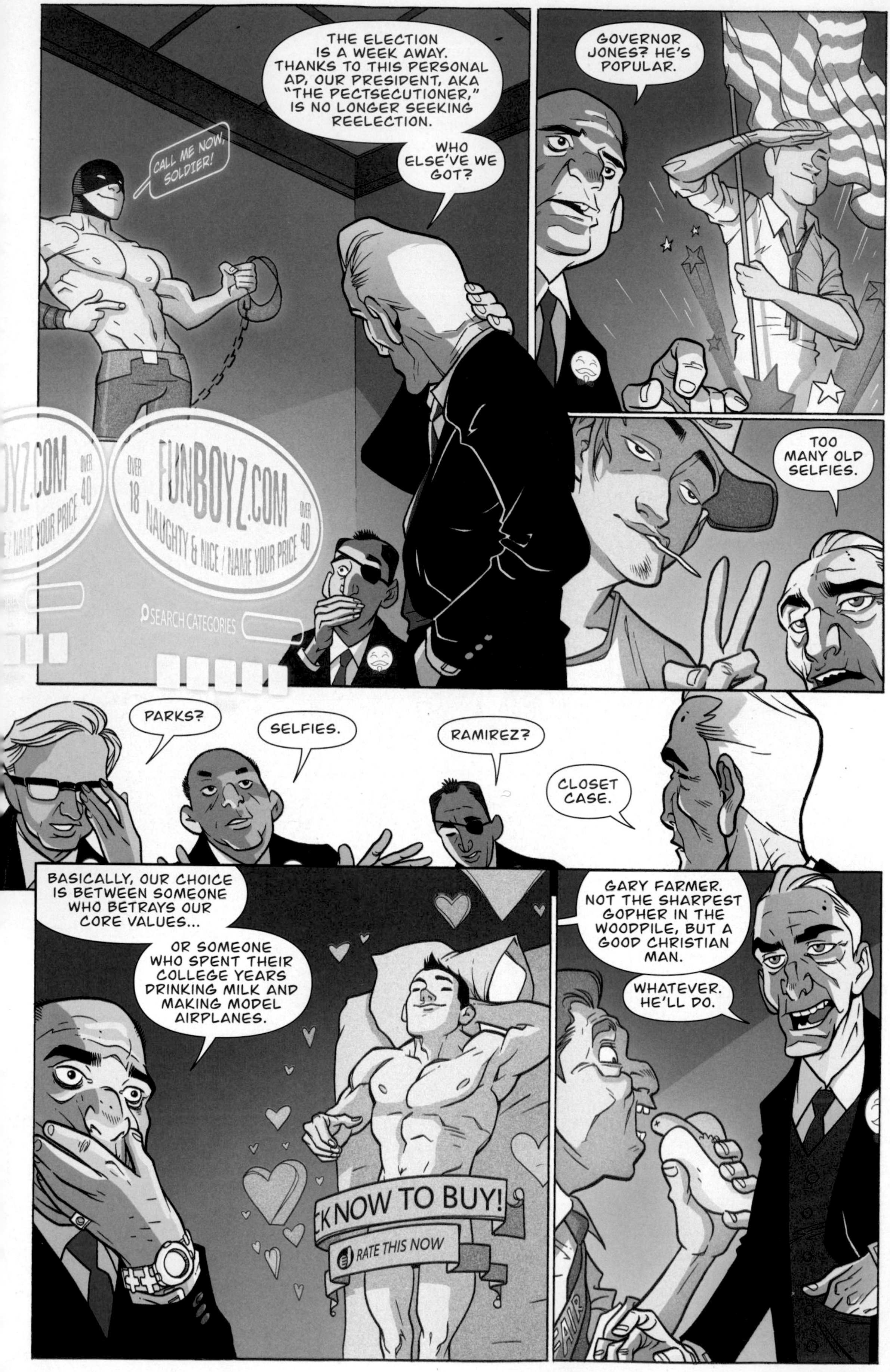

THE ELECTION IS A WEEK AWAY. THANKS TO THIS PERSONAL AD, OUR PRESIDENT, AKA "THE PECTSECUTIONER," IS NO LONGER SEEKING REELECTION.
CALL ME NOW, SOLDIER!
WHO ELSE'VE WE GOT?
FUNBOYZ.COM
OVER 18
NAUGHTY & NICE / NAME YOUR PRICE
OVER 40
SEARCH CATEGORIES
GOVERNOR JONES? HE'S POPULAR.
TOO MANY OLD SELFIES.
PARKS?
SELFIES.
RAMIREZ?
CLOSET CASE.
BASICALLY, OUR CHOICE IS BETWEEN SOMEONE WHO BETRAYS OUR CORE VALUES...
OR SOMEONE WHO SPENT THEIR COLLEGE YEARS DRINKING MILK AND MAKING MODEL AIRPLANES.
NOW TO BUY!
RATE THIS NOW
GARY FARMER. NOT THE SHARPEST GOPHER IN THE WOODPILE, BUT A GOOD CHRISTIAN MAN.
WHATEVER. HE'LL DO.

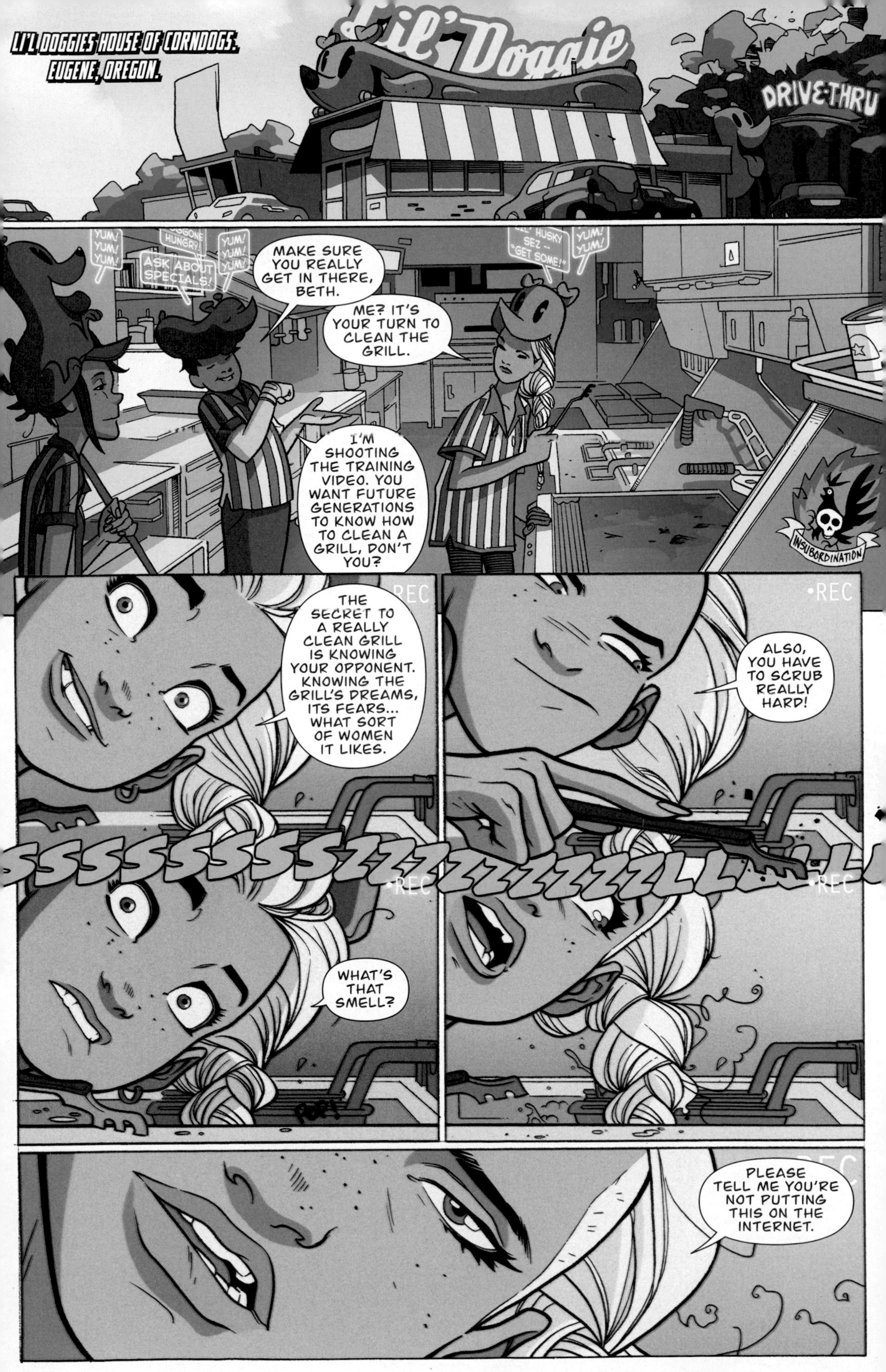
LI'L DOGGIES HOUSE OF CORNDOGS: EUGENE, OREGON.
Lil' Doggie
DRIVE-THRU
YUM! YUM! YUM!
DOGGONE HUNGRY!
ASK ABOUT SPECIALS!
YUM! YUM! YUM!
MAKE SURE YOU REALLY GET IN THERE, BETH.
LIL' HUSKY SEZ -- "GET SOME!"
YUM! YUM!
ME? IT'S YOUR TURN TO CLEAN THE GRILL.
I'M SHOOTING THE TRAINING VIDEO. YOU WANT FUTURE GENERATIONS TO KNOW HOW TO CLEAN A GRILL, DON'T YOU?
INSUBORDINATION
•REC
THE SECRET TO A REALLY CLEAN GRILL IS KNOWING YOUR OPPONENT. KNOWING THE GRILL'S DREAMS, ITS FEARS... WHAT SORT OF WOMEN IT LIKES.
•REC
ALSO, YOU HAVE TO SCRUB REALLY HARD!
SSSSSSSSSZZZZZZZZZZZLLLLLL
•REC
WHAT'S THAT SMELL?
POP!
•REC
PLEASE TELL ME YOU'RE NOT PUTTING THIS ON THE INTERNET.

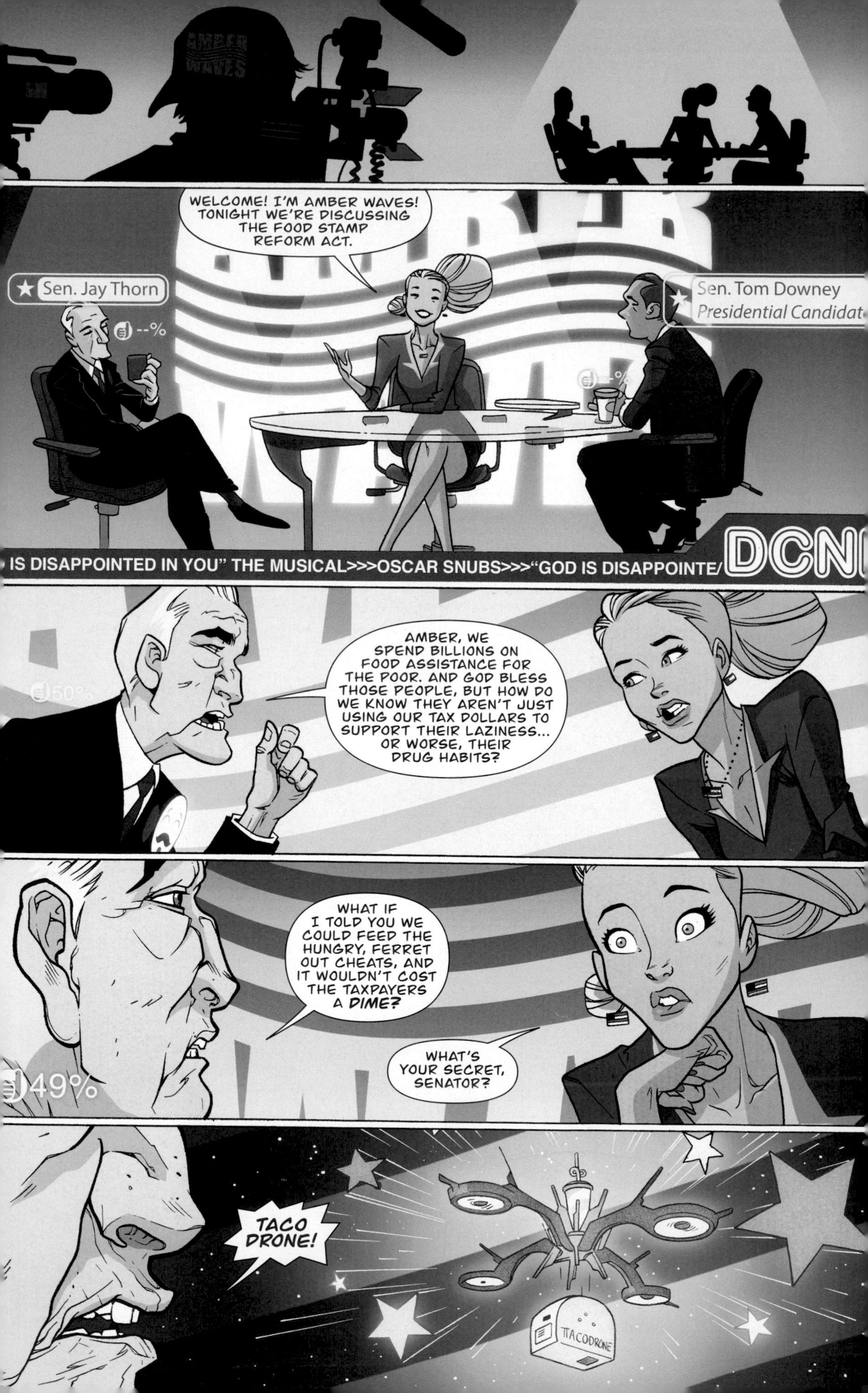
AMBER WAVES
WELCOME! I'M AMBER WAVES! TONIGHT WE'RE DISCUSSING THE FOOD STAMP REFORM ACT.
Sen. Jay Thorn
--%
Sen. Tom Downey
Presidential Candidat
IS DISAPPOINTED IN YOU" THE MUSICAL>>>OSCAR SNUBS>>>"GOD IS DISAPPOINTE/
DCN
50%
AMBER, WE SPEND BILLIONS ON FOOD ASSISTANCE FOR THE POOR. AND GOD BLESS THOSE PEOPLE, BUT HOW DO WE KNOW THEY AREN'T JUST USING OUR TAX DOLLARS TO SUPPORT THEIR LAZINESS... OR WORSE, THEIR DRUG HABITS?
WHAT IF I TOLD YOU WE COULD FEED THE HUNGRY, FERRET OUT CHEATS, AND IT WOULDN'T COST THE TAXPAYERS A *DIME?*
49%
WHAT'S YOUR SECRET, SENATOR?
TACO DRONE!
TACODRONE

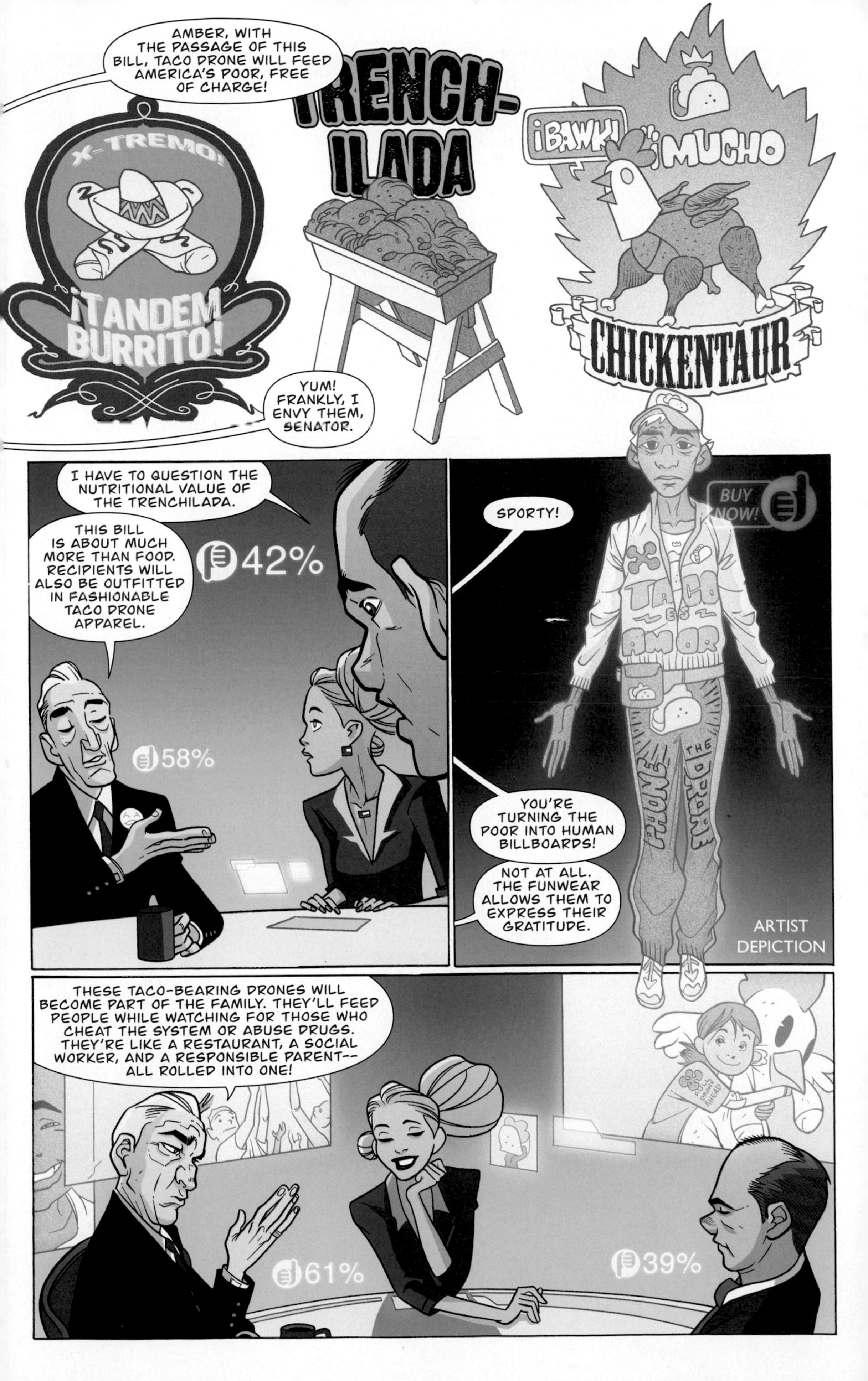
AMBER, WITH THE PASSAGE OF THIS BILL, TACO DRONE WILL FEED AMERICA'S POOR, FREE OF CHARGE!
X-TREMO!
¡TANDEM BURRITO!
TRENCH-ILADA
¡BAWK! ¡MUCHO
CHICKENTAUR
YUM! FRANKLY, I ENVY THEM, SENATOR.
I HAVE TO QUESTION THE NUTRITIONAL VALUE OF THE TRENCHILADA.
THIS BILL IS ABOUT MUCH MORE THAN FOOD. RECIPIENTS WILL ALSO BE OUTFITTED IN FASHIONABLE TACO DRONE APPAREL.
42%
58%
SPORTY!
BUY NOW!
TACO ES AMOR
PHONE THE DRONE
YOU'RE TURNING THE POOR INTO HUMAN BILLBOARDS!
NOT AT ALL. THE FUNWEAR ALLOWS THEM TO EXPRESS THEIR GRATITUDE.
ARTIST DEPICTION
THESE TACO-BEARING DRONES WILL BECOME PART OF THE FAMILY. THEY'LL FEED PEOPLE WHILE WATCHING FOR THOSE WHO CHEAT THE SYSTEM OR ABUSE DRUGS. THEY'RE LIKE A RESTAURANT, A SOCIAL WORKER, AND A RESPONSIBLE PARENT--ALL ROLLED INTO ONE!
FULL DRONE AHEAD
61%
39%

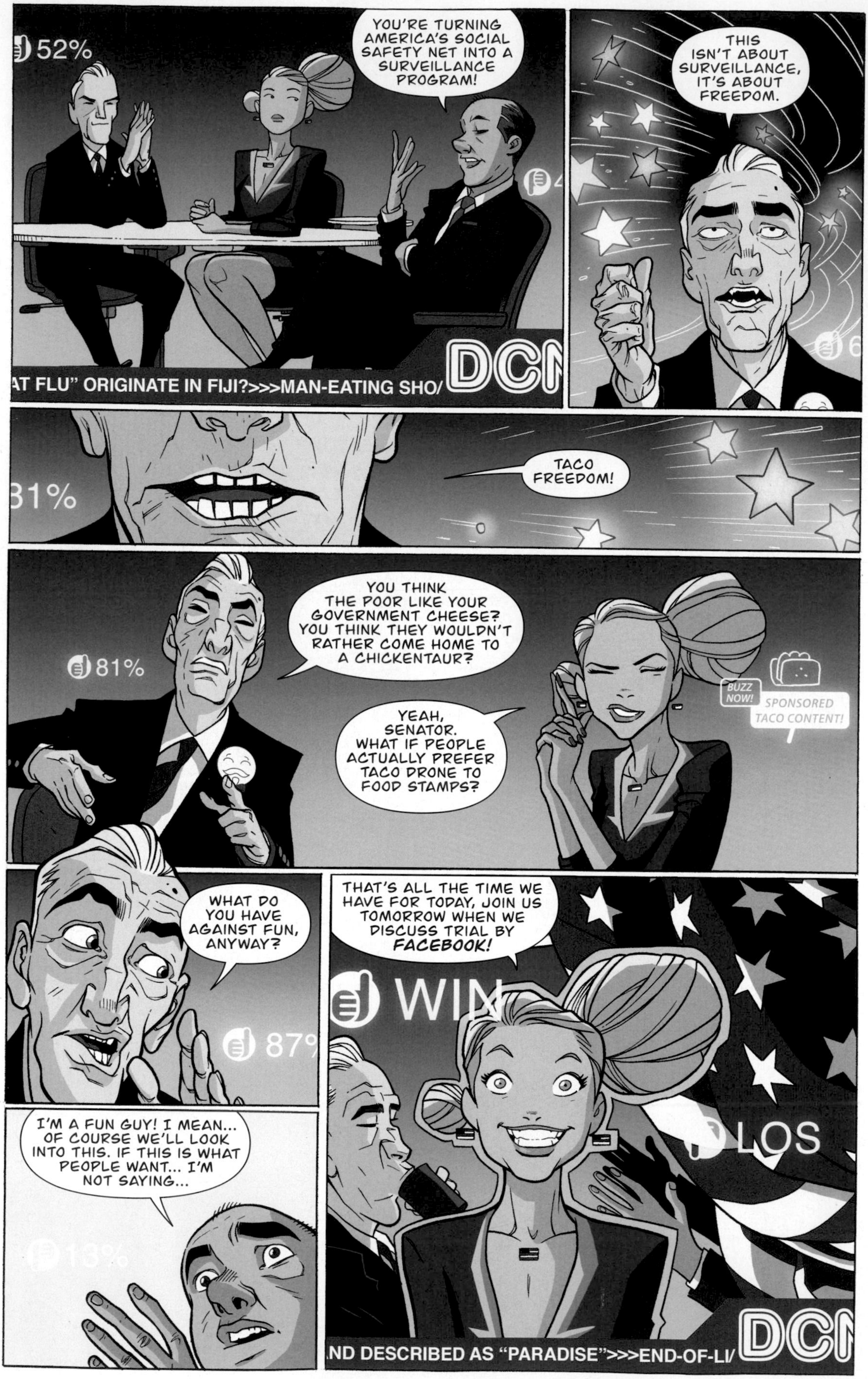
52%
YOU'RE TURNING AMERICA'S SOCIAL SAFETY NET INTO A SURVEILLANCE PROGRAM!
AT FLU" ORIGINATE IN FIJI?>>>MAN-EATING SHO/
DCN
THIS ISN'T ABOUT SURVEILLANCE, IT'S ABOUT FREEDOM.
31%
TACO FREEDOM!
81%
YOU THINK THE POOR LIKE YOUR GOVERNMENT CHEESE? YOU THINK THEY WOULDN'T RATHER COME HOME TO A CHICKENTAUR?
BUZZ NOW!
SPONSORED TACO CONTENT!
YEAH, SENATOR. WHAT IF PEOPLE ACTUALLY PREFER TACO DRONE TO FOOD STAMPS?
WHAT DO YOU HAVE AGAINST FUN, ANYWAY?
87%
I'M A FUN GUY! I MEAN... OF COURSE WE'LL LOOK INTO THIS. IF THIS IS WHAT PEOPLE WANT... I'M NOT SAYING...
13%
THAT'S ALL THE TIME WE HAVE FOR TODAY, JOIN US TOMORROW WHEN WE DISCUSS TRIAL BY FACEBOOK!
WIN
LOS
ND DESCRIBED AS "PARADISE">>>END-OF-LI/
DCN

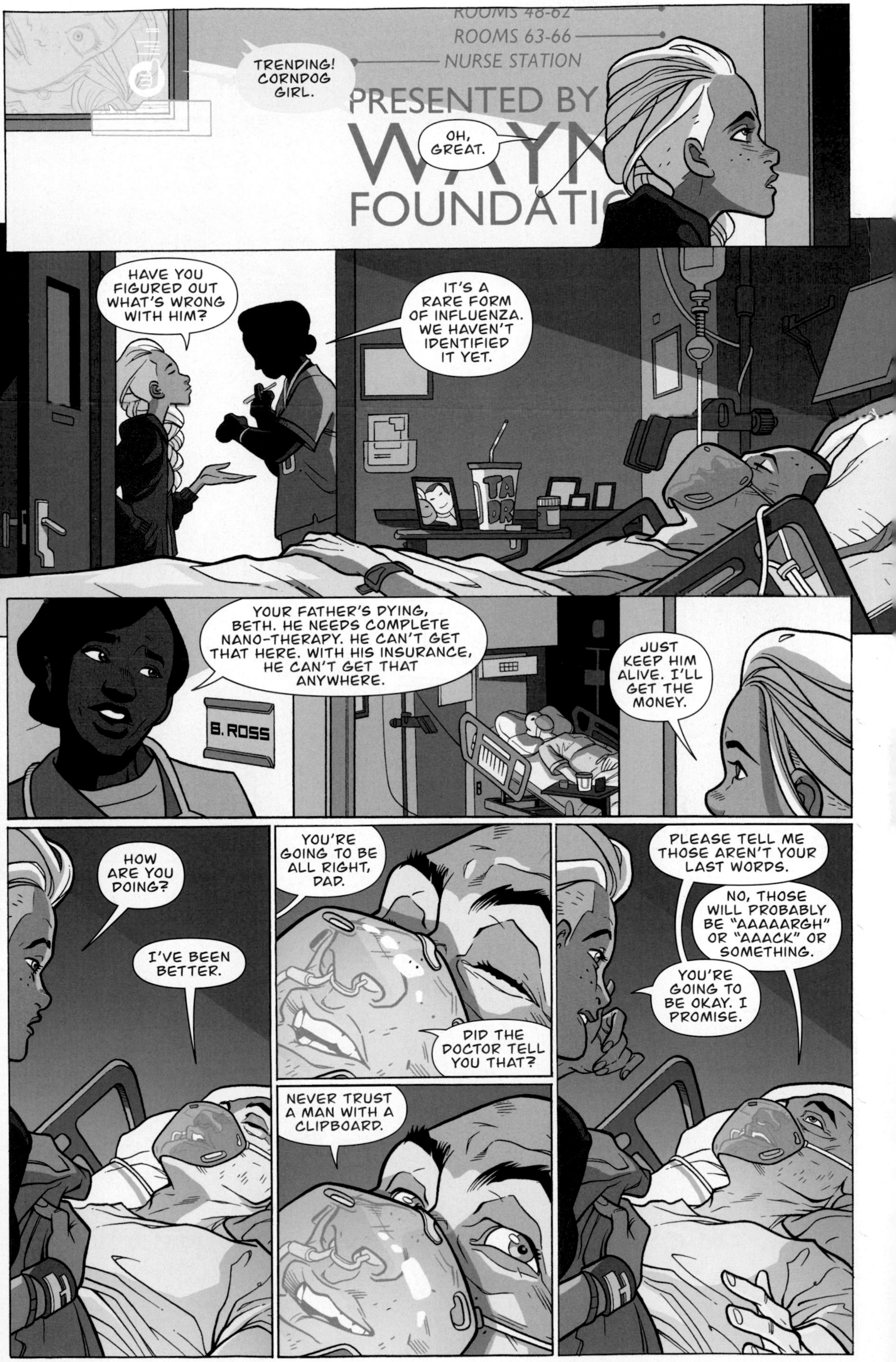
ROOMS 48-62
ROOMS 63-66
NURSE STATION
TRENDING! CORNDOG GIRL.
PRESENTED BY
WAYN
FOUNDATIO
OH, GREAT.
HAVE YOU FIGURED OUT WHAT'S WRONG WITH HIM?
IT'S A RARE FORM OF INFLUENZA. WE HAVEN'T IDENTIFIED IT YET.
YOUR FATHER'S DYING, BETH. HE NEEDS COMPLETE NANO-THERAPY. HE CAN'T GET THAT HERE. WITH HIS INSURANCE, HE CAN'T GET THAT ANYWHERE.
B. ROSS
JUST KEEP HIM ALIVE. I'LL GET THE MONEY.
HOW ARE YOU DOING?
I'VE BEEN BETTER.
YOU'RE GOING TO BE ALL RIGHT, DAD.
DID THE DOCTOR TELL YOU THAT?
NEVER TRUST A MAN WITH A CLIPBOARD.
PLEASE TELL ME THOSE AREN'T YOUR LAST WORDS.
NO, THOSE WILL PROBABLY BE "AAAAARGH" OR "AAACK" OR SOMETHING.
YOU'RE GOING TO BE OKAY. I PROMISE.

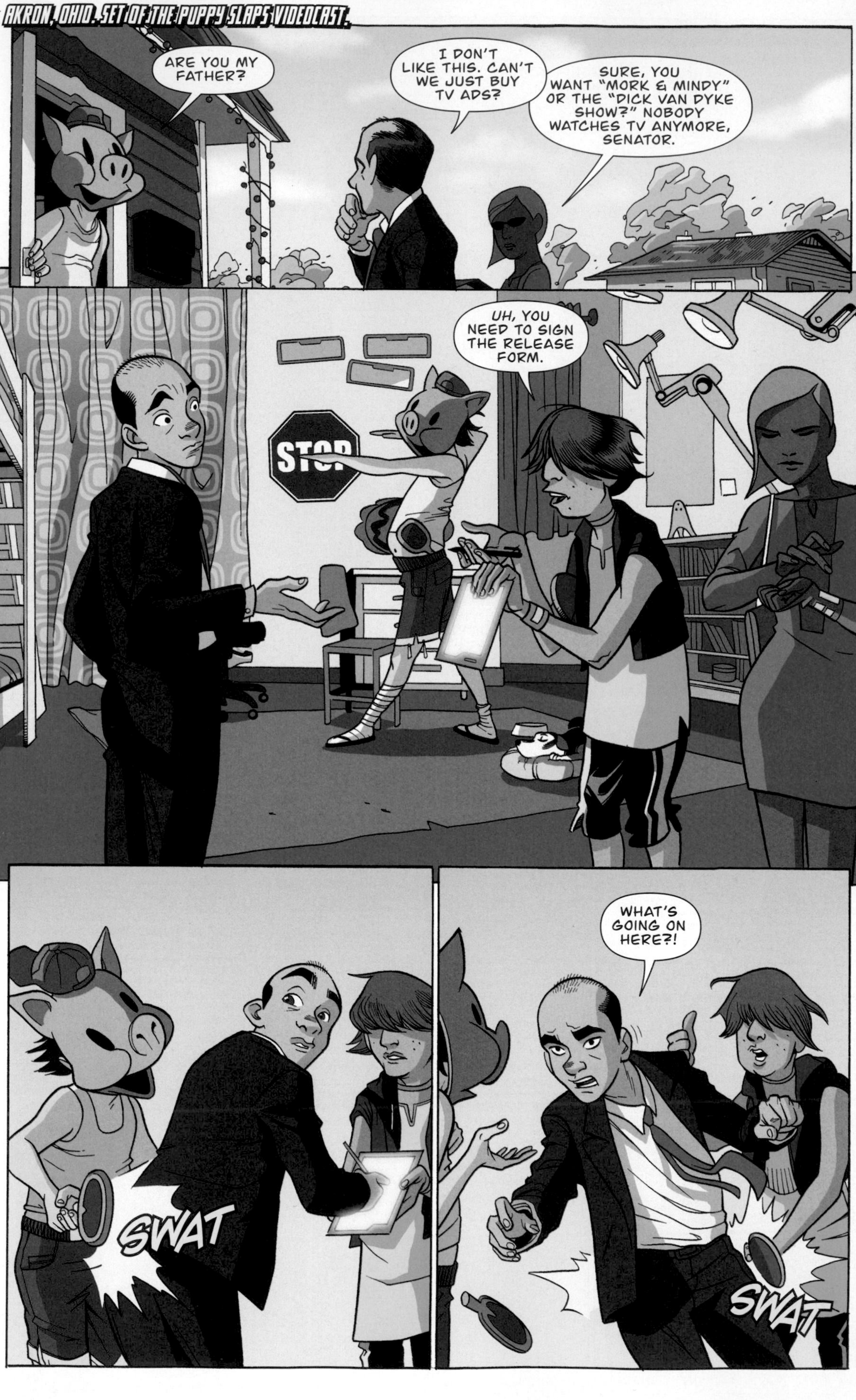
AKRON, OHIO. SET OF THE PUPPY SLAPS VIDEOCAST.
ARE YOU MY FATHER?
I DON'T LIKE THIS. CAN'T WE JUST BUY TV ADS?
SURE, YOU WANT "MORK & MINDY" OR THE "DICK VAN DYKE SHOW?" NOBODY WATCHES TV ANYMORE, SENATOR.
UH, YOU NEED TO SIGN THE RELEASE FORM.
STOP
SWAT
WHAT'S GOING ON HERE?!
SWAT

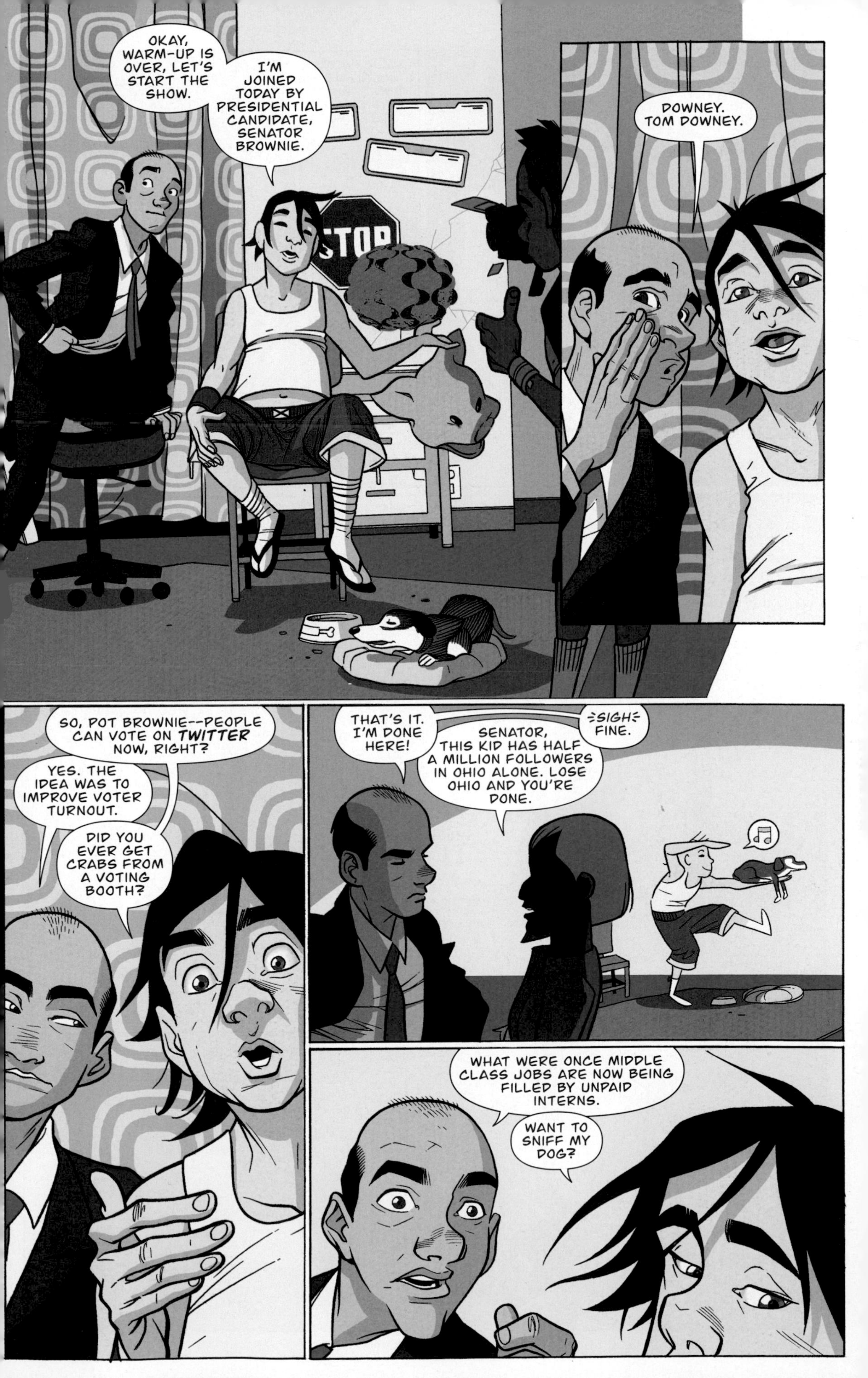
OKAY, WARM-UP IS OVER, LET'S START THE SHOW.
I'M JOINED TODAY BY PRESIDENTIAL CANDIDATE, SENATOR BROWNIE.
STOP
DOWNEY. TOM DOWNEY.
SO, POT BROWNIE--PEOPLE CAN VOTE ON TWITTER NOW, RIGHT?
YES. THE IDEA WAS TO IMPROVE VOTER TURNOUT.
DID YOU EVER GET CRABS FROM A VOTING BOOTH?
THAT'S IT. I'M DONE HERE!
SENATOR, THIS KID HAS HALF A MILLION FOLLOWERS IN OHIO ALONE. LOSE OHIO AND YOU'RE DONE.
SIGH FINE.
WHAT WERE ONCE MIDDLE CLASS JOBS ARE NOW BEING FILLED BY UNPAID INTERNS.
WANT TO SNIFF MY DOG?

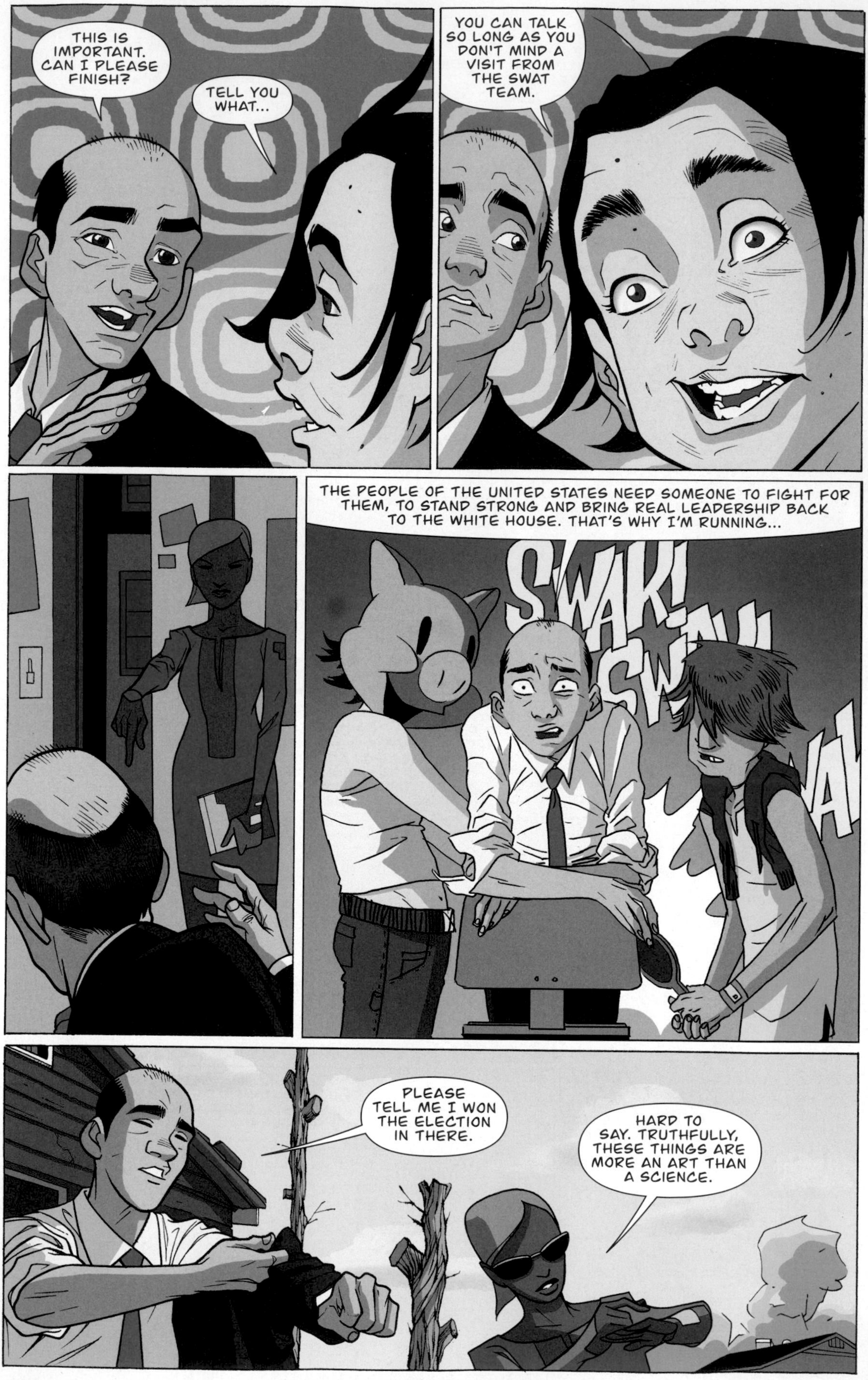
THIS IS IMPORTANT. CAN I PLEASE FINISH?
TELL YOU WHAT...
YOU CAN TALK SO LONG AS YOU DON'T MIND A VISIT FROM THE SWAT TEAM.
THE PEOPLE OF THE UNITED STATES NEED SOMEONE TO FIGHT FOR THEM, TO STAND STRONG AND BRING REAL LEADERSHIP BACK TO THE WHITE HOUSE. THAT'S WHY I'M RUNNING...
SWAK!
PLEASE TELL ME I WON THE ELECTION IN THERE.
HARD TO SAY. TRUTHFULLY, THESE THINGS ARE MORE AN ART THAN A SCIENCE.

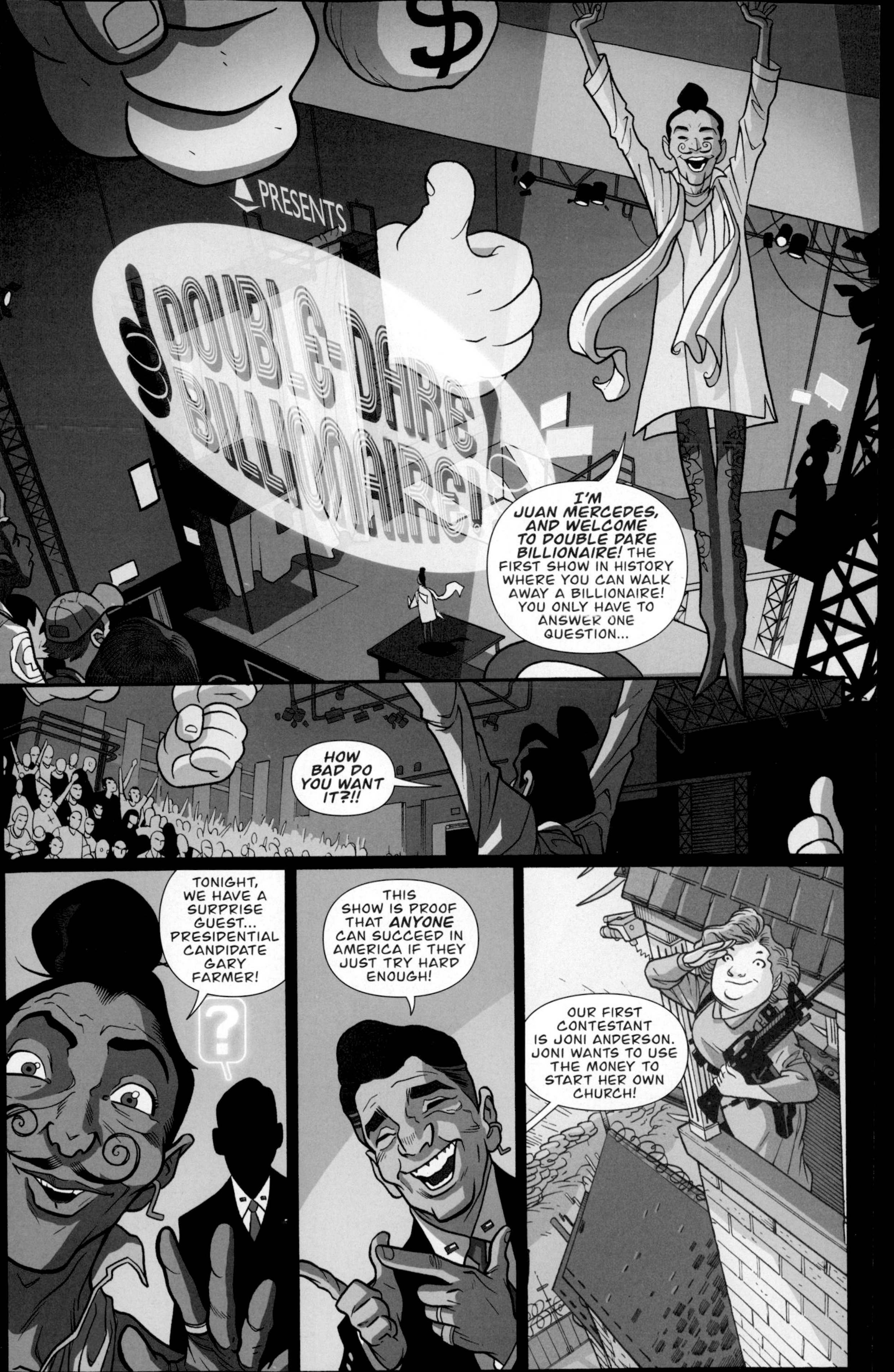
PRESENTS
DOUBLE-DARE BILLIONAIRE!
I'M JUAN MERCEDES, AND WELCOME TO DOUBLE DARE BILLIONAIRE! THE FIRST SHOW IN HISTORY WHERE YOU CAN WALK AWAY A BILLIONAIRE! YOU ONLY HAVE TO ANSWER ONE QUESTION...
HOW BAD DO YOU WANT IT?!!
TONIGHT, WE HAVE A SURPRISE GUEST... PRESIDENTIAL CANDIDATE GARY FARMER!
?
THIS SHOW IS PROOF THAT ANYONE CAN SUCCEED IN AMERICA IF THEY JUST TRY HARD ENOUGH!
OUR FIRST CONTESTANT IS JONI ANDERSON. JONI WANTS TO USE THE MONEY TO START HER OWN CHURCH!

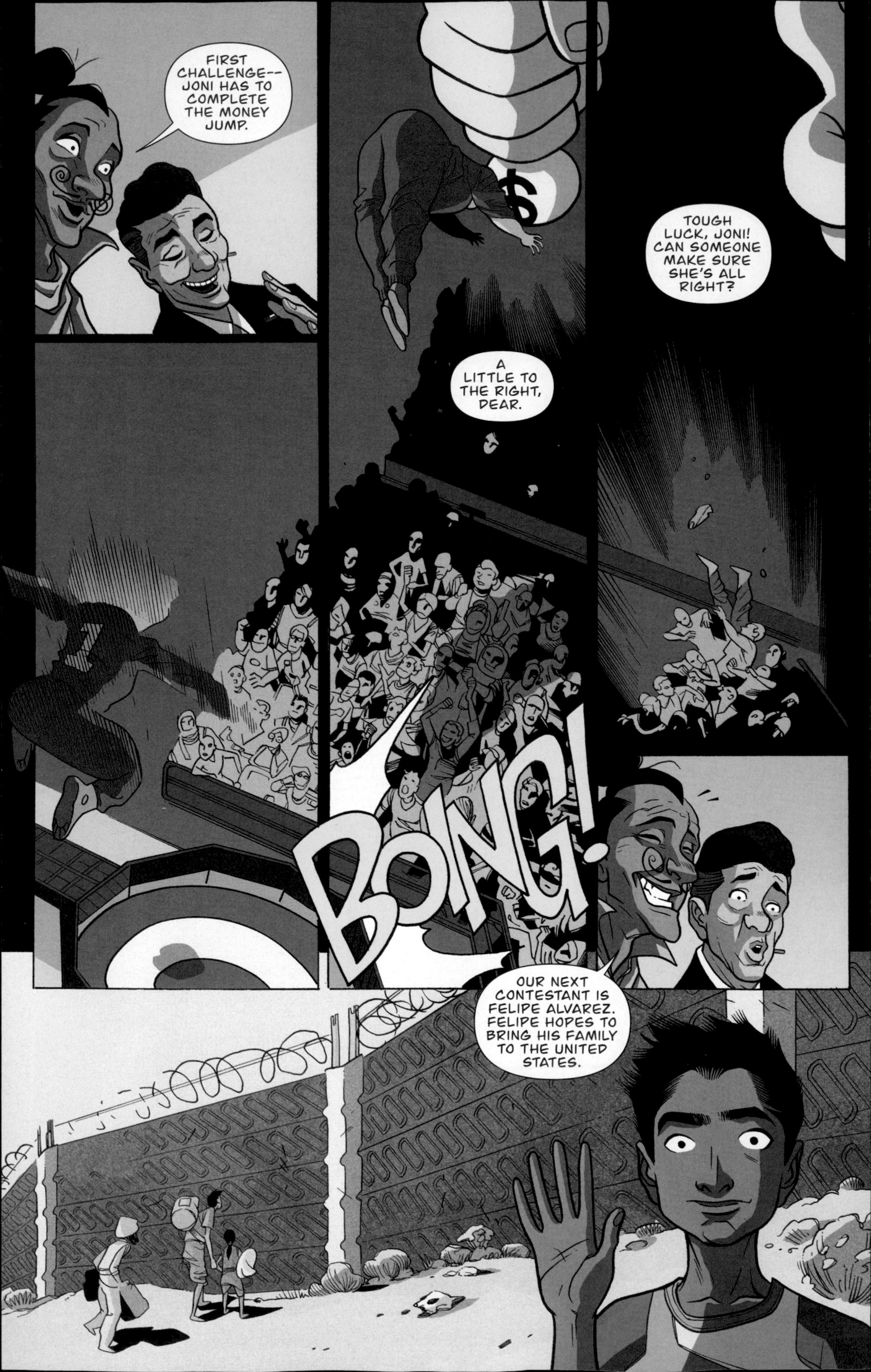
FIRST CHALLENGE-- JONI HAS TO COMPLETE THE MONEY JUMP.
A LITTLE TO THE RIGHT, DEAR.
BONG!
TOUGH LUCK, JONI! CAN SOMEONE MAKE SURE SHE'S ALL RIGHT?
OUR NEXT CONTESTANT IS FELIPE ALVAREZ. FELIPE HOPES TO BRING HIS FAMILY TO THE UNITED STATES.

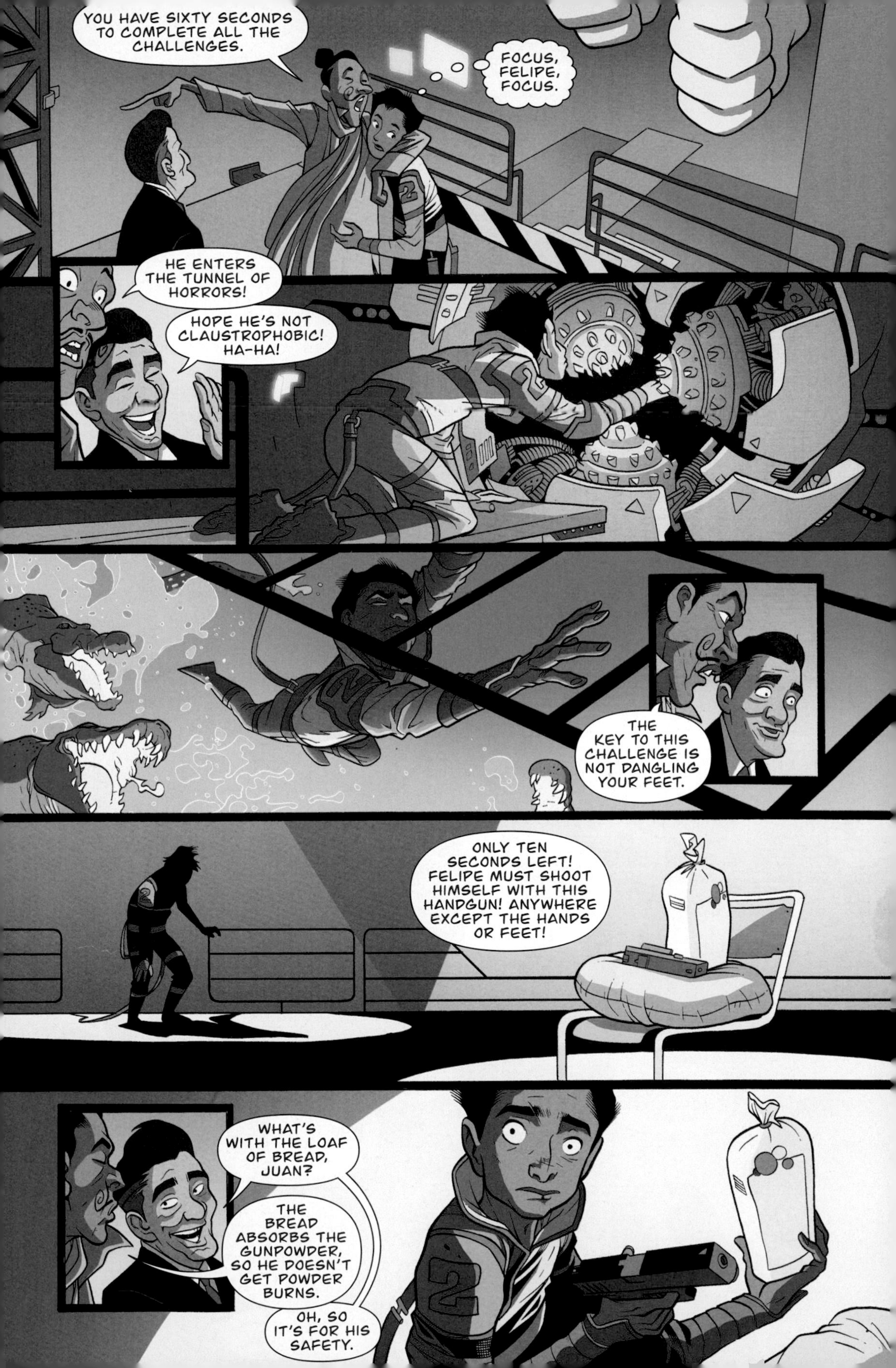
YOU HAVE SIXTY SECONDS TO COMPLETE ALL THE CHALLENGES.
FOCUS, FELIPE, FOCUS.
HE ENTERS THE TUNNEL OF HORRORS!
HOPE HE'S NOT CLAUSTROPHOBIC! HA-HA!
THE KEY TO THIS CHALLENGE IS NOT DANGLING YOUR FEET.
ONLY TEN SECONDS LEFT! FELIPE MUST SHOOT HIMSELF WITH THIS HANDGUN! ANYWHERE EXCEPT THE HANDS OR FEET!
WHAT'S WITH THE LOAF OF BREAD, JUAN?
THE BREAD ABSORBS THE GUNPOWDER, SO HE DOESN'T GET POWDER BURNS.
OH, SO IT'S FOR HIS SAFETY.

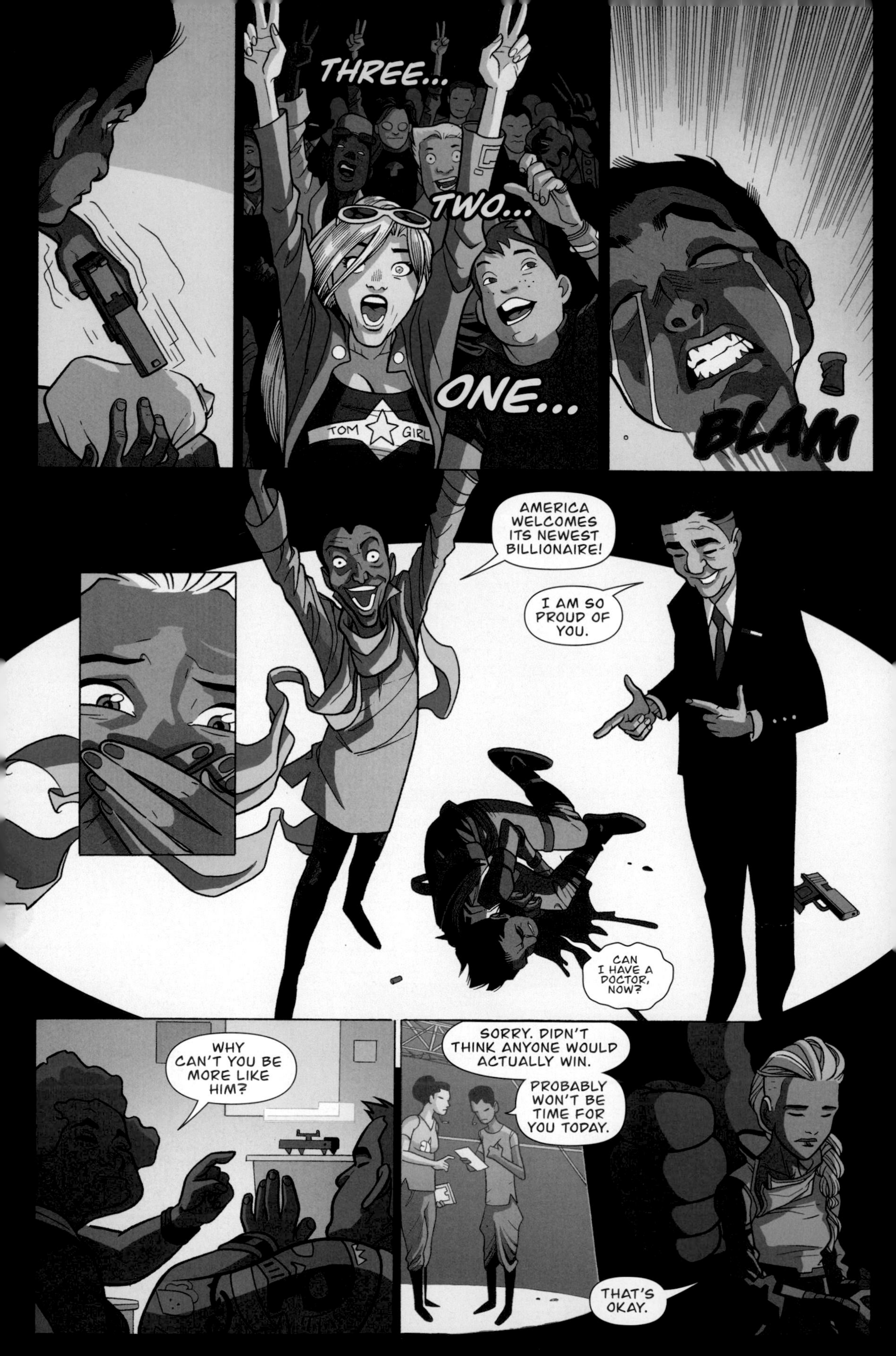
THREE...
TWO...
ONE...
TOM GIRL
BLAM
AMERICA WELCOMES ITS NEWEST BILLIONAIRE!
I AM SO PROUD OF YOU.
CAN I HAVE A DOCTOR, NOW?
WHY CAN'T YOU BE MORE LIKE HIM?
SORRY. DIDN'T THINK ANYONE WOULD ACTUALLY WIN.
PROBABLY WON'T BE TIME FOR YOU TODAY.
THAT'S OKAY.

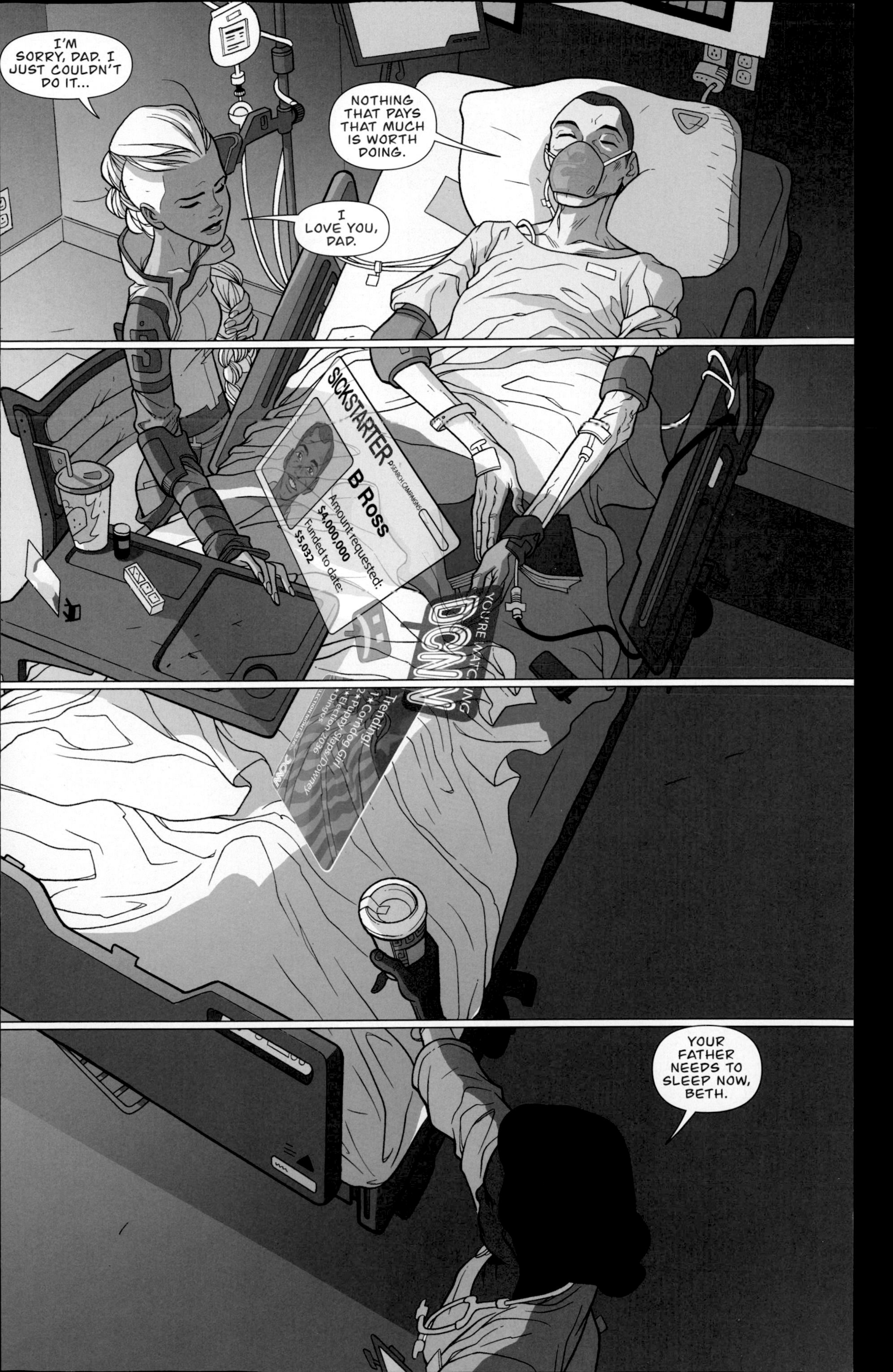

I'M SORRY, DAD. I JUST COULDN'T DO IT...
NOTHING THAT PAYS THAT MUCH IS WORTH DOING.
I LOVE YOU, DAD.
SICKSTARTER
SEARCH CAMPAIGNS
B Ross
Amount requested:
$4,000,000
Funded to date:
$5,032
YOU'RE WATCHING
DCNN
Trending!
YOUR FATHER NEEDS TO SLEEP NOW, BETH.

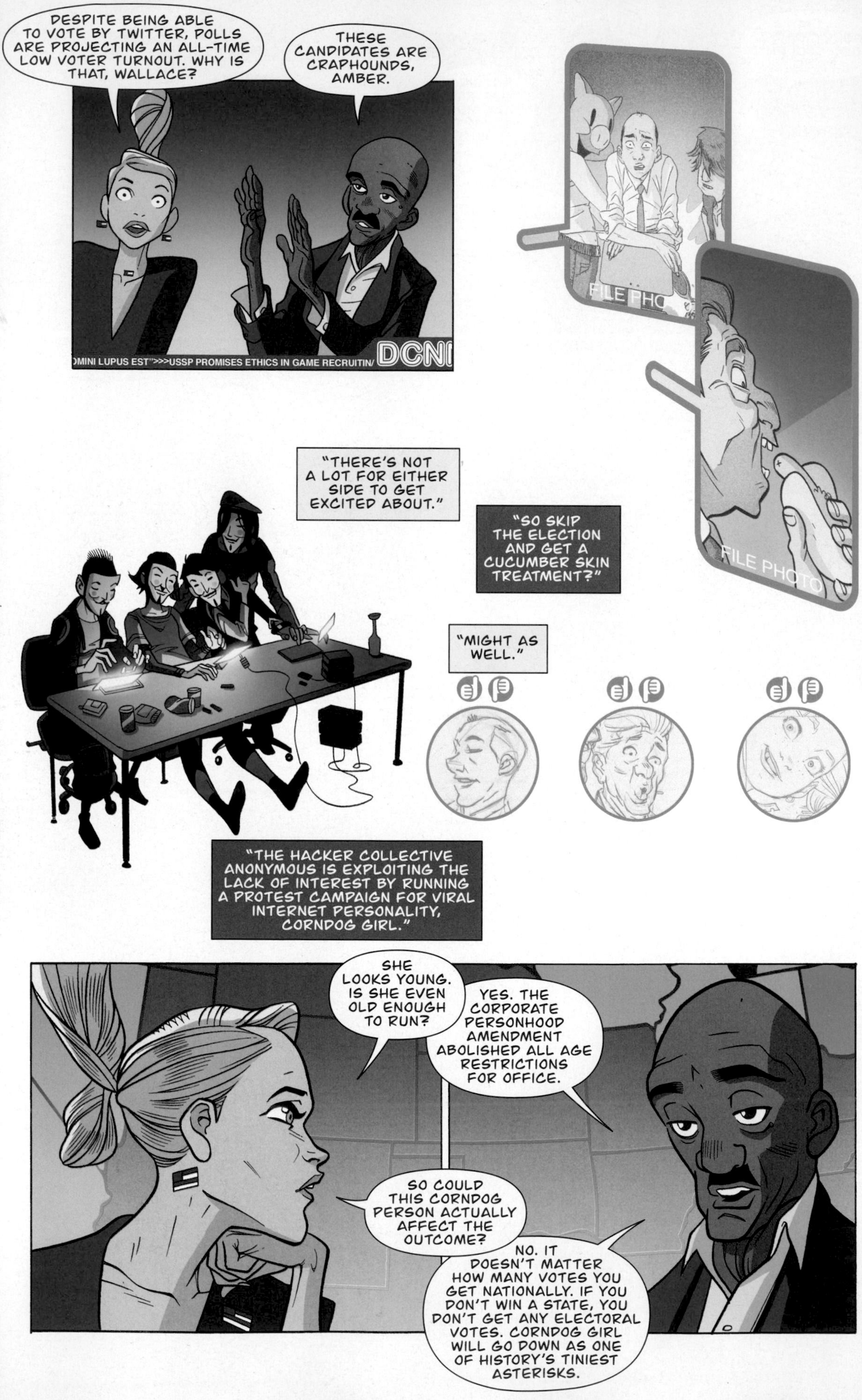
DESPITE BEING ABLE TO VOTE BY TWITTER, POLLS ARE PROJECTING AN ALL-TIME LOW VOTER TURNOUT. WHY IS THAT, WALLACE?
THESE CANDIDATES ARE CRAPHOUNDS, AMBER.
OMINI LUPUS EST">>>USSP PROMISES ETHICS IN GAME RECRUITIN/
DCN
FILE PHOTO
FILE PHOTO
"THERE'S NOT A LOT FOR EITHER SIDE TO GET EXCITED ABOUT."
"SO SKIP THE ELECTION AND GET A CUCUMBER SKIN TREATMENT?"
"MIGHT AS WELL."
"THE HACKER COLLECTIVE ANONYMOUS IS EXPLOITING THE LACK OF INTEREST BY RUNNING A PROTEST CAMPAIGN FOR VIRAL INTERNET PERSONALITY, CORNDOG GIRL."
SHE LOOKS YOUNG. IS SHE EVEN OLD ENOUGH TO RUN?
YES. THE CORPORATE PERSONHOOD AMENDMENT ABOLISHED ALL AGE RESTRICTIONS FOR OFFICE.
SO COULD THIS CORNDOG PERSON ACTUALLY AFFECT THE OUTCOME?
NO. IT DOESN'T MATTER HOW MANY VOTES YOU GET NATIONALLY. IF YOU DON'T WIN A STATE, YOU DON'T GET ANY ELECTORAL VOTES. CORNDOG GIRL WILL GO DOWN AS ONE OF HISTORY'S TINIEST ASTERISKS.

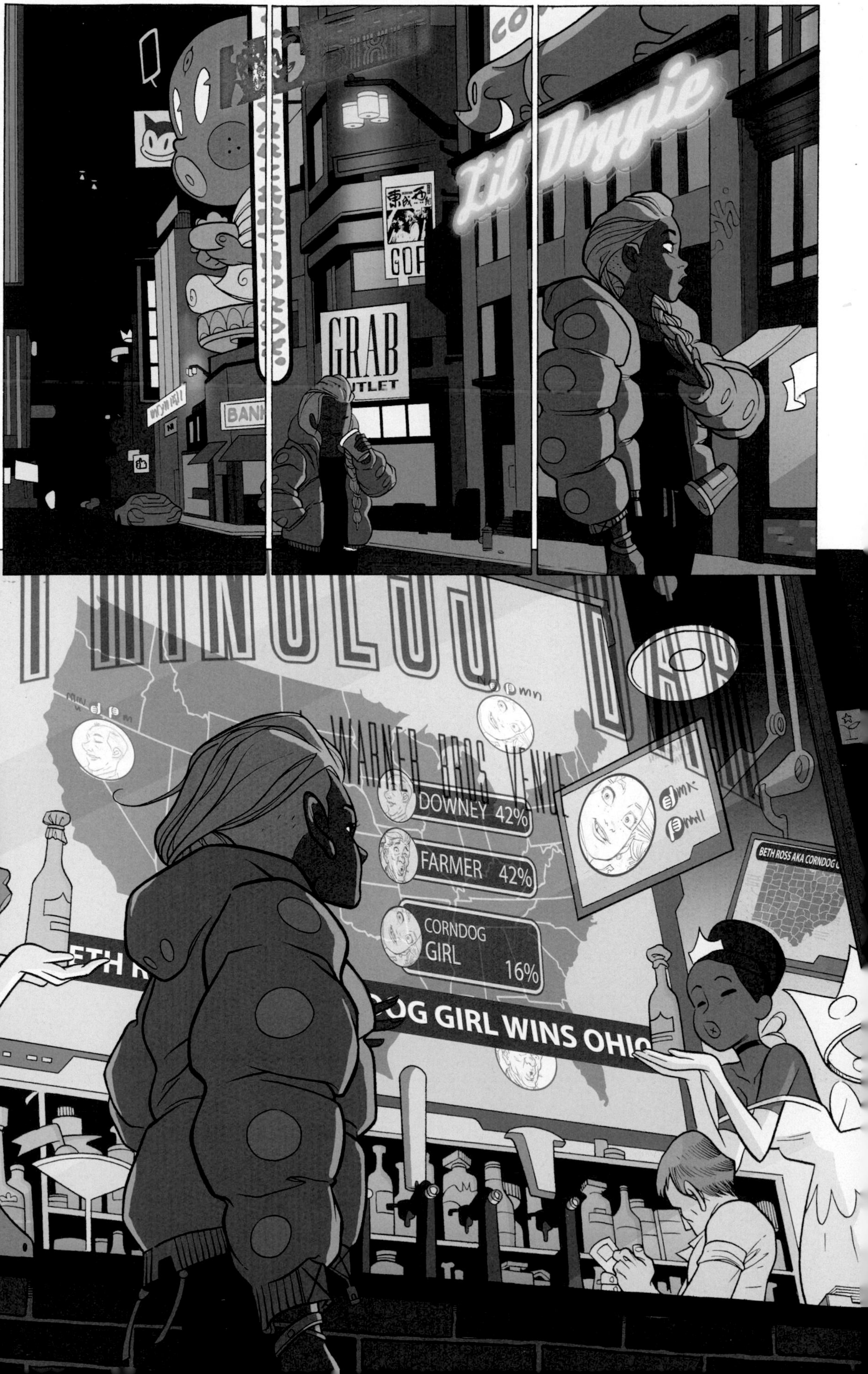
BANK
GRAB
UTLET
GOF
Lil' Doggie
WARNER BROS VENUE
DOWNEY 42%
FARMER 42%
CORNDOG GIRL 16%
ETH R
OG GIRL WINS OHIO
BETH ROSS AKA CORNDOG

IN A STUNNING DEVELOPMENT, CORNDOG GIRL WINS OHIO AFTER A LATE ENDORSEMENT FROM INTERNET PERSONALITY PUPPY SLAPS.

SO IS SHE ACTUALLY MADE OUT OF CORNDOGS?

THIS COUNTRY JUST GETS STUPIDER.

DOWNEY:261   FARMER:259   C-DOG GIR

NOBODY GOT ENOUGH ELECTORAL VOTES TO WIN.

ARMER:259   CDOG GIR

SO NO PRESIDENT? WHAT DOES THIS MEAN?

ACCORDING TO THE CONSTITUTION, THE ELECTION MOVES TO THE HOUSE OF REPRESENTATIVES, WHERE EACH STATE RECEIVES ONE VOTE. THERE'S NOTHING TO WORRY ABOUT.

ARME   C-D

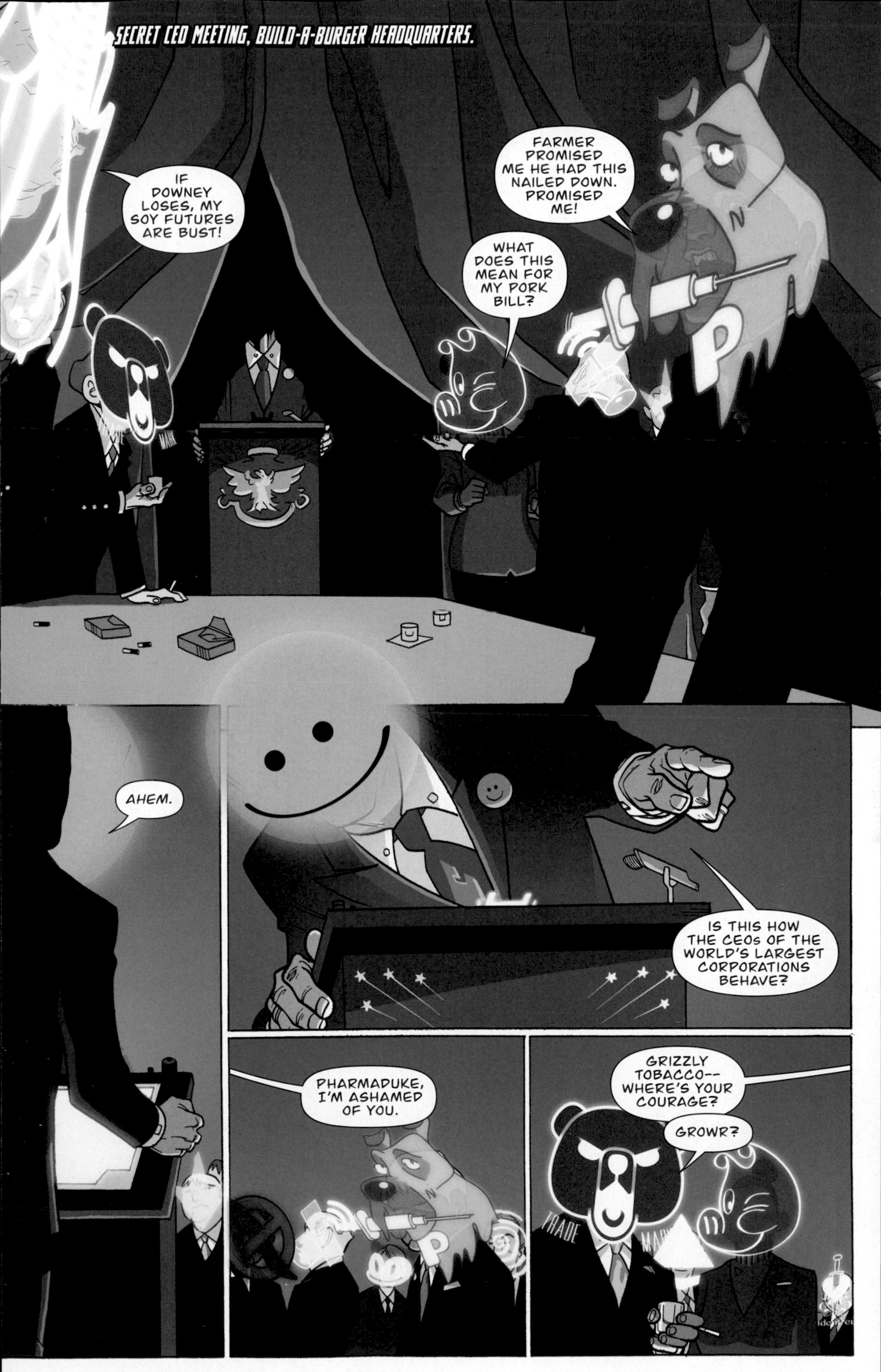
SECRET CEO MEETING, BUILD-A-BURGER HEADQUARTERS.
IF DOWNEY LOSES, MY SOY FUTURES ARE BUST!
FARMER PROMISED ME HE HAD THIS NAILED DOWN. PROMISED ME!
WHAT DOES THIS MEAN FOR MY PORK BILL?
AHEM.
IS THIS HOW THE CEOs OF THE WORLD'S LARGEST CORPORATIONS BEHAVE?
PHARMADUKE, I'M ASHAMED OF YOU.
GRIZZLY TOBACCO-- WHERE'S YOUR COURAGE?
GROWR?

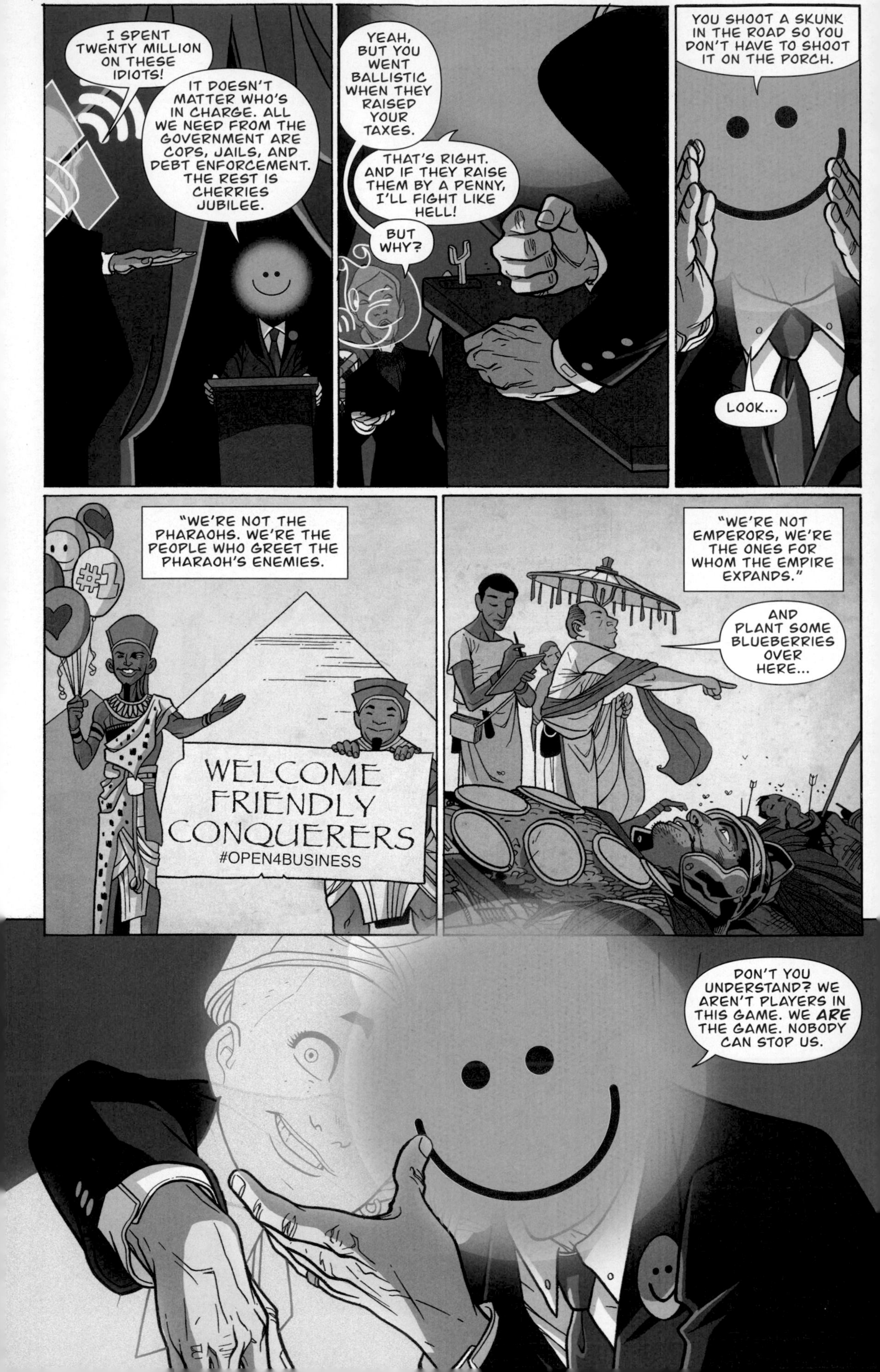
I SPENT TWENTY MILLION ON THESE IDIOTS!
IT DOESN'T MATTER WHO'S IN CHARGE. ALL WE NEED FROM THE GOVERNMENT ARE COPS, JAILS, AND DEBT ENFORCEMENT. THE REST IS CHERRIES JUBILEE.
YEAH, BUT YOU WENT BALLISTIC WHEN THEY RAISED YOUR TAXES.
THAT'S RIGHT. AND IF THEY RAISE THEM BY A PENNY, I'LL FIGHT LIKE HELL!
BUT WHY?
YOU SHOOT A SKUNK IN THE ROAD SO YOU DON'T HAVE TO SHOOT IT ON THE PORCH.
LOOK...
"WE'RE NOT THE PHARAOHS. WE'RE THE PEOPLE WHO GREET THE PHARAOH'S ENEMIES.
#1
WELCOME FRIENDLY CONQUERERS
#OPEN4BUSINESS
"WE'RE NOT EMPERORS, WE'RE THE ONES FOR WHOM THE EMPIRE EXPANDS."
AND PLANT SOME BLUEBERRIES OVER HERE...
DON'T YOU UNDERSTAND? WE AREN'T PLAYERS IN THIS GAME. WE ARE THE GAME. NOBODY CAN STOP US.

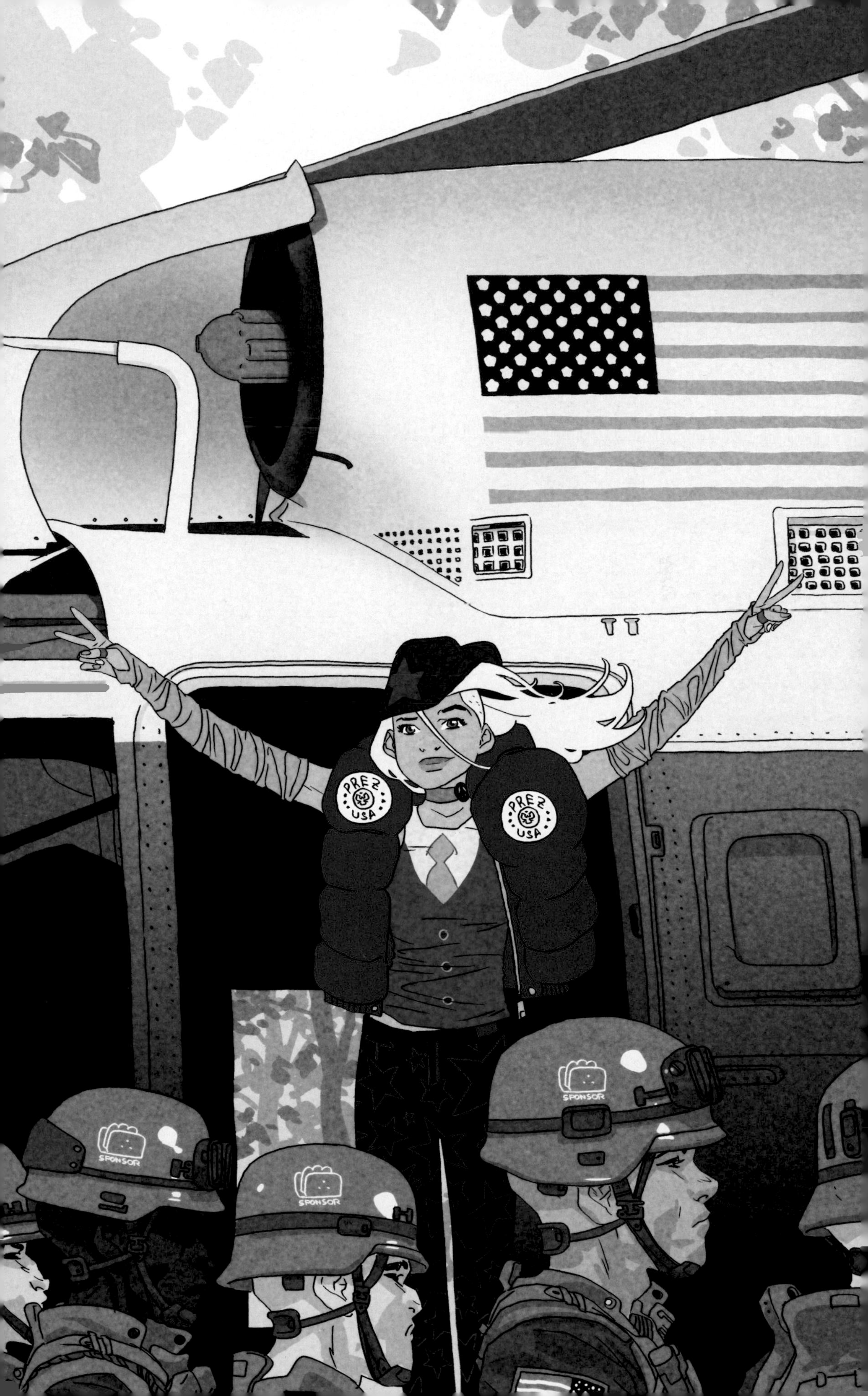
PREZ
USA
PREZ
USA
SPONSOR
SPONSOR
SPONSOR

THE DEMOCRATIC CIRCUS

MARK RUSSELL writer BEN CALDWELL penciller MARK MORALES with SEAN PARSONS inkers JEREMY LAWSON colorist

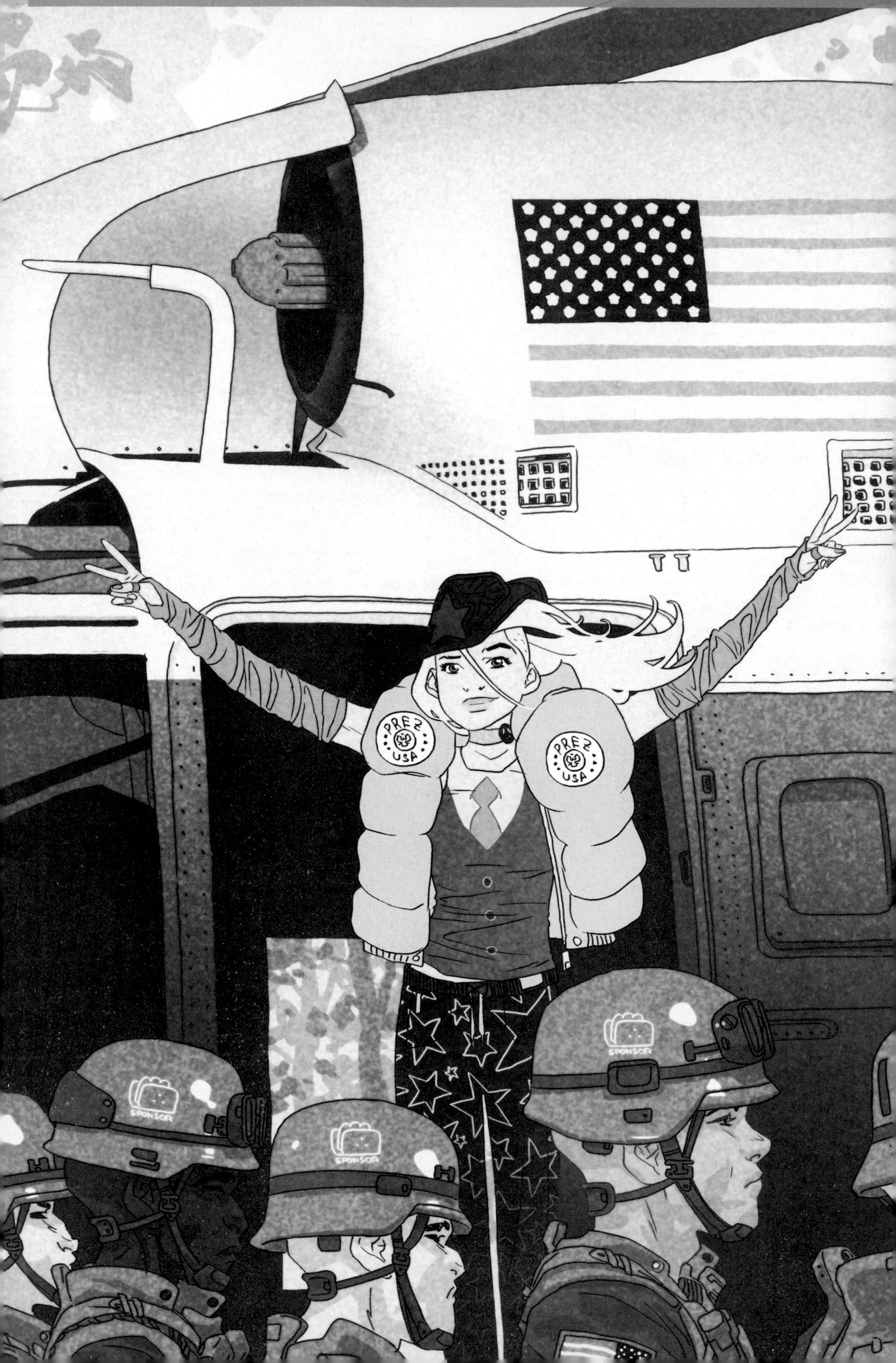
PREZ USA
PREZ USA
SPONSOR
SPONSOR
SPONSOR

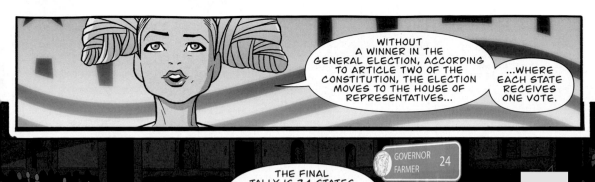

WITHOUT A WINNER IN THE GENERAL ELECTION, ACCORDING TO ARTICLE TWO OF THE CONSTITUTION, THE ELECTION MOVES TO THE HOUSE OF REPRESENTATIVES...

...WHERE EACH STATE RECEIVES ONE VOTE.

THE FINAL TALLY IS 24 STATES FOR GARY FARMER, 24 FOR THOMAS DOWNEY, WITH OHIO VOTING FOR BETH ROSS AND DELAWARE ABSTAINING.

GOVERNOR FARMER   24

SENATOR DOWNEY   24

CORNDOG ROSS   1

ABSTAIN   1

"LADIES AND GENTLEMEN, WE HAVE A TIE."

GRROOOOAANN!

OHIO'S HOLDING OUT FOR SOME CANDY. YOU NEED TO OFFER HIM SOMETHING.

LIKE WHAT?

HOW ABOUT NASA? IT'S NOT LIKE TEXAS IS USING IT.

ANYONE WANT TO TAKE A STAB AT WHY THE ROMAN EMPIRE FELL? BETH?

BECAUSE THEY WON TOO MUCH?

EXPLAIN.

PARIS HILTON COMMUNITY COLLEGE

THE ROMANS WERE SO USED TO WINNING THAT THEY NEVER SAW ANY NEED TO CHANGE, EVEN AS THEIR EMPIRE GOT TOO BIG TO DEFEND.

CORRECT. WHEN CRISIS COMES, AN EMPIRE WILL EITHER CHANGE WITH THE WORLD, OR ENTRENCH ITSELF IN PAST GREATNESS. IF IT DOES THE LATTER, IT DIES.

IT'S HER!

CORNDOG GIRL!

BECAUSE THEY COULD NOT ADAPT, THE ROMANS WERE OVERRUN.

LOADING SITE...

THE GOTHS SACKED ROME. DEPOSED EMPERORS AT WILL.

HIPSTAGRAM #CORNDOGGIRL

BUT EVEN AS THE NATION COLLAPSED AROUND THEM, EVERYONE ASSUMED LIFE WOULD GO BACK TO NORMAL. THE ROMAN EMPIRE WAS DEAD FOR FORTY YEARS BEFORE ANYONE REALIZED IT WAS GONE.

HIPSTAGRAM #CORNDOGGIRL

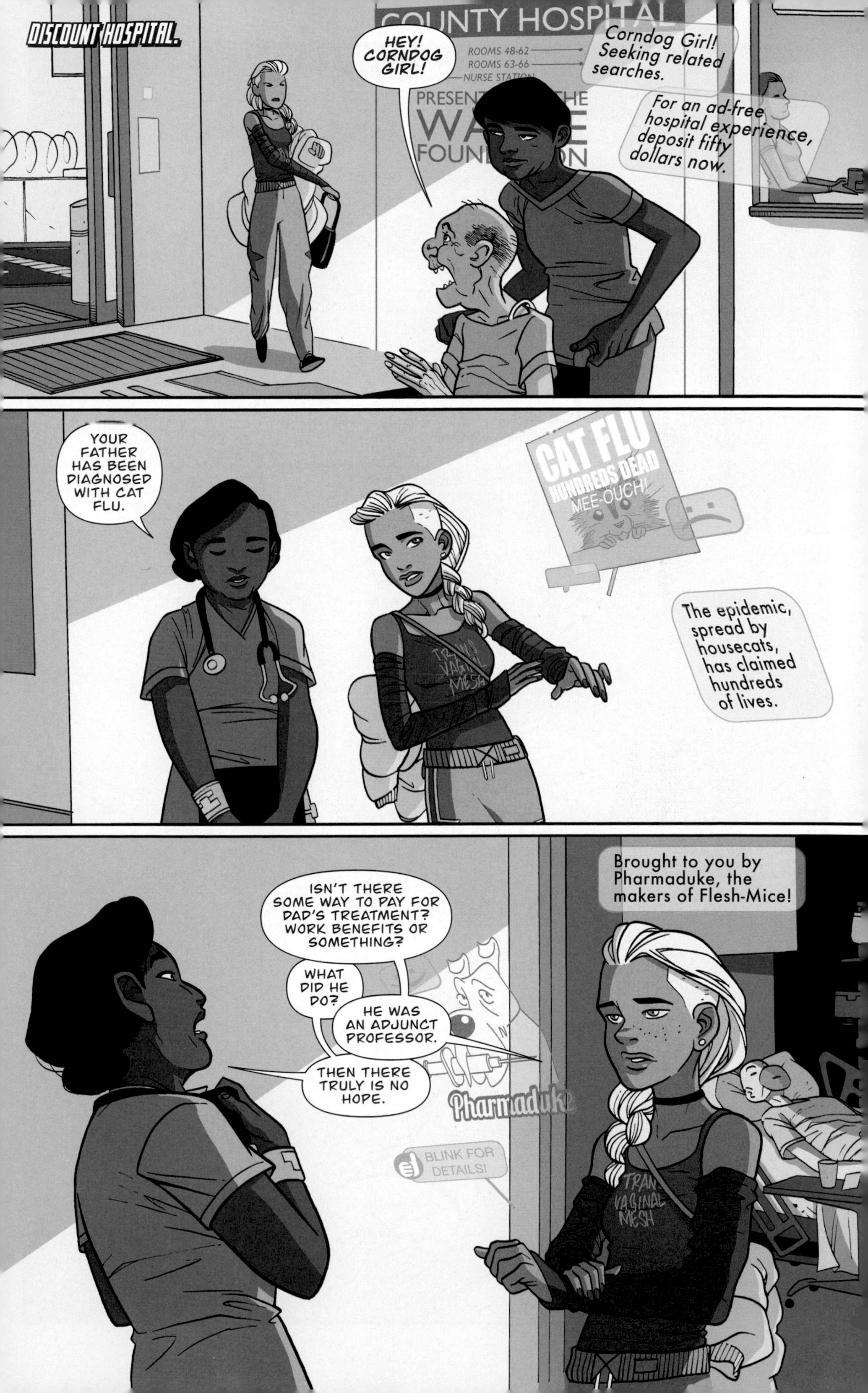
DISCOUNT HOSPITAL.
COUNTY HOSPITAL
ROOMS 48-62
ROOMS 63-66
NURSE STATION
HEY! CORNDOG GIRL!
Corndog Girl! Seeking related searches.
For an ad-free hospital experience, deposit fifty dollars now.
YOUR FATHER HAS BEEN DIAGNOSED WITH CAT FLU.
CAT FLU
HUNDREDS DEAD
MEE-OUCH!
The epidemic, spread by housecats, has claimed hundreds of lives.
TRANS VAGINAL MESH
Brought to you by Pharmaduke, the makers of Flesh-Mice!
ISN'T THERE SOME WAY TO PAY FOR DAD'S TREATMENT? WORK BENEFITS OR SOMETHING?
WHAT DID HE DO?
HE WAS AN ADJUNCT PROFESSOR.
THEN THERE TRULY IS NO HOPE.
Pharmaduke
BLINK FOR DETAILS!

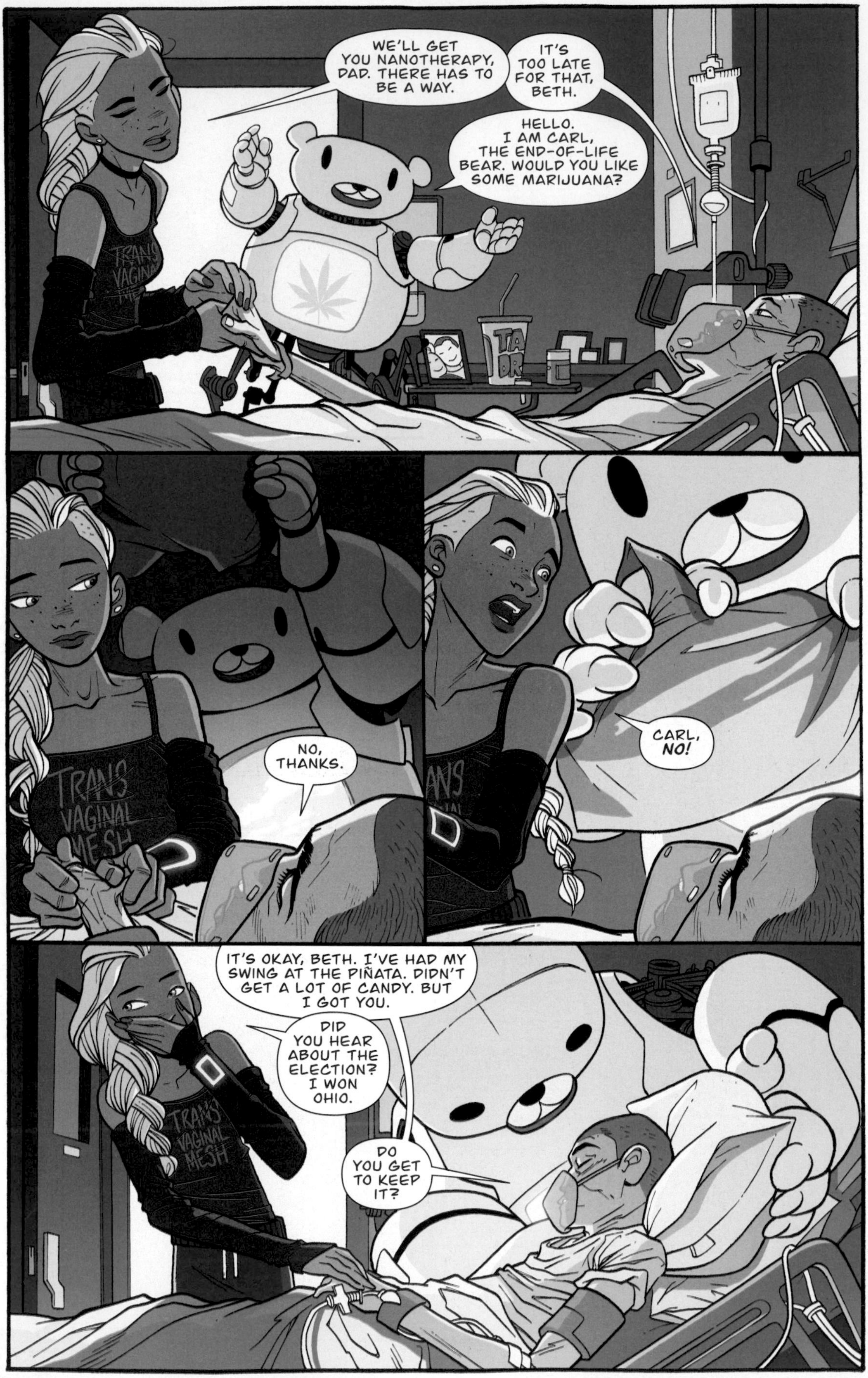
WE'LL GET YOU NANOTHERAPY, DAD. THERE HAS TO BE A WAY.
IT'S TOO LATE FOR THAT, BETH.
HELLO. I AM CARL, THE END-OF-LIFE BEAR. WOULD YOU LIKE SOME MARIJUANA?
TRANS VAGINAL MESH
NO, THANKS.
CARL, NO!
IT'S OKAY, BETH. I'VE HAD MY SWING AT THE PIÑATA. DIDN'T GET A LOT OF CANDY. BUT I GOT YOU.
DID YOU HEAR ABOUT THE ELECTION? I WON OHIO.
DO YOU GET TO KEEP IT?

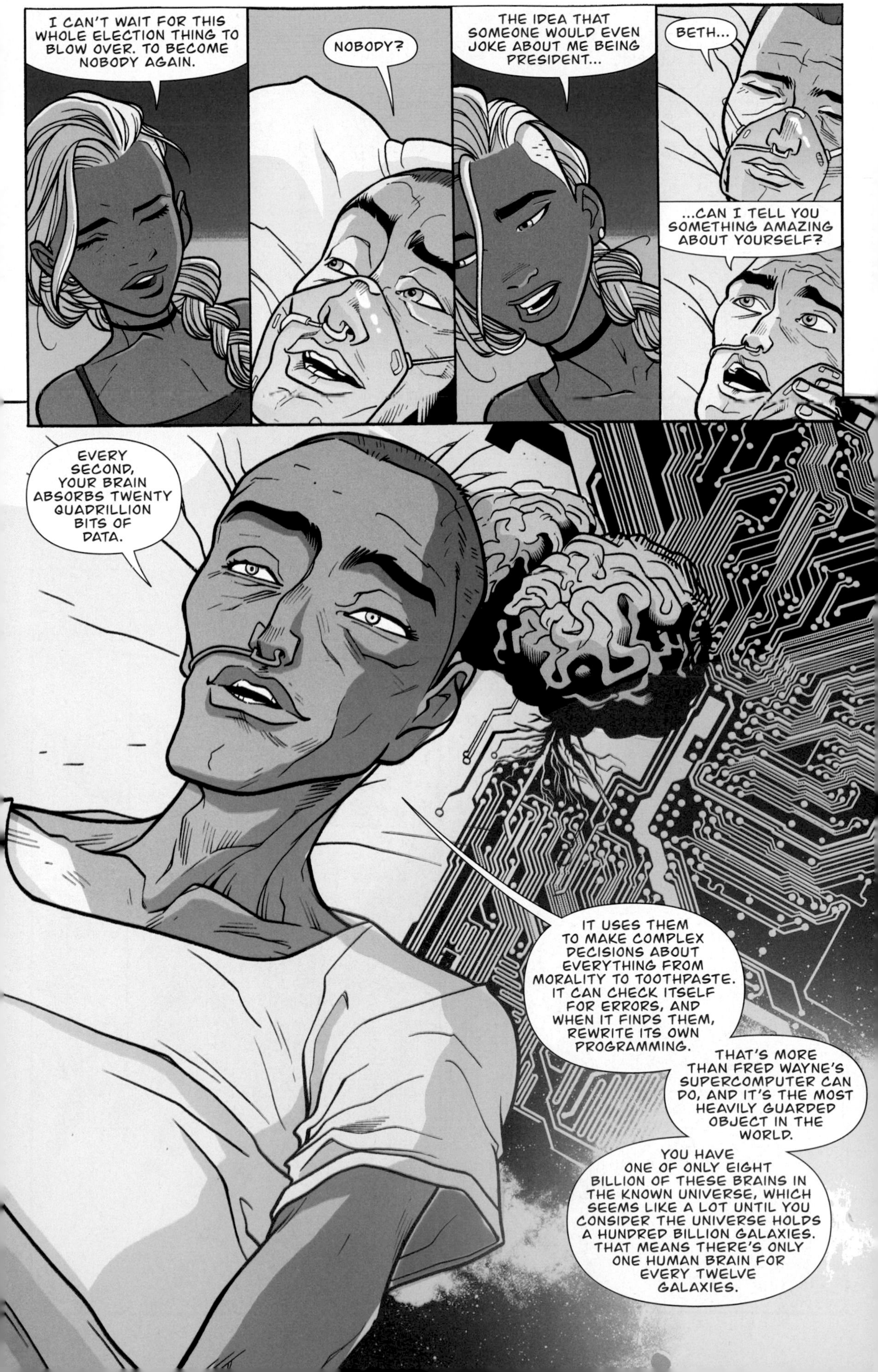
I CAN'T WAIT FOR THIS WHOLE ELECTION THING TO BLOW OVER. TO BECOME NOBODY AGAIN.
NOBODY?
THE IDEA THAT SOMEONE WOULD EVEN JOKE ABOUT ME BEING PRESIDENT...
BETH...
...CAN I TELL YOU SOMETHING AMAZING ABOUT YOURSELF?
EVERY SECOND, YOUR BRAIN ABSORBS TWENTY QUADRILLION BITS OF DATA.
IT USES THEM TO MAKE COMPLEX DECISIONS ABOUT EVERYTHING FROM MORALITY TO TOOTHPASTE. IT CAN CHECK ITSELF FOR ERRORS, AND WHEN IT FINDS THEM, REWRITE ITS OWN PROGRAMMING.
THAT'S MORE THAN FRED WAYNE'S SUPERCOMPUTER CAN DO, AND IT'S THE MOST HEAVILY GUARDED OBJECT IN THE WORLD.
YOU HAVE ONE OF ONLY EIGHT BILLION OF THESE BRAINS IN THE KNOWN UNIVERSE, WHICH SEEMS LIKE A LOT UNTIL YOU CONSIDER THE UNIVERSE HOLDS A HUNDRED BILLION GALAXIES. THAT MEANS THERE'S ONLY ONE HUMAN BRAIN FOR EVERY TWELVE GALAXIES.

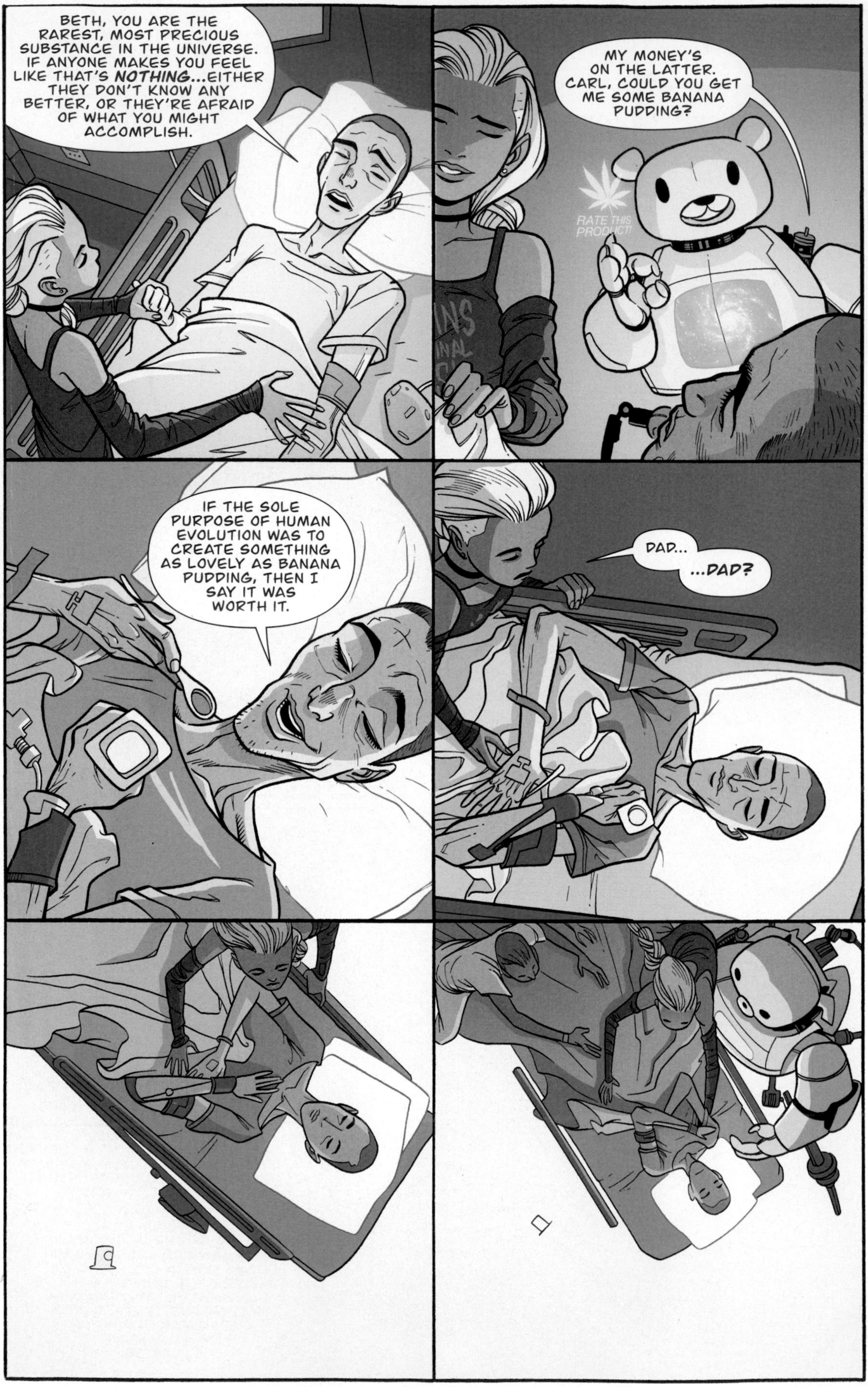
BETH, YOU ARE THE RAREST, MOST PRECIOUS SUBSTANCE IN THE UNIVERSE. IF ANYONE MAKES YOU FEEL LIKE THAT'S NOTHING...EITHER THEY DON'T KNOW ANY BETTER, OR THEY'RE AFRAID OF WHAT YOU MIGHT ACCOMPLISH.
MY MONEY'S ON THE LATTER. CARL, COULD YOU GET ME SOME BANANA PUDDING?
RATE THIS PRODUCT!
IF THE SOLE PURPOSE OF HUMAN EVOLUTION WAS TO CREATE SOMETHING AS LOVELY AS BANANA PUDDING, THEN I SAY IT WAS WORTH IT.
DAD...
...DAD?

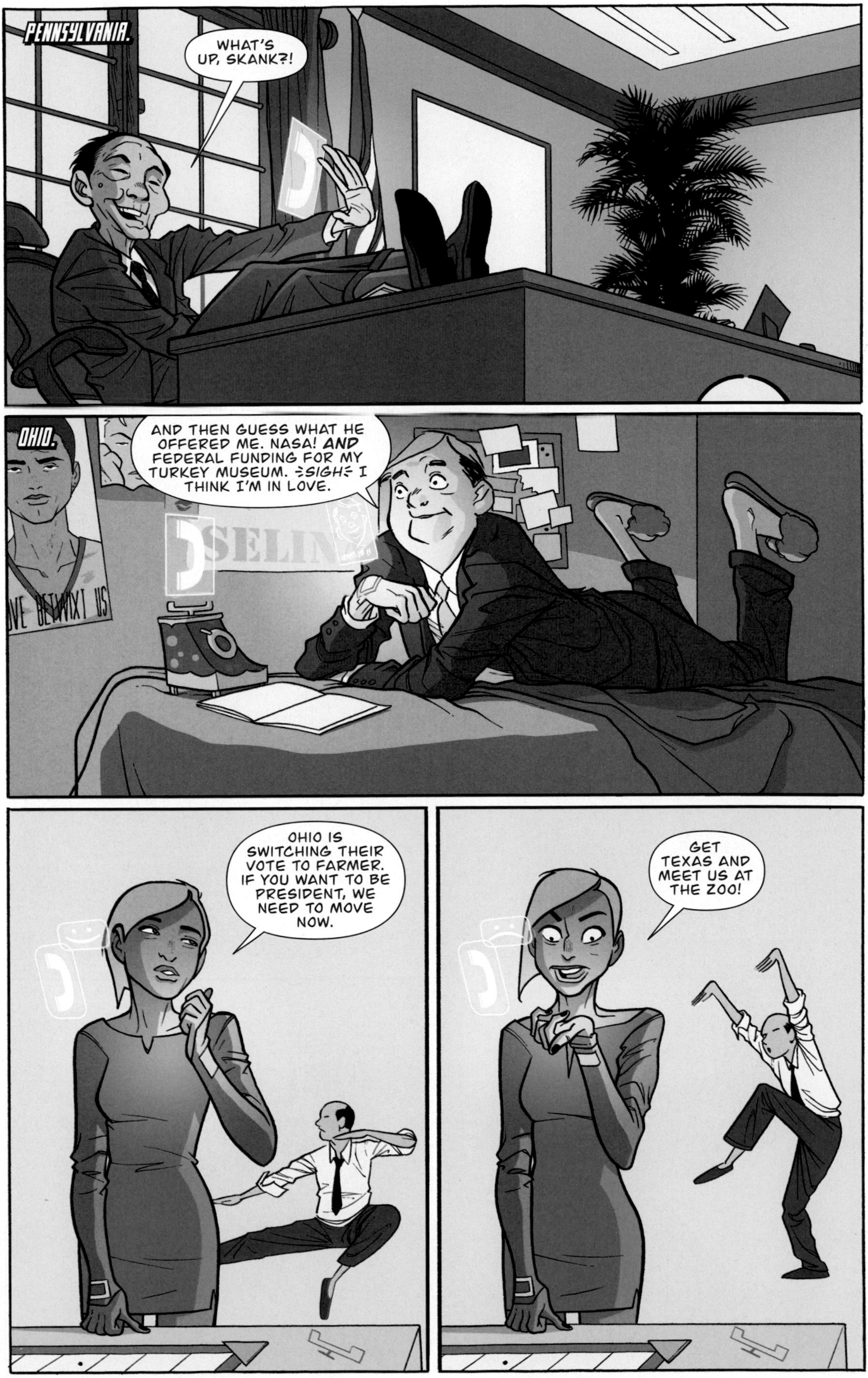
PENNSYLVANIA.
WHAT'S UP, SKANK?!
OHIO.
AND THEN GUESS WHAT HE OFFERED ME. NASA! AND FEDERAL FUNDING FOR MY TURKEY MUSEUM. *SIGH* I THINK I'M IN LOVE.
SELIN
OVE BETWIXT US
OHIO IS SWITCHING THEIR VOTE TO FARMER. IF YOU WANT TO BE PRESIDENT, WE NEED TO MOVE NOW.
GET TEXAS AND MEET US AT THE ZOO!

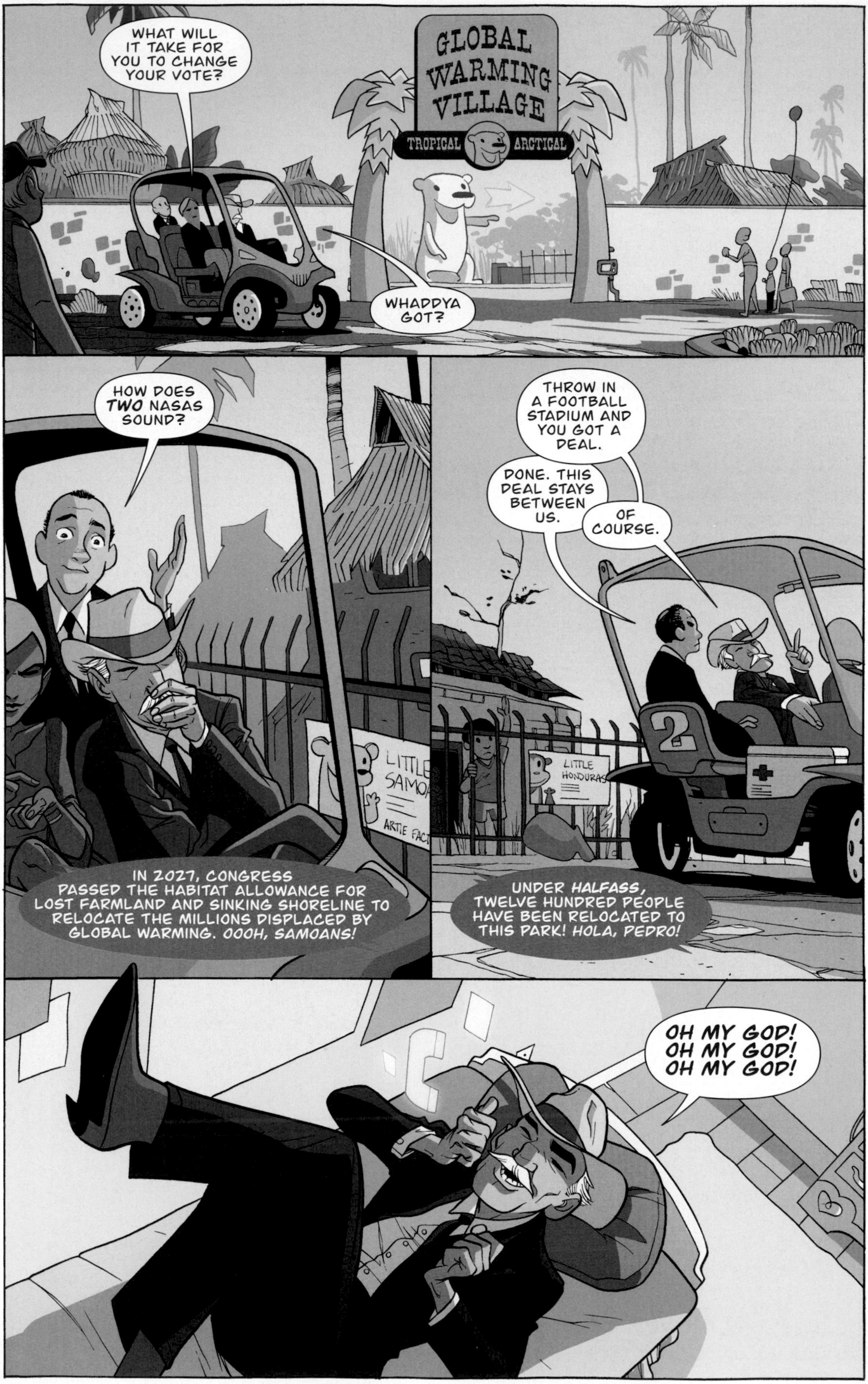
GLOBAL WARMING VILLAGE
TROPICAL ARCTICAL
WHAT WILL IT TAKE FOR YOU TO CHANGE YOUR VOTE?
WHADDYA GOT?
HOW DOES *TWO* NASAS SOUND?
IN 2027, CONGRESS PASSED THE HABITAT ALLOWANCE FOR LOST FARMLAND AND SINKING SHORELINE TO RELOCATE THE MILLIONS DISPLACED BY GLOBAL WARMING. *OOOH, SAMOANS!*
THROW IN A FOOTBALL STADIUM AND YOU GOT A DEAL.
DONE. THIS DEAL STAYS BETWEEN US.
OF COURSE.
LITTLE HONDURAS
UNDER *HALFASS*, TWELVE HUNDRED PEOPLE HAVE BEEN RELOCATED TO THIS PARK! *HOLA, PEDRO!*
OH MY GOD! OH MY GOD! OH MY GOD!

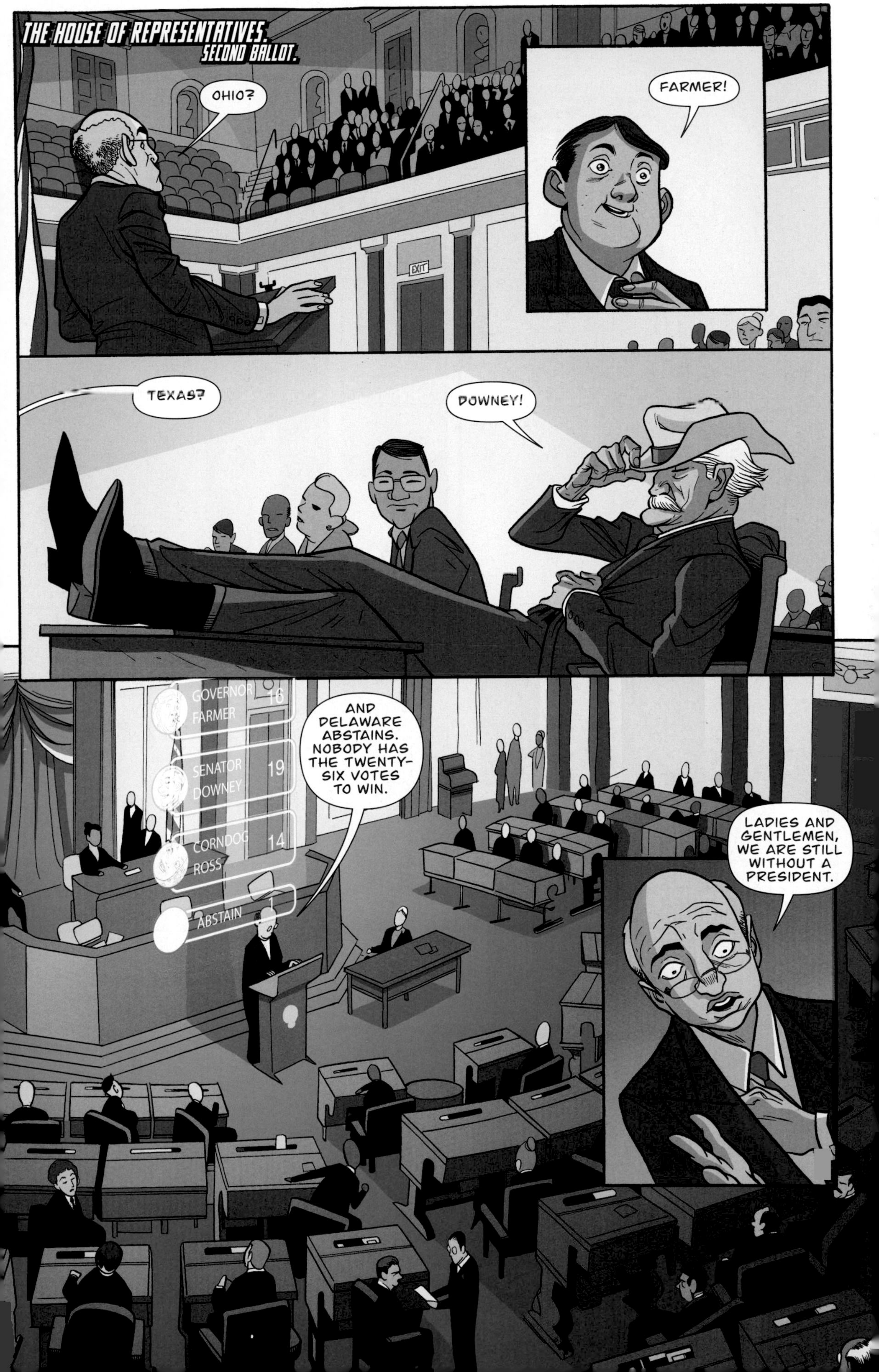
THE HOUSE OF REPRESENTATIVES.
SECOND BALLOT.
OHIO?
FARMER!
EXIT
TEXAS?
DOWNEY!
GOVERNOR FARMER 16
SENATOR DOWNEY 19
CORNDOG ROSS 14
ABSTAIN 1
AND DELAWARE ABSTAINS. NOBODY HAS THE TWENTY-SIX VOTES TO WIN.
LADIES AND GENTLEMEN, WE ARE STILL WITHOUT A PRESIDENT.

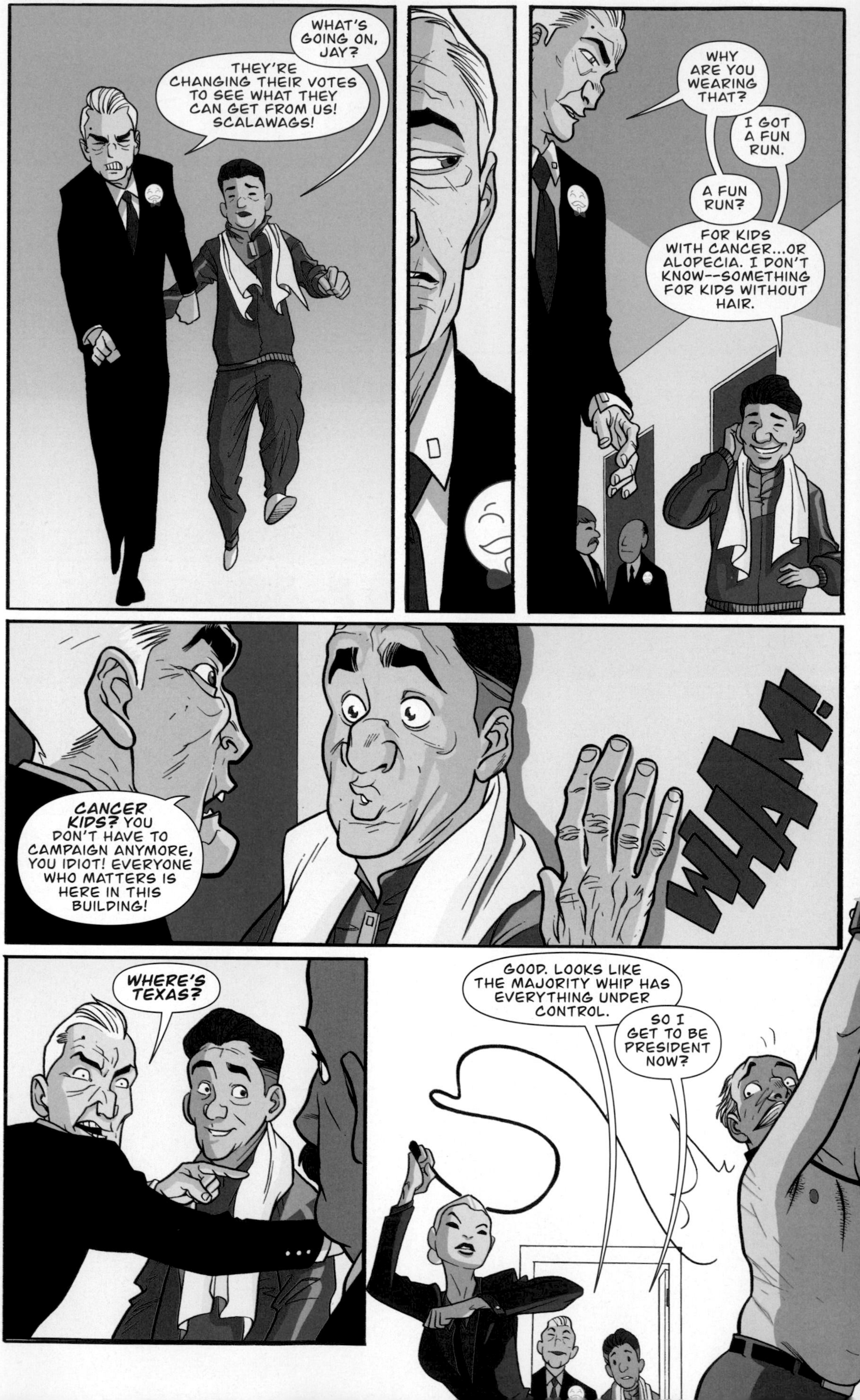
WHAT'S GOING ON, JAY?
THEY'RE CHANGING THEIR VOTES TO SEE WHAT THEY CAN GET FROM US! SCALAWAGS!
WHY ARE YOU WEARING THAT?
I GOT A FUN RUN.
A FUN RUN?
FOR KIDS WITH CANCER...OR ALOPECIA. I DON'T KNOW--SOMETHING FOR KIDS WITHOUT HAIR.
CANCER KIDS? YOU DON'T HAVE TO CAMPAIGN ANYMORE, YOU IDIOT! EVERYONE WHO MATTERS IS HERE IN THIS BUILDING!
WHAM!
WHERE'S TEXAS?
GOOD. LOOKS LIKE THE MAJORITY WHIP HAS EVERYTHING UNDER CONTROL.
SO I GET TO BE PRESIDENT NOW?

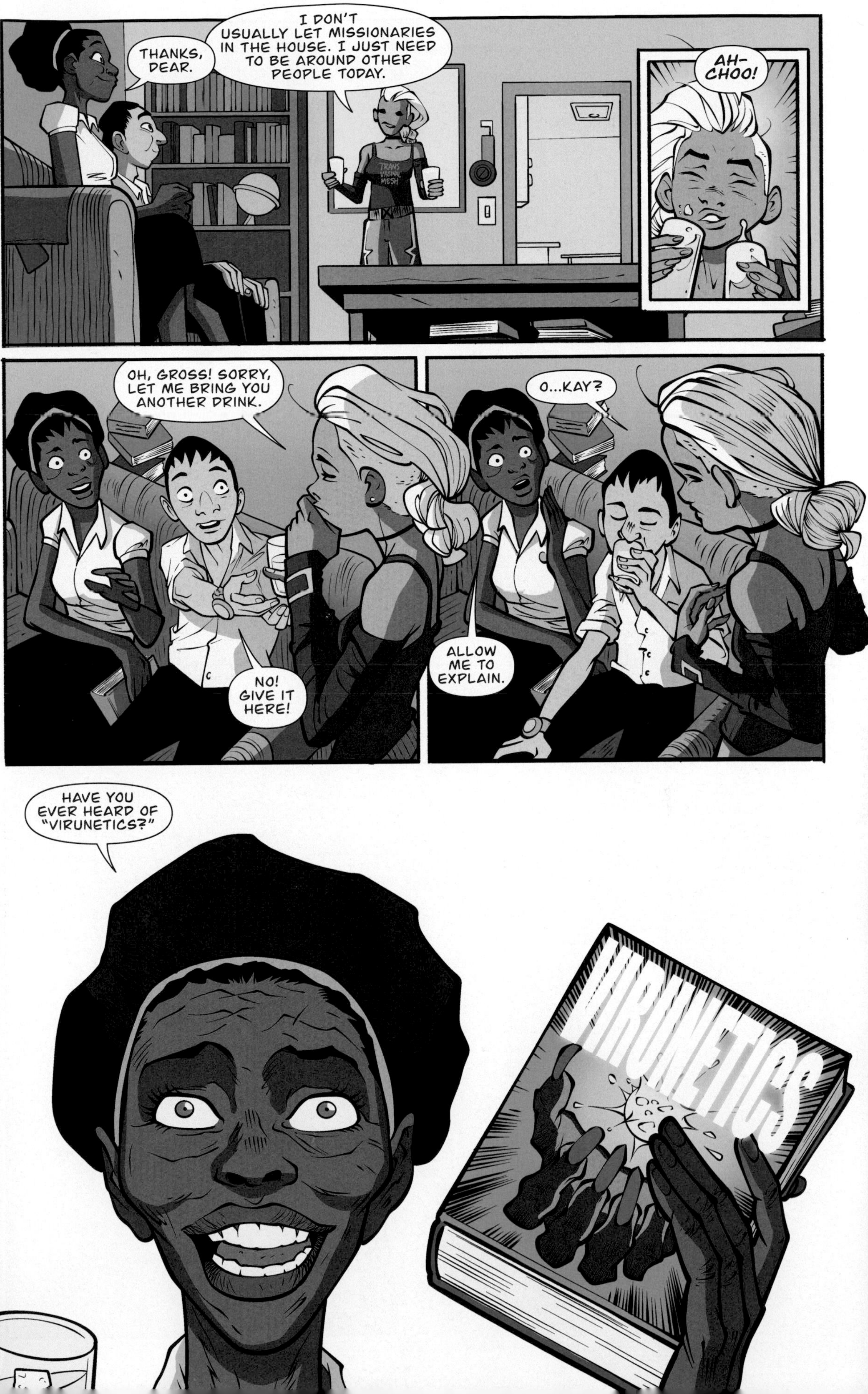
THANKS, DEAR.
I DON'T USUALLY LET MISSIONARIES IN THE HOUSE. I JUST NEED TO BE AROUND OTHER PEOPLE TODAY.
TRANS VAGINAL MESH
AH-CHOO!
OH, GROSS! SORRY, LET ME BRING YOU ANOTHER DRINK.
NO! GIVE IT HERE!
O...KAY?
ALLOW ME TO EXPLAIN.
HAVE YOU EVER HEARD OF "VIRUNETICS?"
VIRUNETICS

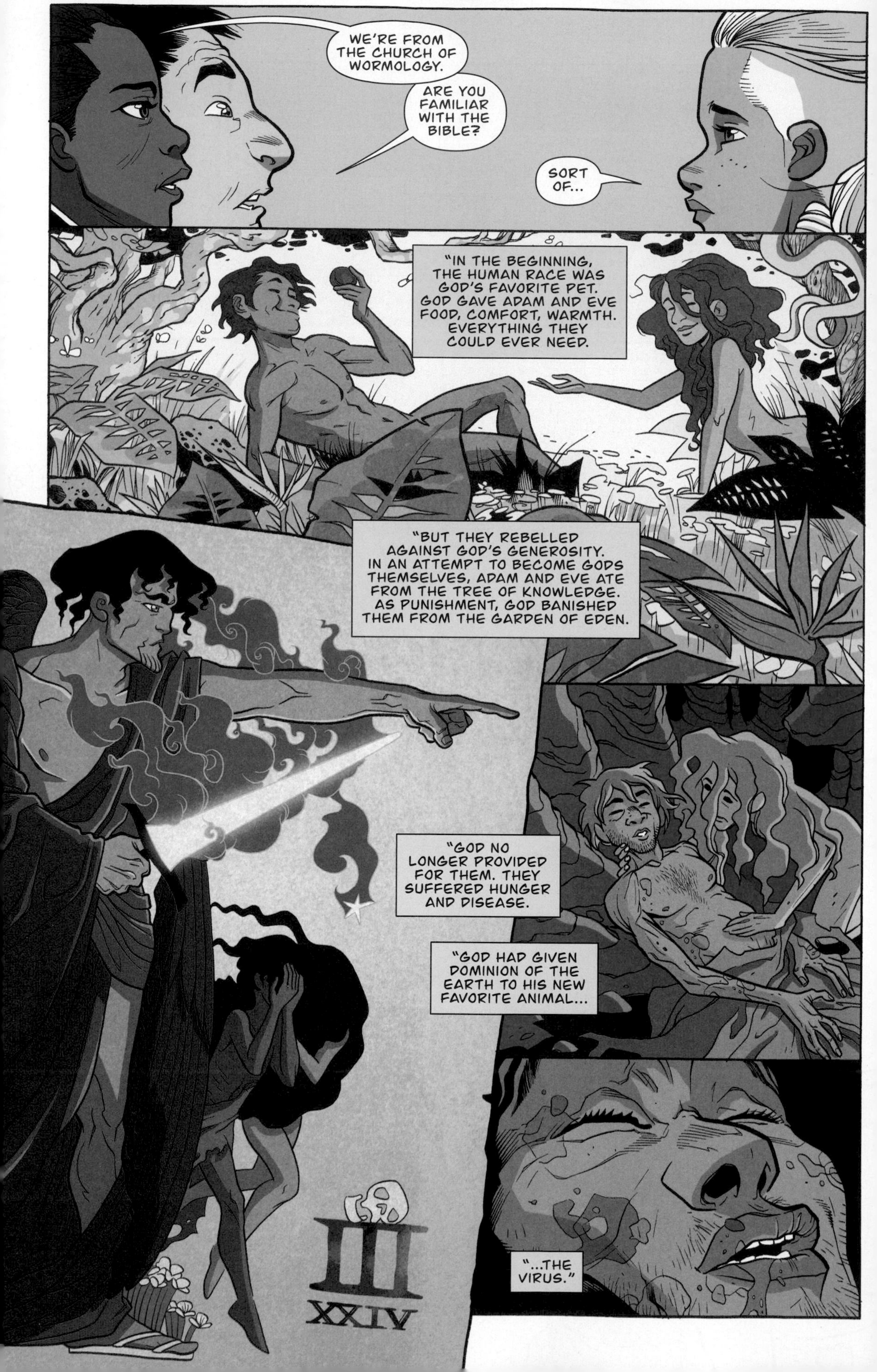
WE'RE FROM THE CHURCH OF WORMOLOGY.
ARE YOU FAMILIAR WITH THE BIBLE?
SORT OF...
"IN THE BEGINNING, THE HUMAN RACE WAS GOD'S FAVORITE PET. GOD GAVE ADAM AND EVE FOOD, COMFORT, WARMTH. EVERYTHING THEY COULD EVER NEED.
"BUT THEY REBELLED AGAINST GOD'S GENEROSITY. IN AN ATTEMPT TO BECOME GODS THEMSELVES, ADAM AND EVE ATE FROM THE TREE OF KNOWLEDGE. AS PUNISHMENT, GOD BANISHED THEM FROM THE GARDEN OF EDEN.
"GOD NO LONGER PROVIDED FOR THEM. THEY SUFFERED HUNGER AND DISEASE.
"GOD HAD GIVEN DOMINION OF THE EARTH TO HIS NEW FAVORITE ANIMAL...
"...THE VIRUS."
III
XXIV

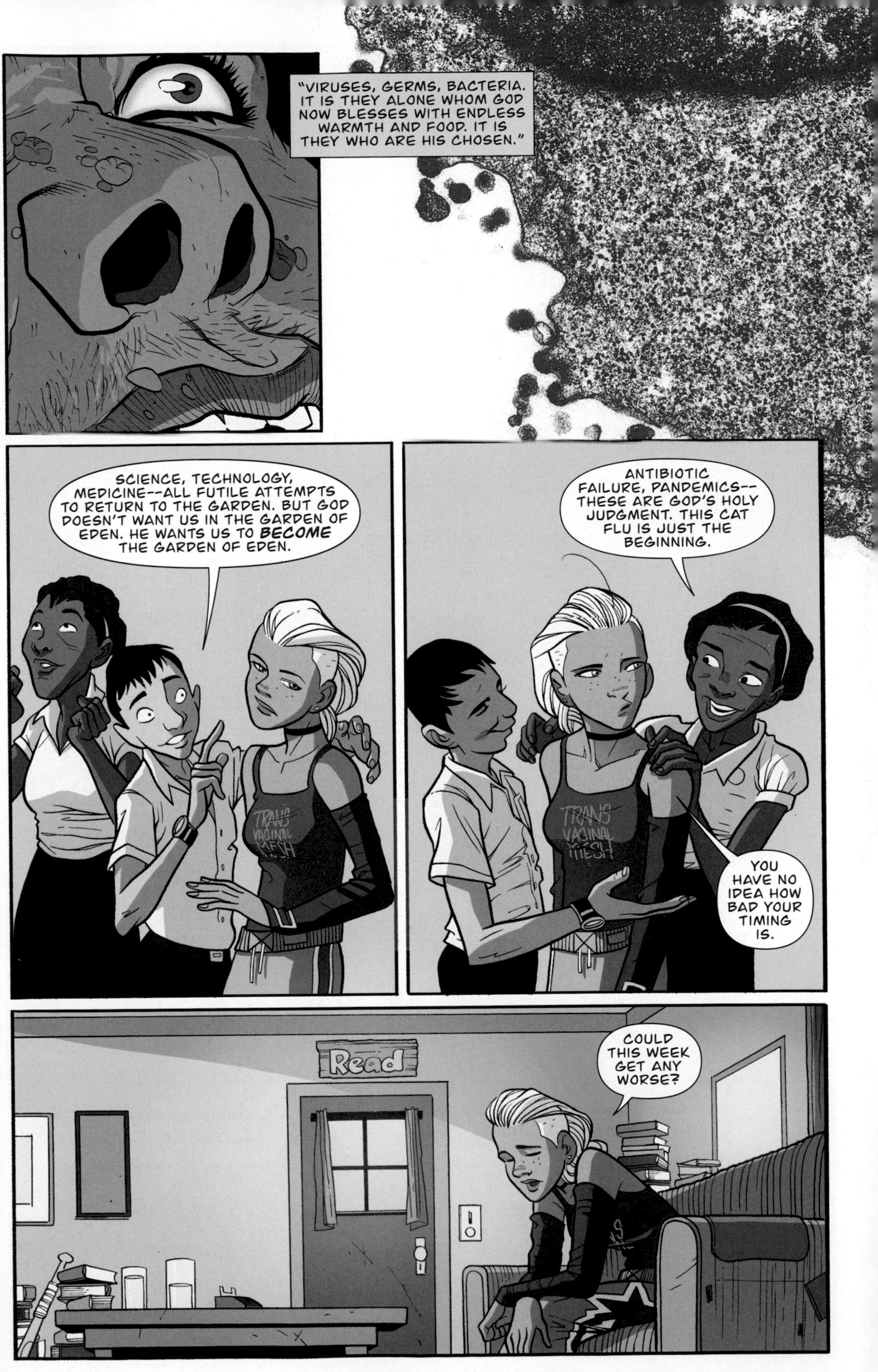
"VIRUSES, GERMS, BACTERIA. IT IS THEY ALONE WHOM GOD NOW BLESSES WITH ENDLESS WARMTH AND FOOD. IT IS THEY WHO ARE HIS CHOSEN."
SCIENCE, TECHNOLOGY, MEDICINE--ALL FUTILE ATTEMPTS TO RETURN TO THE GARDEN. BUT GOD DOESN'T WANT US IN THE GARDEN OF EDEN. HE WANTS US TO *BECOME* THE GARDEN OF EDEN.
TRANS VAGINAL MESH
ANTIBIOTIC FAILURE, PANDEMICS--THESE ARE GOD'S HOLY JUDGMENT. THIS CAT FLU IS JUST THE BEGINNING.
TRANS VAGINAL MESH
YOU HAVE NO IDEA HOW BAD YOUR TIMING IS.
Read
COULD THIS WEEK GET ANY WORSE?

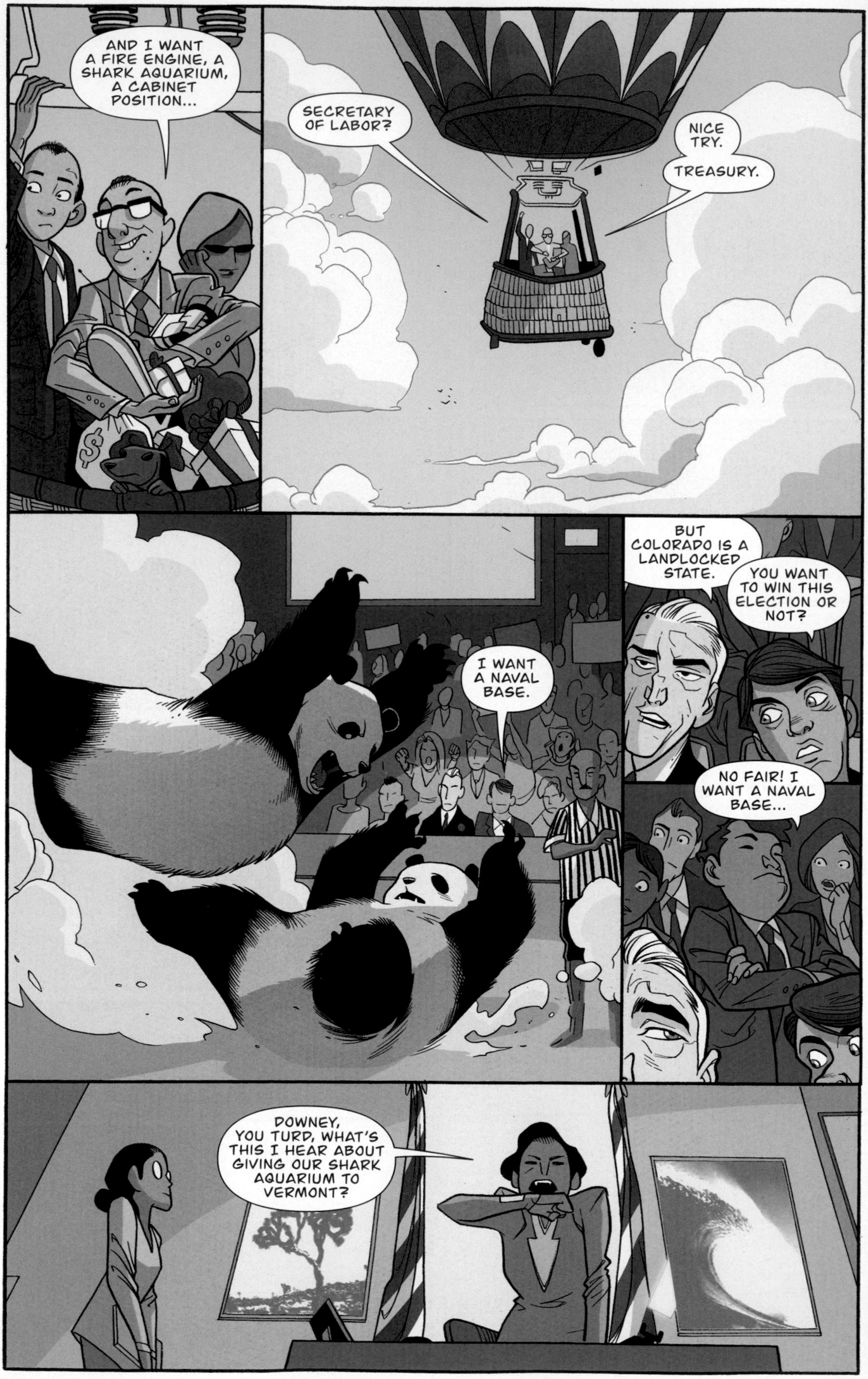
AND I WANT A FIRE ENGINE, A SHARK AQUARIUM, A CABINET POSITION...
SECRETARY OF LABOR?
NICE TRY.
TREASURY.
I WANT A NAVAL BASE.
BUT COLORADO IS A LANDLOCKED STATE.
YOU WANT TO WIN THIS ELECTION OR NOT?
NO FAIR! I WANT A NAVAL BASE...
DOWNEY, YOU TURD, WHAT'S THIS I HEAR ABOUT GIVING OUR SHARK AQUARIUM TO VERMONT?

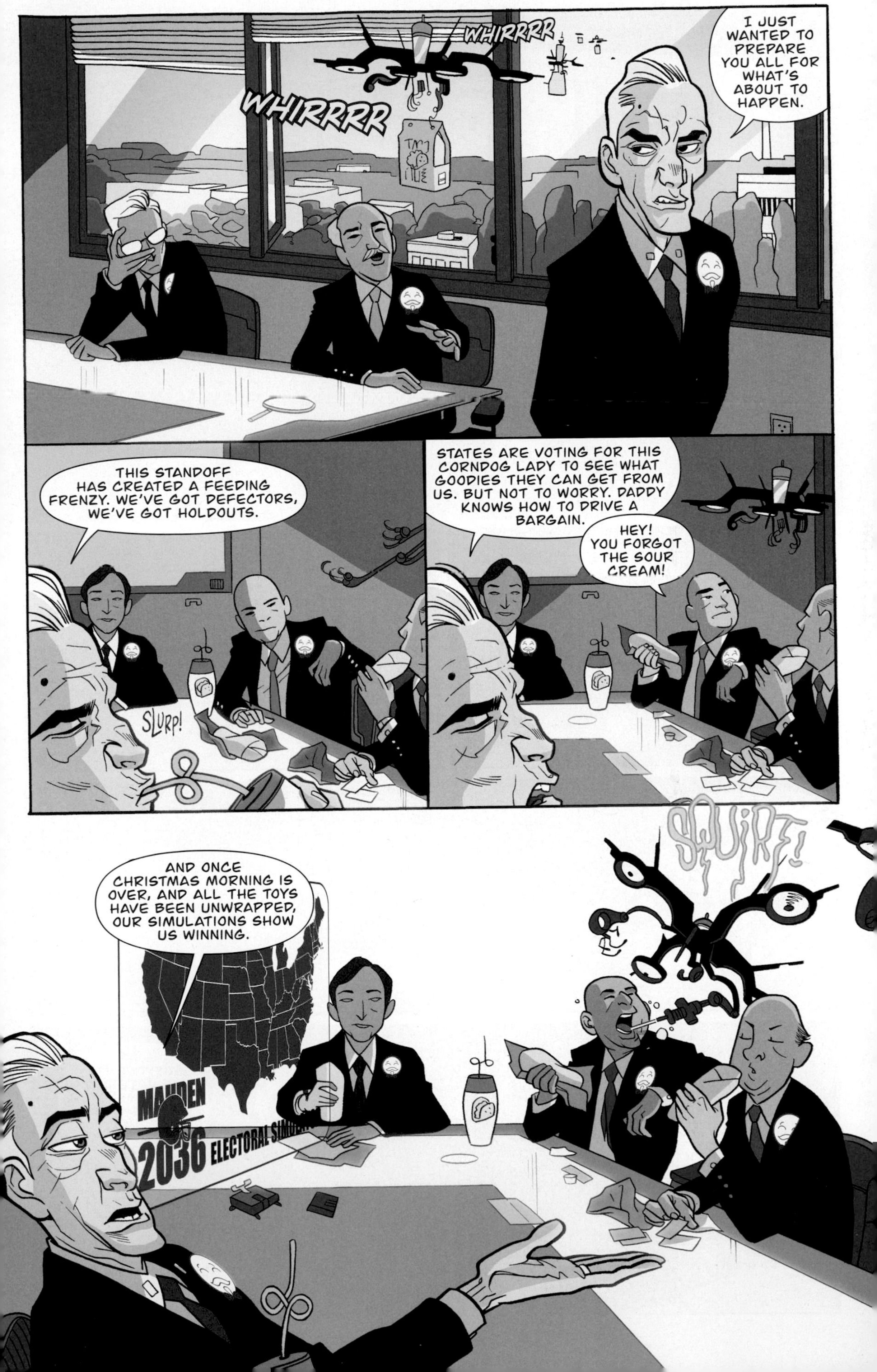
WHIRRRR
WHIRRRR
I JUST WANTED TO PREPARE YOU ALL FOR WHAT'S ABOUT TO HAPPEN.
THIS STANDOFF HAS CREATED A FEEDING FRENZY. WE'VE GOT DEFECTORS, WE'VE GOT HOLDOUTS.
SLURP!
STATES ARE VOTING FOR THIS CORNDOG LADY TO SEE WHAT GOODIES THEY CAN GET FROM US. BUT NOT TO WORRY. DADDY KNOWS HOW TO DRIVE A BARGAIN.
HEY! YOU FORGOT THE SOUR CREAM!
AND ONCE CHRISTMAS MORNING IS OVER, AND ALL THE TOYS HAVE BEEN UNWRAPPED, OUR SIMULATIONS SHOW US WINNING.
MAUDEN
2036 ELECTORAL
SQUIRT!

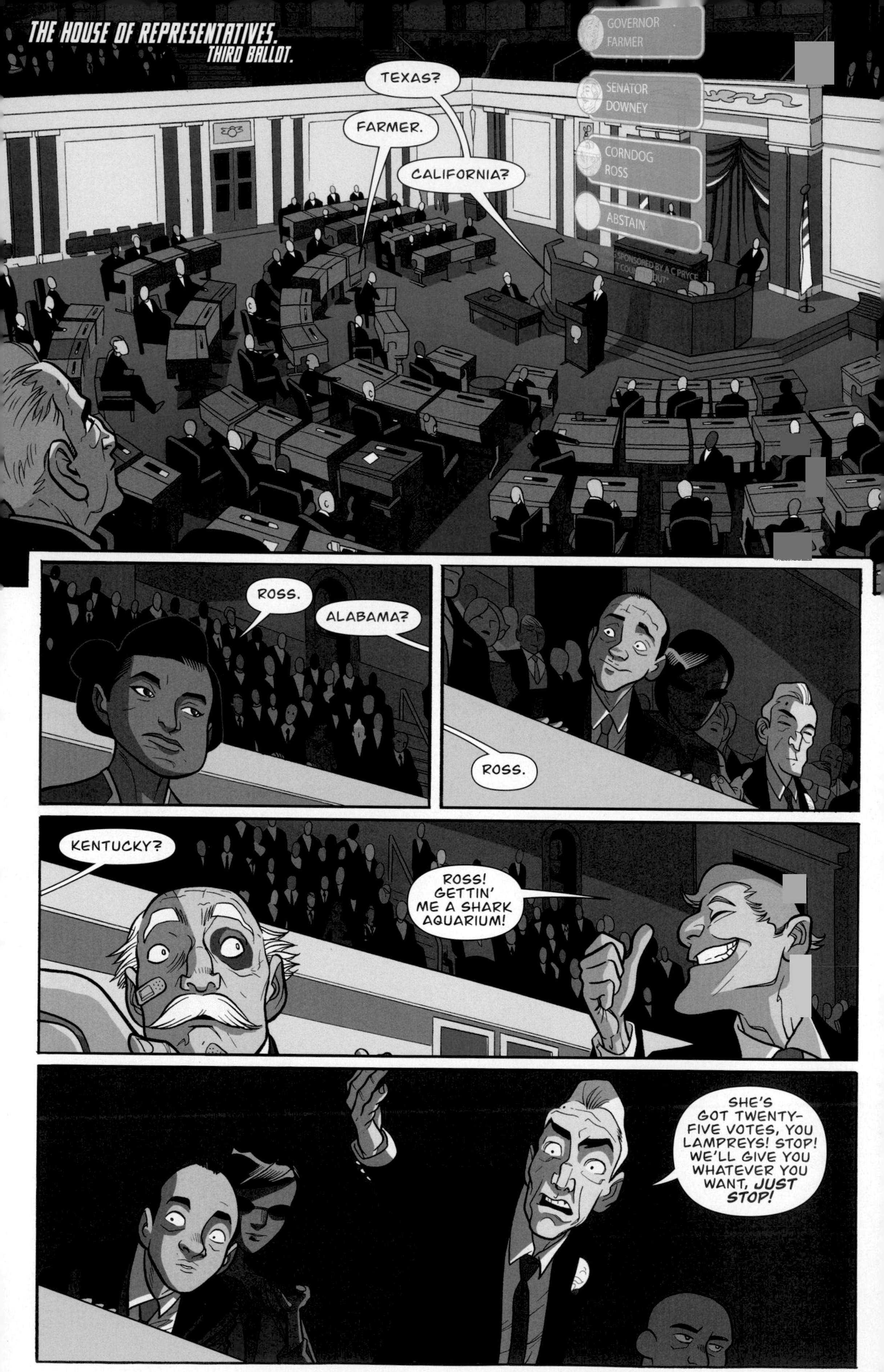
THE HOUSE OF REPRESENTATIVES.
THIRD BALLOT.
GOVERNOR FARMER
SENATOR DOWNEY
CORNDOG ROSS
ABSTAIN
TEXAS?
FARMER.
CALIFORNIA?
ROSS.
ALABAMA?
ROSS.
KENTUCKY?
ROSS! GETTIN' ME A SHARK AQUARIUM!
SHE'S GOT TWENTY-FIVE VOTES, YOU LAMPREYS! STOP! WE'LL GIVE YOU WHATEVER YOU WANT, JUST STOP!

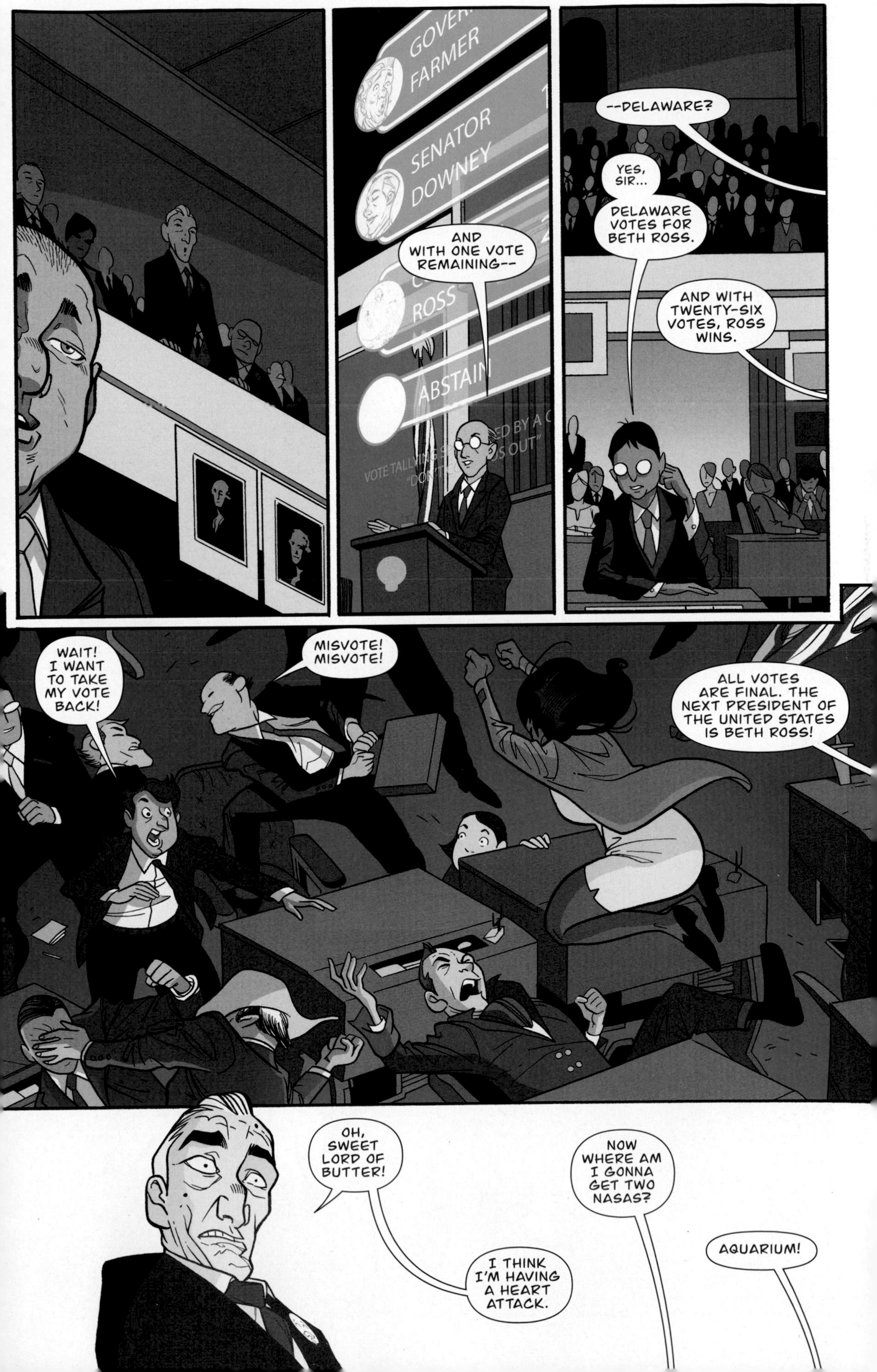
FARMER
SENATOR DOWNEY
ROSS
ABSTAIN
AND WITH ONE VOTE REMAINING--
--DELAWARE?
YES, SIR...
DELAWARE VOTES FOR BETH ROSS.
AND WITH TWENTY-SIX VOTES, ROSS WINS.
WAIT! I WANT TO TAKE MY VOTE BACK!
MISVOTE! MISVOTE!
ALL VOTES ARE FINAL. THE NEXT PRESIDENT OF THE UNITED STATES IS BETH ROSS!
OH, SWEET LORD OF BUTTER!
I THINK I'M HAVING A HEART ATTACK.
NOW WHERE AM I GONNA GET TWO NASAS?
AQUARIUM!

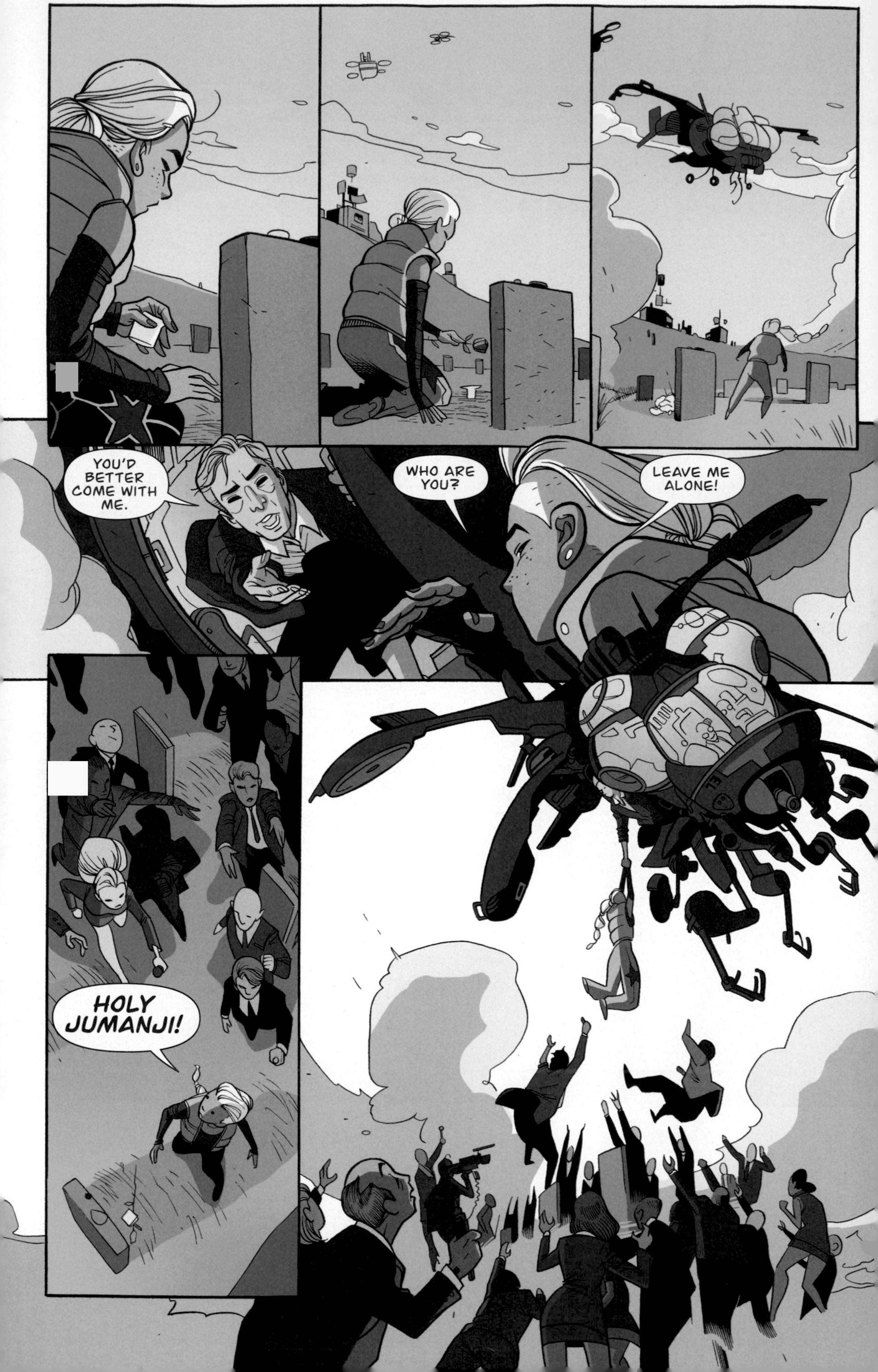
YOU'D BETTER COME WITH ME.
WHO ARE YOU?
LEAVE ME ALONE!
HOLY JUMANJI!

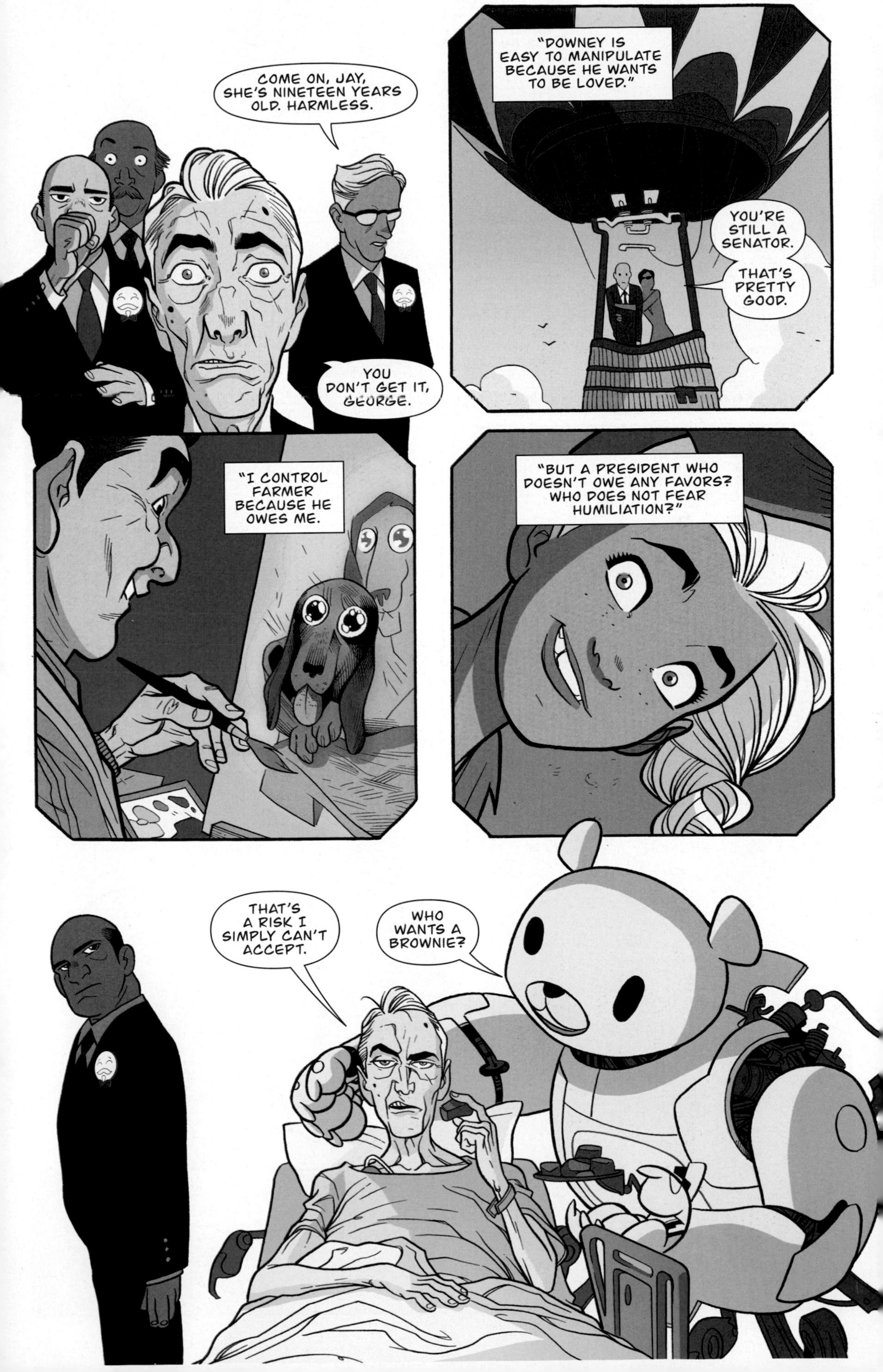
COME ON, JAY, SHE'S NINETEEN YEARS OLD. HARMLESS.
YOU DON'T GET IT, GEORGE.
"DOWNEY IS EASY TO MANIPULATE BECAUSE HE WANTS TO BE LOVED."
YOU'RE STILL A SENATOR.
THAT'S PRETTY GOOD.
"I CONTROL FARMER BECAUSE HE OWES ME.
"BUT A PRESIDENT WHO DOESN'T OWE ANY FAVORS? WHO DOES NOT FEAR HUMILIATION?"
THAT'S A RISK I SIMPLY CAN'T ACCEPT.
WHO WANTS A BROWNIE?

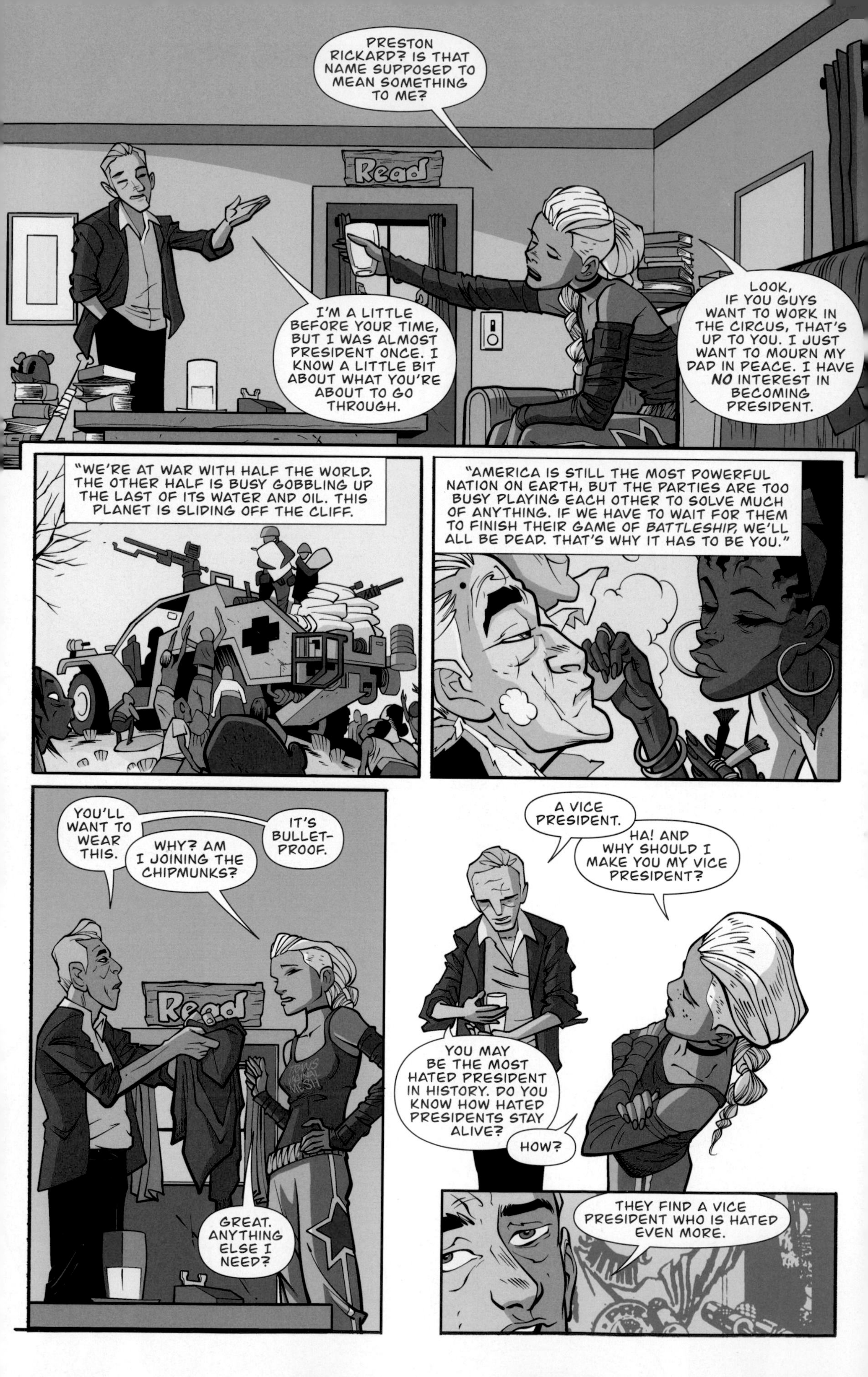
PRESTON RICKARD? IS THAT NAME SUPPOSED TO MEAN SOMETHING TO ME?
Read
I'M A LITTLE BEFORE YOUR TIME, BUT I WAS ALMOST PRESIDENT ONCE. I KNOW A LITTLE BIT ABOUT WHAT YOU'RE ABOUT TO GO THROUGH.
LOOK, IF YOU GUYS WANT TO WORK IN THE CIRCUS, THAT'S UP TO YOU. I JUST WANT TO MOURN MY DAD IN PEACE. I HAVE NO INTEREST IN BECOMING PRESIDENT.
"WE'RE AT WAR WITH HALF THE WORLD. THE OTHER HALF IS BUSY GOBBLING UP THE LAST OF ITS WATER AND OIL. THIS PLANET IS SLIDING OFF THE CLIFF.
"AMERICA IS STILL THE MOST POWERFUL NATION ON EARTH, BUT THE PARTIES ARE TOO BUSY PLAYING EACH OTHER TO SOLVE MUCH OF ANYTHING. IF WE HAVE TO WAIT FOR THEM TO FINISH THEIR GAME OF BATTLESHIP, WE'LL ALL BE DEAD. THAT'S WHY IT HAS TO BE YOU."
YOU'LL WANT TO WEAR THIS.
IT'S BULLET-PROOF.
WHY? AM I JOINING THE CHIPMUNKS?
Read
GREAT. ANYTHING ELSE I NEED?
A VICE PRESIDENT.
HA! AND WHY SHOULD I MAKE YOU MY VICE PRESIDENT?
YOU MAY BE THE MOST HATED PRESIDENT IN HISTORY. DO YOU KNOW HOW HATED PRESIDENTS STAY ALIVE?
HOW?
THEY FIND A VICE PRESIDENT WHO IS HATED EVEN MORE.

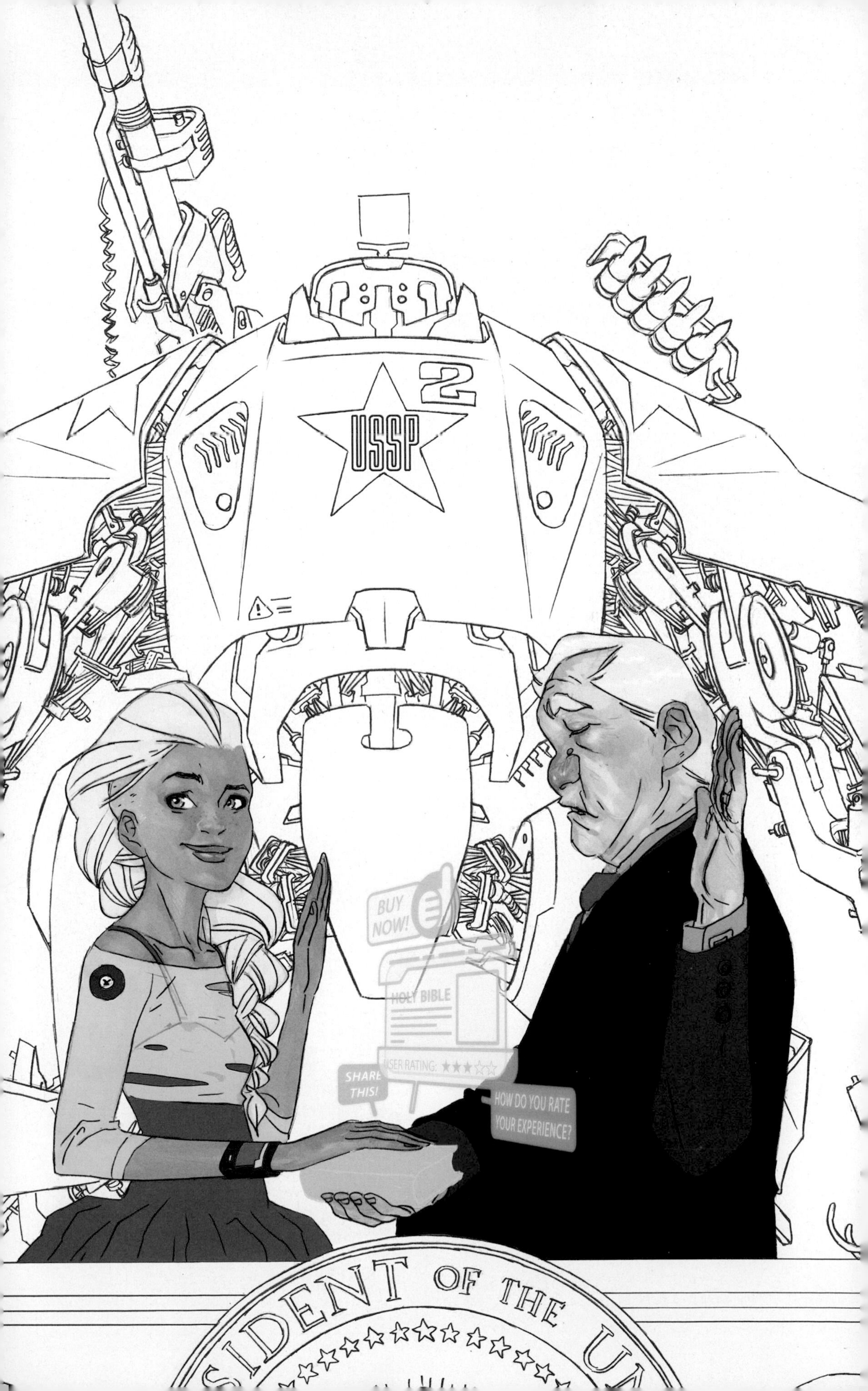

USSP
2
BUY NOW!
HOLY BIBLE
USER RATING:
SHARE THIS!
HOW DO YOU RATE YOUR EXPERIENCE?
SIDENT OF THE U

ADVENTURES IN CABINETRY

MARK RUSSELL writer BEN CALDWELL penciller MARK MORALES inker JEREMY LAWSON colorist

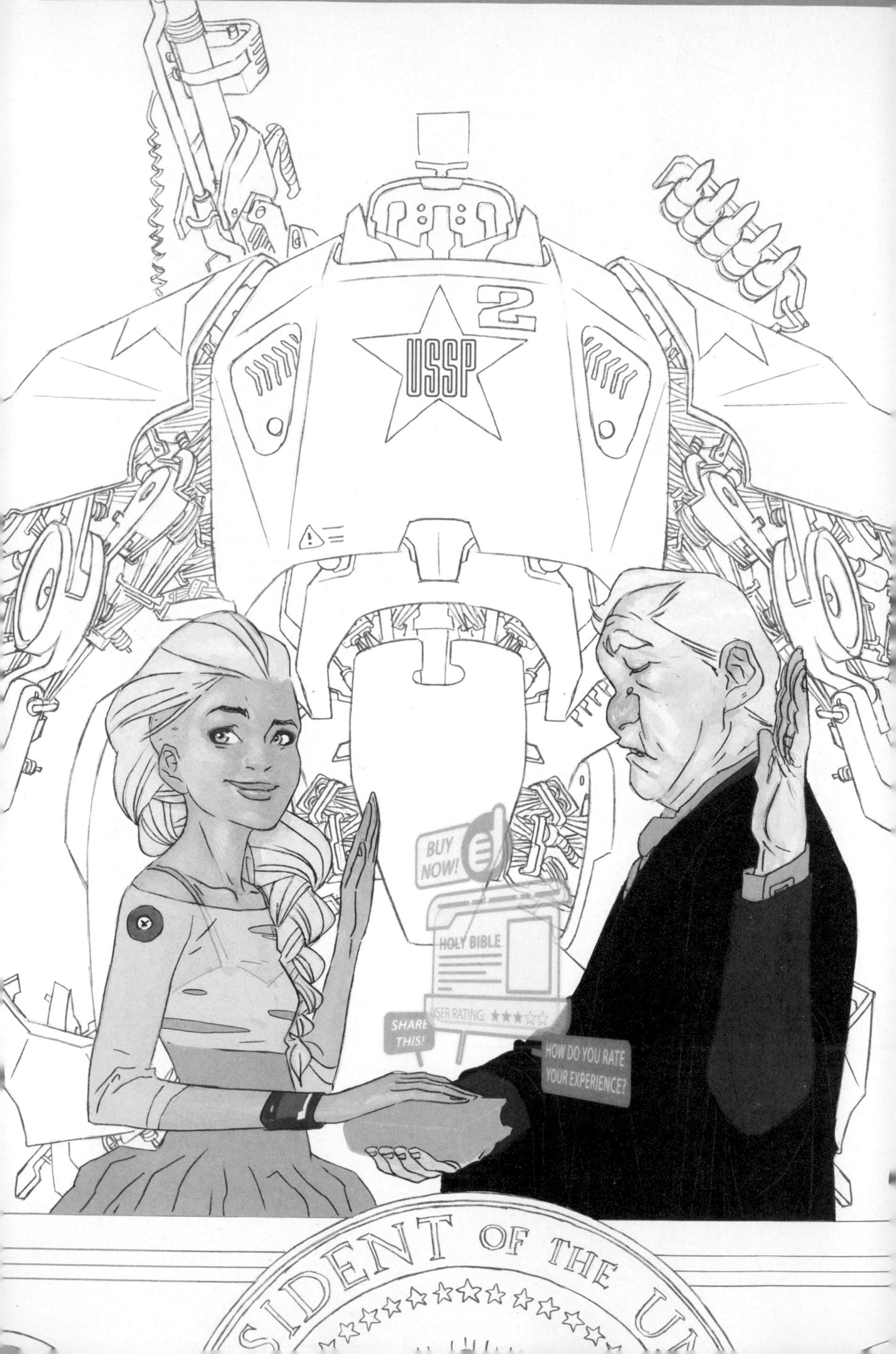

USSP
2
BUY NOW!
HOLY BIBLE
USER RATING:
SHARE THIS!
HOW DO YOU RATE YOUR EXPERIENCE?

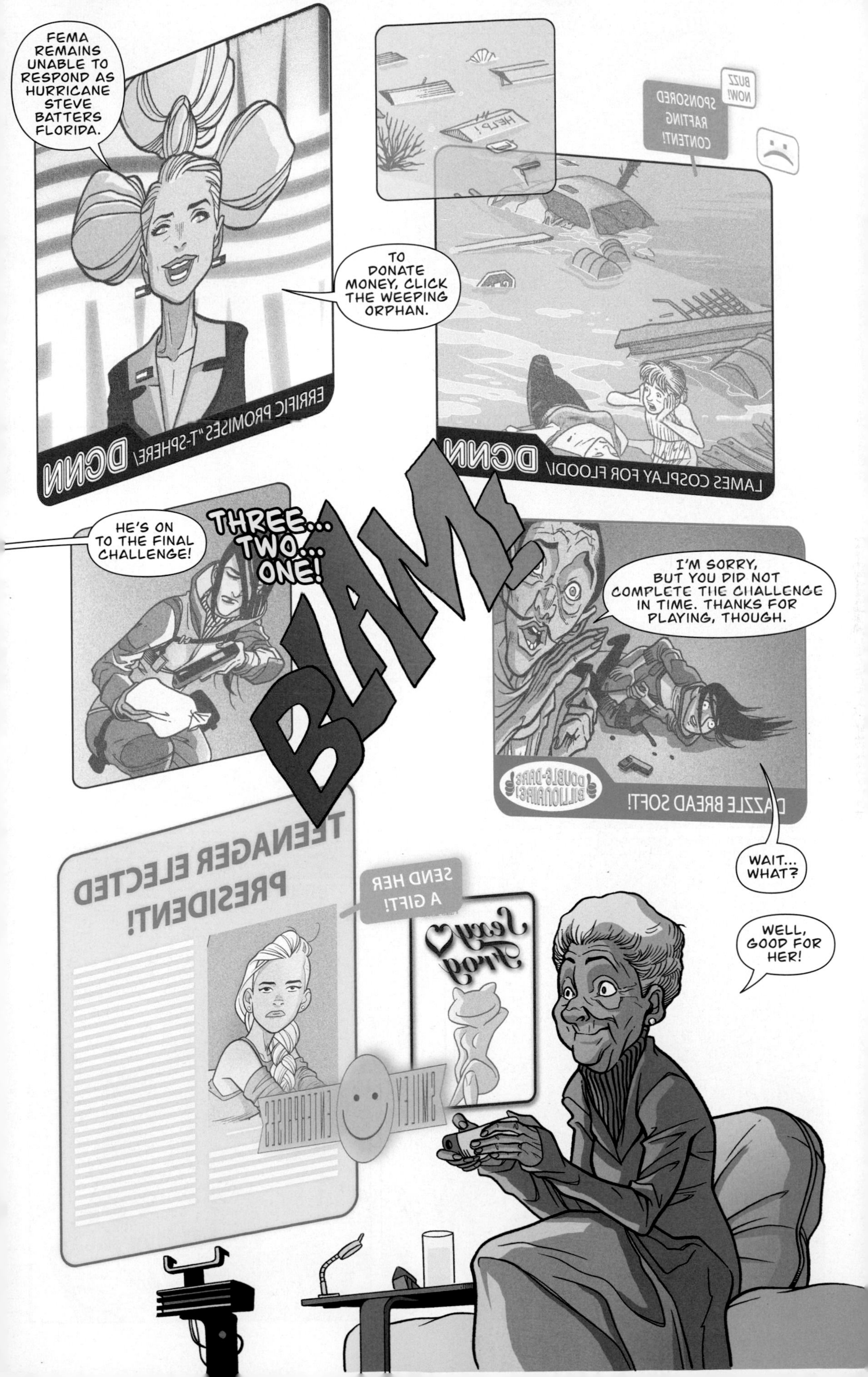
FEMA REMAINS UNABLE TO RESPOND AS HURRICANE STEVE BATTERS FLORIDA.
TO DONATE MONEY, CLICK THE WEEPING ORPHAN.
HE'S ON TO THE FINAL CHALLENGE!
THREE... TWO... ONE!
BLAM!
I'M SORRY, BUT YOU DID NOT COMPLETE THE CHALLENGE IN TIME. THANKS FOR PLAYING, THOUGH.
WAIT... WHAT?
WELL, GOOD FOR HER!

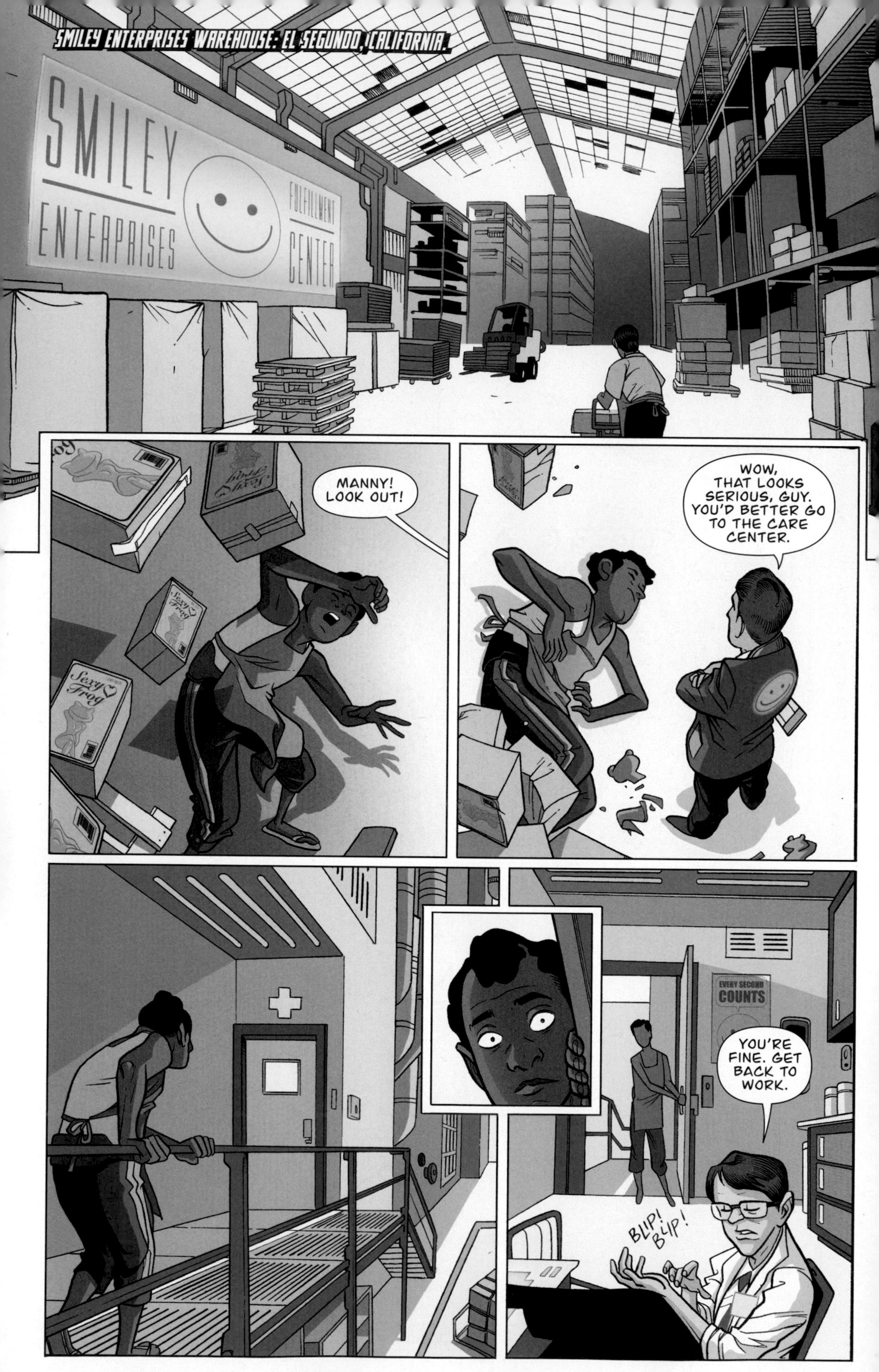
SMILEY ENTERPRISES WAREHOUSE: EL SEGUNDO, CALIFORNIA.
SMILEY ENTERPRISES
FULFILLMENT CENTER
MANNY! LOOK OUT!
Sexy Frog
WOW, THAT LOOKS SERIOUS, GUY. YOU'D BETTER GO TO THE CARE CENTER.
EVERY SECOND COUNTS
YOU'RE FINE. GET BACK TO WORK.
BLIP! BLIP!

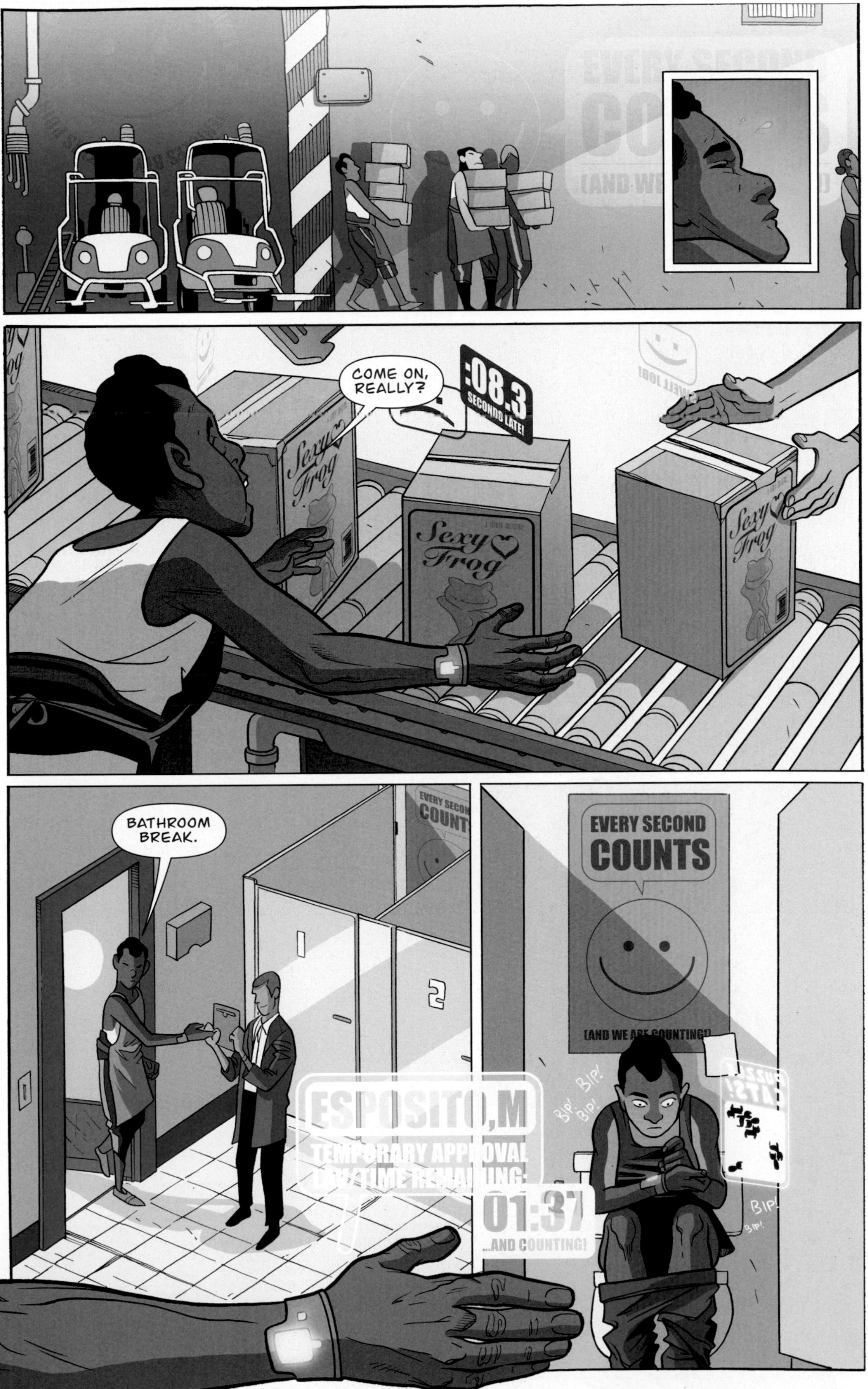
COME ON, REALLY?
:08.3
SECONDS LATE!
Sexy Frog
Sexy Frog
Sexy Frog
BATHROOM BREAK.
EVERY SECOND COUNTS
EVERY SECOND
COUNTS
(AND WE ARE COUNTING!)
BIP! BIP! BIP!
ESPOSITO,M
TEMPORARY APPROVAL
LAV/TIME REMAINING:
01:37
...AND COUNTING!
BIP! BIP!

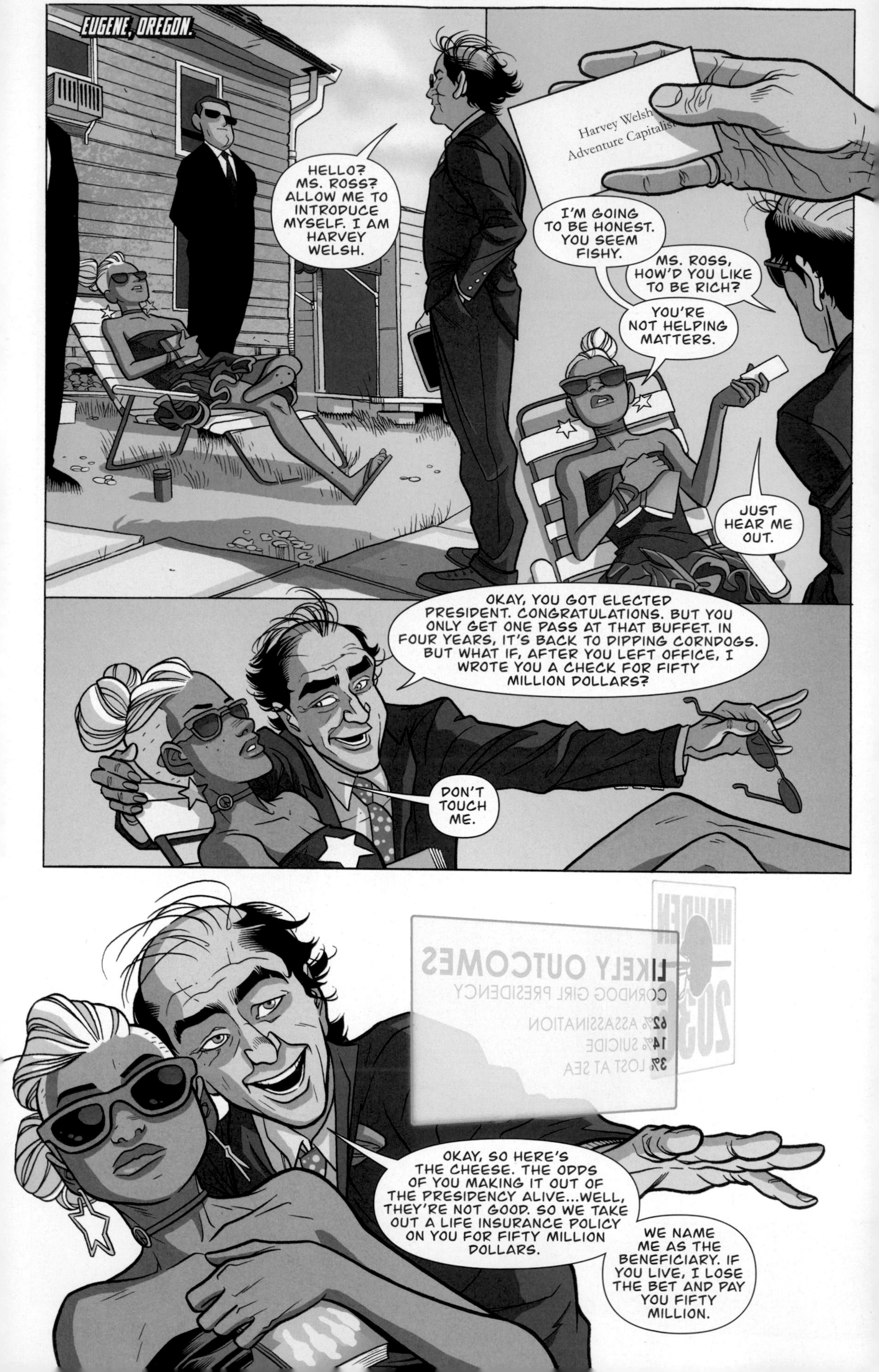
EUGENE, OREGON.
HELLO? MS. ROSS? ALLOW ME TO INTRODUCE MYSELF. I AM HARVEY WELSH.
Harvey Welsh
Adventure Capitalist
I'M GOING TO BE HONEST. YOU SEEM FISHY.
MS. ROSS, HOW'D YOU LIKE TO BE RICH?
YOU'RE NOT HELPING MATTERS.
JUST HEAR ME OUT.
OKAY, YOU GOT ELECTED PRESIDENT. CONGRATULATIONS. BUT YOU ONLY GET ONE PASS AT THAT BUFFET. IN FOUR YEARS, IT'S BACK TO DIPPING CORNDOGS. BUT WHAT IF, AFTER YOU LEFT OFFICE, I WROTE YOU A CHECK FOR FIFTY MILLION DOLLARS?
DON'T TOUCH ME.
LIKELY OUTCOMES
CORNDOG GIRL PRESIDENCY
62% ASSASSINATION
14% SUICIDE
3% LOST AT SEA
OKAY, SO HERE'S THE CHEESE. THE ODDS OF YOU MAKING IT OUT OF THE PRESIDENCY ALIVE...WELL, THEY'RE NOT GOOD. SO WE TAKE OUT A LIFE INSURANCE POLICY ON YOU FOR FIFTY MILLION DOLLARS.
WE NAME ME AS THE BENEFICIARY. IF YOU LIVE, I LOSE THE BET AND PAY YOU FIFTY MILLION.

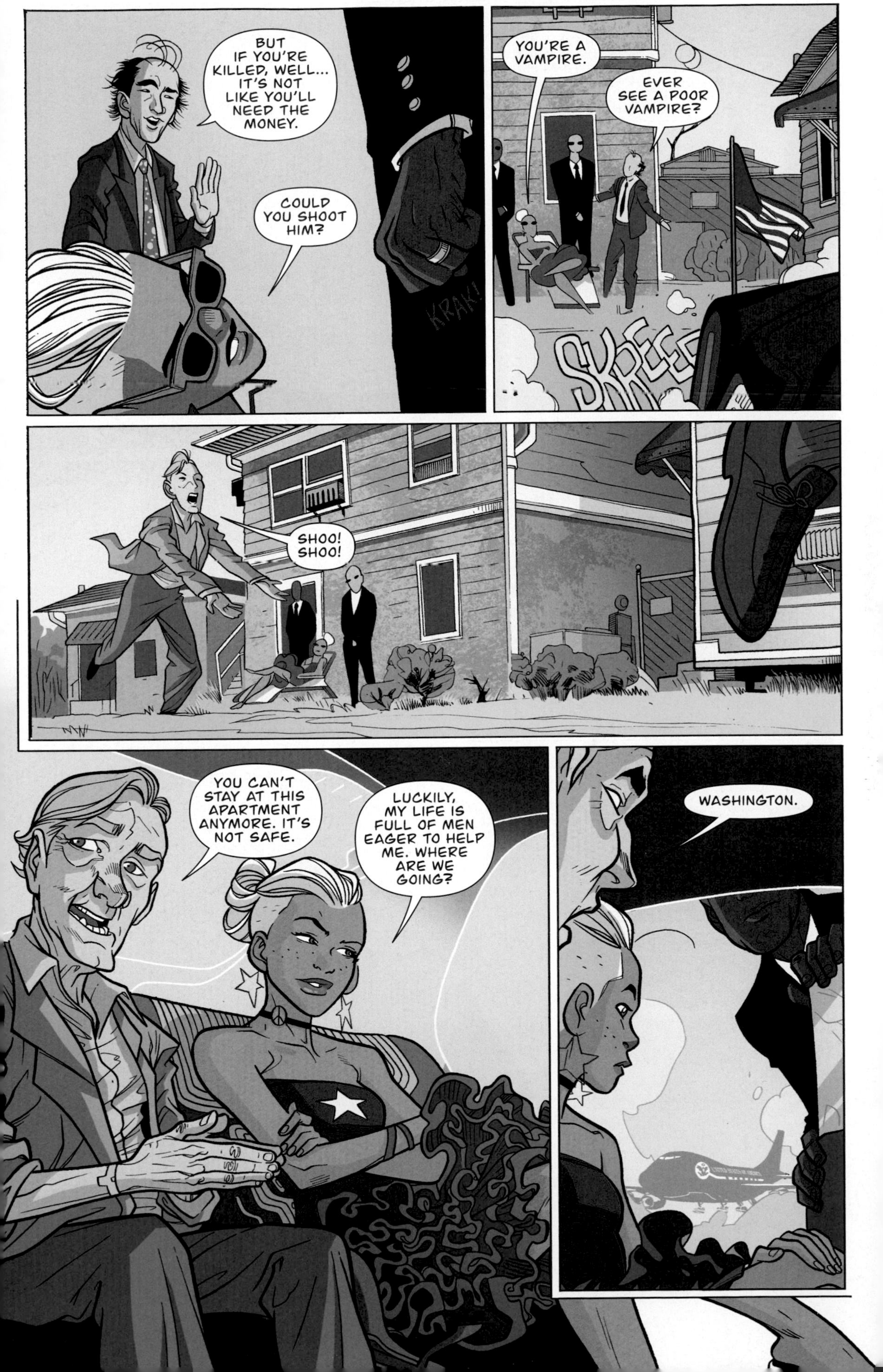
BUT IF YOU'RE KILLED, WELL... IT'S NOT LIKE YOU'LL NEED THE MONEY.
COULD YOU SHOOT HIM?
KRAK!
YOU'RE A VAMPIRE.
EVER SEE A POOR VAMPIRE?
SKREEE
SHOO! SHOO!
YOU CAN'T STAY AT THIS APARTMENT ANYMORE. IT'S NOT SAFE.
LUCKILY, MY LIFE IS FULL OF MEN EAGER TO HELP ME. WHERE ARE WE GOING?
WASHINGTON.

GENTLEMEN, IN LESS THAN A WEEK, WE WILL HAVE A NEW PRESIDENT. MY SOURCES SAY SHE INTENDS TO MAKE CONGRESSMAN RICKARD HER VICE PRESIDENT.

THAT TRAITOR? VICE PRESIDENT?!

NOBODY WANTS RICKARD TO BECOME PRESIDENT. ONCE HE'S SWORN IN AS VICE PRESIDENT, NOBODY IN WASHINGTON IS GOING TO KNOCK HER OFF. MAYBE SHE'S NOT AS DUMB AS THE CORNDOG SCARS SUGGEST.

KLIK!

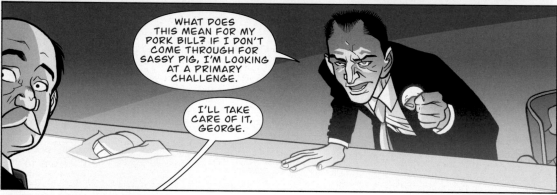

WHAT DOES THIS MEAN FOR MY PORK BILL? IF I DON'T COME THROUGH FOR SASSY PIG, I'M LOOKING AT A PRIMARY CHALLENGE.

I'LL TAKE CARE OF IT, GEORGE.

AS FOR PRESIDENT CORNDOG, THERE'S STILL A WEEK BEFORE SHE'S SWORN IN. A LOT CAN HAPPEN BEFORE THEN.

JUST HACKED INTO SENATOR LONGWATER'S EYEBALL. TEN POINTS.

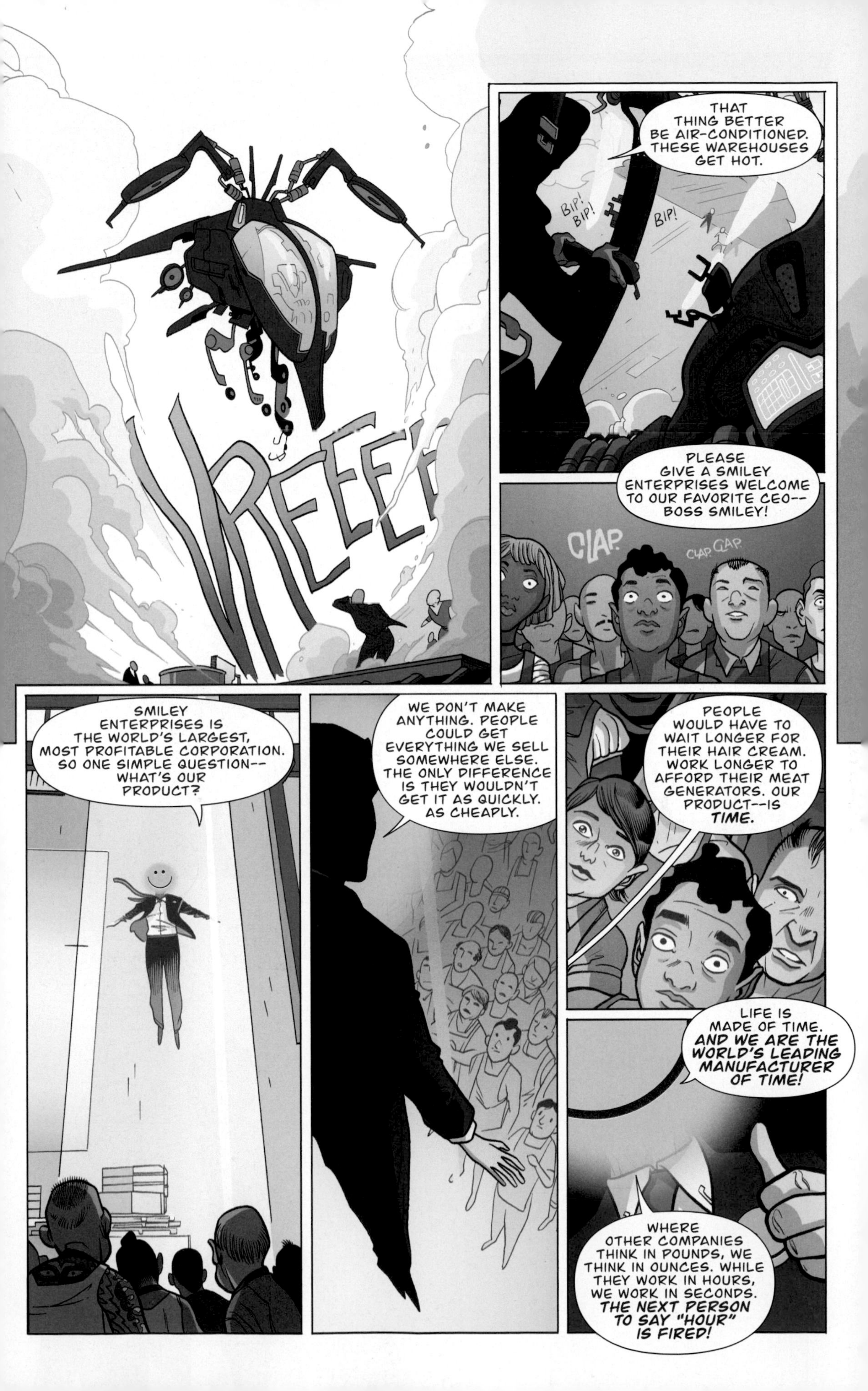
VREEEE
THAT THING BETTER BE AIR-CONDITIONED. THESE WAREHOUSES GET HOT.
BIP! BIP!
BIP!
PLEASE GIVE A SMILEY ENTERPRISES WELCOME TO OUR FAVORITE CEO--BOSS SMILEY!
CLAP
CLAP CLAP
SMILEY ENTERPRISES IS THE WORLD'S LARGEST, MOST PROFITABLE CORPORATION. SO ONE SIMPLE QUESTION--WHAT'S OUR PRODUCT?
WE DON'T MAKE ANYTHING. PEOPLE COULD GET EVERYTHING WE SELL SOMEWHERE ELSE. THE ONLY DIFFERENCE IS THEY WOULDN'T GET IT AS QUICKLY. AS CHEAPLY.
PEOPLE WOULD HAVE TO WAIT LONGER FOR THEIR HAIR CREAM. WORK LONGER TO AFFORD THEIR MEAT GENERATORS. OUR PRODUCT--IS TIME.
LIFE IS MADE OF TIME. AND WE ARE THE WORLD'S LEADING MANUFACTURER OF TIME!
WHERE OTHER COMPANIES THINK IN POUNDS, WE THINK IN OUNCES. WHILE THEY WORK IN HOURS, WE WORK IN SECONDS. THE NEXT PERSON TO SAY "HOUR" IS FIRED!

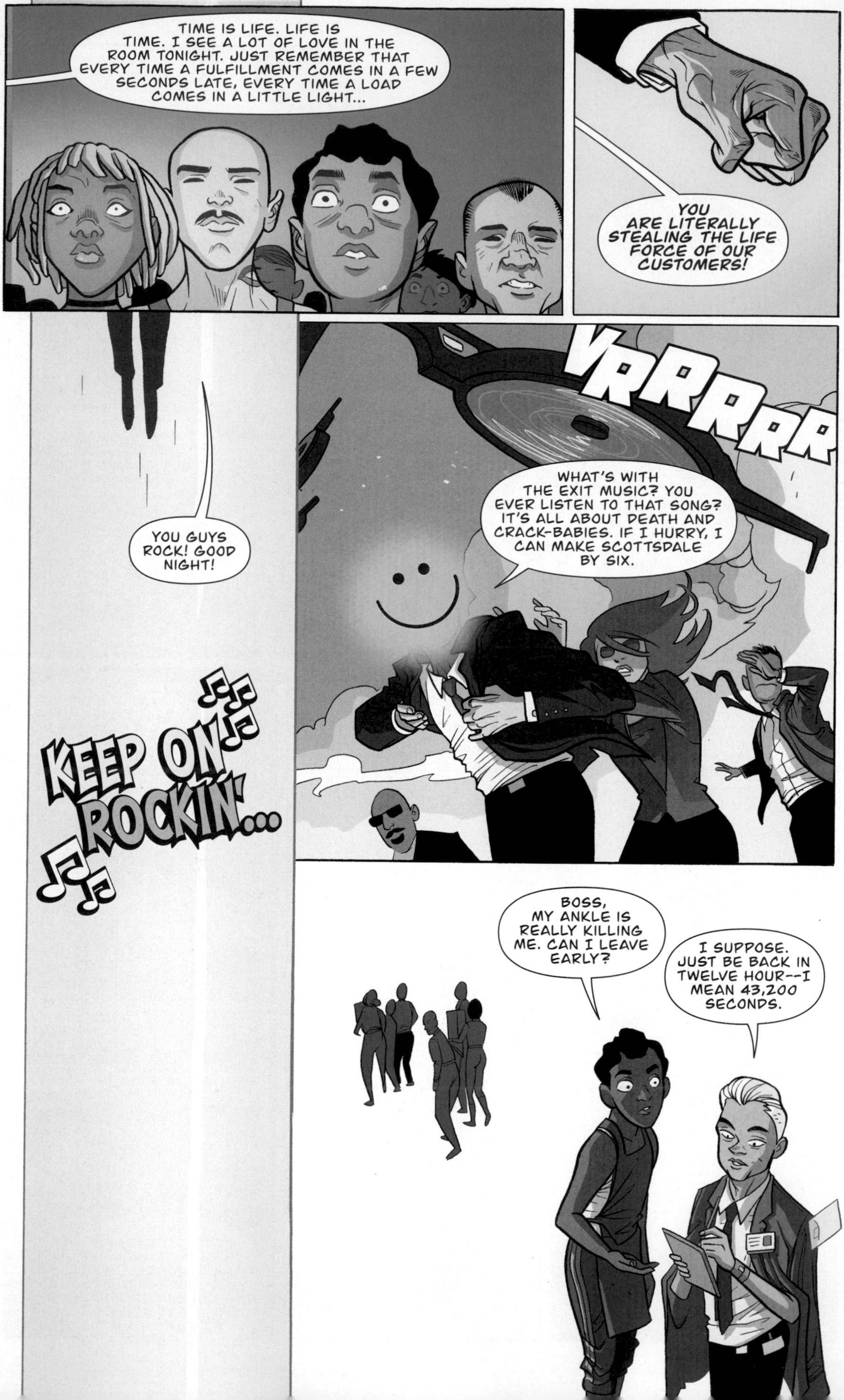
TIME IS LIFE. LIFE IS TIME. I SEE A LOT OF LOVE IN THE ROOM TONIGHT. JUST REMEMBER THAT EVERY TIME A FULFILLMENT COMES IN A FEW SECONDS LATE, EVERY TIME A LOAD COMES IN A LITTLE LIGHT...
YOU ARE LITERALLY STEALING THE LIFE FORCE OF OUR CUSTOMERS!
YOU GUYS ROCK! GOOD NIGHT!
VRRRRR
WHAT'S WITH THE EXIT MUSIC? YOU EVER LISTEN TO THAT SONG? IT'S ALL ABOUT DEATH AND CRACK-BABIES. IF I HURRY, I CAN MAKE SCOTTSDALE BY SIX.
KEEP ON ROCKIN'...
BOSS, MY ANKLE IS REALLY KILLING ME. CAN I LEAVE EARLY?
I SUPPOSE. JUST BE BACK IN TWELVE HOUR--I MEAN 43,200 SECONDS.

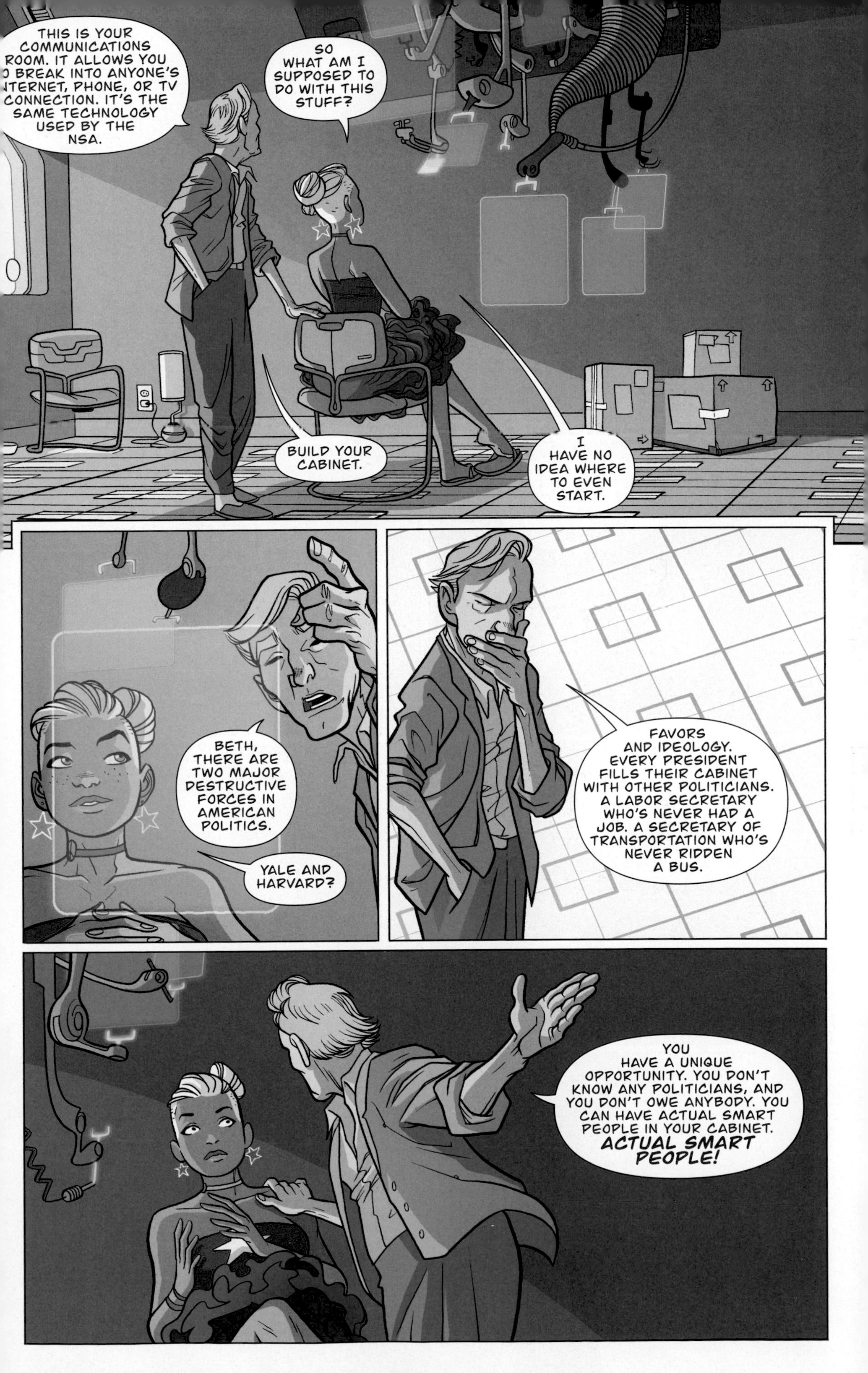
THIS IS YOUR COMMUNICATIONS ROOM. IT ALLOWS YOU TO BREAK INTO ANYONE'S INTERNET, PHONE, OR TV CONNECTION. IT'S THE SAME TECHNOLOGY USED BY THE NSA.
SO WHAT AM I SUPPOSED TO DO WITH THIS STUFF?
BUILD YOUR CABINET.
I HAVE NO IDEA WHERE TO EVEN START.
BETH, THERE ARE TWO MAJOR DESTRUCTIVE FORCES IN AMERICAN POLITICS.
YALE AND HARVARD?
FAVORS AND IDEOLOGY. EVERY PRESIDENT FILLS THEIR CABINET WITH OTHER POLITICIANS. A LABOR SECRETARY WHO'S NEVER HAD A JOB. A SECRETARY OF TRANSPORTATION WHO'S NEVER RIDDEN A BUS.
YOU HAVE A UNIQUE OPPORTUNITY. YOU DON'T KNOW ANY POLITICIANS, AND YOU DON'T OWE ANYBODY. YOU CAN HAVE ACTUAL SMART PEOPLE IN YOUR CABINET. ACTUAL SMART PEOPLE!

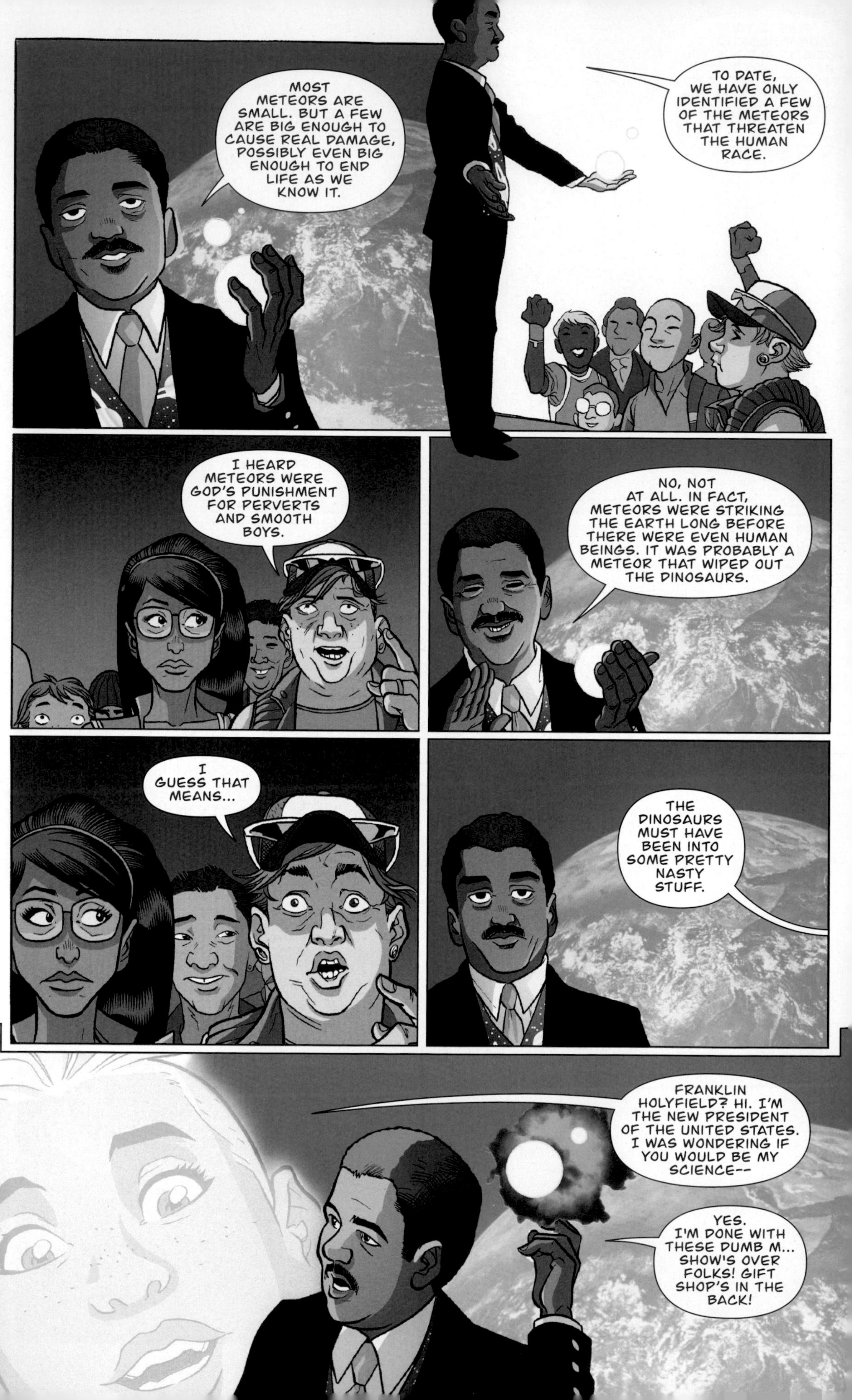
MOST METEORS ARE SMALL. BUT A FEW ARE BIG ENOUGH TO CAUSE REAL DAMAGE, POSSIBLY EVEN BIG ENOUGH TO END LIFE AS WE KNOW IT.
TO DATE, WE HAVE ONLY IDENTIFIED A FEW OF THE METEORS THAT THREATEN THE HUMAN RACE.
I HEARD METEORS WERE GOD'S PUNISHMENT FOR PERVERTS AND SMOOTH BOYS.
NO, NOT AT ALL. IN FACT, METEORS WERE STRIKING THE EARTH LONG BEFORE THERE WERE EVEN HUMAN BEINGS. IT WAS PROBABLY A METEOR THAT WIPED OUT THE DINOSAURS.
I GUESS THAT MEANS...
THE DINOSAURS MUST HAVE BEEN INTO SOME PRETTY NASTY STUFF.
FRANKLIN HOLYFIELD? HI. I'M THE NEW PRESIDENT OF THE UNITED STATES. I WAS WONDERING IF YOU WOULD BE MY SCIENCE--
YES. I'M DONE WITH THESE DUMB M... SHOW'S OVER FOLKS! GIFT SHOP'S IN THE BACK!

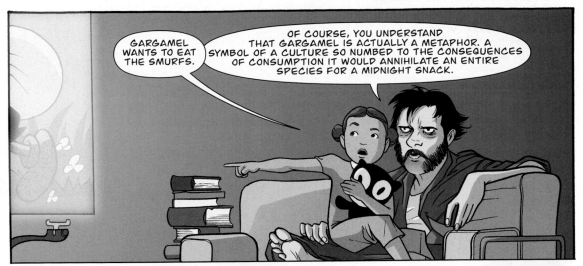

GARGAMEL WANTS TO EAT THE SMURFS.

OF COURSE, YOU UNDERSTAND THAT GARGAMEL IS ACTUALLY A METAPHOR. A SYMBOL OF A CULTURE SO NUMBED TO THE CONSEQUENCES OF CONSUMPTION IT WOULD ANNIHILATE AN ENTIRE SPECIES FOR A MIDNIGHT SNACK.

A MAN SO BORED WITH LIFE THAT HE CREATES ENEMIES SIMPLY SO THEY CAN EITHER INVIGORATE OR DESTROY HIM. IT DOES NOT MATTER WHICH.

GARGAMEL IS LATE STAGE CAPITALISM, REFLECTED BACK TO US IN A BROKEN MIRROR. HE ALLOWS US TO DESPISE WHAT WE HAVE BECOME, WITHOUT RECOGNIZING IT AS OURSELVES.

GARGAMEL BLOWS, DADDY.

HELLO? MISTER WYZCHEK? MY NAME IS BETH ROSS. THE NEW PRESIDENT? I WAS WONDERING IF YOU'D BE MY SECRETARY OF STATE?

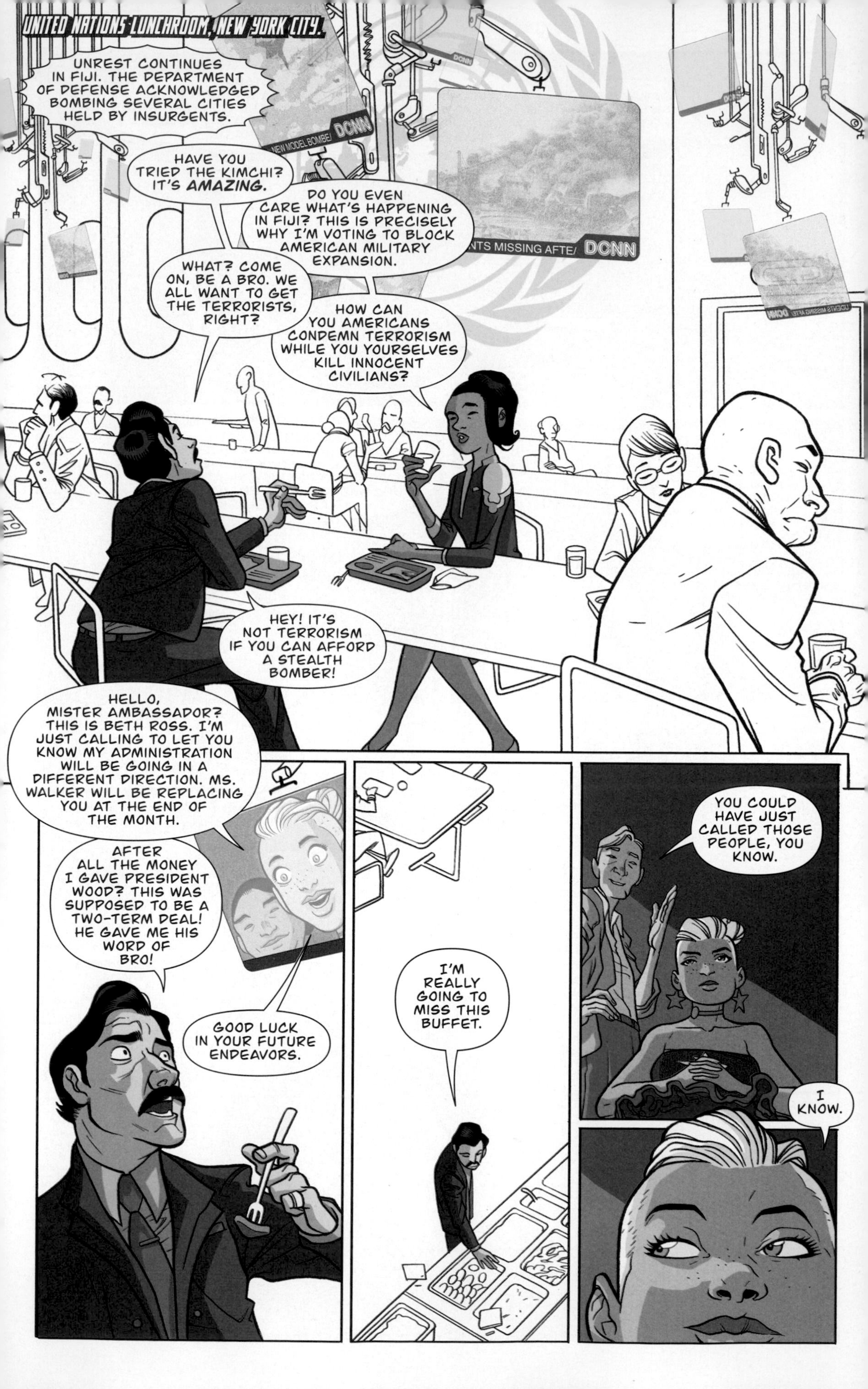

UNITED NATIONS LUNCHROOM, NEW YORK CITY.
UNREST CONTINUES IN FIJI. THE DEPARTMENT OF DEFENSE ACKNOWLEDGED BOMBING SEVERAL CITIES HELD BY INSURGENTS.
NEW MODEL BOMBE/ DCNN
HAVE YOU TRIED THE KIMCHI? IT'S AMAZING.
DO YOU EVEN CARE WHAT'S HAPPENING IN FIJI? THIS IS PRECISELY WHY I'M VOTING TO BLOCK AMERICAN MILITARY EXPANSION.
NTS MISSING AFTE/ DCNN
WHAT? COME ON, BE A BRO. WE ALL WANT TO GET THE TERRORISTS, RIGHT?
HOW CAN YOU AMERICANS CONDEMN TERRORISM WHILE YOU YOURSELVES KILL INNOCENT CIVILIANS?
HEY! IT'S NOT TERRORISM IF YOU CAN AFFORD A STEALTH BOMBER!
HELLO, MISTER AMBASSADOR? THIS IS BETH ROSS. I'M JUST CALLING TO LET YOU KNOW MY ADMINISTRATION WILL BE GOING IN A DIFFERENT DIRECTION. MS. WALKER WILL BE REPLACING YOU AT THE END OF THE MONTH.
AFTER ALL THE MONEY I GAVE PRESIDENT WOOD? THIS WAS SUPPOSED TO BE A TWO-TERM DEAL! HE GAVE ME HIS WORD OF BRO!
GOOD LUCK IN YOUR FUTURE ENDEAVORS.
I'M REALLY GOING TO MISS THIS BUFFET.
YOU COULD HAVE JUST CALLED THOSE PEOPLE, YOU KNOW.
I KNOW.

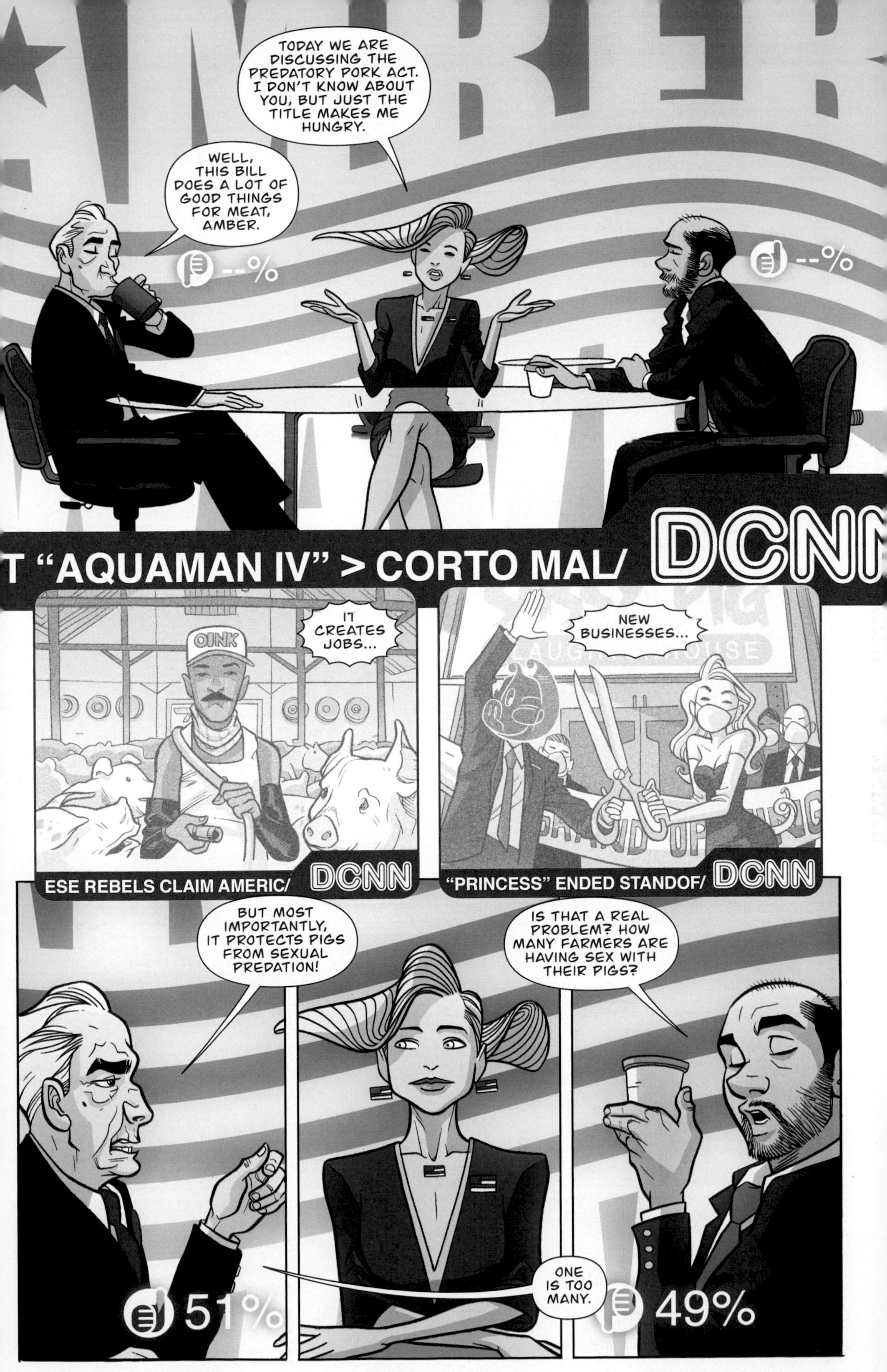
TODAY WE ARE DISCUSSING THE PREDATORY PORK ACT. I DON'T KNOW ABOUT YOU, BUT JUST THE TITLE MAKES ME HUNGRY.
WELL, THIS BILL DOES A LOT OF GOOD THINGS FOR MEAT, AMBER.
--%
--%
T "AQUAMAN IV" > CORTO MAL/
DCNN
IT CREATES JOBS...
OINK
ESE REBELS CLAIM AMERIC/
DCNN
NEW BUSINESSES...
"PRINCESS" ENDED STANDOF/
DCNN
BUT MOST IMPORTANTLY, IT PROTECTS PIGS FROM SEXUAL PREDATION!
IS THAT A REAL PROBLEM? HOW MANY FARMERS ARE HAVING SEX WITH THEIR PIGS?
51%
ONE IS TOO MANY.
49%

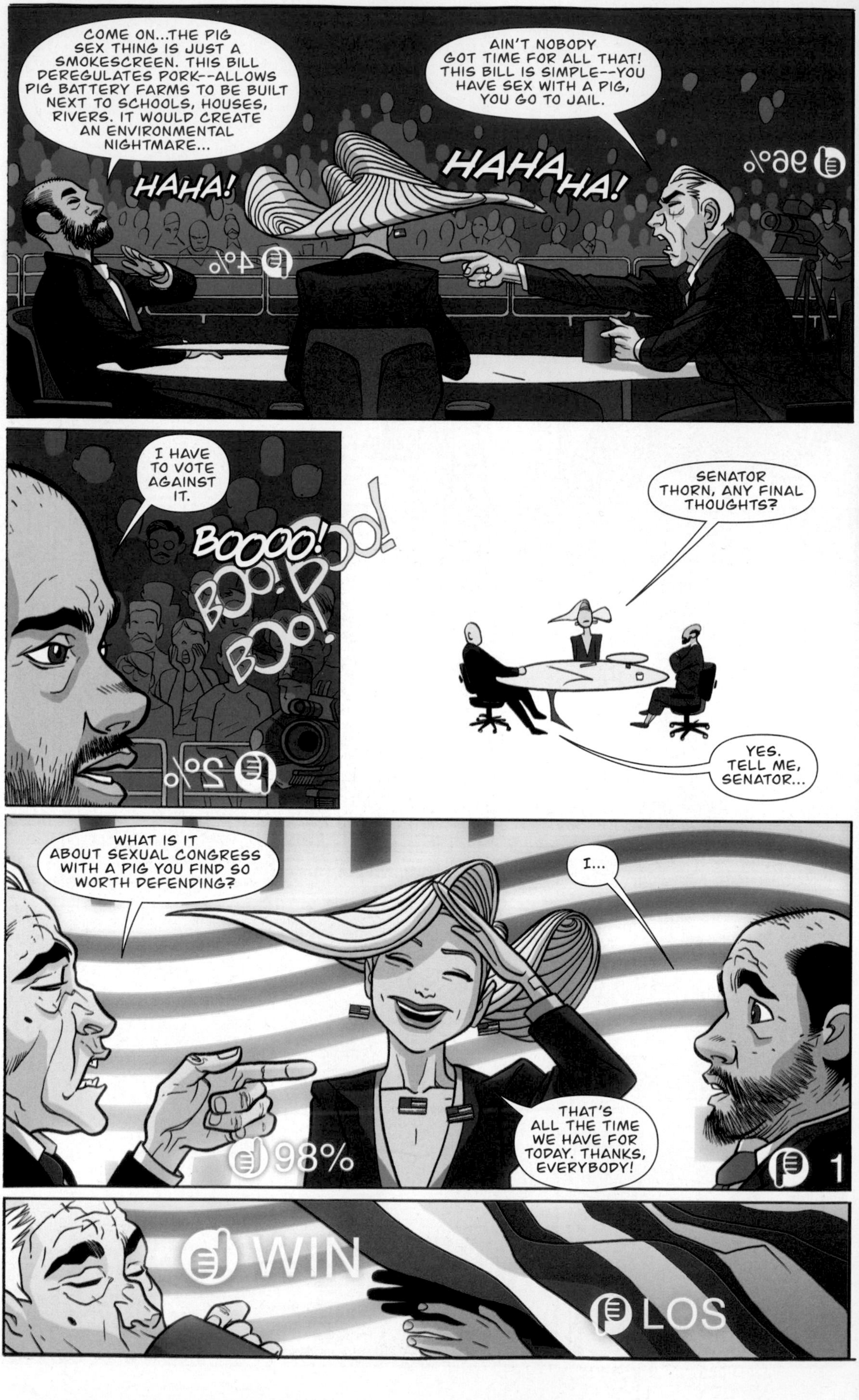
COME ON...THE PIG SEX THING IS JUST A SMOKESCREEN. THIS BILL DEREGULATES PORK--ALLOWS PIG BATTERY FARMS TO BE BUILT NEXT TO SCHOOLS, HOUSES, RIVERS. IT WOULD CREATE AN ENVIRONMENTAL NIGHTMARE...
AIN'T NOBODY GOT TIME FOR ALL THAT! THIS BILL IS SIMPLE--YOU HAVE SEX WITH A PIG, YOU GO TO JAIL.
HAHA!
HAHAHAHA!
96%
4%
I HAVE TO VOTE AGAINST IT.
BOOOO!
BOO!
BOO!
BOO!
2%
SENATOR THORN, ANY FINAL THOUGHTS?
YES. TELL ME, SENATOR...
WHAT IS IT ABOUT SEXUAL CONGRESS WITH A PIG YOU FIND SO WORTH DEFENDING?
I...
THAT'S ALL THE TIME WE HAVE FOR TODAY. THANKS, EVERYBODY!
98%
1
WIN
LOS

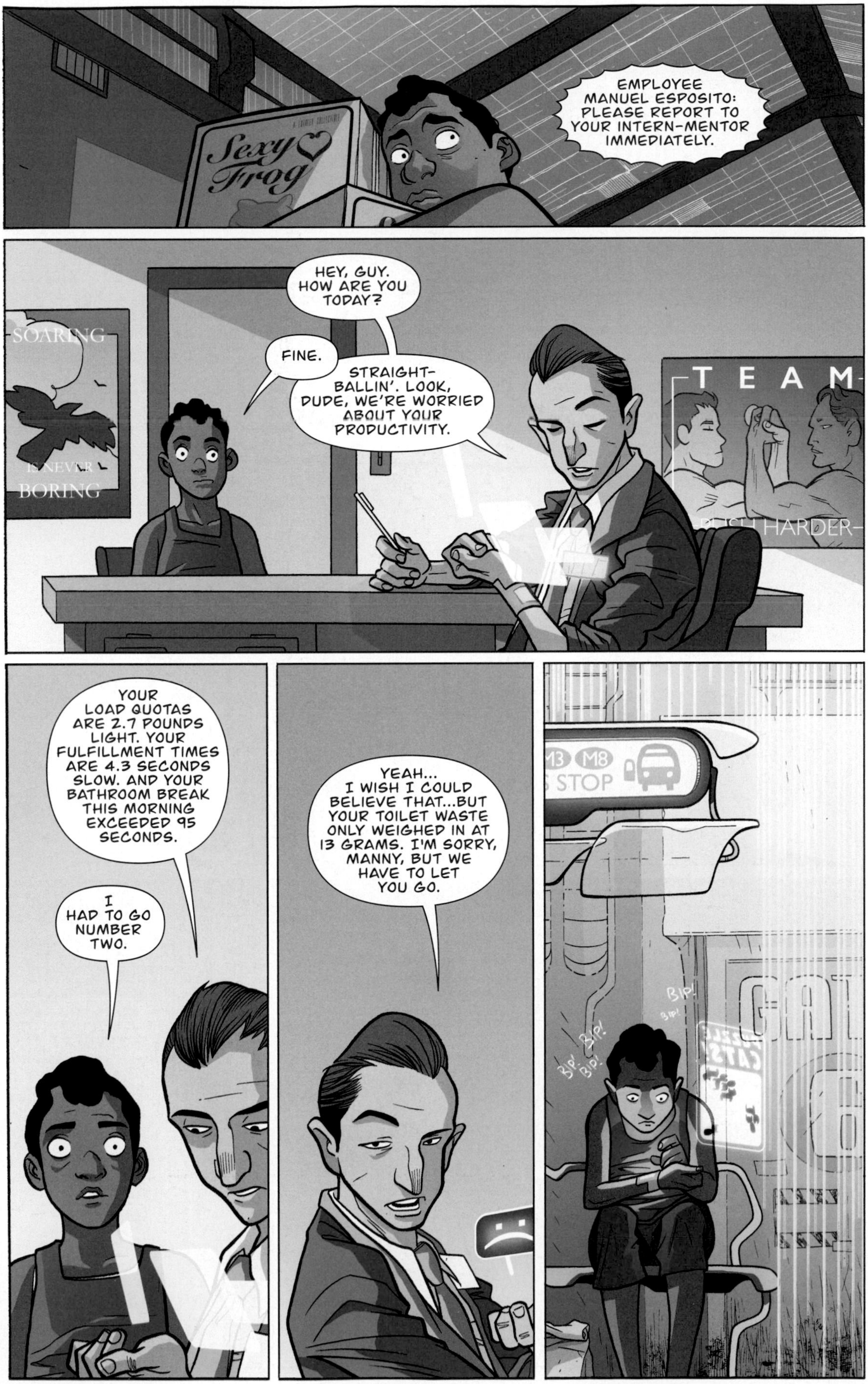
Sexy Frog
EMPLOYEE MANUEL ESPOSITO: PLEASE REPORT TO YOUR INTERN-MENTOR IMMEDIATELY.
SOARING IS NEVER BORING
TEAM
HARDER
HEY, GUY. HOW ARE YOU TODAY?
FINE.
STRAIGHT-BALLIN'. LOOK, DUDE, WE'RE WORRIED ABOUT YOUR PRODUCTIVITY.
YOUR LOAD QUOTAS ARE 2.7 POUNDS LIGHT. YOUR FULFILLMENT TIMES ARE 4.3 SECONDS SLOW. AND YOUR BATHROOM BREAK THIS MORNING EXCEEDED 95 SECONDS.
I HAD TO GO NUMBER TWO.
YEAH... I WISH I COULD BELIEVE THAT...BUT YOUR TOILET WASTE ONLY WEIGHED IN AT 13 GRAMS. I'M SORRY, MANNY, BUT WE HAVE TO LET YOU GO.
M3 M8
STOP
BIP! BIP! BIP! BIP! BIP! BIP!

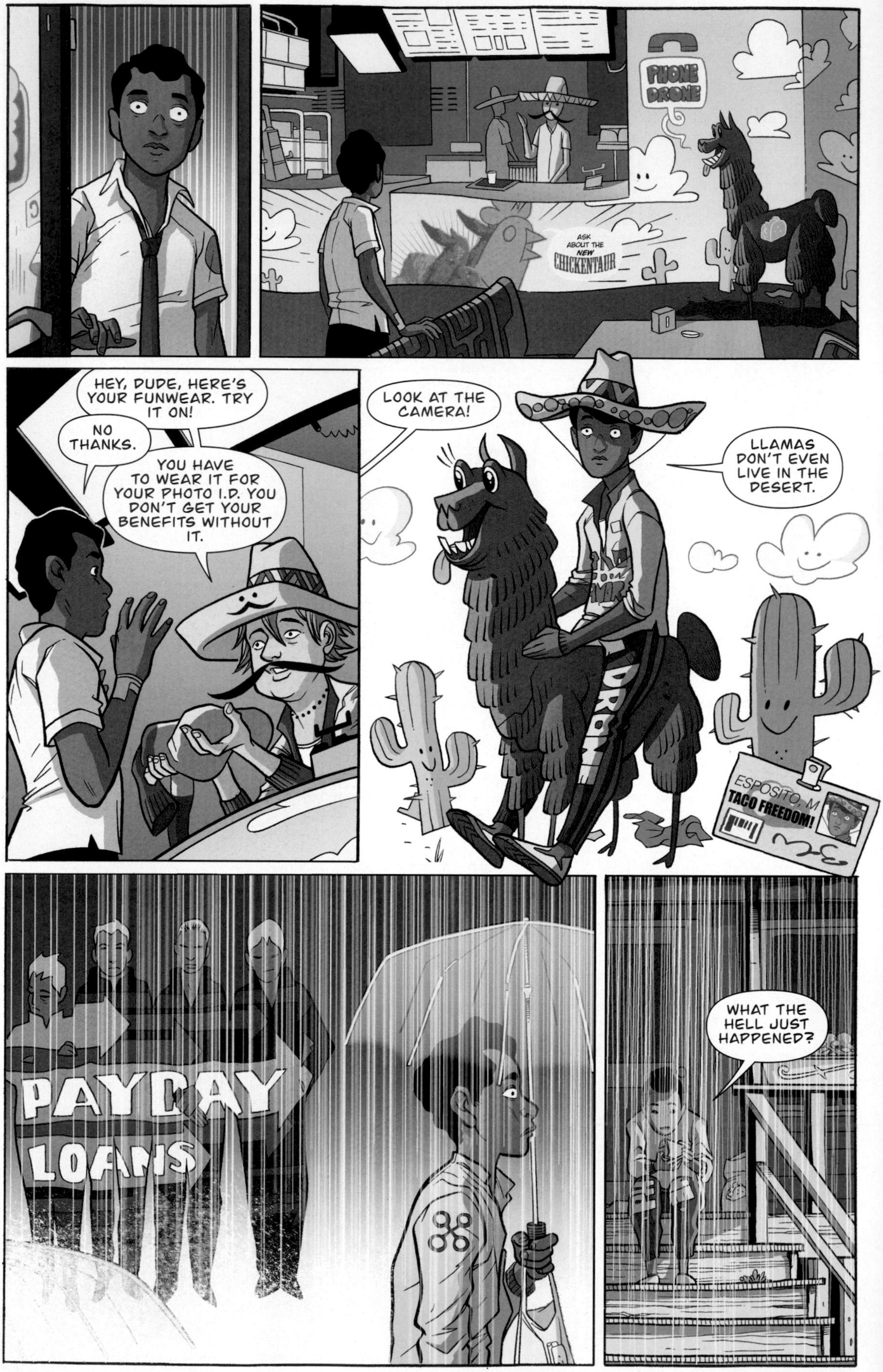
PHONE DRONE
ASK ABOUT THE NEW CHICKENTAUR
HEY, DUDE, HERE'S YOUR FUNWEAR. TRY IT ON!
NO THANKS.
YOU HAVE TO WEAR IT FOR YOUR PHOTO I.D. YOU DON'T GET YOUR BENEFITS WITHOUT IT.
LOOK AT THE CAMERA!
LLAMAS DON'T EVEN LIVE IN THE DESERT.
DRONE
ESPOSITO, M
TACO FREEDOM!
PAYDAY LOANS
WHAT THE HELL JUST HAPPENED?

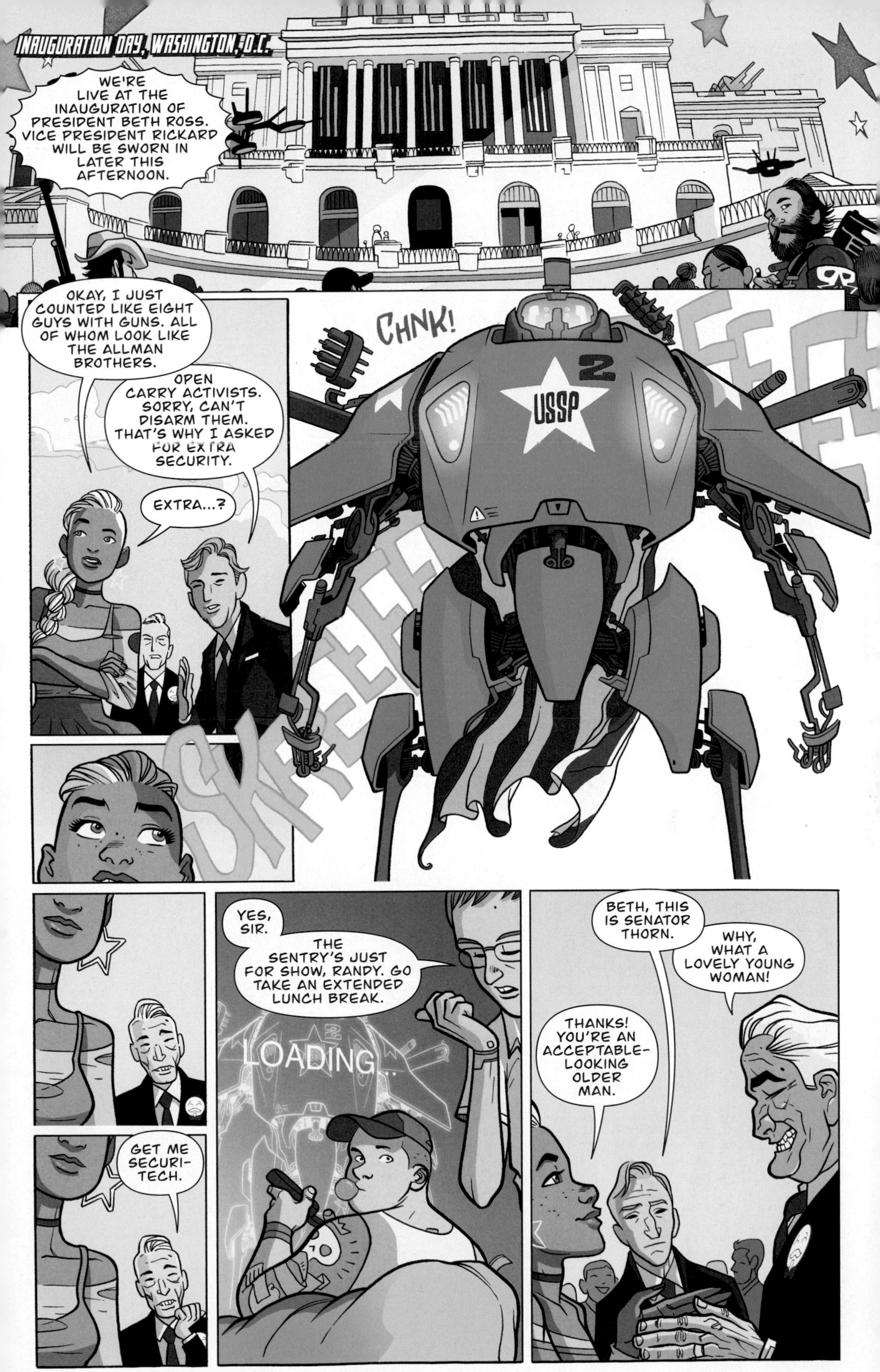
INAUGURATION DAY, WASHINGTON, D.C.
WE'RE LIVE AT THE INAUGURATION OF PRESIDENT BETH ROSS. VICE PRESIDENT RICKARD WILL BE SWORN IN LATER THIS AFTERNOON.
OKAY, I JUST COUNTED LIKE EIGHT GUYS WITH GUNS. ALL OF WHOM LOOK LIKE THE ALLMAN BROTHERS.
OPEN CARRY ACTIVISTS. SORRY, CAN'T DISARM THEM. THAT'S WHY I ASKED FOR EXTRA SECURITY.
EXTRA...?
CHNK!
USSP
2
GET ME SECURI-TECH.
YES, SIR.
THE SENTRY'S JUST FOR SHOW, RANDY. GO TAKE AN EXTENDED LUNCH BREAK.
LOADING...
BETH, THIS IS SENATOR THORN.
WHY, WHAT A LOVELY YOUNG WOMAN!
THANKS! YOU'RE AN ACCEPTABLE-LOOKING OLDER MAN.

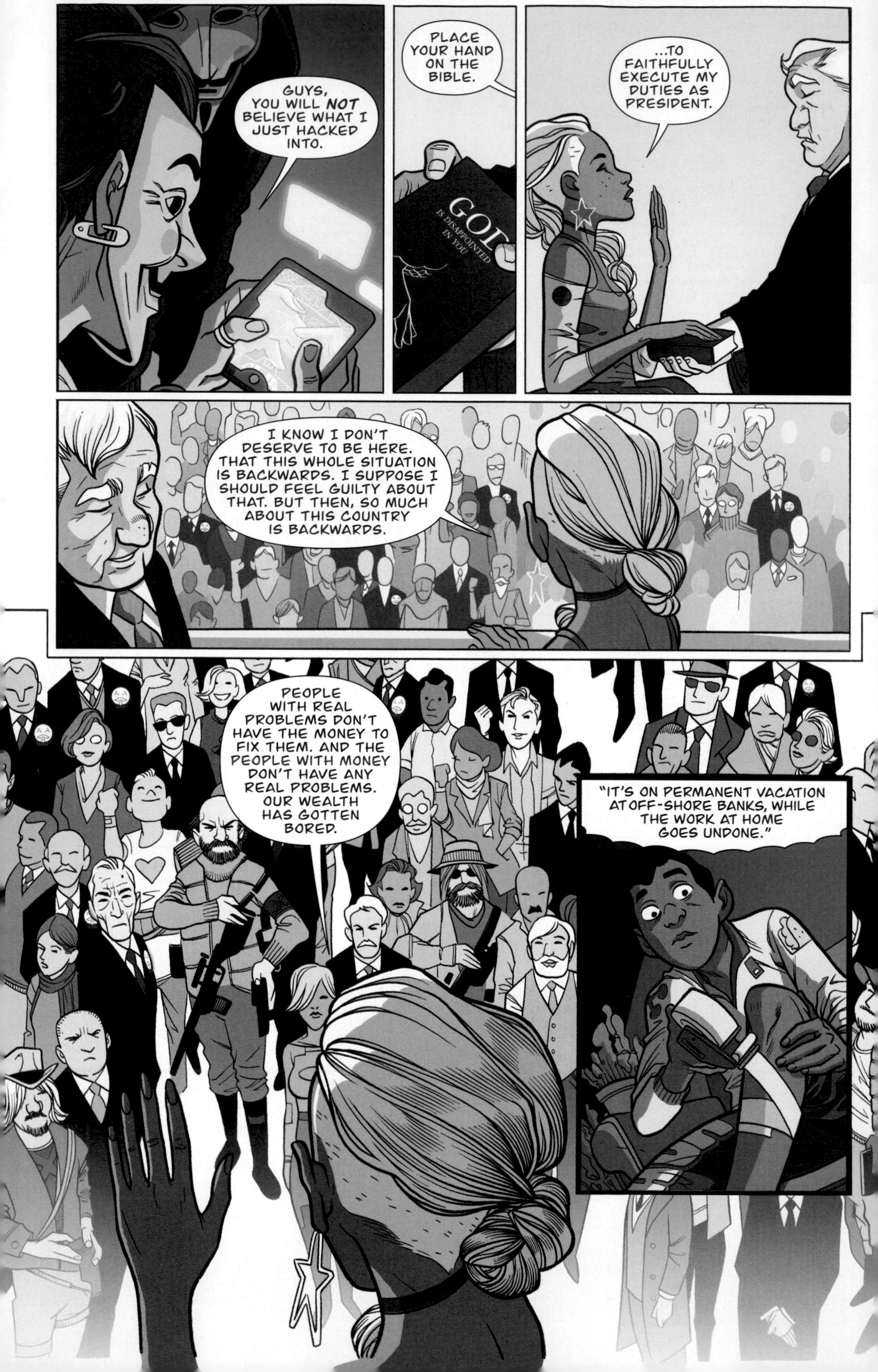
GUYS, YOU WILL NOT BELIEVE WHAT I JUST HACKED INTO.
PLACE YOUR HAND ON THE BIBLE.
GOD IS DISAPPOINTED IN YOU
...TO FAITHFULLY EXECUTE MY DUTIES AS PRESIDENT.
I KNOW I DON'T DESERVE TO BE HERE. THAT THIS WHOLE SITUATION IS BACKWARDS. I SUPPOSE I SHOULD FEEL GUILTY ABOUT THAT. BUT THEN, SO MUCH ABOUT THIS COUNTRY IS BACKWARDS.
PEOPLE WITH REAL PROBLEMS DON'T HAVE THE MONEY TO FIX THEM. AND THE PEOPLE WITH MONEY DON'T HAVE ANY REAL PROBLEMS. OUR WEALTH HAS GOTTEN BORED.
"IT'S ON PERMANENT VACATION AT OFF-SHORE BANKS, WHILE THE WORK AT HOME GOES UNDONE."

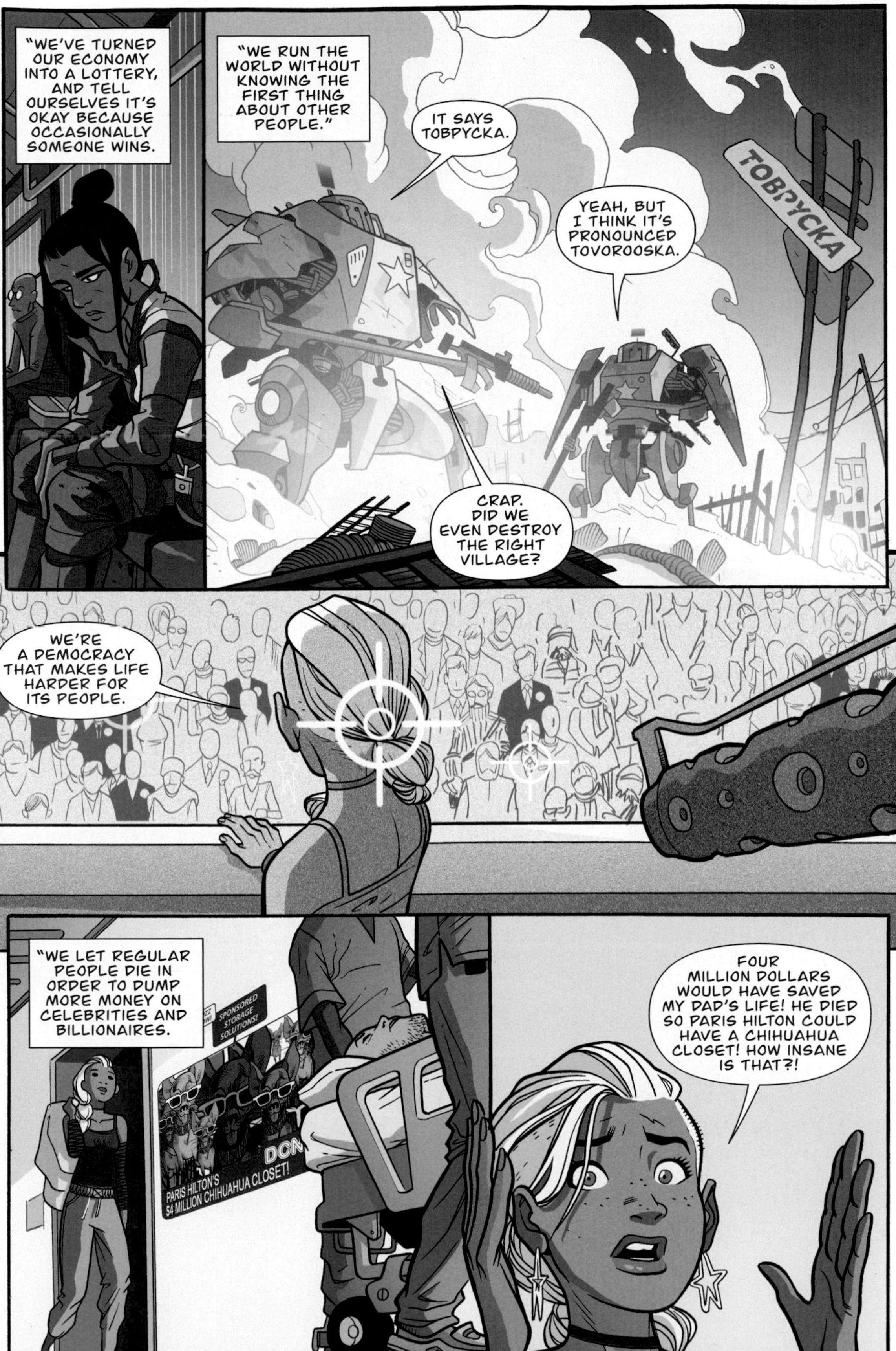
"WE'VE TURNED OUR ECONOMY INTO A LOTTERY, AND TELL OURSELVES IT'S OKAY BECAUSE OCCASIONALLY SOMEONE WINS.
"WE RUN THE WORLD WITHOUT KNOWING THE FIRST THING ABOUT OTHER PEOPLE."
IT SAYS TOBPYCKA.
TOBPYCKA
YEAH, BUT I THINK IT'S PRONOUNCED TOVOROOSKA.
CRAP. DID WE EVEN DESTROY THE RIGHT VILLAGE?
WE'RE A DEMOCRACY THAT MAKES LIFE HARDER FOR ITS PEOPLE.
"WE LET REGULAR PEOPLE DIE IN ORDER TO DUMP MORE MONEY ON CELEBRITIES AND BILLIONAIRES.
SPONSORED STORAGE SOLUTIONS!
DCN
PARIS HILTON'S $4 MILLION CHIHUAHUA CLOSET!
FOUR MILLION DOLLARS WOULD HAVE SAVED MY DAD'S LIFE! HE DIED SO PARIS HILTON COULD HAVE A CHIHUAHUA CLOSET! HOW INSANE IS THAT?!

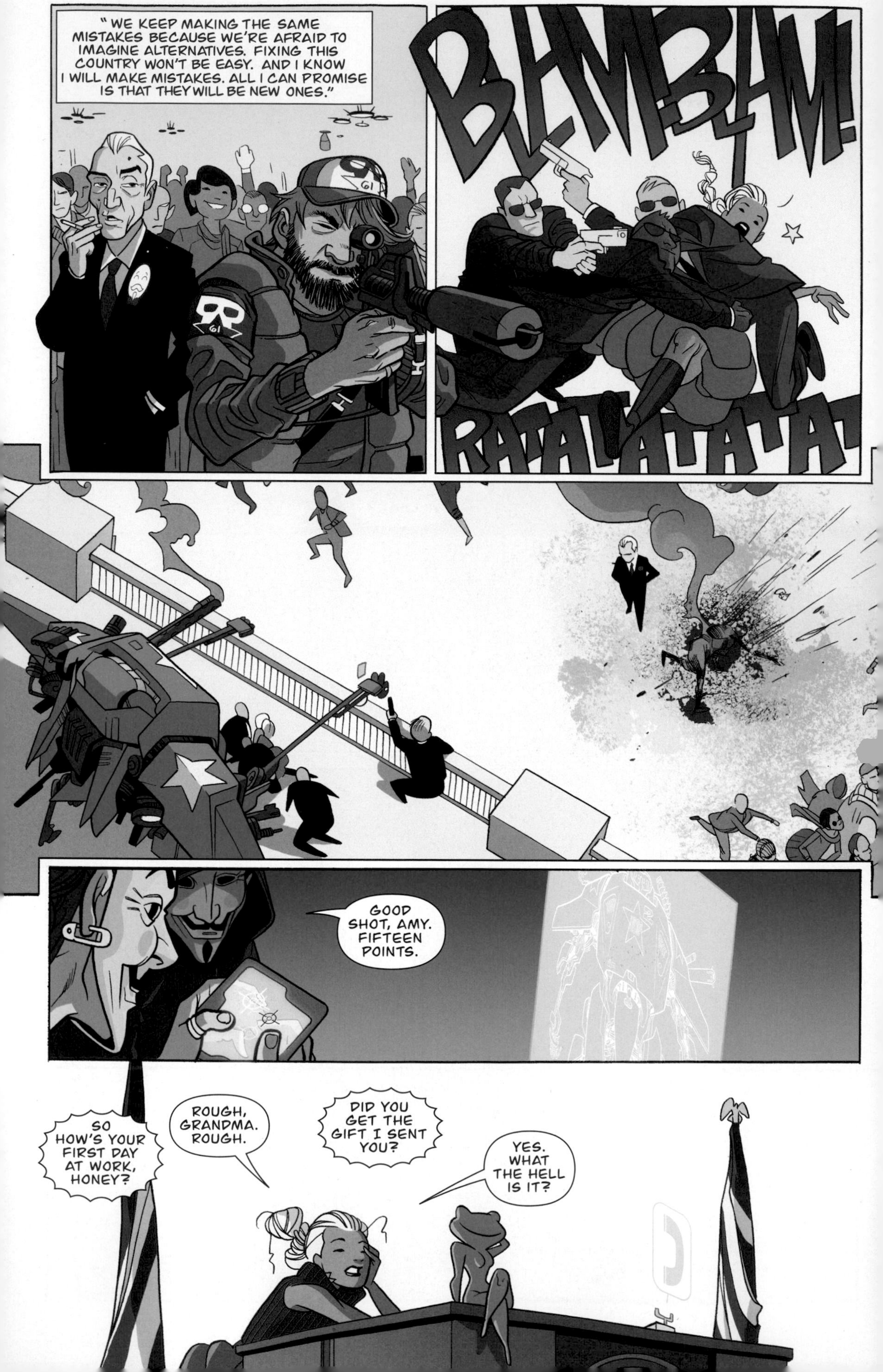
"WE KEEP MAKING THE SAME MISTAKES BECAUSE WE'RE AFRAID TO IMAGINE ALTERNATIVES. FIXING THIS COUNTRY WON'T BE EASY. AND I KNOW I WILL MAKE MISTAKES. ALL I CAN PROMISE IS THAT THEY WILL BE NEW ONES."
BLAMBLAM!
BAM!
RATATATATAT
GOOD SHOT, AMY. FIFTEEN POINTS.
SO HOW'S YOUR FIRST DAY AT WORK, HONEY?
ROUGH, GRANDMA. ROUGH.
DID YOU GET THE GIFT I SENT YOU?
YES. WHAT THE HELL IS IT?

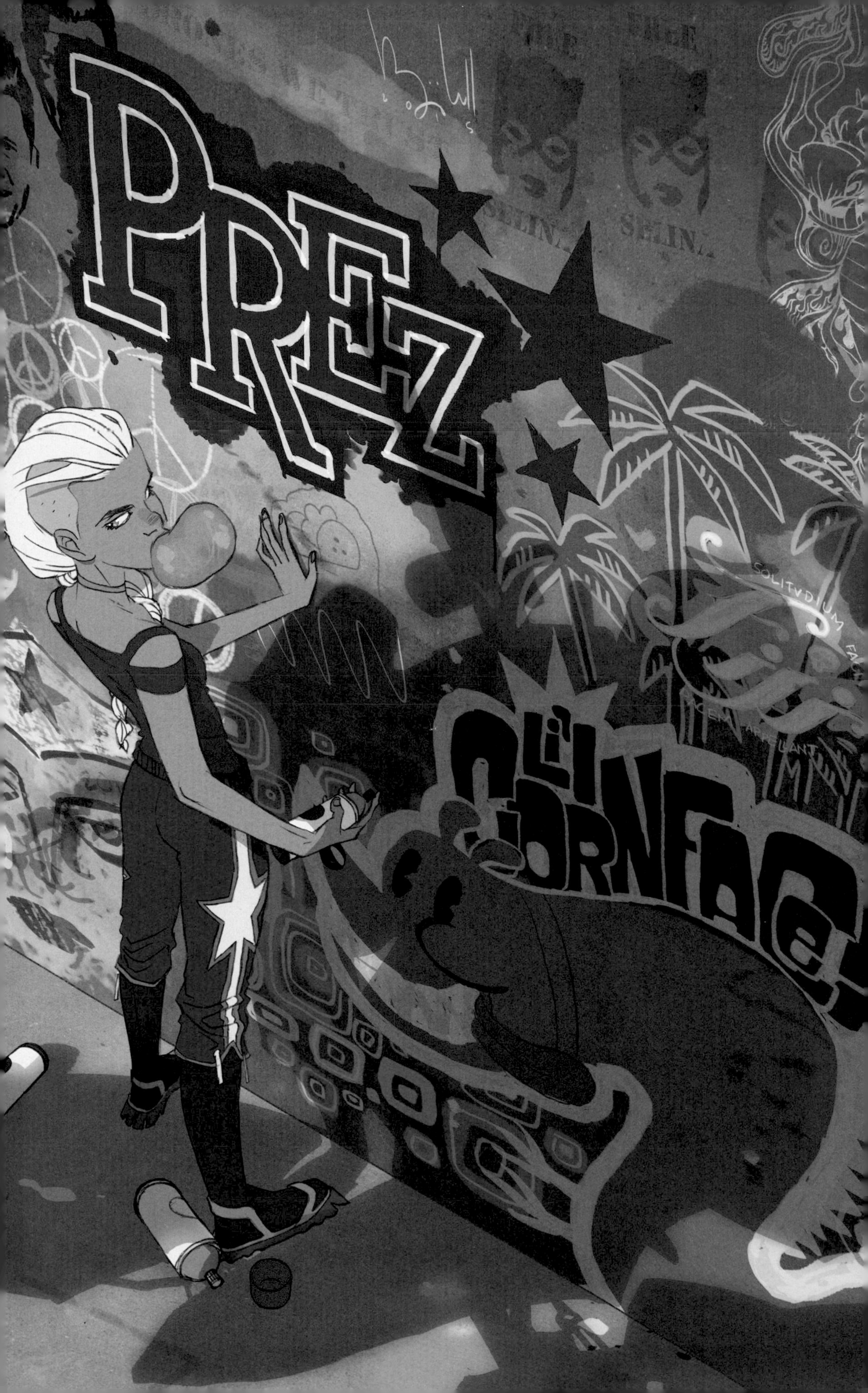
PREZ
SOLITVDIUM

THE BEAST OF WAR

MARK RUSSELL writer **DOMINIKE "DOMO" STANTON** penciller **MARK MORALES & SEAN PARSONS** inkers **JEREMY LAWSON** colorist

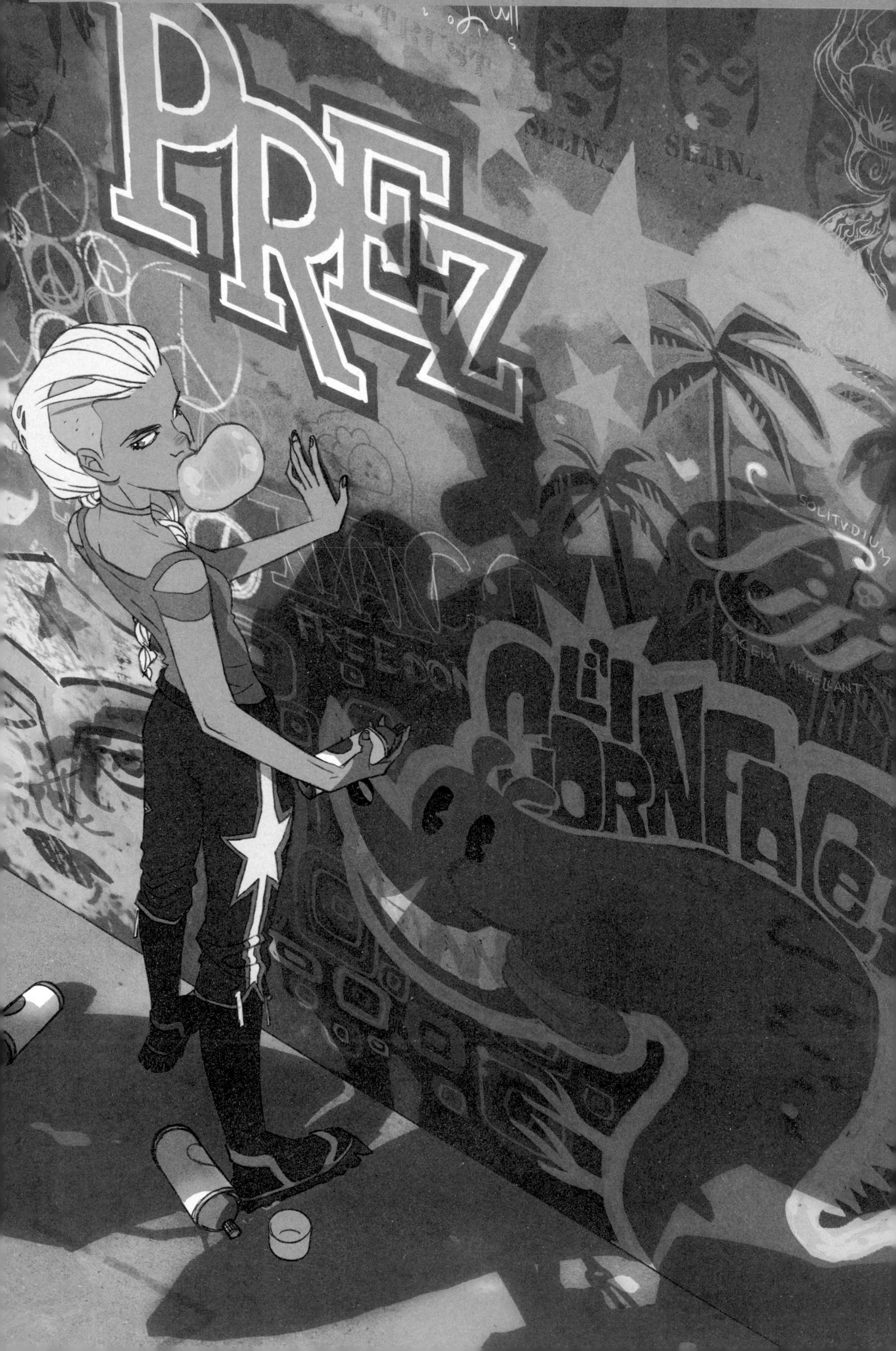
PREZ
SOLITVDIUM

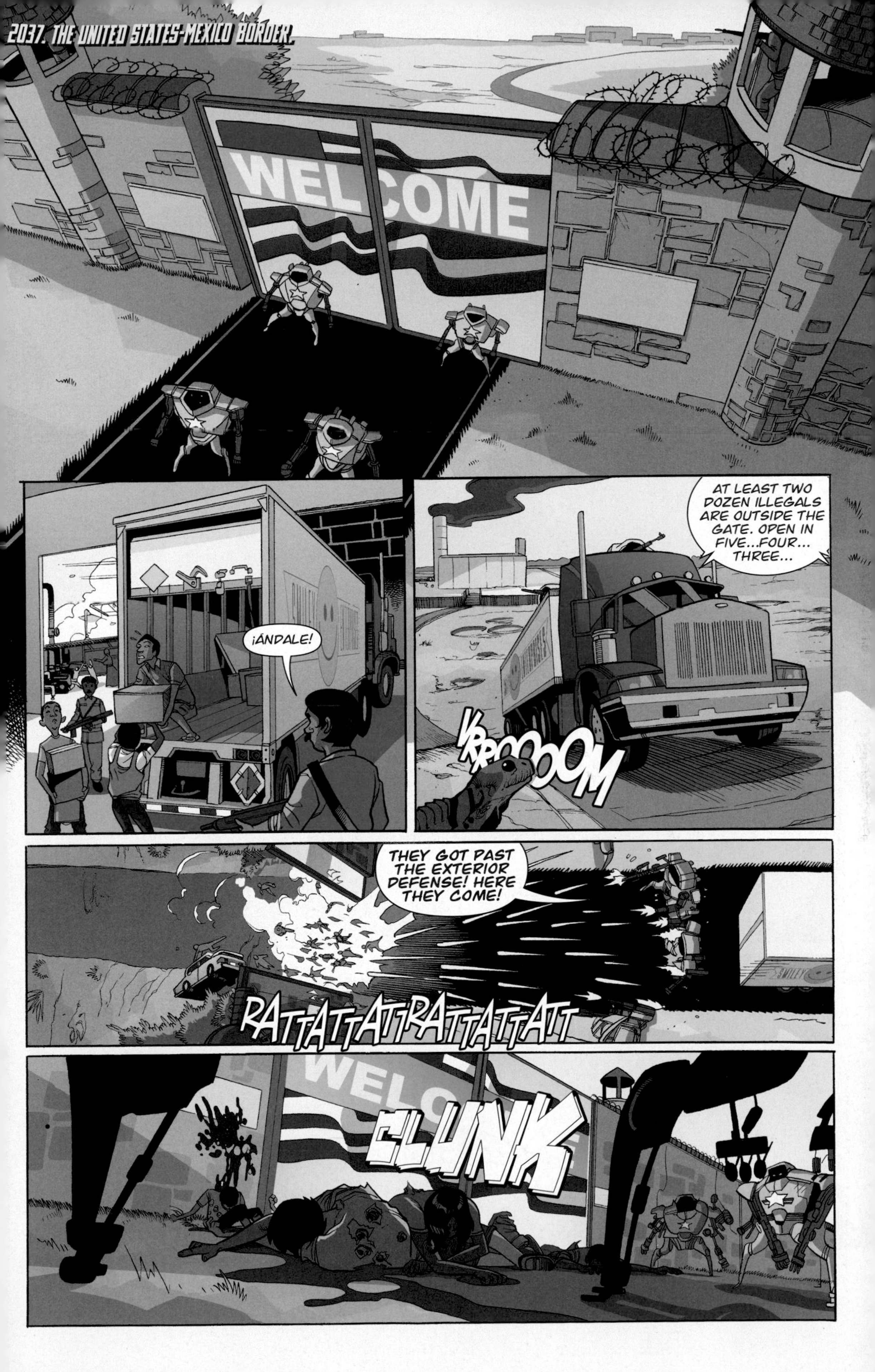
2037. THE UNITED STATES-MEXICO BORDER.
WELCOME
¡ÁNDALE!
AT LEAST TWO DOZEN ILLEGALS ARE OUTSIDE THE GATE. OPEN IN FIVE...FOUR... THREE...
VRROOOOOM
THEY GOT PAST THE EXTERIOR DEFENSE! HERE THEY COME!
RATTATTATTRATTATTATT
CLUNK

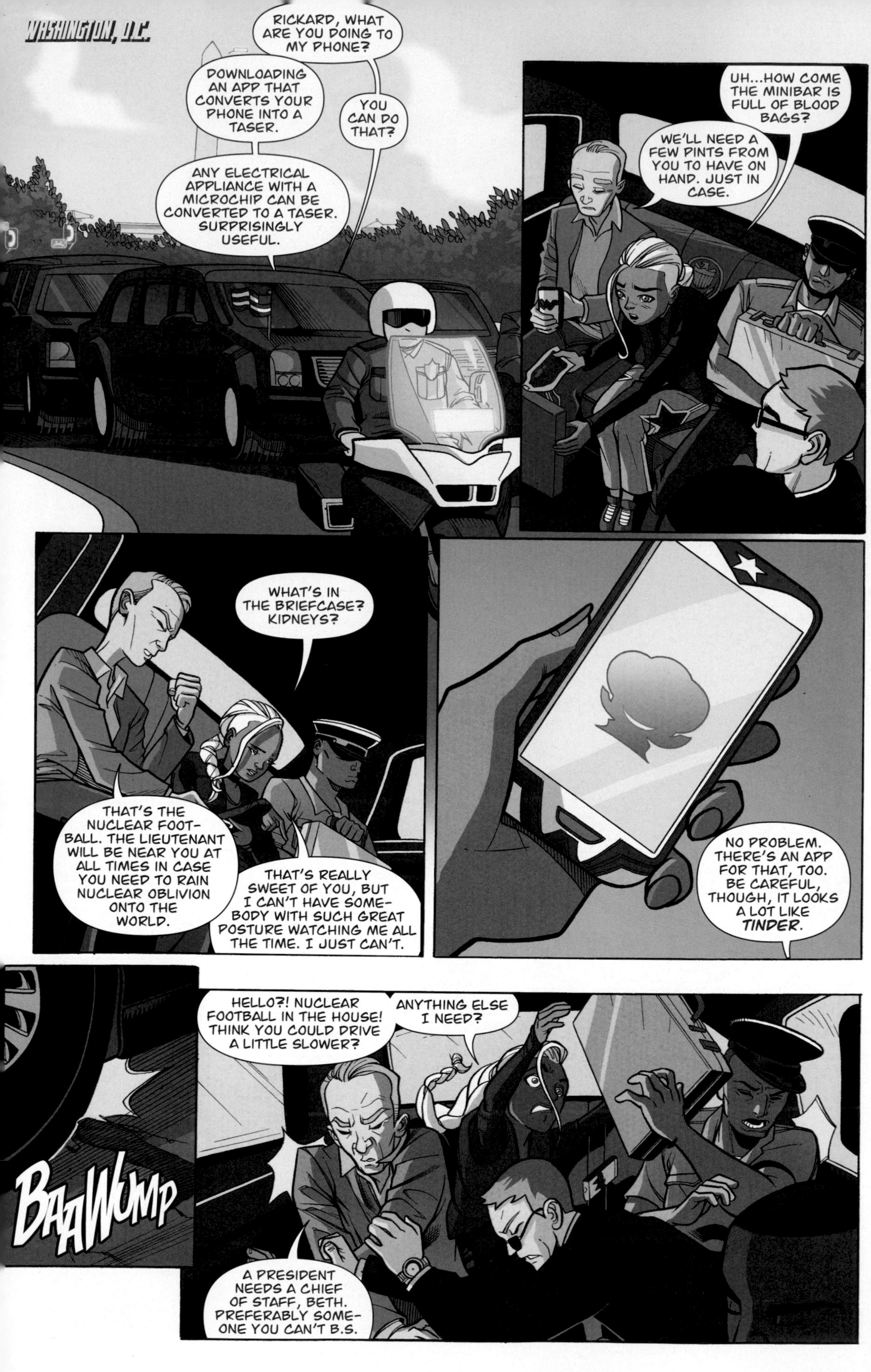
WASHINGTON, D.C.
RICKARD, WHAT ARE YOU DOING TO MY PHONE?
DOWNLOADING AN APP THAT CONVERTS YOUR PHONE INTO A TASER.
YOU CAN DO THAT?
ANY ELECTRICAL APPLIANCE WITH A MICROCHIP CAN BE CONVERTED TO A TASER. SURPRISINGLY USEFUL.
UH...HOW COME THE MINIBAR IS FULL OF BLOOD BAGS?
WE'LL NEED A FEW PINTS FROM YOU TO HAVE ON HAND. JUST IN CASE.
WHAT'S IN THE BRIEFCASE? KIDNEYS?
THAT'S THE NUCLEAR FOOT-BALL. THE LIEUTENANT WILL BE NEAR YOU AT ALL TIMES IN CASE YOU NEED TO RAIN NUCLEAR OBLIVION ONTO THE WORLD.
THAT'S REALLY SWEET OF YOU, BUT I CAN'T HAVE SOME-BODY WITH SUCH GREAT POSTURE WATCHING ME ALL THE TIME. I JUST CAN'T.
NO PROBLEM. THERE'S AN APP FOR THAT, TOO. BE CAREFUL, THOUGH, IT LOOKS A LOT LIKE TINDER.
ANYTHING ELSE I NEED?
A PRESIDENT NEEDS A CHIEF OF STAFF, BETH. PREFERABLY SOME-ONE YOU CAN'T B.S.
BAAWOMP
HELLO?! NUCLEAR FOOTBALL IN THE HOUSE! THINK YOU COULD DRIVE A LITTLE SLOWER?

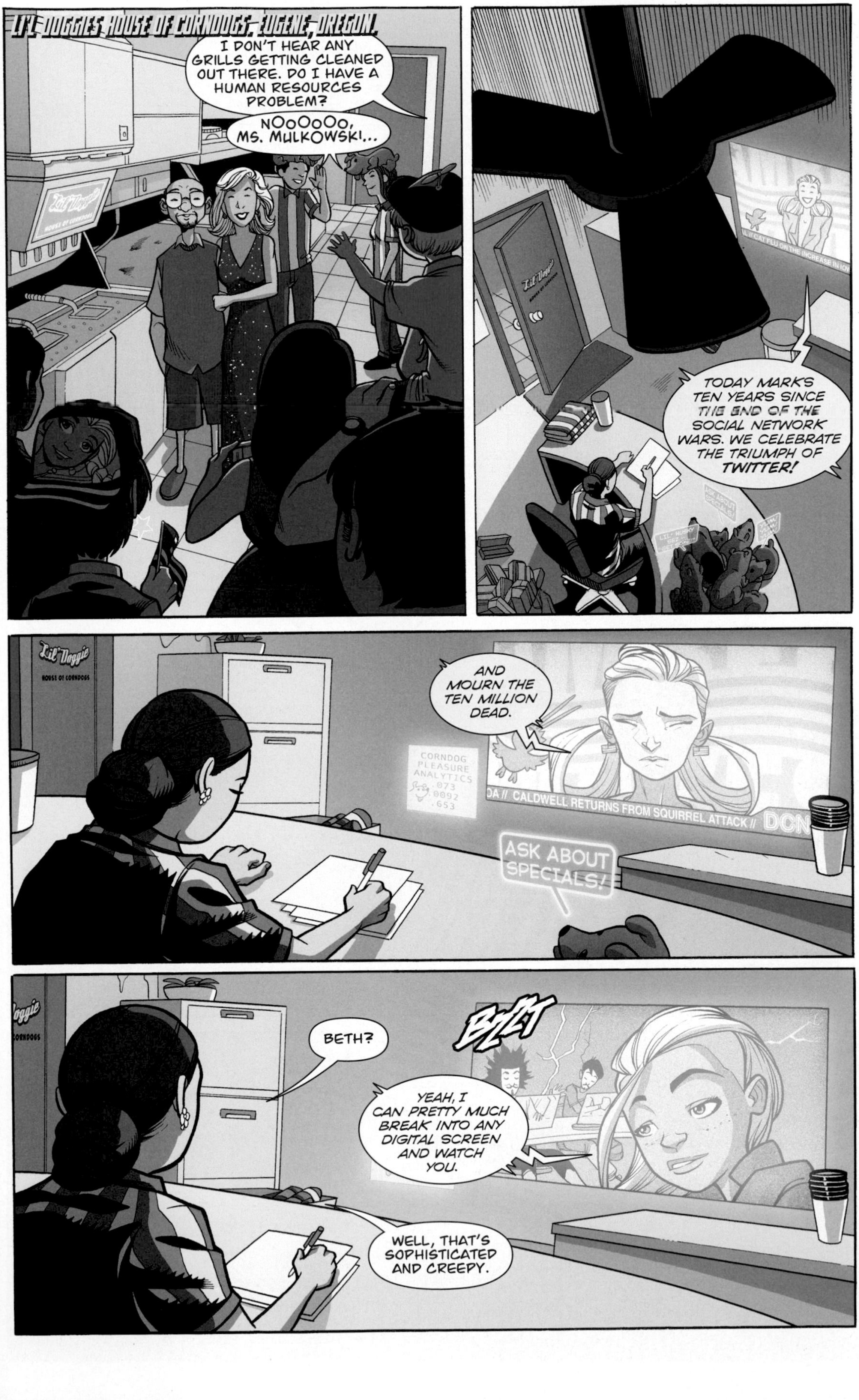
LI'L DOGGIES HOUSE OF CORNDOGS, EUGENE, OREGON.
I DON'T HEAR ANY GRILLS GETTING CLEANED OUT THERE. DO I HAVE A HUMAN RESOURCES PROBLEM?
NOoOoOo, MS. MULKOWSKI...
TODAY MARKS TEN YEARS SINCE THE END OF THE SOCIAL NETWORK WARS. WE CELEBRATE THE TRIUMPH OF TWITTER!
AND MOURN THE TEN MILLION DEAD.
Lil' Doggie
HOUSE OF CORNDOGS
CORNDOG PLEASURE ANALYTICS .073 .0092 .653
CALDWELL RETURNS FROM SQUIRREL ATTACK //
DCN
ASK ABOUT SPECIALS!
BZZT
BETH?
YEAH, I CAN PRETTY MUCH BREAK INTO ANY DIGITAL SCREEN AND WATCH YOU.
WELL, THAT'S SOPHISTICATED AND CREEPY.

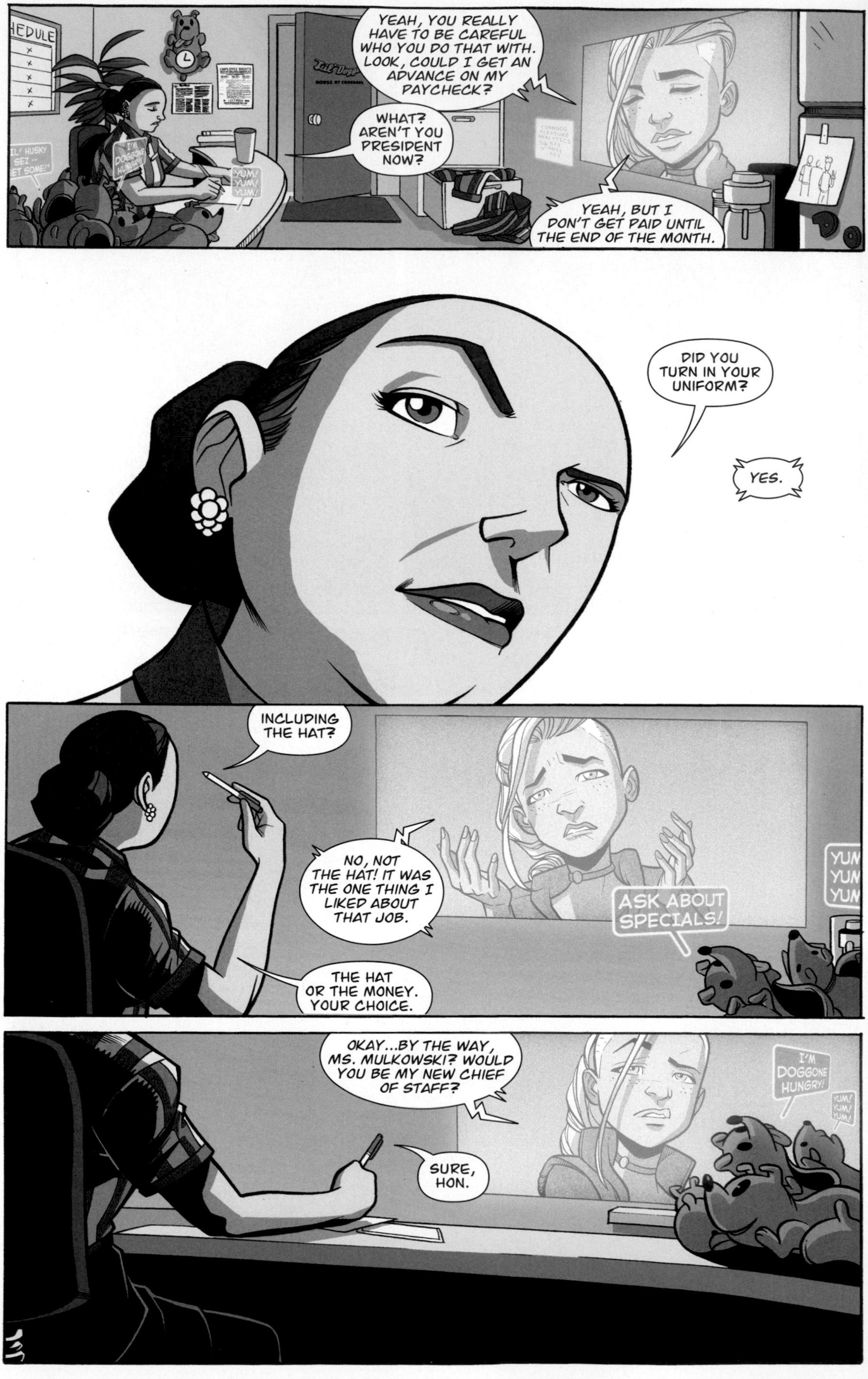
YEAH, YOU REALLY HAVE TO BE CAREFUL WHO YOU DO THAT WITH. LOOK, COULD I GET AN ADVANCE ON MY PAYCHECK?
WHAT? AREN'T YOU PRESIDENT NOW?
YEAH, BUT I DON'T GET PAID UNTIL THE END OF THE MONTH.
DID YOU TURN IN YOUR UNIFORM?
YES.
INCLUDING THE HAT?
NO, NOT THE HAT! IT WAS THE ONE THING I LIKED ABOUT THAT JOB.
ASK ABOUT SPECIALS!
THE HAT OR THE MONEY. YOUR CHOICE.
OKAY...BY THE WAY, MS. MULKOWSKI? WOULD YOU BE MY NEW CHIEF OF STAFF?
I'M DOGGONE HUNGRY!
YUM! YUM! YUM!
SURE, HON.

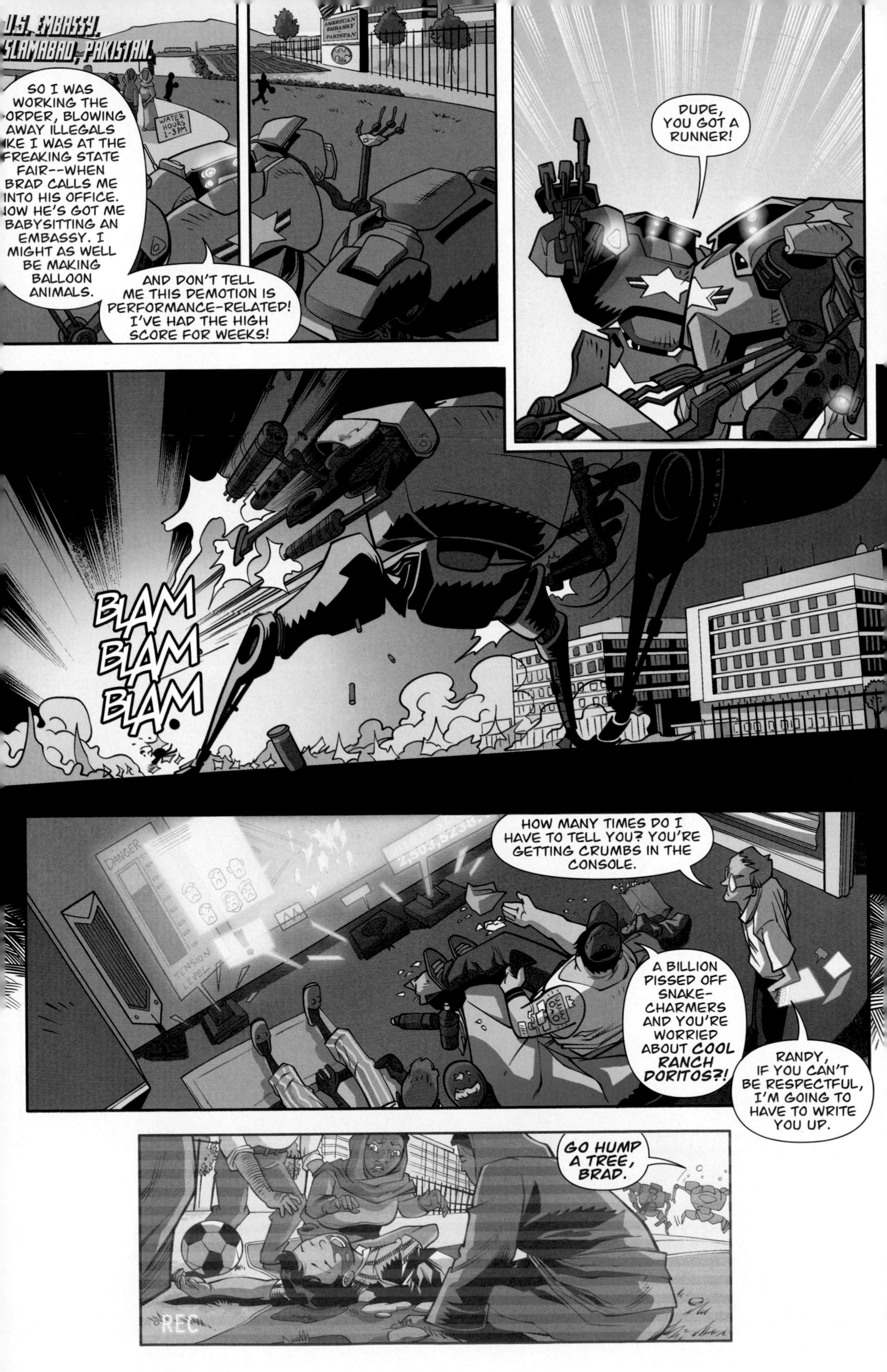

U.S. EMBASSY, ISLAMABAD, PAKISTAN.
AMERICAN EMBASSY PAKISTAN
WATER HOURS 1-3PM
SO I WAS WORKING THE BORDER, BLOWING AWAY ILLEGALS LIKE I WAS AT THE FREAKING STATE FAIR--WHEN BRAD CALLS ME INTO HIS OFFICE. NOW HE'S GOT ME BABYSITTING AN EMBASSY. I MIGHT AS WELL BE MAKING BALLOON ANIMALS.
AND DON'T TELL ME THIS DEMOTION IS PERFORMANCE-RELATED! I'VE HAD THE HIGH SCORE FOR WEEKS!
DUDE, YOU GOT A RUNNER!
BLAM BLAM BLAM
DANGER
TENSION LEVEL
HOW MANY TIMES DO I HAVE TO TELL YOU? YOU'RE GETTING CRUMBS IN THE CONSOLE.
A BILLION PISSED OFF SNAKE-CHARMERS AND YOU'RE WORRIED ABOUT COOL RANCH DORITOS?!
RANDY, IF YOU CAN'T BE RESPECTFUL, I'M GOING TO HAVE TO WRITE YOU UP.
GO HUMP A TREE, BRAD.
REC

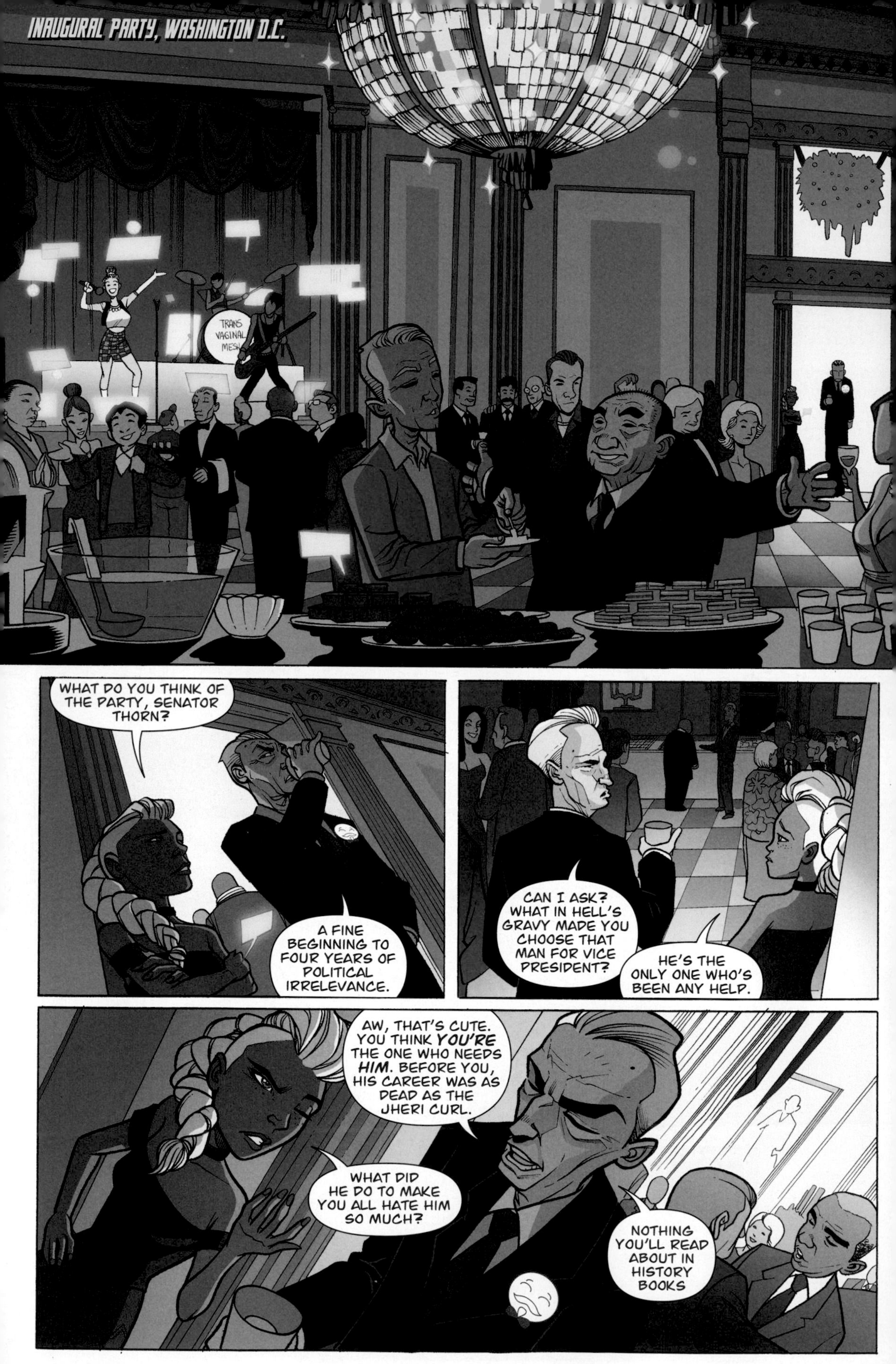
INAUGURAL PARTY, WASHINGTON D.C.
TRANS VAGINAL MESH
WHAT DO YOU THINK OF THE PARTY, SENATOR THORN?
A FINE BEGINNING TO FOUR YEARS OF POLITICAL IRRELEVANCE.
CAN I ASK? WHAT IN HELL'S GRAVY MADE YOU CHOOSE THAT MAN FOR VICE PRESIDENT?
HE'S THE ONLY ONE WHO'S BEEN ANY HELP.
AW, THAT'S CUTE. YOU THINK *YOU'RE* THE ONE WHO NEEDS *HIM*. BEFORE YOU, HIS CAREER WAS AS DEAD AS THE JHERI CURL.
WHAT DID HE DO TO MAKE YOU ALL HATE HIM SO MUCH?
NOTHING YOU'LL READ ABOUT IN HISTORY BOOKS

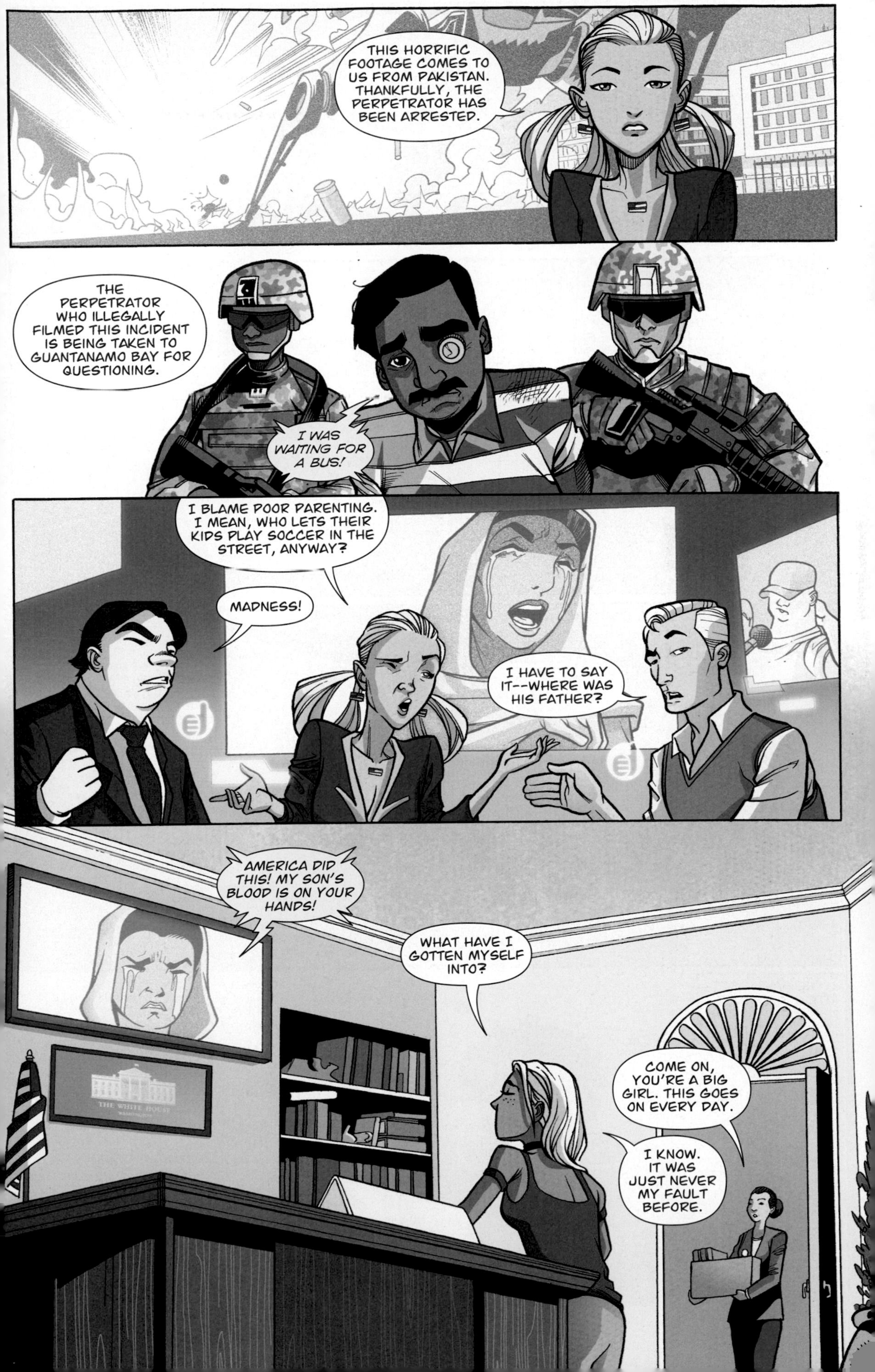
THIS HORRIFIC FOOTAGE COMES TO US FROM PAKISTAN. THANKFULLY, THE PERPETRATOR HAS BEEN ARRESTED.
THE PERPETRATOR WHO ILLEGALLY FILMED THIS INCIDENT IS BEING TAKEN TO GUANTANAMO BAY FOR QUESTIONING.
I WAS WAITING FOR A BUS!
I BLAME POOR PARENTING. I MEAN, WHO LETS THEIR KIDS PLAY SOCCER IN THE STREET, ANYWAY?
MADNESS!
I HAVE TO SAY IT--WHERE WAS HIS FATHER?
AMERICA DID THIS! MY SON'S BLOOD IS ON YOUR HANDS!
WHAT HAVE I GOTTEN MYSELF INTO?
COME ON, YOU'RE A BIG GIRL. THIS GOES ON EVERY DAY.
I KNOW. IT WAS JUST NEVER MY FAULT BEFORE.
THE WHITE HOUSE

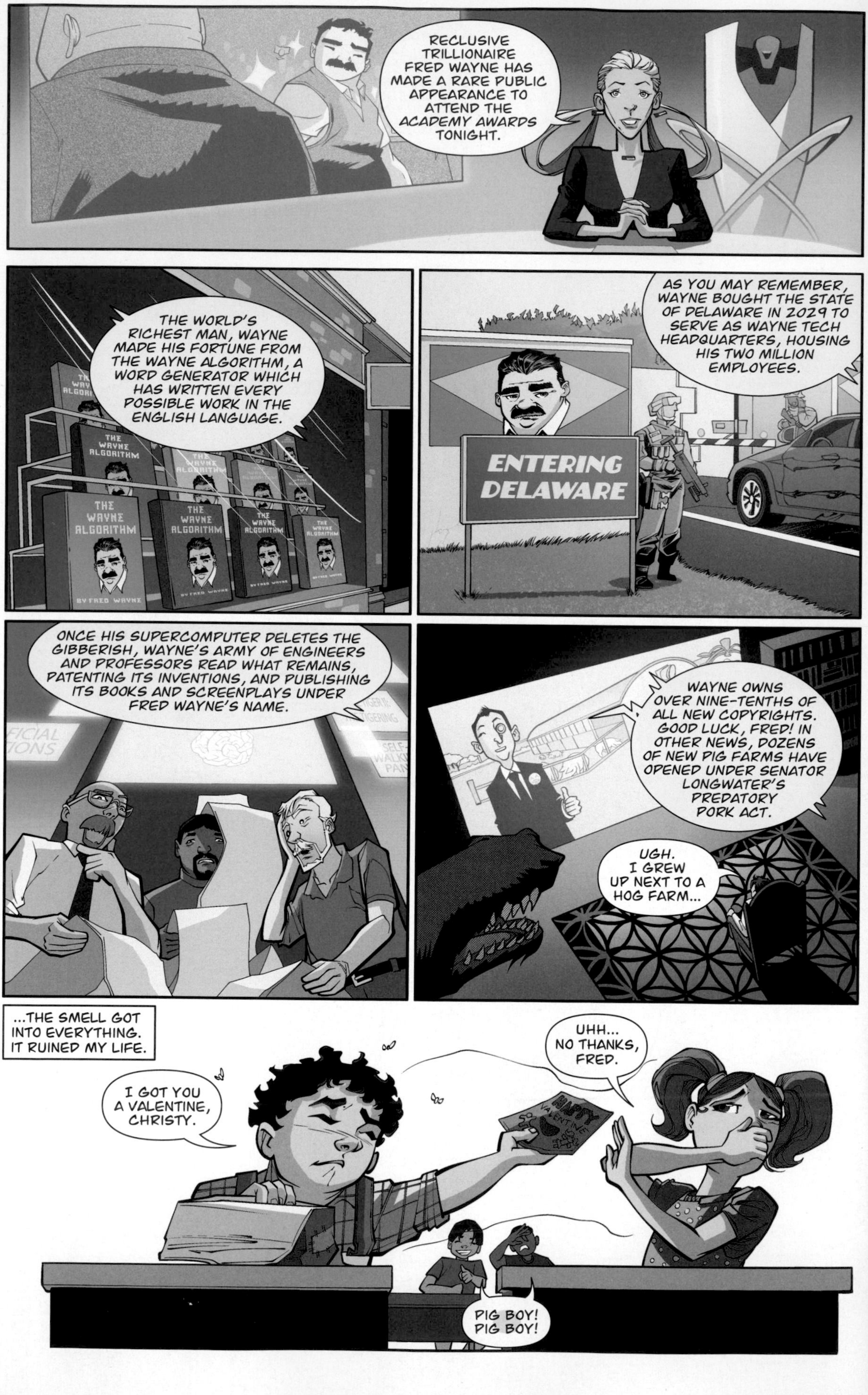
RECLUSIVE TRILLIONAIRE FRED WAYNE HAS MADE A RARE PUBLIC APPEARANCE TO ATTEND THE ACADEMY AWARDS TONIGHT.
THE WORLD'S RICHEST MAN, WAYNE MADE HIS FORTUNE FROM THE WAYNE ALGORITHM, A WORD GENERATOR WHICH HAS WRITTEN EVERY POSSIBLE WORK IN THE ENGLISH LANGUAGE.
THE WAYNE ALGORITHM
BY FRED WAYNE
AS YOU MAY REMEMBER, WAYNE BOUGHT THE STATE OF DELAWARE IN 2029 TO SERVE AS WAYNE TECH HEADQUARTERS, HOUSING HIS TWO MILLION EMPLOYEES.
ENTERING DELAWARE
ONCE HIS SUPERCOMPUTER DELETES THE GIBBERISH, WAYNE'S ARMY OF ENGINEERS AND PROFESSORS READ WHAT REMAINS, PATENTING ITS INVENTIONS, AND PUBLISHING ITS BOOKS AND SCREENPLAYS UNDER FRED WAYNE'S NAME.
WAYNE OWNS OVER NINE-TENTHS OF ALL NEW COPYRIGHTS. GOOD LUCK, FRED! IN OTHER NEWS, DOZENS OF NEW PIG FARMS HAVE OPENED UNDER SENATOR LONGWATER'S PREDATORY PORK ACT.
UGH. I GREW UP NEXT TO A HOG FARM...
...THE SMELL GOT INTO EVERYTHING. IT RUINED MY LIFE.
I GOT YOU A VALENTINE, CHRISTY.
UHH... NO THANKS, FRED.
HAPPY VALENTINE
PIG BOY! PIG BOY!

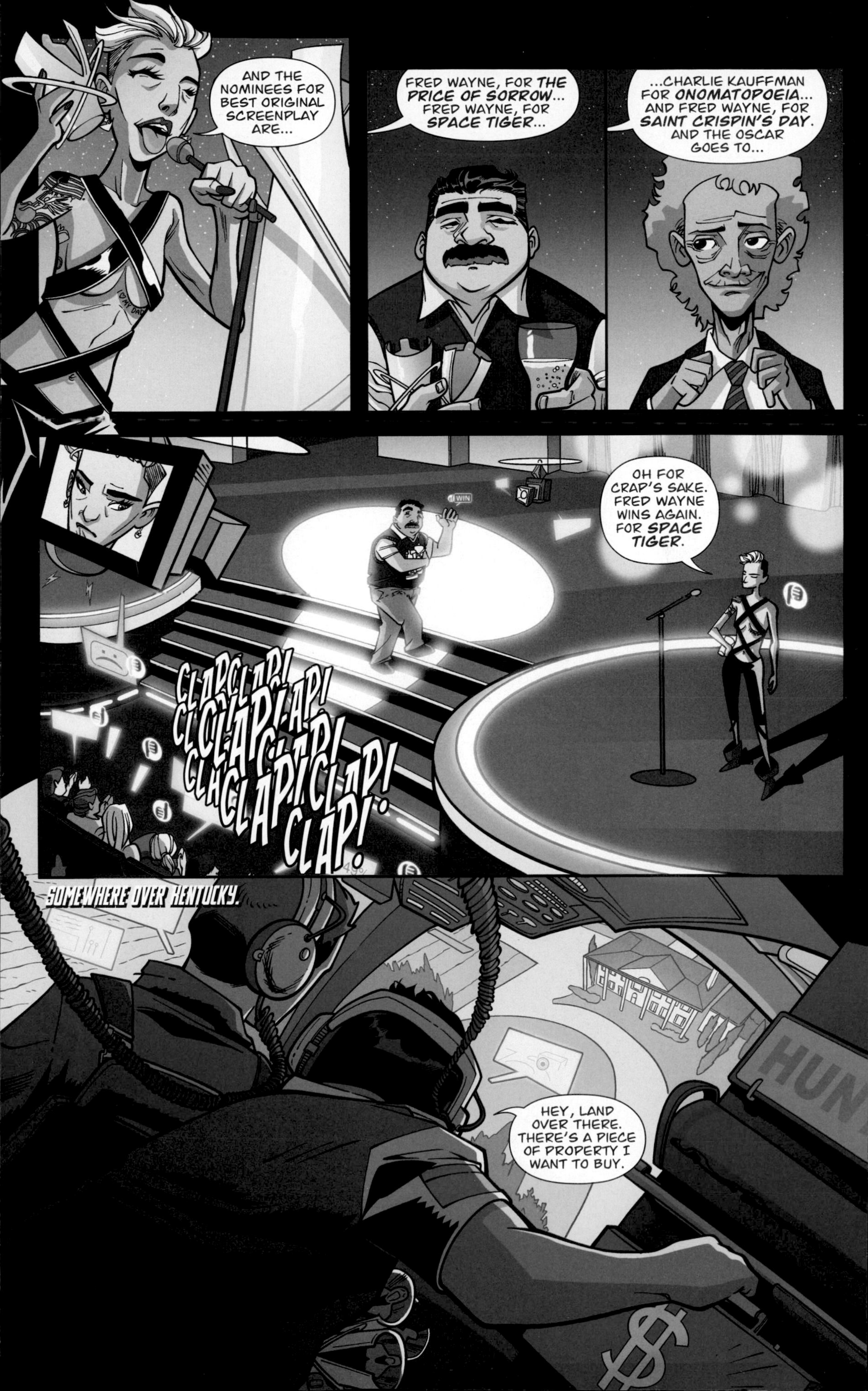
AND THE NOMINEES FOR BEST ORIGINAL SCREENPLAY ARE...
FRED WAYNE, FOR THE PRICE OF SORROW... FRED WAYNE, FOR SPACE TIGER...
...CHARLIE KAUFFMAN FOR ONOMATOPOEIA... AND FRED WAYNE, FOR SAINT CRISPIN'S DAY. AND THE OSCAR GOES TO...
OH FOR CRAP'S SAKE. FRED WAYNE WINS AGAIN. FOR SPACE TIGER.
CLAP! CLAP! CLAP! CLAP! CLAP! CLAP! CLAP! CLAP!
SOMEWHERE OVER KENTUCKY.
HEY, LAND OVER THERE. THERE'S A PIECE OF PROPERTY I WANT TO BUY.

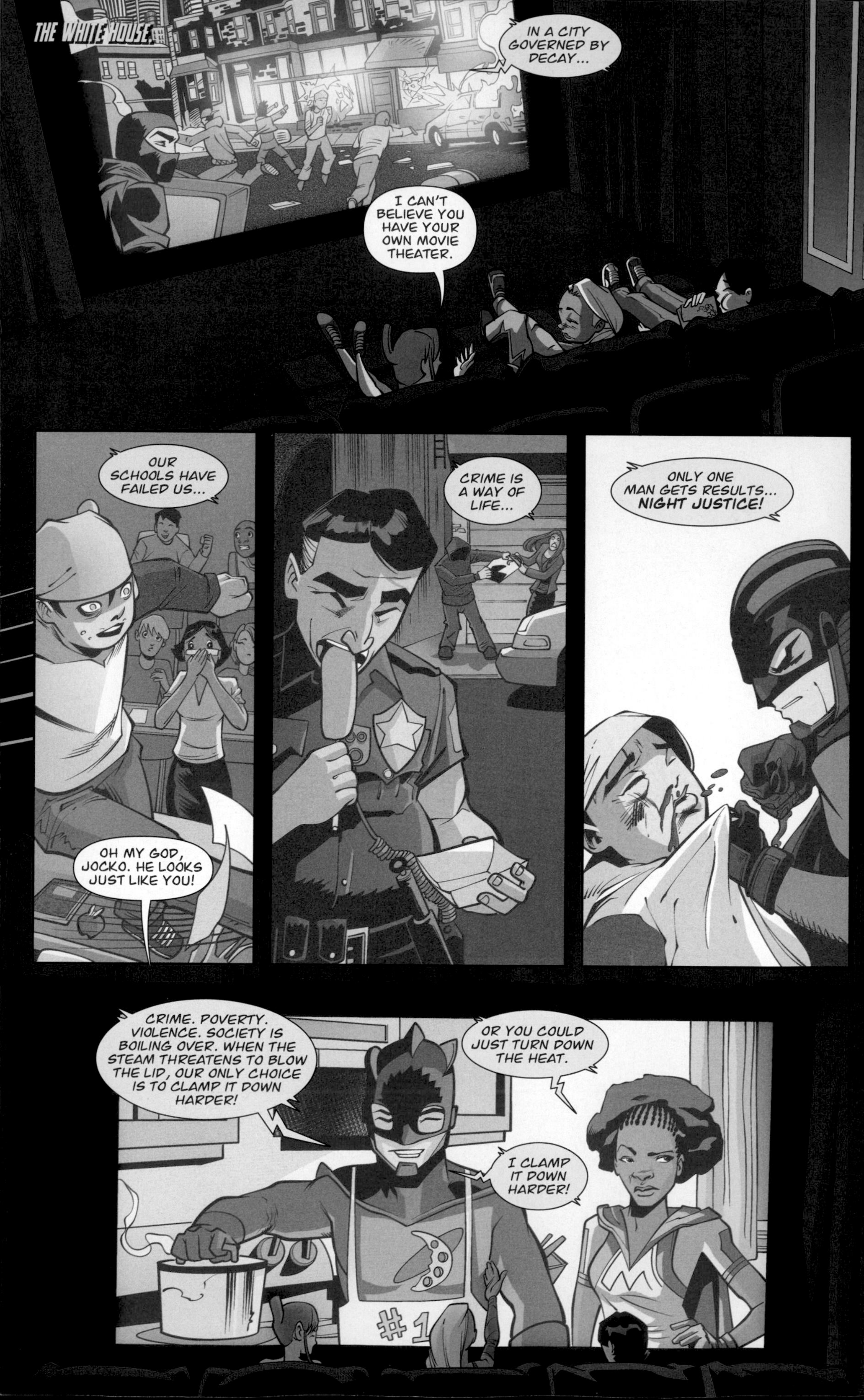
THE WHITE HOUSE.
IN A CITY GOVERNED BY DECAY...
I CAN'T BELIEVE YOU HAVE YOUR OWN MOVIE THEATER.
OUR SCHOOLS HAVE FAILED US...
OH MY GOD, JOCKO. HE LOOKS JUST LIKE YOU!
CRIME IS A WAY OF LIFE...
ONLY ONE MAN GETS RESULTS... NIGHT JUSTICE!
CRIME. POVERTY. VIOLENCE. SOCIETY IS BOILING OVER. WHEN THE STEAM THREATENS TO BLOW THE LID, OUR ONLY CHOICE IS TO CLAMP IT DOWN HARDER!
OR YOU COULD JUST TURN DOWN THE HEAT.
I CLAMP IT DOWN HARDER!
#1

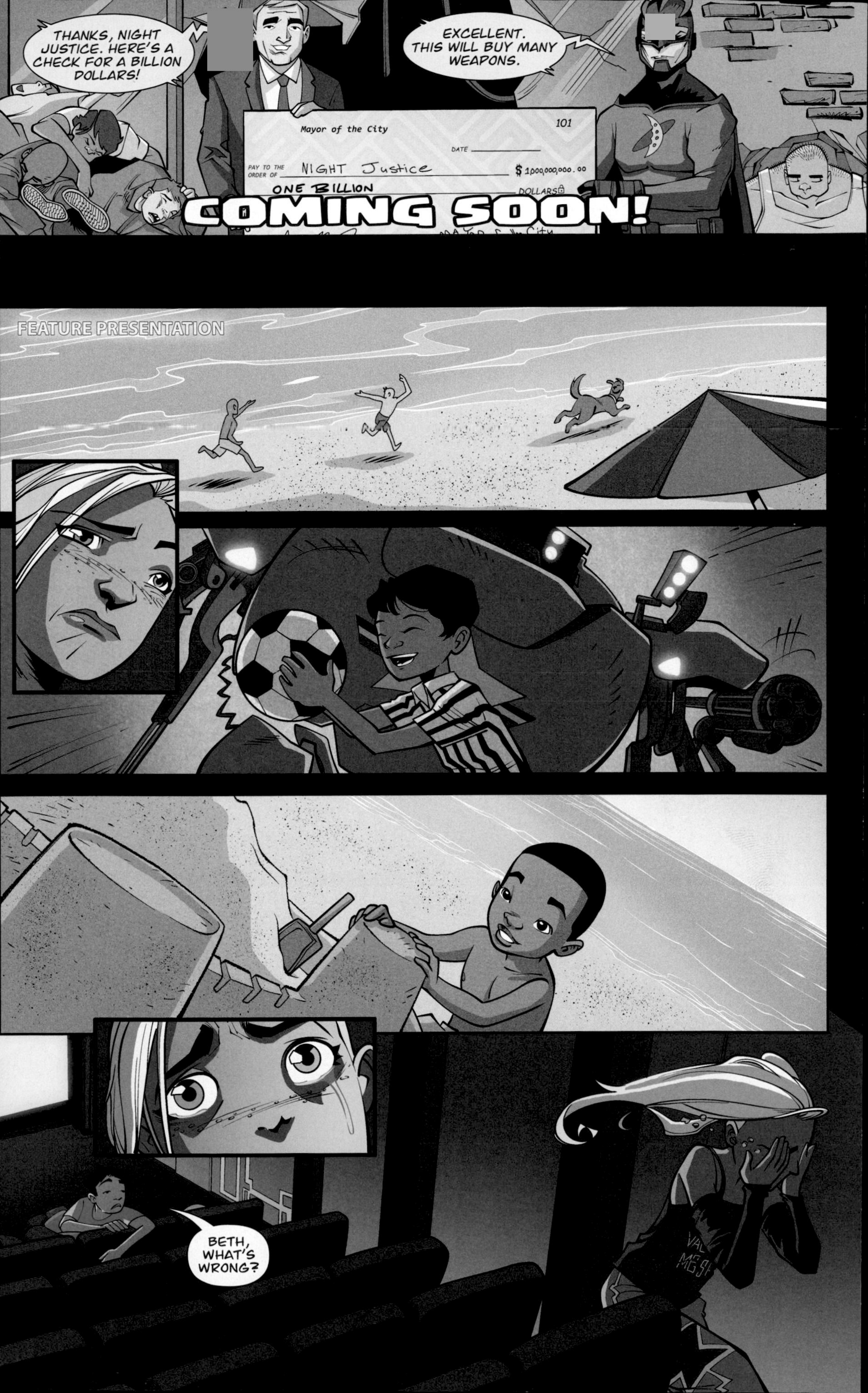
THANKS, NIGHT JUSTICE. HERE'S A CHECK FOR A BILLION DOLLARS!
EXCELLENT. THIS WILL BUY MANY WEAPONS.
Mayor of the City
101
DATE
PAY TO THE ORDER OF
NIGHT Justice
$1,000,000,000.00
ONE BILLION
DOLLARS
COMING SOON!
FEATURE PRESENTATION
BETH, WHAT'S WRONG?

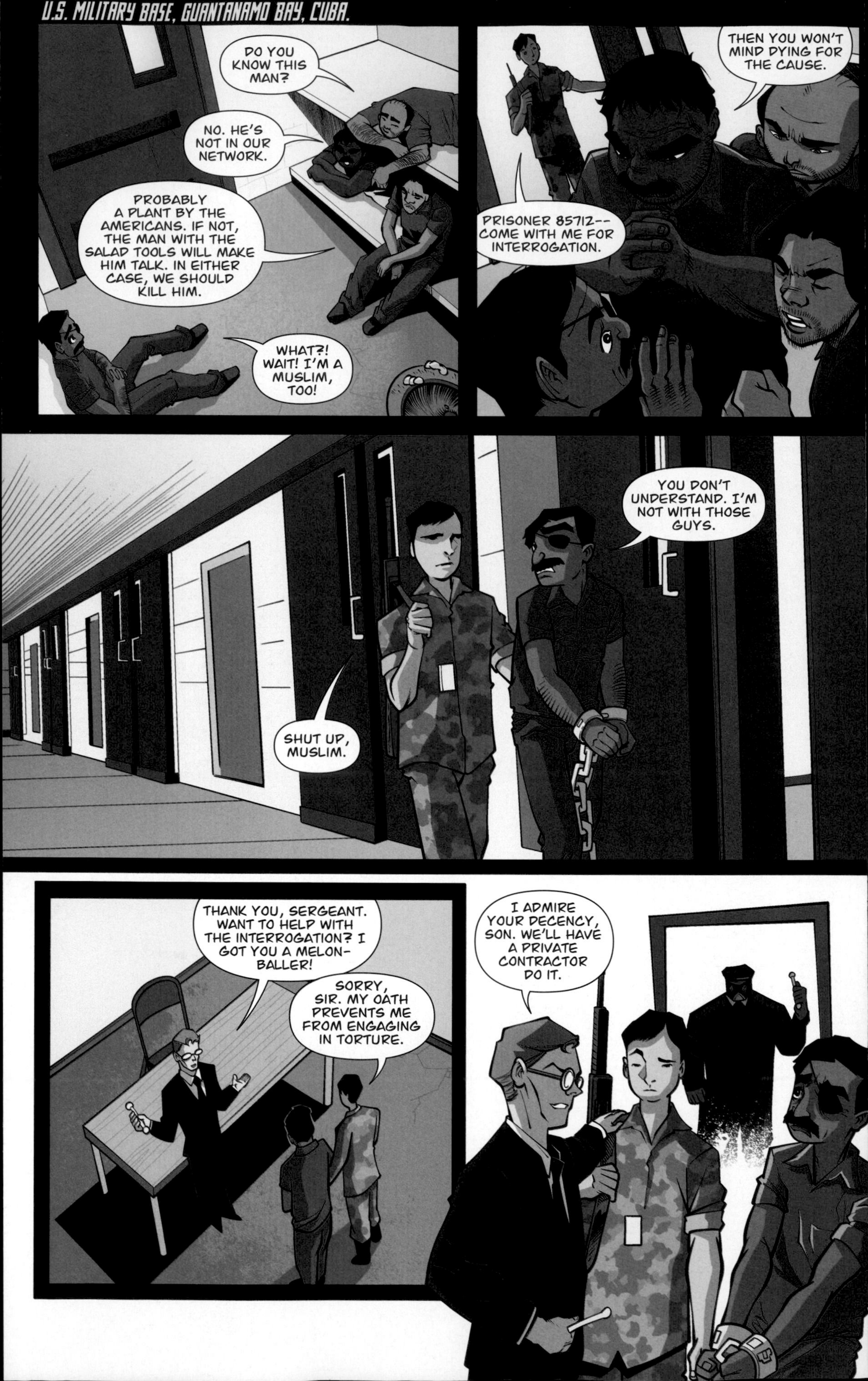
U.S. MILITARY BASE, GUANTANAMO BAY, CUBA.
DO YOU KNOW THIS MAN?
NO. HE'S NOT IN OUR NETWORK.
PROBABLY A PLANT BY THE AMERICANS. IF NOT, THE MAN WITH THE SALAD TOOLS WILL MAKE HIM TALK. IN EITHER CASE, WE SHOULD KILL HIM.
WHAT?! WAIT! I'M A MUSLIM, TOO!
THEN YOU WON'T MIND DYING FOR THE CAUSE.
PRISONER 85712-- COME WITH ME FOR INTERROGATION.
YOU DON'T UNDERSTAND. I'M NOT WITH THOSE GUYS.
SHUT UP, MUSLIM.
THANK YOU, SERGEANT. WANT TO HELP WITH THE INTERROGATION? I GOT YOU A MELON-BALLER!
SORRY, SIR. MY OATH PREVENTS ME FROM ENGAGING IN TORTURE.
I ADMIRE YOUR DECENCY, SON. WE'LL HAVE A PRIVATE CONTRACTOR DO IT.

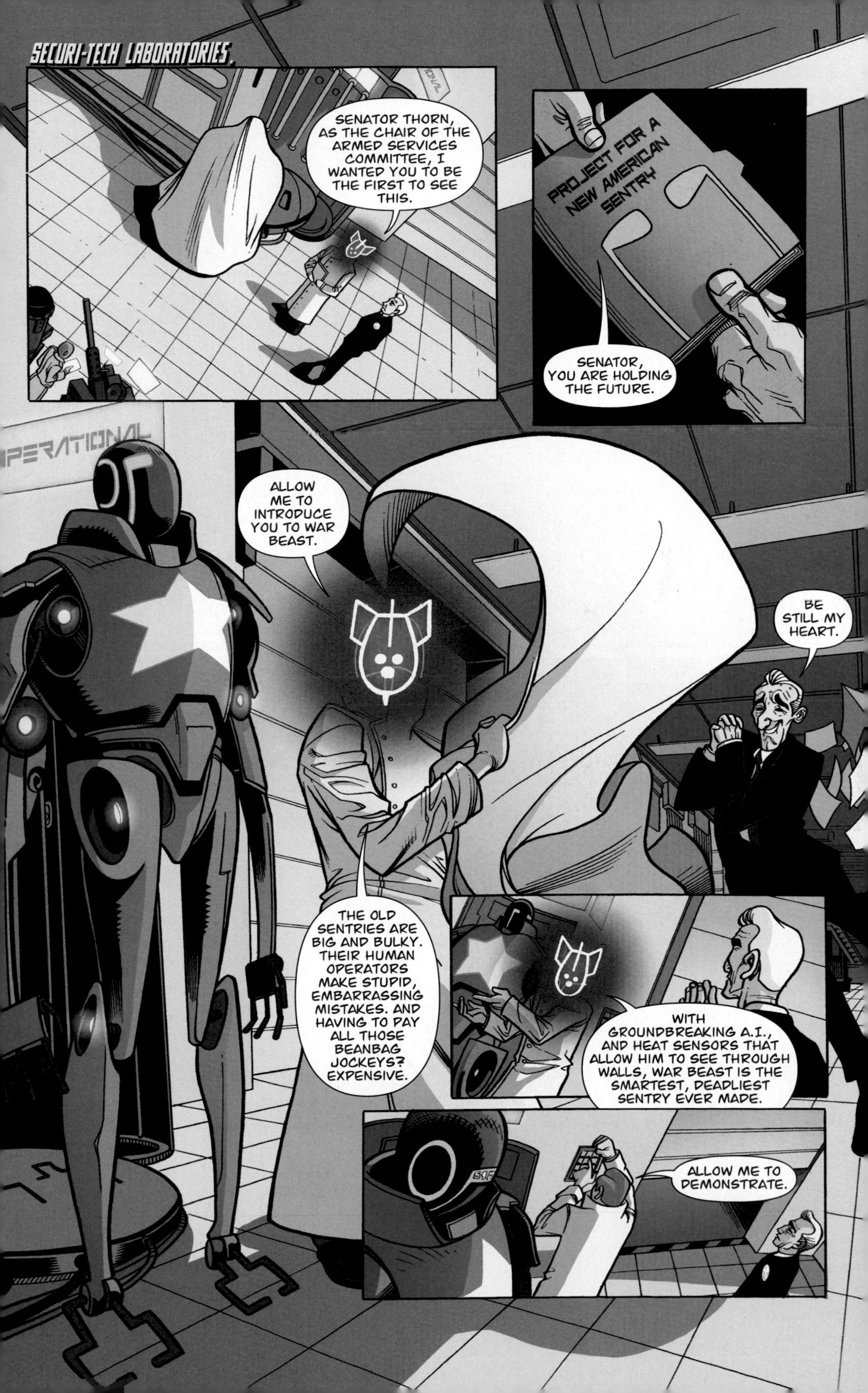
SECURI-TECH LABORATORIES.
SENATOR THORN, AS THE CHAIR OF THE ARMED SERVICES COMMITTEE, I WANTED YOU TO BE THE FIRST TO SEE THIS.
PROJECT FOR A NEW AMERICAN SENTRY
SENATOR, YOU ARE HOLDING THE FUTURE.
OPERATIONAL
ALLOW ME TO INTRODUCE YOU TO WAR BEAST.
BE STILL MY HEART.
THE OLD SENTRIES ARE BIG AND BULKY. THEIR HUMAN OPERATORS MAKE STUPID, EMBARRASSING MISTAKES. AND HAVING TO PAY ALL THOSE BEANBAG JOCKEYS? EXPENSIVE.
WITH GROUNDBREAKING A.I., AND HEAT SENSORS THAT ALLOW HIM TO SEE THROUGH WALLS, WAR BEAST IS THE SMARTEST, DEADLIEST SENTRY EVER MADE.
ALLOW ME TO DEMONSTRATE.

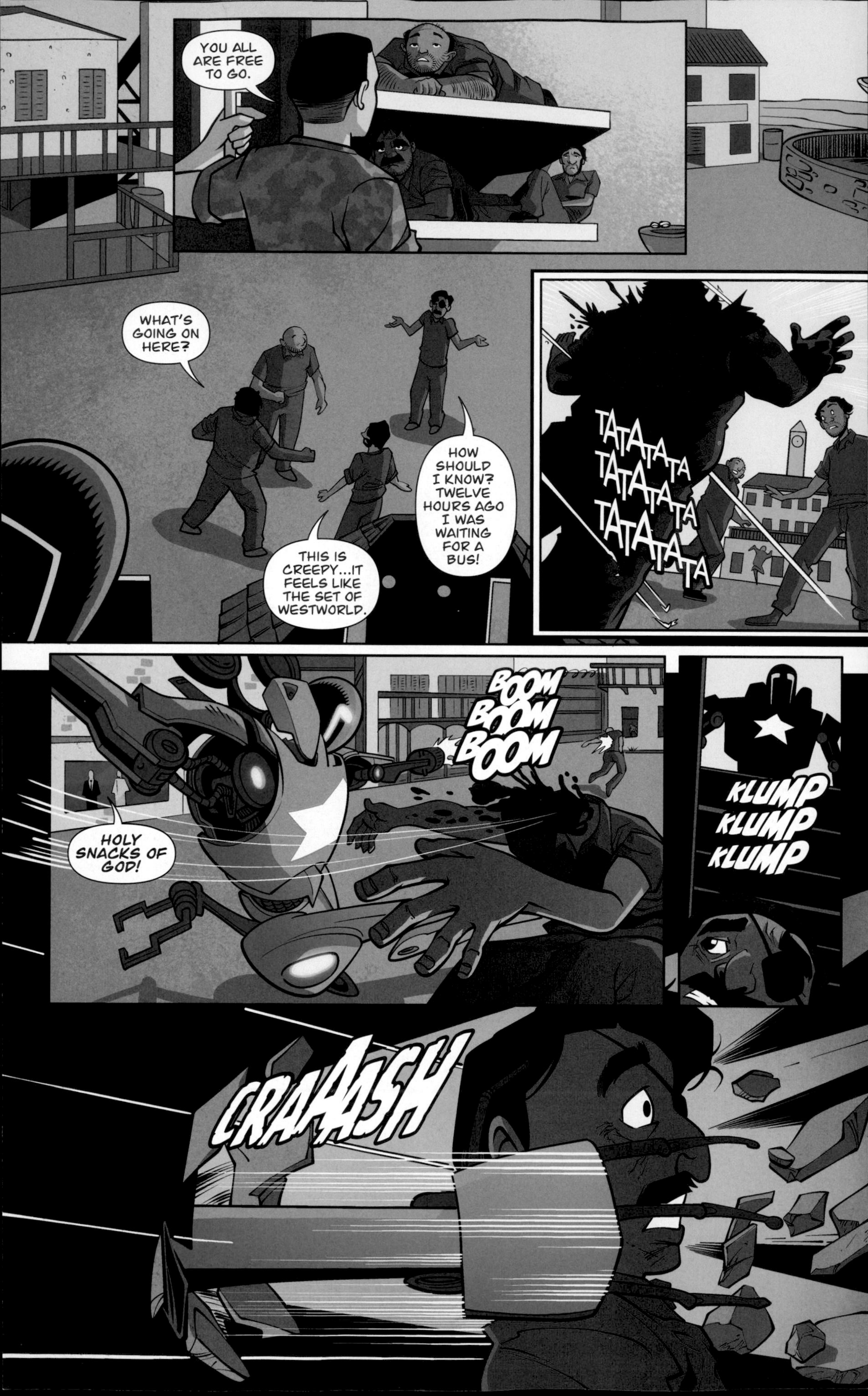
YOU ALL ARE FREE TO GO.
WHAT'S GOING ON HERE?
HOW SHOULD I KNOW? TWELVE HOURS AGO I WAS WAITING FOR A BUS!
THIS IS CREEPY...IT FEELS LIKE THE SET OF WESTWORLD.
TATATATATA TATATATATA TATATATATA
BOOM BOOM BOOM
HOLY SNACKS OF GOD!
KLUMP KLUMP KLUMP
CRAAAASH

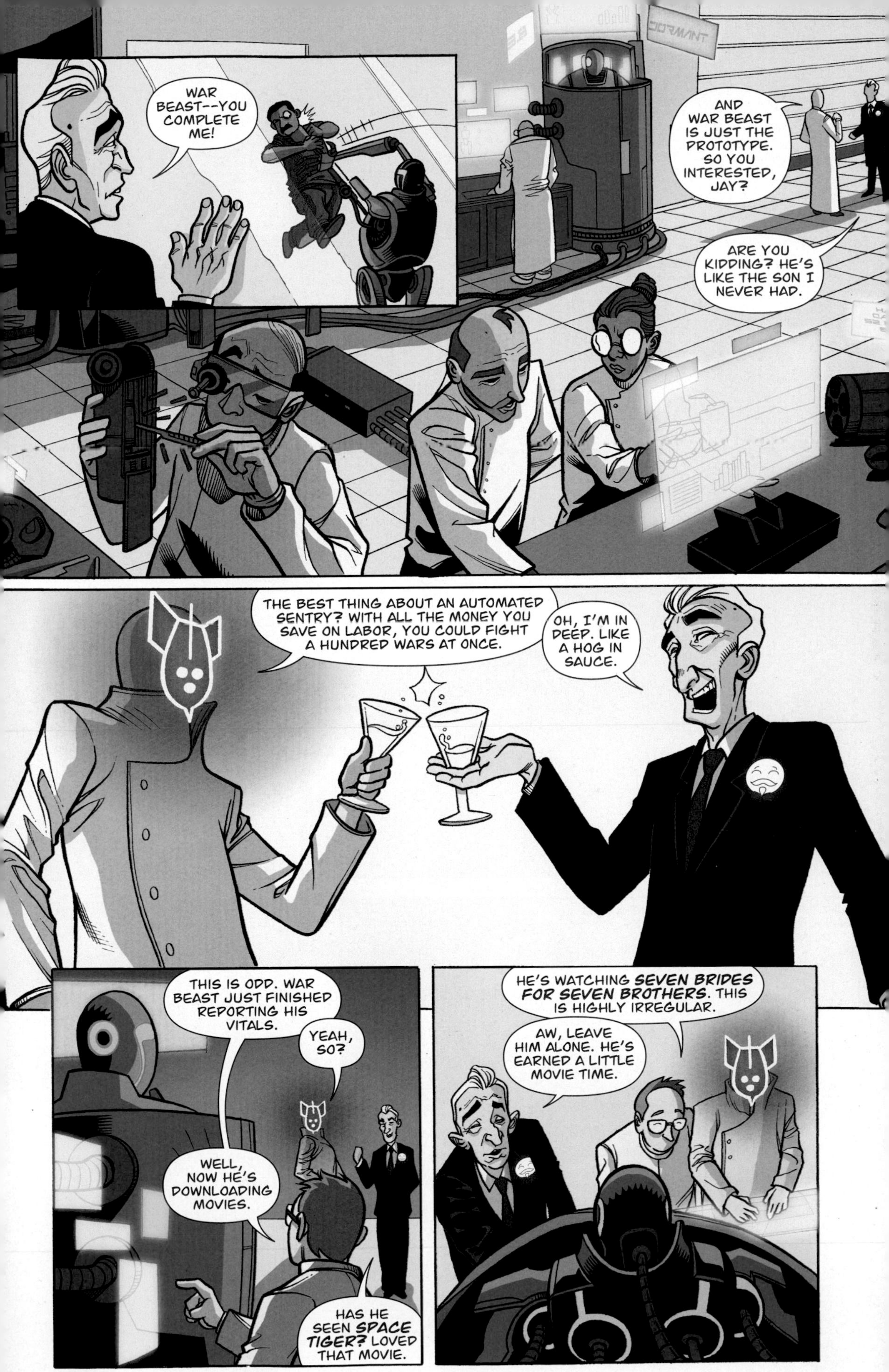
WAR BEAST--YOU COMPLETE ME!
AND WAR BEAST IS JUST THE PROTOTYPE. SO YOU INTERESTED, JAY?
ARE YOU KIDDING? HE'S LIKE THE SON I NEVER HAD.
DORMANT
THE BEST THING ABOUT AN AUTOMATED SENTRY? WITH ALL THE MONEY YOU SAVE ON LABOR, YOU COULD FIGHT A HUNDRED WARS AT ONCE.
OH, I'M IN DEEP. LIKE A HOG IN SAUCE.
THIS IS ODD. WAR BEAST JUST FINISHED REPORTING HIS VITALS.
YEAH, SO?
WELL, NOW HE'S DOWNLOADING MOVIES.
HAS HE SEEN SPACE TIGER? LOVED THAT MOVIE.
HE'S WATCHING SEVEN BRIDES FOR SEVEN BROTHERS. THIS IS HIGHLY IRREGULAR.
AW, LEAVE HIM ALONE. HE'S EARNED A LITTLE MOVIE TIME.

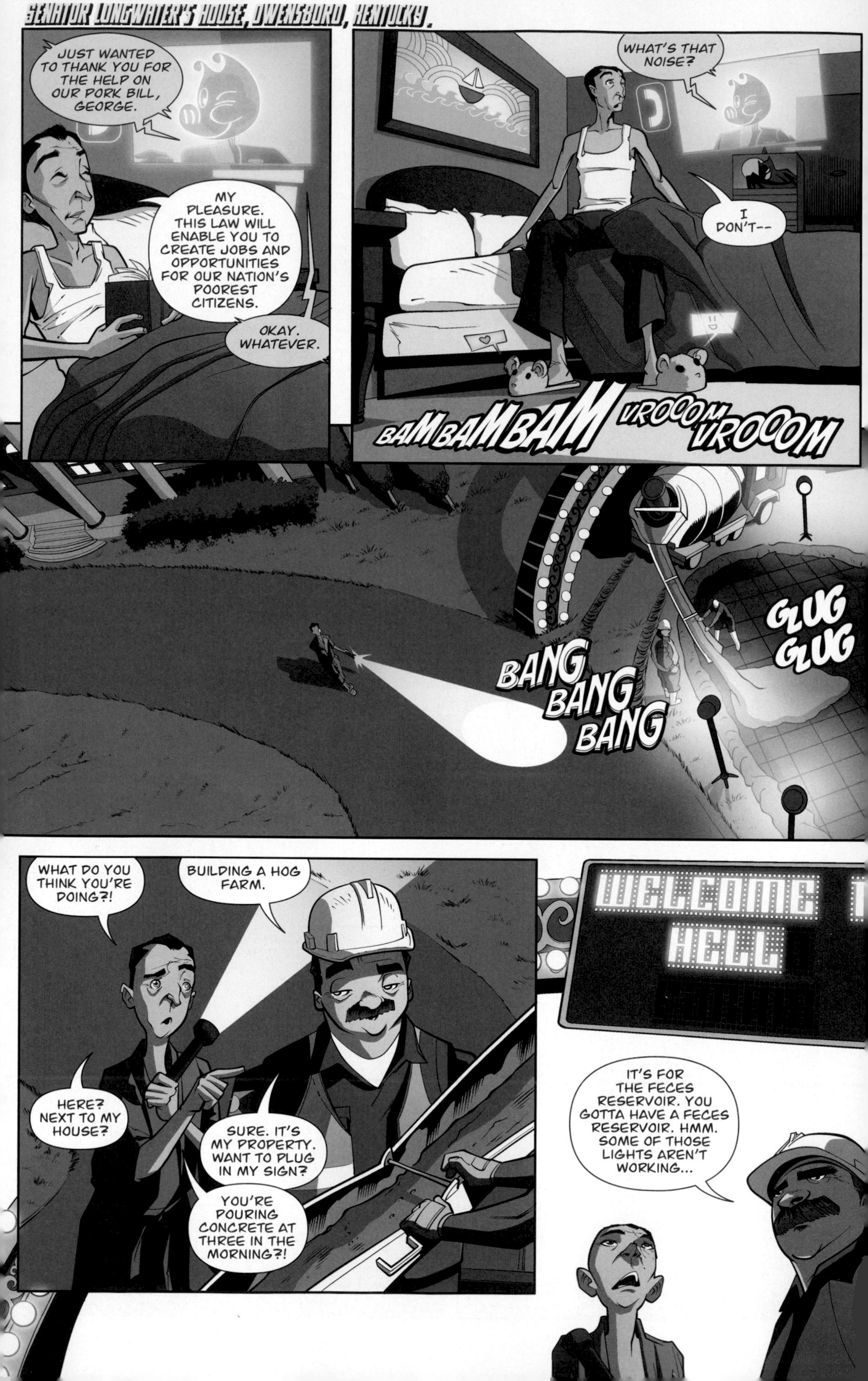
SENATOR LONGWATER'S HOUSE, OWENSBORO, KENTUCKY.
JUST WANTED TO THANK YOU FOR THE HELP ON OUR PORK BILL, GEORGE.
MY PLEASURE. THIS LAW WILL ENABLE YOU TO CREATE JOBS AND OPPORTUNITIES FOR OUR NATION'S POOREST CITIZENS.
OKAY. WHATEVER.
WHAT'S THAT NOISE?
I DON'T--
BAMBAMBAM VROOOM VROOOM
BANG BANG BANG
GLUG GLUG
WHAT DO YOU THINK YOU'RE DOING?!
BUILDING A HOG FARM.
HERE? NEXT TO MY HOUSE?
SURE. IT'S MY PROPERTY. WANT TO PLUG IN MY SIGN?
YOU'RE POURING CONCRETE AT THREE IN THE MORNING?!
WELCOME T HELL
IT'S FOR THE FECES RESERVOIR. YOU GOTTA HAVE A FECES RESERVOIR. HMM. SOME OF THOSE LIGHTS AREN'T WORKING...

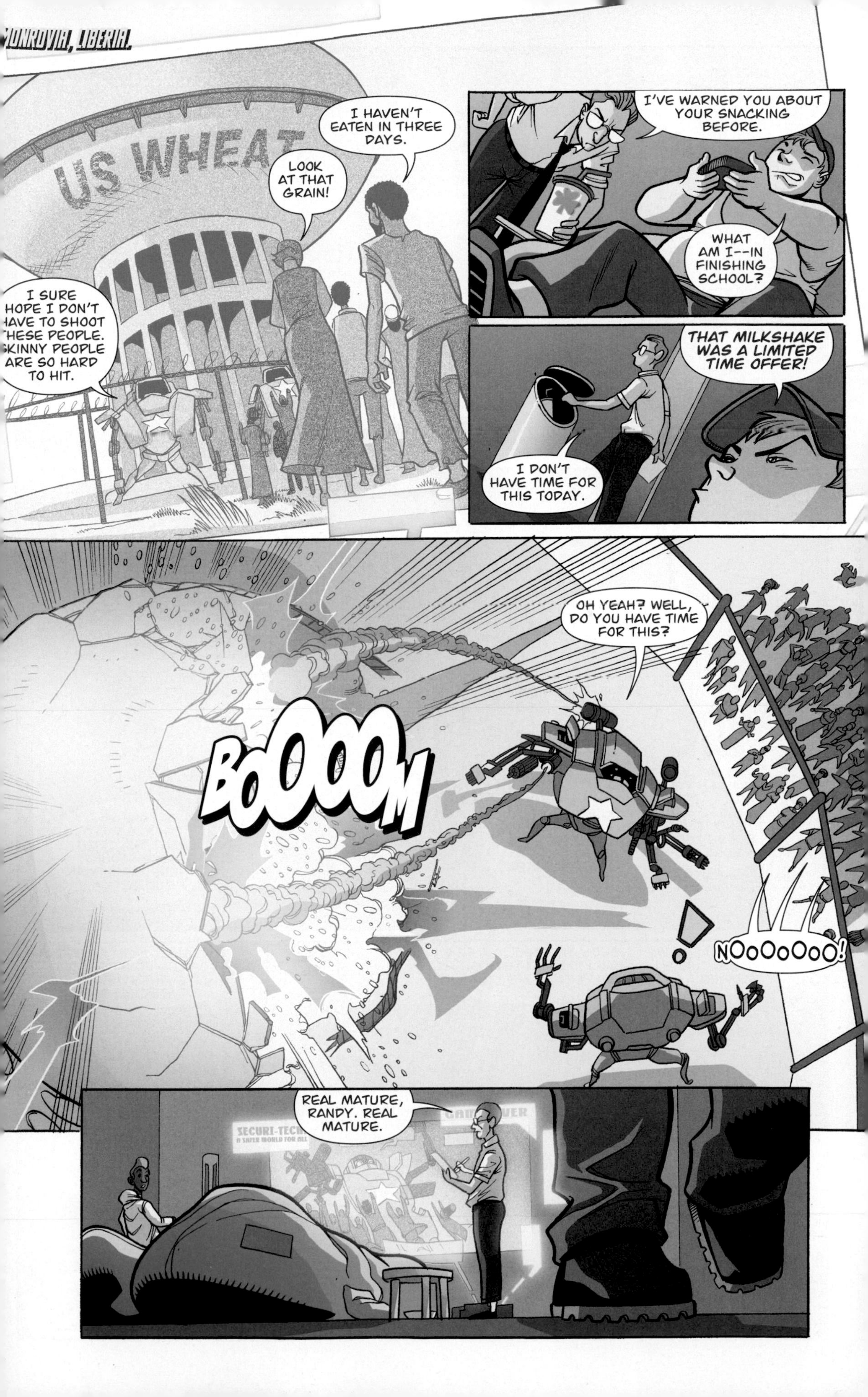
MONROVIA, LIBERIA.
US WHEAT
I HAVEN'T EATEN IN THREE DAYS.
LOOK AT THAT GRAIN!
I SURE HOPE I DON'T HAVE TO SHOOT THESE PEOPLE. SKINNY PEOPLE ARE SO HARD TO HIT.
I'VE WARNED YOU ABOUT YOUR SNACKING BEFORE.
WHAT AM I--IN FINISHING SCHOOL?
THAT MILKSHAKE WAS A LIMITED TIME OFFER!
I DON'T HAVE TIME FOR THIS TODAY.
OH YEAH? WELL, DO YOU HAVE TIME FOR THIS?
BOOOOM
!
NOOOOOOO!
REAL MATURE, RANDY. REAL MATURE.
SECURI-TECH
A SAFER WORLD FOR ALL

YOU LOOK HAPPY, SENATOR.

DO I? DO I LOOK LIKE A BOY IN LOVE?

HAPPINESS IS FOR DOGS AND CHILDREN.

SITUATION ROOM

SITUATION ROOM

I'M GLAD YOU CALLED THIS MEETING, MADAM PRESIDENT. I THINK I KNOW HOW WE CAN IMPROVE OUR SENTRY FORCES.

ACTUALLY, I CALLED YOU ALL HERE BECAUSE I WANT TO SHUT DOWN THE SENTRY PROGRAM.

WHAT?! YOU'RE GOING TO PUT OUR SECURITY AT RISK BECAUSE OF ONE KID? A *SOCCER PLAYER*, NO LESS?!

HE WAS NOT THE ONLY ONE. I FOUND HUNDREDS OF CLASSIFIED INCIDENTS. THOUSANDS DEAD. AT THE VERY LEAST, PEOPLE NEED TO KNOW THE TRUTH.

ANYONE WHO THINKS THEY WANT THE TRUTH NEVER FOUND THEIR DAD'S PORN COLLECTION.

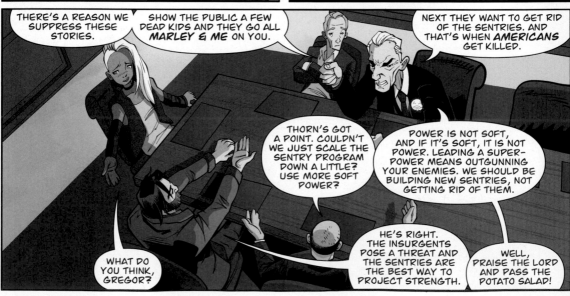

THERE'S A REASON WE SUPPRESS THESE STORIES.

SHOW THE PUBLIC A FEW DEAD KIDS AND THEY GO ALL *MARLEY & ME* ON YOU.

NEXT THEY WANT TO GET RID OF THE SENTRIES. AND THAT'S WHEN *AMERICANS* GET KILLED.

THORN'S GOT A POINT. COULDN'T WE JUST SCALE THE SENTRY PROGRAM DOWN A LITTLE? USE MORE SOFT POWER?

POWER IS NOT SOFT, AND IF IT'S SOFT, IT IS NOT POWER. LEADING A SUPER-POWER MEANS OUTGUNNING YOUR ENEMIES. WE SHOULD BE BUILDING NEW SENTRIES, NOT GETTING RID OF THEM.

WHAT DO YOU THINK, GREGOR?

HE'S RIGHT. THE INSURGENTS POSE A THREAT AND THE SENTRIES ARE THE BEST WAY TO PROJECT STRENGTH.

WELL, PRAISE THE LORD AND PASS THE POTATO SALAD!

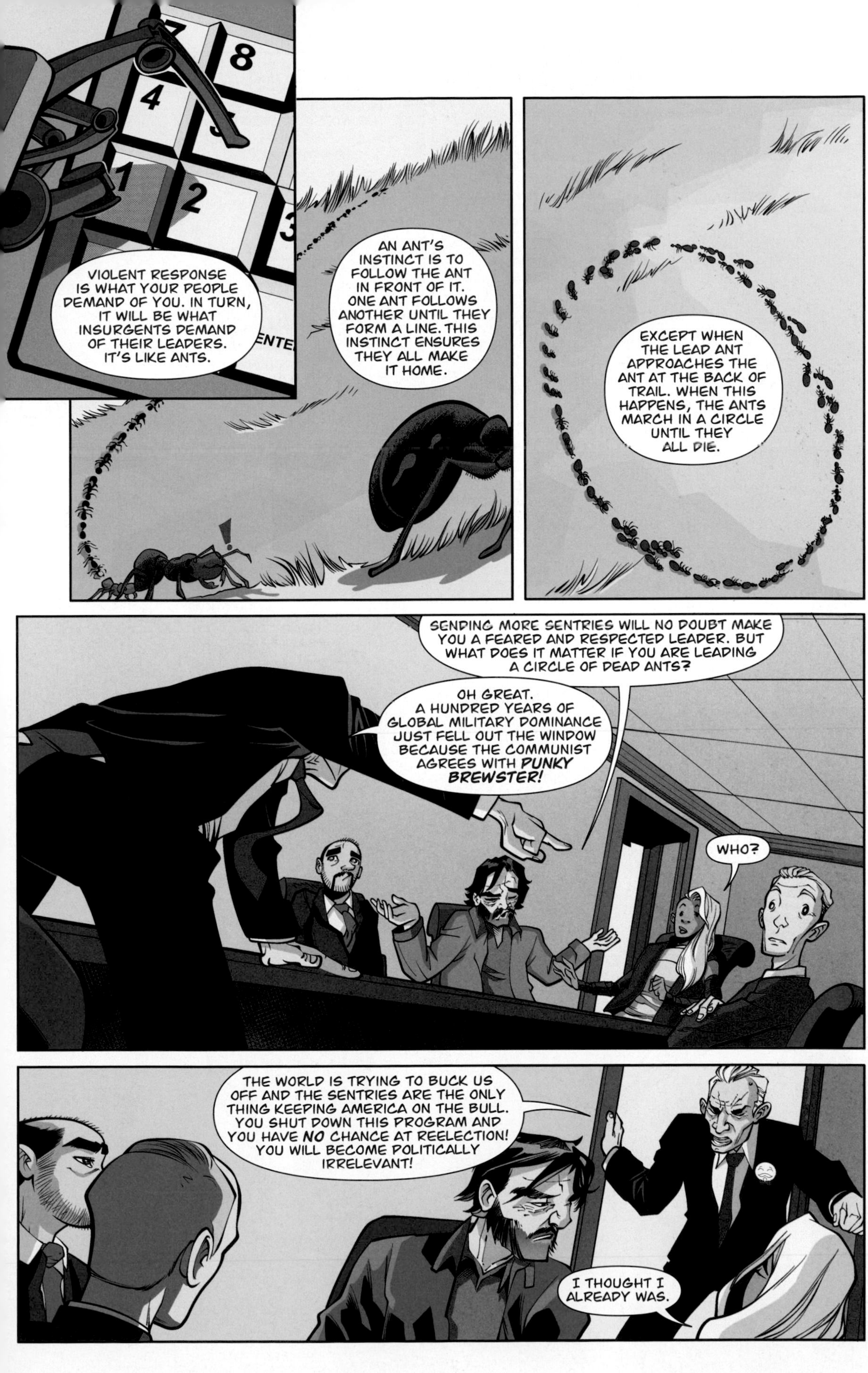
8
4
1
2
3
VIOLENT RESPONSE IS WHAT YOUR PEOPLE DEMAND OF YOU. IN TURN, IT WILL BE WHAT INSURGENTS DEMAND OF THEIR LEADERS. IT'S LIKE ANTS.
AN ANT'S INSTINCT IS TO FOLLOW THE ANT IN FRONT OF IT. ONE ANT FOLLOWS ANOTHER UNTIL THEY FORM A LINE. THIS INSTINCT ENSURES THEY ALL MAKE IT HOME.
!
EXCEPT WHEN THE LEAD ANT APPROACHES THE ANT AT THE BACK OF TRAIL. WHEN THIS HAPPENS, THE ANTS MARCH IN A CIRCLE UNTIL THEY ALL DIE.
SENDING MORE SENTRIES WILL NO DOUBT MAKE YOU A FEARED AND RESPECTED LEADER. BUT WHAT DOES IT MATTER IF YOU ARE LEADING A CIRCLE OF DEAD ANTS?
OH GREAT. A HUNDRED YEARS OF GLOBAL MILITARY DOMINANCE JUST FELL OUT THE WINDOW BECAUSE THE COMMUNIST AGREES WITH *PUNKY BREWSTER!*
WHO?
THE WORLD IS TRYING TO BUCK US OFF AND THE SENTRIES ARE THE ONLY THING KEEPING AMERICA ON THE BULL. YOU SHUT DOWN THIS PROGRAM AND YOU HAVE *NO* CHANCE AT REELECTION! YOU WILL BECOME POLITICALLY IRRELEVANT!
I THOUGHT I ALREADY WAS.

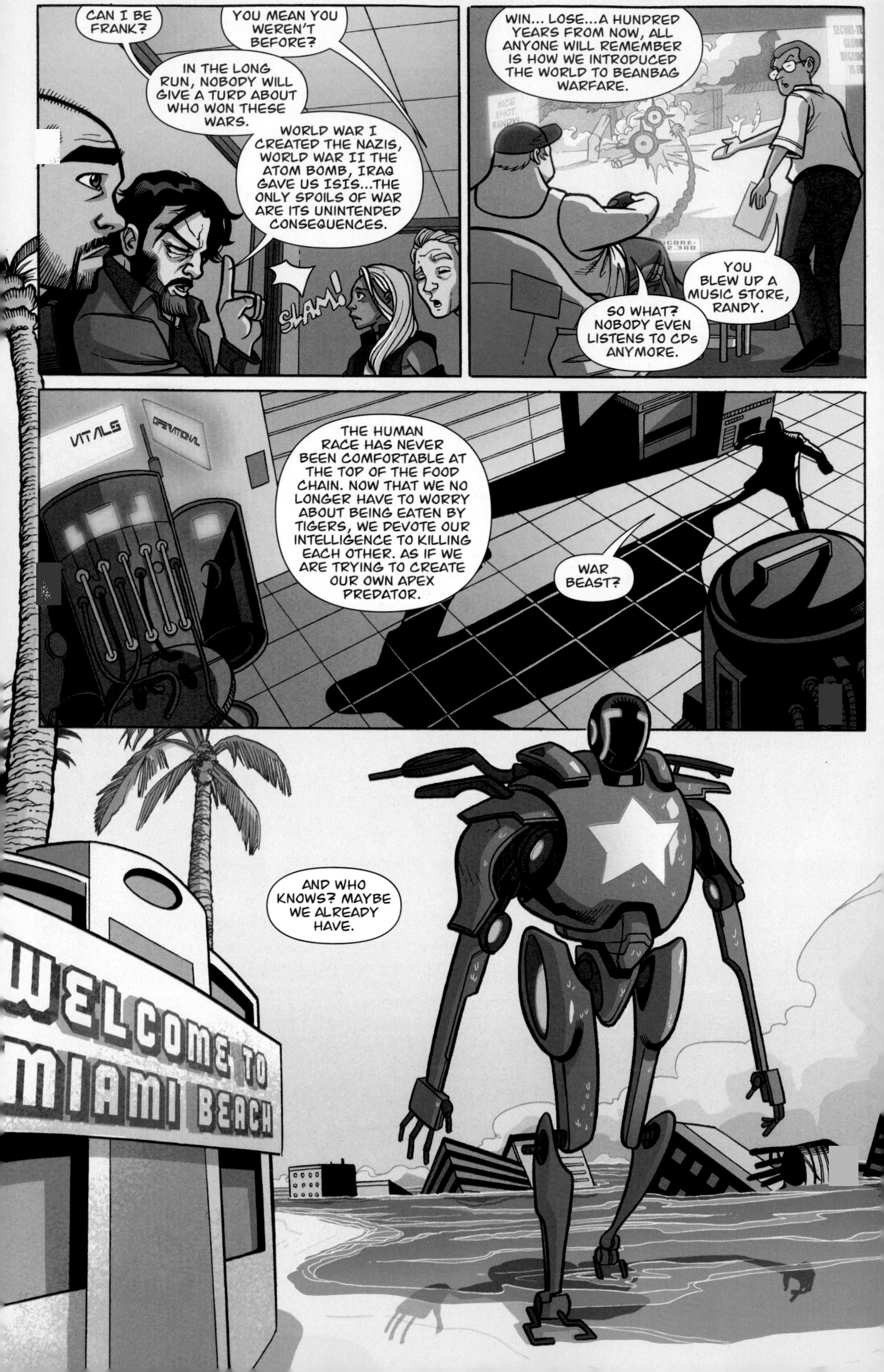
CAN I BE FRANK?
YOU MEAN YOU WEREN'T BEFORE?
IN THE LONG RUN, NOBODY WILL GIVE A TURD ABOUT WHO WON THESE WARS.
WORLD WAR I CREATED THE NAZIS, WORLD WAR II THE ATOM BOMB, IRAQ GAVE US ISIS...THE ONLY SPOILS OF WAR ARE ITS UNINTENDED CONSEQUENCES.
SLAM!
WIN... LOSE...A HUNDRED YEARS FROM NOW, ALL ANYONE WILL REMEMBER IS HOW WE INTRODUCED THE WORLD TO BEANBAG WARFARE.
YOU BLEW UP A MUSIC STORE, RANDY.
SO WHAT? NOBODY EVEN LISTENS TO CDs ANYMORE.
VITALS
OPERATIONAL
THE HUMAN RACE HAS NEVER BEEN COMFORTABLE AT THE TOP OF THE FOOD CHAIN. NOW THAT WE NO LONGER HAVE TO WORRY ABOUT BEING EATEN BY TIGERS, WE DEVOTE OUR INTELLIGENCE TO KILLING EACH OTHER. AS IF WE ARE TRYING TO CREATE OUR OWN APEX PREDATOR.
WAR BEAST?
AND WHO KNOWS? MAYBE WE ALREADY HAVE.
WELCOME TO MIAMI BEACH

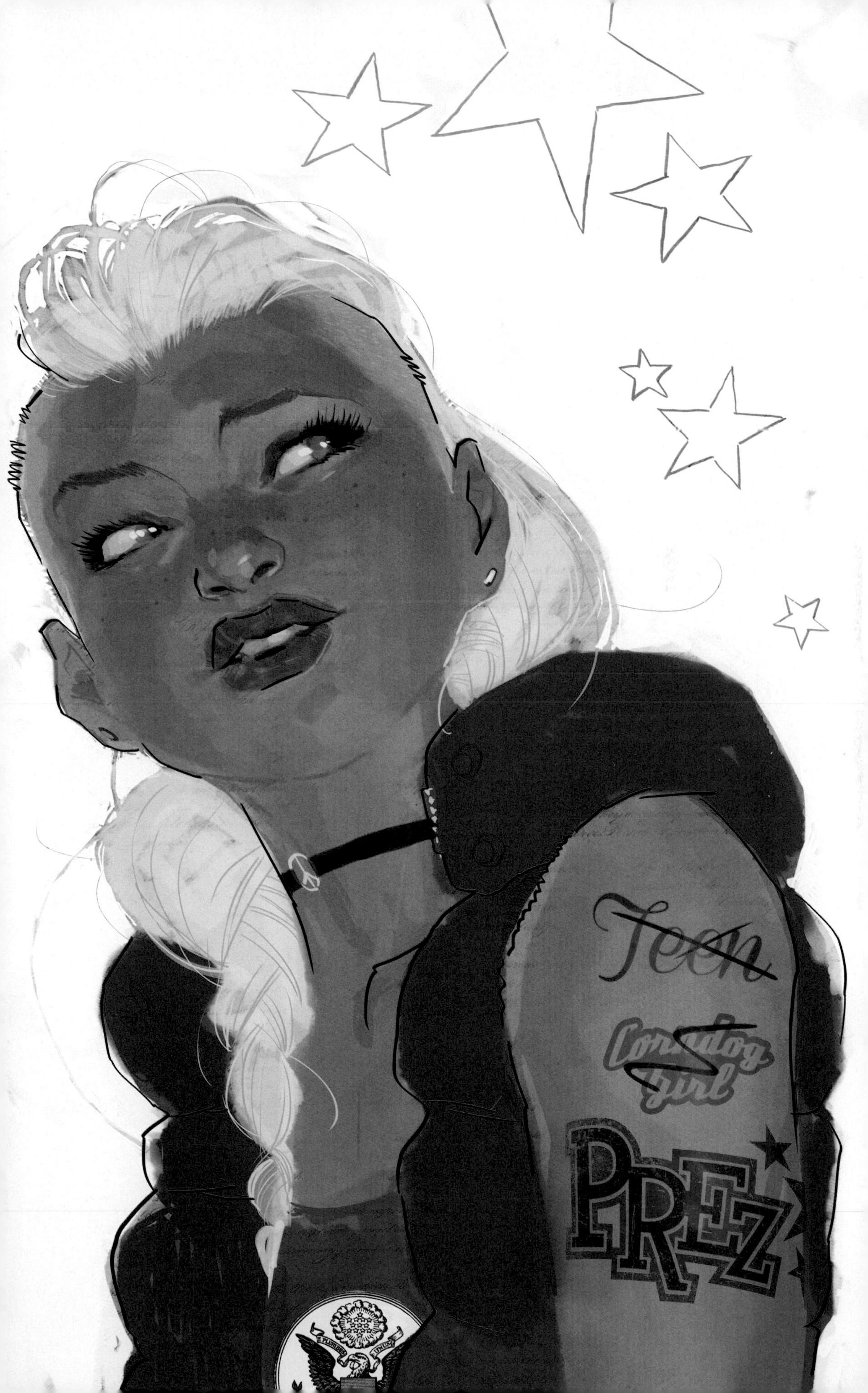
Teen
Corndog Girl
PREZ

APOLOGIES IN ADVANCE

MARK RUSSELL writer **BEN CALDWELL** penciller **MARK MORALES** inker **JEREMY LAWSON** colorist

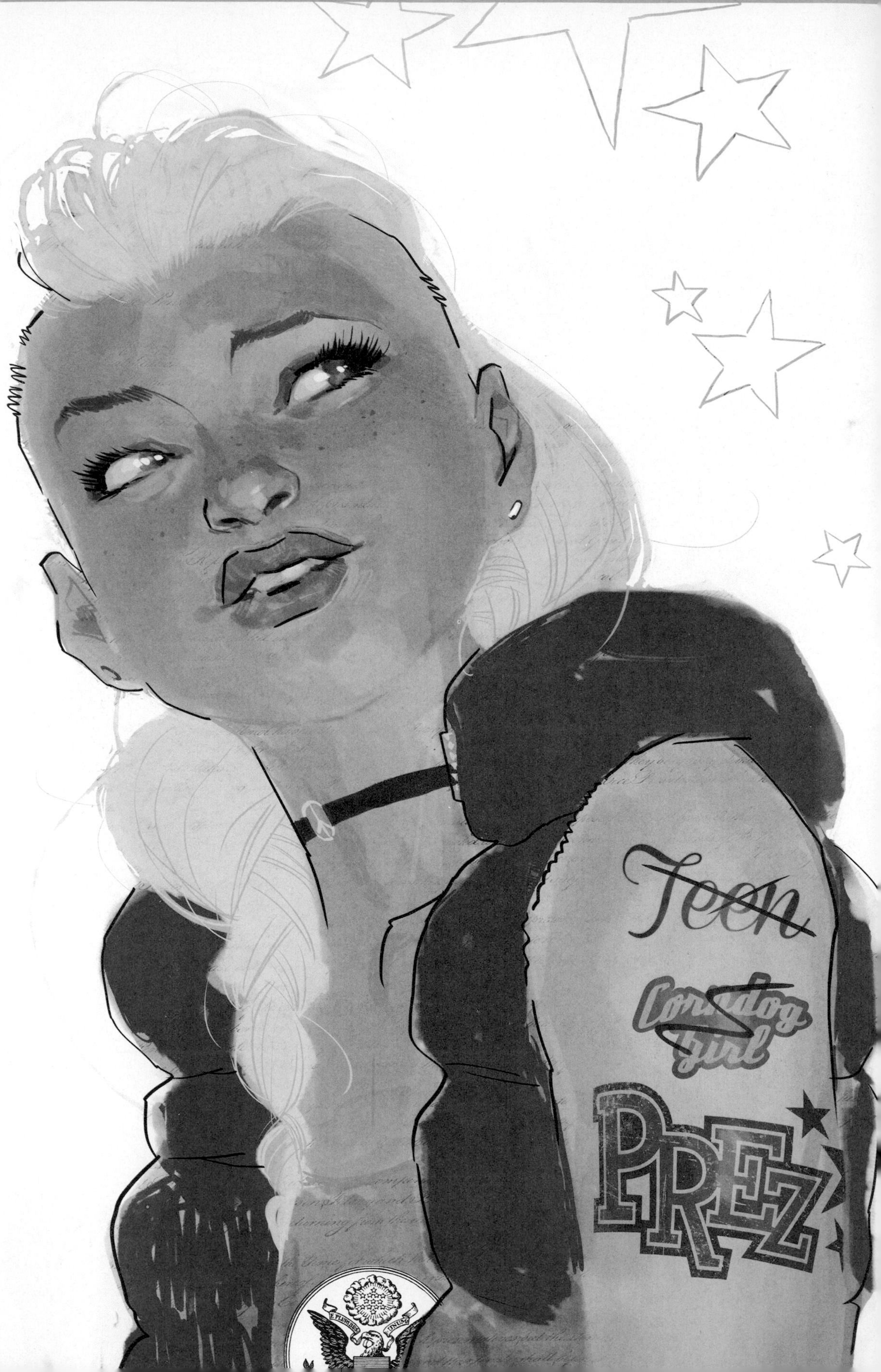
Teen
Corndog girl
PREZ

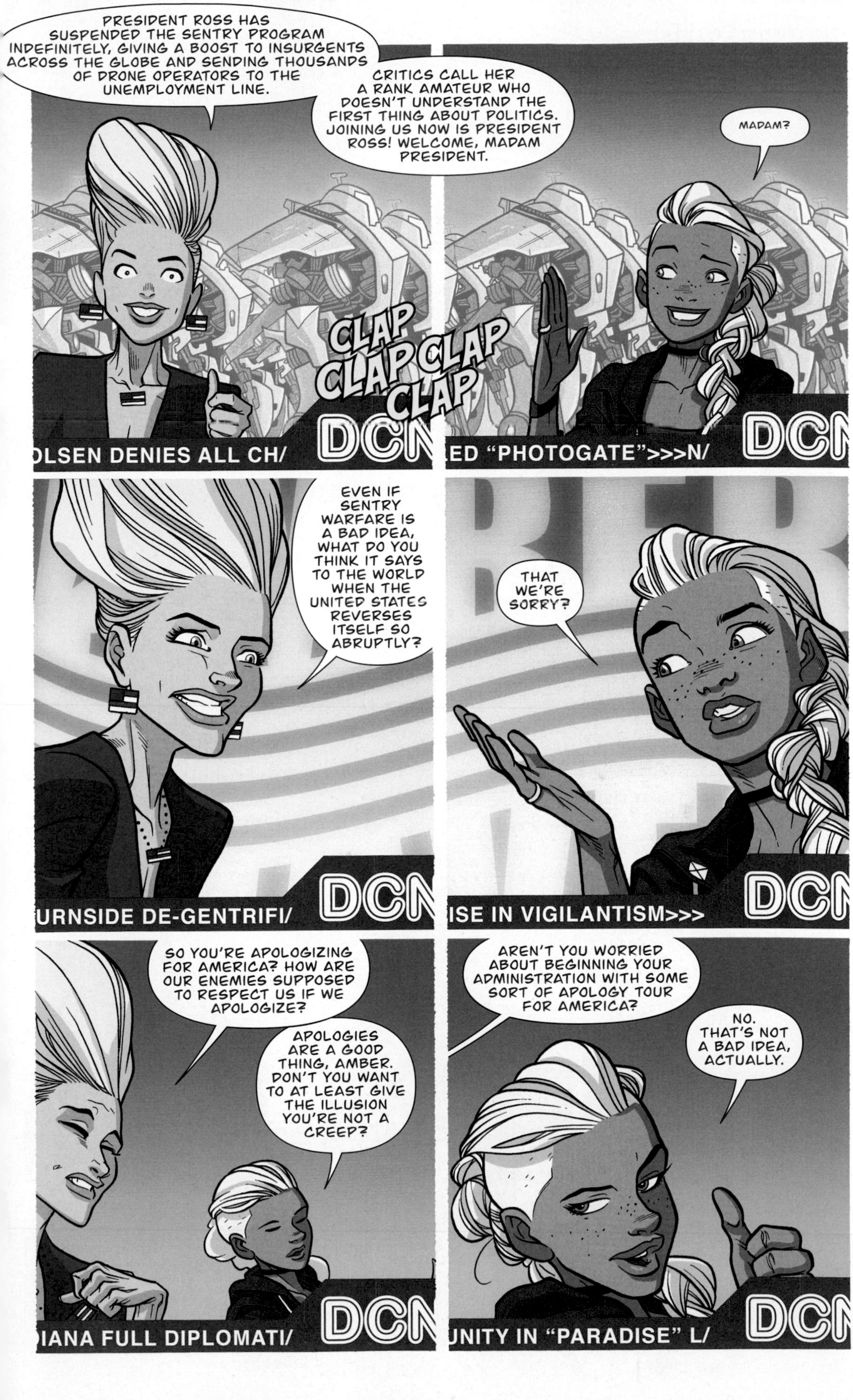
PRESIDENT ROSS HAS SUSPENDED THE SENTRY PROGRAM INDEFINITELY, GIVING A BOOST TO INSURGENTS ACROSS THE GLOBE AND SENDING THOUSANDS OF DRONE OPERATORS TO THE UNEMPLOYMENT LINE.
CRITICS CALL HER A RANK AMATEUR WHO DOESN'T UNDERSTAND THE FIRST THING ABOUT POLITICS. JOINING US NOW IS PRESIDENT ROSS! WELCOME, MADAM PRESIDENT.
CLAP CLAP CLAP CLAP
DCN
OLSEN DENIES ALL CH/
MADAM?
DCN
ED "PHOTOGATE">>>N/
EVEN IF SENTRY WARFARE IS A BAD IDEA, WHAT DO YOU THINK IT SAYS TO THE WORLD WHEN THE UNITED STATES REVERSES ITSELF SO ABRUPTLY?
DCN
URNSIDE DE-GENTRIFI/
THAT WE'RE SORRY?
DCN
ISE IN VIGILANTISM>>>
SO YOU'RE APOLOGIZING FOR AMERICA? HOW ARE OUR ENEMIES SUPPOSED TO RESPECT US IF WE APOLOGIZE?
APOLOGIES ARE A GOOD THING, AMBER. DON'T YOU WANT TO AT LEAST GIVE THE ILLUSION YOU'RE NOT A CREEP?
DCN
DIANA FULL DIPLOMATI/
AREN'T YOU WORRIED ABOUT BEGINNING YOUR ADMINISTRATION WITH SOME SORT OF APOLOGY TOUR FOR AMERICA?
NO. THAT'S NOT A BAD IDEA, ACTUALLY.
DCN
UNITY IN "PARADISE" L/

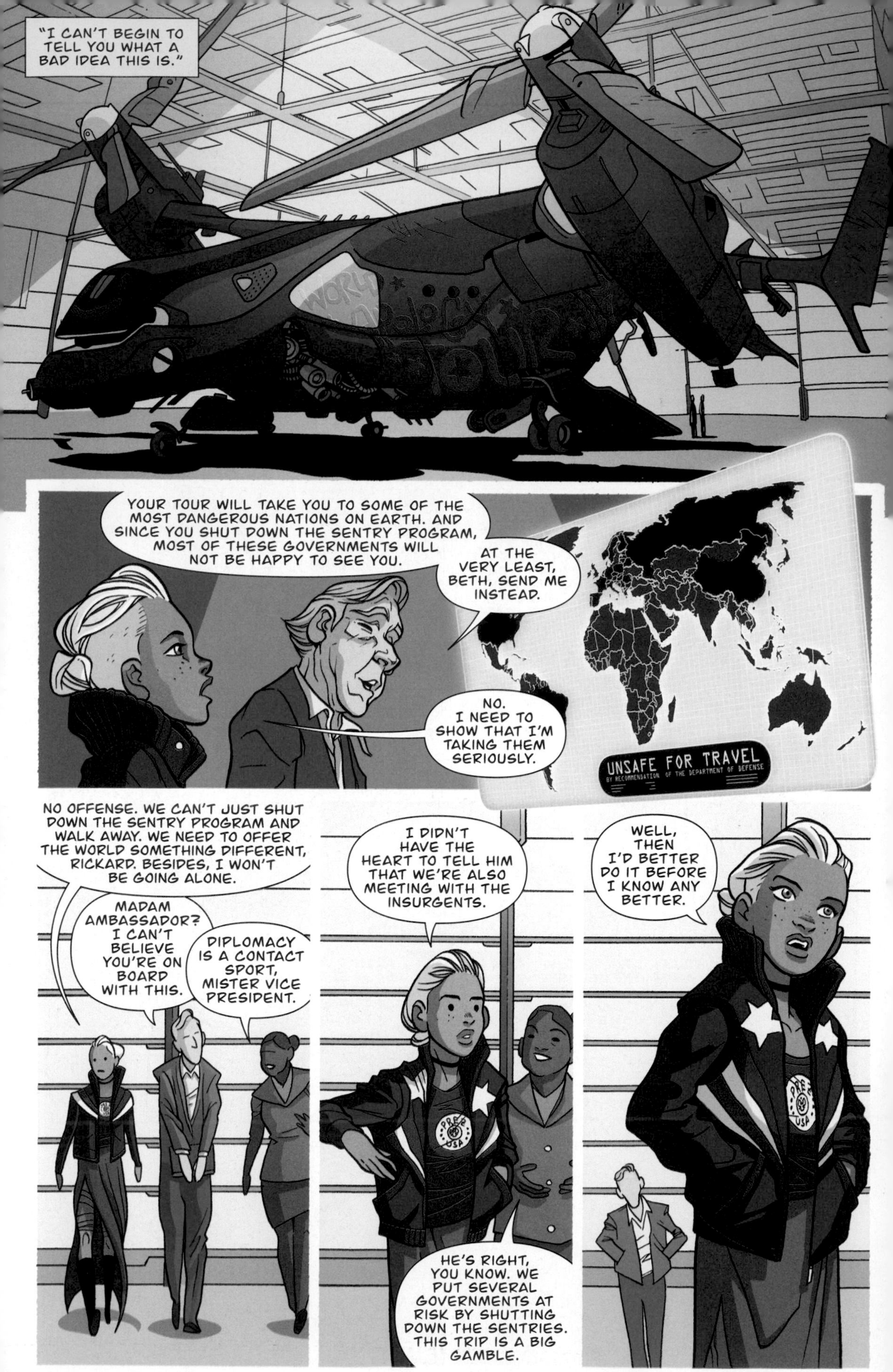
"I CAN'T BEGIN TO TELL YOU WHAT A BAD IDEA THIS IS."
YOUR TOUR WILL TAKE YOU TO SOME OF THE MOST DANGEROUS NATIONS ON EARTH. AND SINCE YOU SHUT DOWN THE SENTRY PROGRAM, MOST OF THESE GOVERNMENTS WILL NOT BE HAPPY TO SEE YOU.
AT THE VERY LEAST, BETH, SEND ME INSTEAD.
NO. I NEED TO SHOW THAT I'M TAKING THEM SERIOUSLY.
UNSAFE FOR TRAVEL
BY RECOMMENDATION OF THE DEPARTMENT OF DEFENSE
NO OFFENSE. WE CAN'T JUST SHUT DOWN THE SENTRY PROGRAM AND WALK AWAY. WE NEED TO OFFER THE WORLD SOMETHING DIFFERENT, RICKARD. BESIDES, I WON'T BE GOING ALONE.
MADAM AMBASSADOR? I CAN'T BELIEVE YOU'RE ON BOARD WITH THIS.
DIPLOMACY IS A CONTACT SPORT, MISTER VICE PRESIDENT.
I DIDN'T HAVE THE HEART TO TELL HIM THAT WE'RE ALSO MEETING WITH THE INSURGENTS.
HE'S RIGHT, YOU KNOW. WE PUT SEVERAL GOVERNMENTS AT RISK BY SHUTTING DOWN THE SENTRIES. THIS TRIP IS A BIG GAMBLE.
WELL, THEN I'D BETTER DO IT BEFORE I KNOW ANY BETTER.

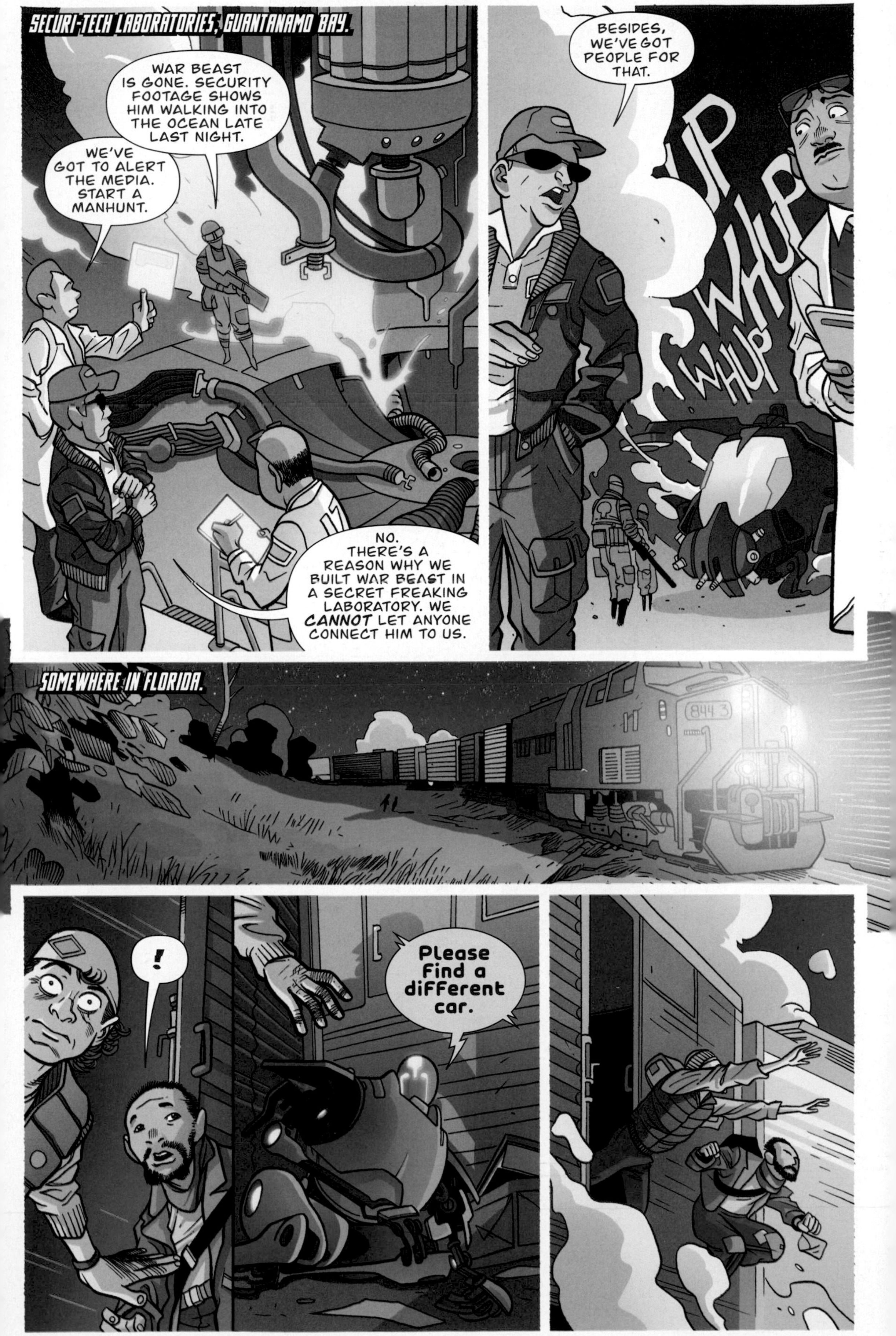
SECURI-TECH LABORATORIES, GUANTANAMO BAY.
WE'VE GOT TO ALERT THE MEDIA. START A MANHUNT.
WAR BEAST IS GONE. SECURITY FOOTAGE SHOWS HIM WALKING INTO THE OCEAN LATE LAST NIGHT.
NO. THERE'S A REASON WHY WE BUILT WAR BEAST IN A SECRET FREAKING LABORATORY. WE CANNOT LET ANYONE CONNECT HIM TO US.
BESIDES, WE'VE GOT PEOPLE FOR THAT.
WHUP WHUP WHUP
SOMEWHERE IN FLORIDA.
8443
!
Please find a different car.

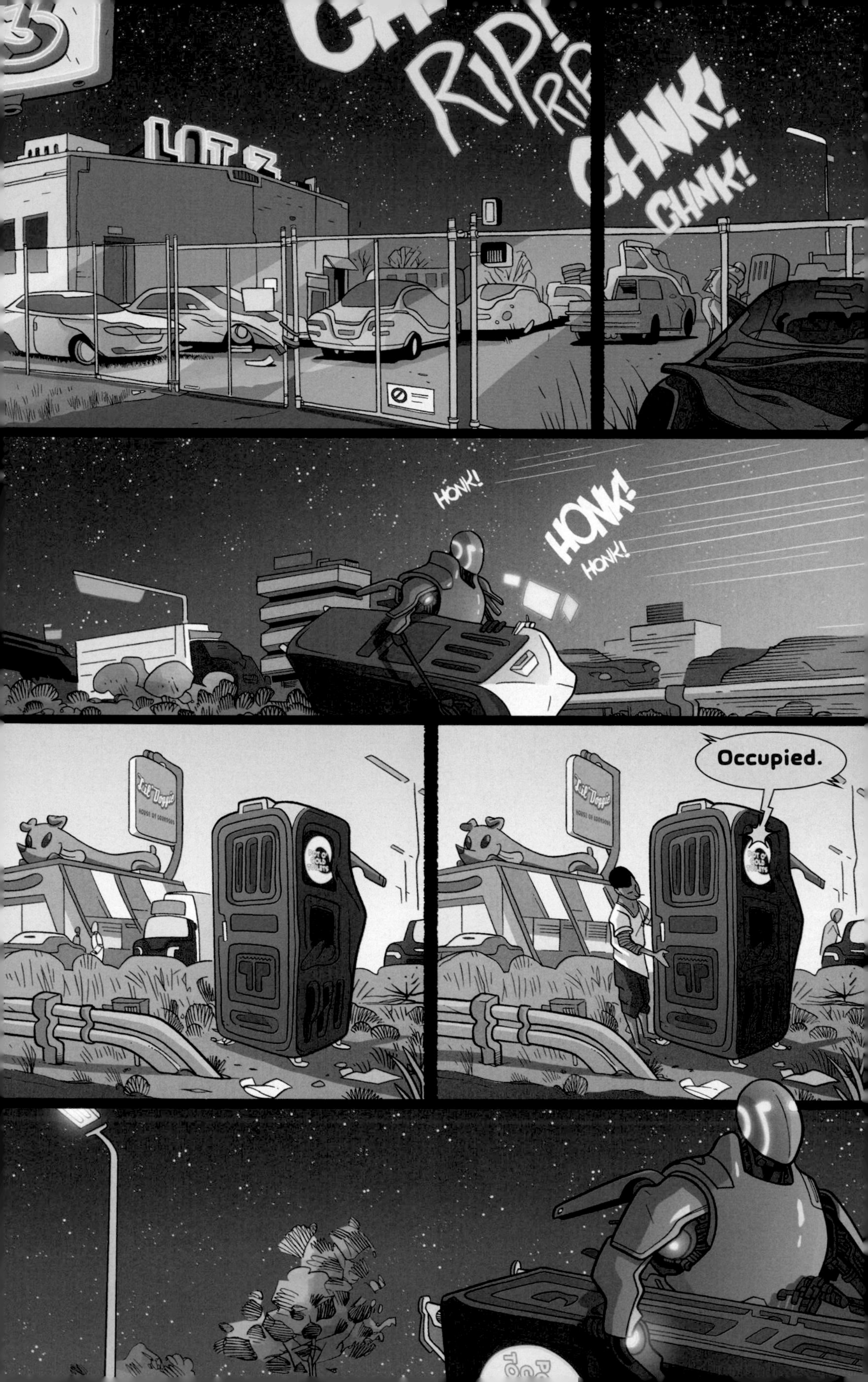
RIP!
CHNK!
CHNK!
CHNK!
HONK!
HONK!
HONK!
Lil' Doggie
HOUSE OF CORNDOGS
POT O' GOLD TOILETS
Occupied.

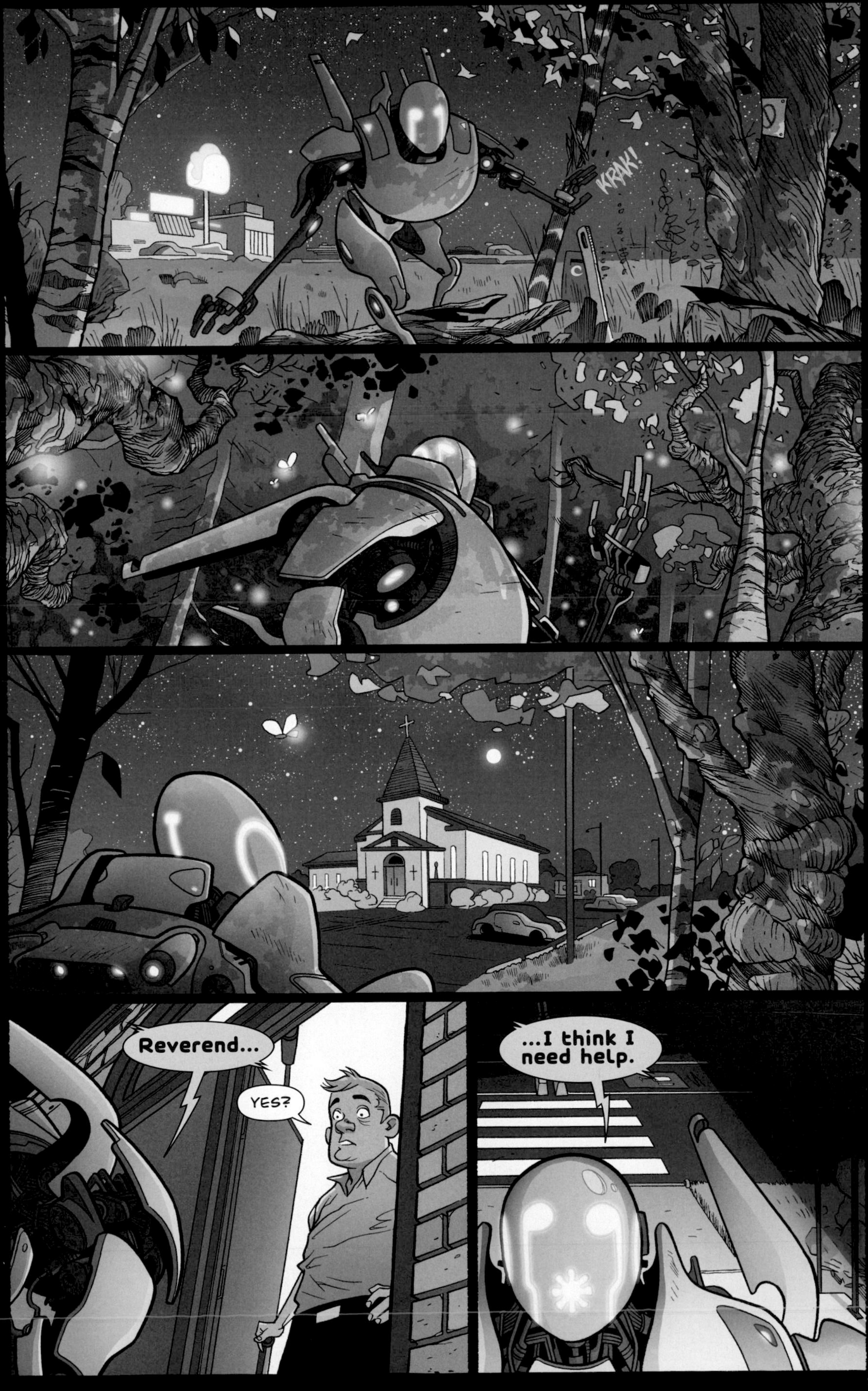
KRAK!
Reverend...
YES?
...I think I
need help.

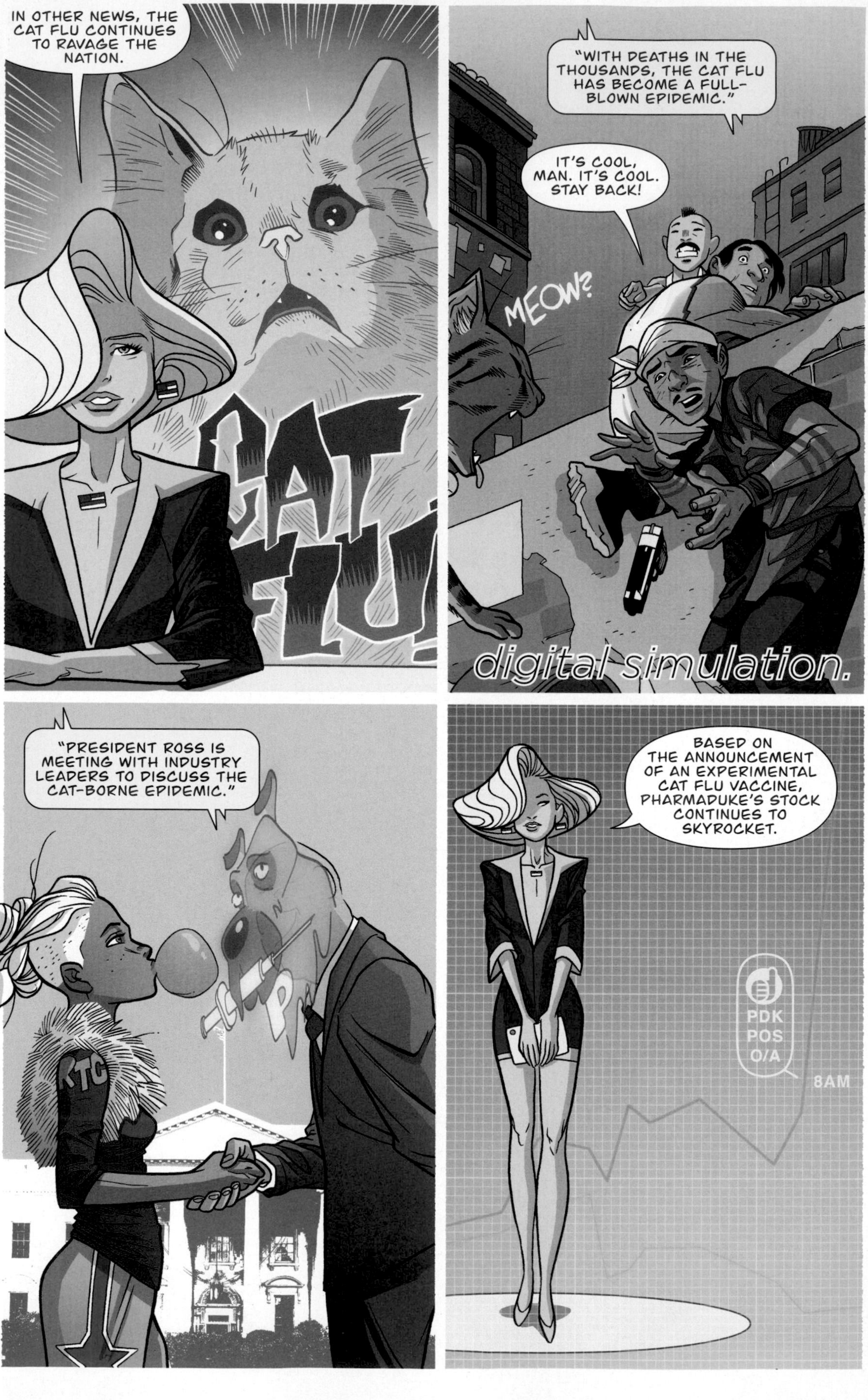

IN OTHER NEWS, THE CAT FLU CONTINUES TO RAVAGE THE NATION.
CAT FLU
"WITH DEATHS IN THE THOUSANDS, THE CAT FLU HAS BECOME A FULL-BLOWN EPIDEMIC."
IT'S COOL, MAN. IT'S COOL. STAY BACK!
MEOW?
digital simulation.
"PRESIDENT ROSS IS MEETING WITH INDUSTRY LEADERS TO DISCUSS THE CAT-BORNE EPIDEMIC."
KTC
BASED ON THE ANNOUNCEMENT OF AN EXPERIMENTAL CAT FLU VACCINE, PHARMADUKE'S STOCK CONTINUES TO SKYROCKET.
PDK
POS
O/A
8AM

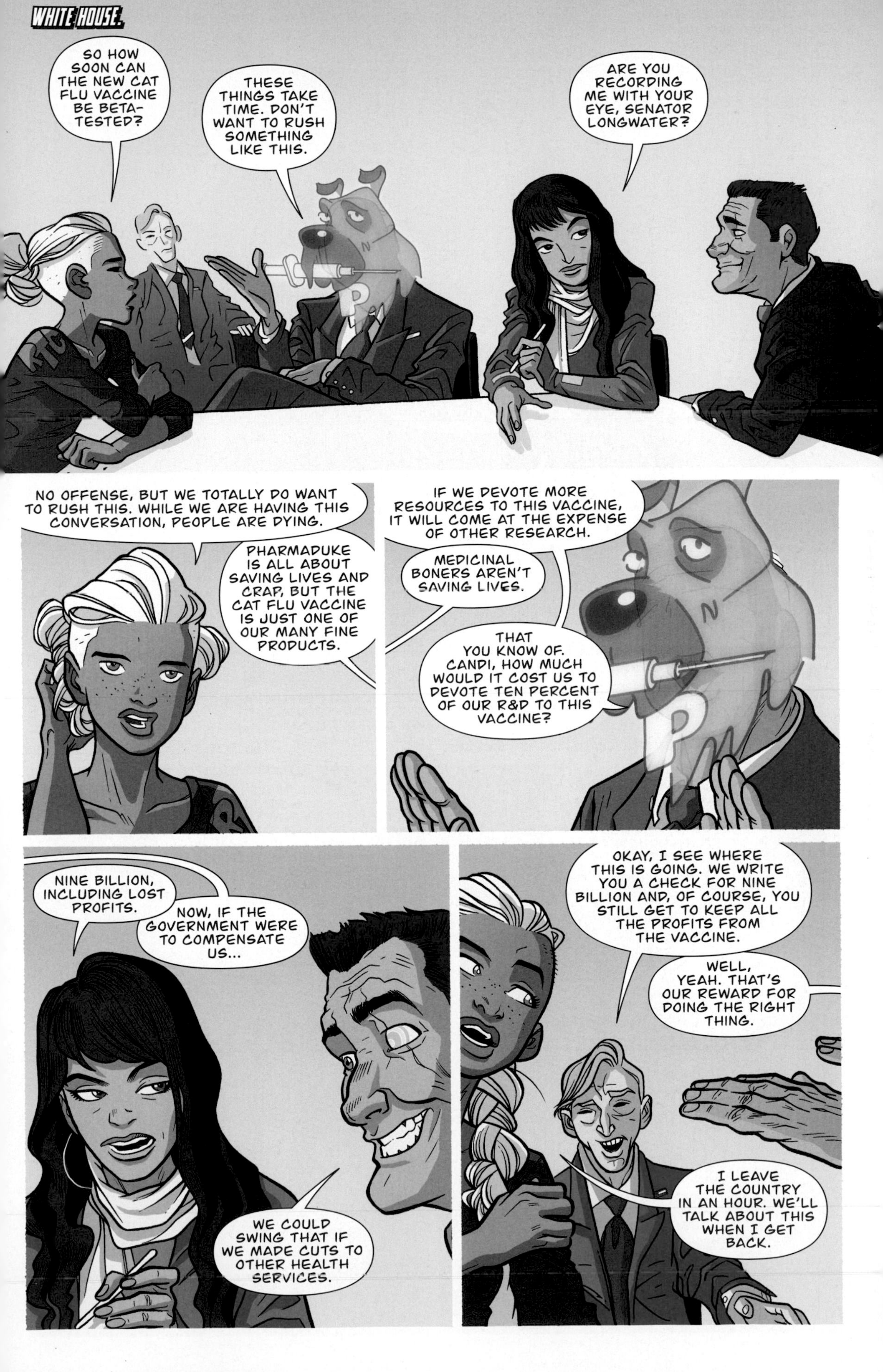
WHITE HOUSE.
SO HOW SOON CAN THE NEW CAT FLU VACCINE BE BETA-TESTED?
THESE THINGS TAKE TIME. DON'T WANT TO RUSH SOMETHING LIKE THIS.
ARE YOU RECORDING ME WITH YOUR EYE, SENATOR LONGWATER?
NO OFFENSE, BUT WE TOTALLY DO WANT TO RUSH THIS. WHILE WE ARE HAVING THIS CONVERSATION, PEOPLE ARE DYING.
PHARMADUKE IS ALL ABOUT SAVING LIVES AND CRAP, BUT THE CAT FLU VACCINE IS JUST ONE OF OUR MANY FINE PRODUCTS.
IF WE DEVOTE MORE RESOURCES TO THIS VACCINE, IT WILL COME AT THE EXPENSE OF OTHER RESEARCH.
MEDICINAL BONERS AREN'T SAVING LIVES.
THAT YOU KNOW OF. CANDI, HOW MUCH WOULD IT COST US TO DEVOTE TEN PERCENT OF OUR R&D TO THIS VACCINE?
NINE BILLION, INCLUDING LOST PROFITS.
NOW, IF THE GOVERNMENT WERE TO COMPENSATE US...
WE COULD SWING THAT IF WE MADE CUTS TO OTHER HEALTH SERVICES.
OKAY, I SEE WHERE THIS IS GOING. WE WRITE YOU A CHECK FOR NINE BILLION AND, OF COURSE, YOU STILL GET TO KEEP ALL THE PROFITS FROM THE VACCINE.
WELL, YEAH. THAT'S OUR REWARD FOR DOING THE RIGHT THING.
I LEAVE THE COUNTRY IN AN HOUR. WE'LL TALK ABOUT THIS WHEN I GET BACK.

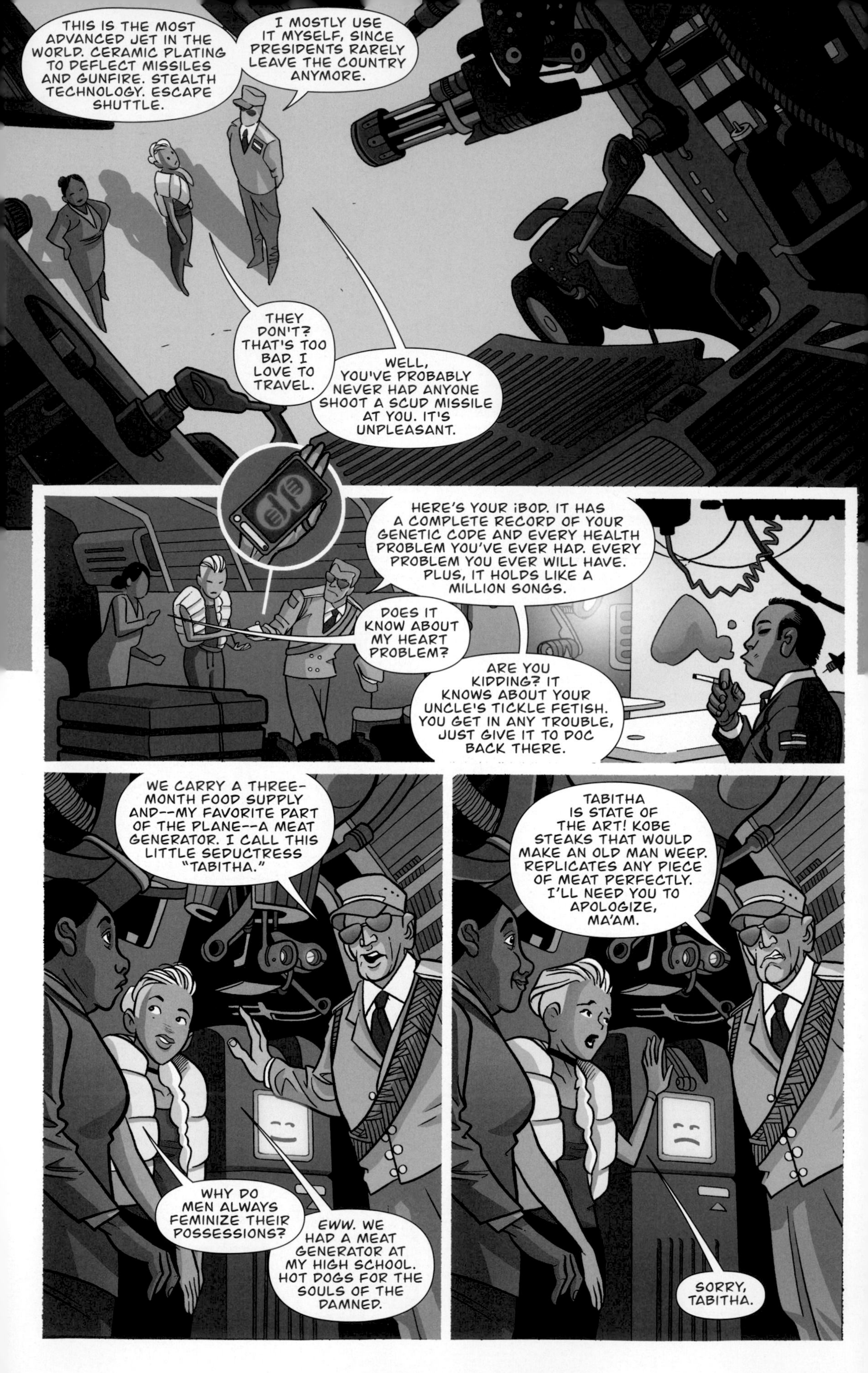
THIS IS THE MOST ADVANCED JET IN THE WORLD. CERAMIC PLATING TO DEFLECT MISSILES AND GUNFIRE. STEALTH TECHNOLOGY. ESCAPE SHUTTLE.
I MOSTLY USE IT MYSELF, SINCE PRESIDENTS RARELY LEAVE THE COUNTRY ANYMORE.
THEY DON'T? THAT'S TOO BAD. I LOVE TO TRAVEL.
WELL, YOU'VE PROBABLY NEVER HAD ANYONE SHOOT A SCUD MISSILE AT YOU. IT'S UNPLEASANT.
HERE'S YOUR iBOD. IT HAS A COMPLETE RECORD OF YOUR GENETIC CODE AND EVERY HEALTH PROBLEM YOU'VE EVER HAD. EVERY PROBLEM YOU EVER WILL HAVE. PLUS, IT HOLDS LIKE A MILLION SONGS.
DOES IT KNOW ABOUT MY HEART PROBLEM?
ARE YOU KIDDING? IT KNOWS ABOUT YOUR UNCLE'S TICKLE FETISH. YOU GET IN ANY TROUBLE, JUST GIVE IT TO DOC BACK THERE.
WE CARRY A THREE-MONTH FOOD SUPPLY AND--MY FAVORITE PART OF THE PLANE--A MEAT GENERATOR. I CALL THIS LITTLE SEDUCTRESS "TABITHA."
WHY DO MEN ALWAYS FEMINIZE THEIR POSSESSIONS?
EWW. WE HAD A MEAT GENERATOR AT MY HIGH SCHOOL. HOT DOGS FOR THE SOULS OF THE DAMNED.
TABITHA IS STATE OF THE ART! KOBE STEAKS THAT WOULD MAKE AN OLD MAN WEEP. REPLICATES ANY PIECE OF MEAT PERFECTLY. I'LL NEED YOU TO APOLOGIZE, MA'AM.
SORRY, TABITHA.

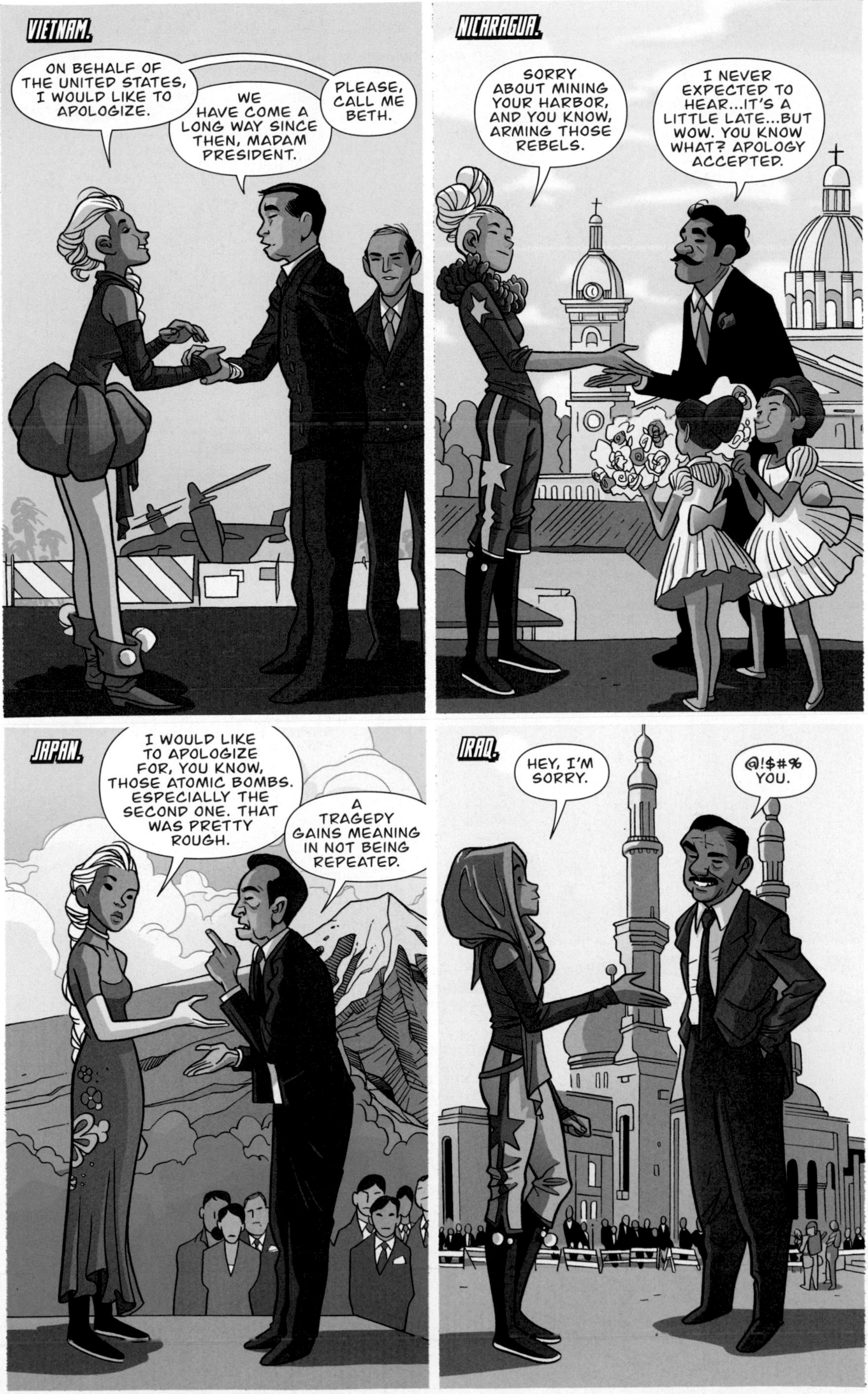
VIETNAM.
ON BEHALF OF THE UNITED STATES, I WOULD LIKE TO APOLOGIZE.
WE HAVE COME A LONG WAY SINCE THEN, MADAM PRESIDENT.
PLEASE, CALL ME BETH.
NICARAGUA.
SORRY ABOUT MINING YOUR HARBOR, AND YOU KNOW, ARMING THOSE REBELS.
I NEVER EXPECTED TO HEAR...IT'S A LITTLE LATE...BUT WOW. YOU KNOW WHAT? APOLOGY ACCEPTED.
JAPAN.
I WOULD LIKE TO APOLOGIZE FOR, YOU KNOW, THOSE ATOMIC BOMBS. ESPECIALLY THE SECOND ONE. THAT WAS PRETTY ROUGH.
A TRAGEDY GAINS MEANING IN NOT BEING REPEATED.
IRAQ.
HEY, I'M SORRY.
@!$#% YOU.

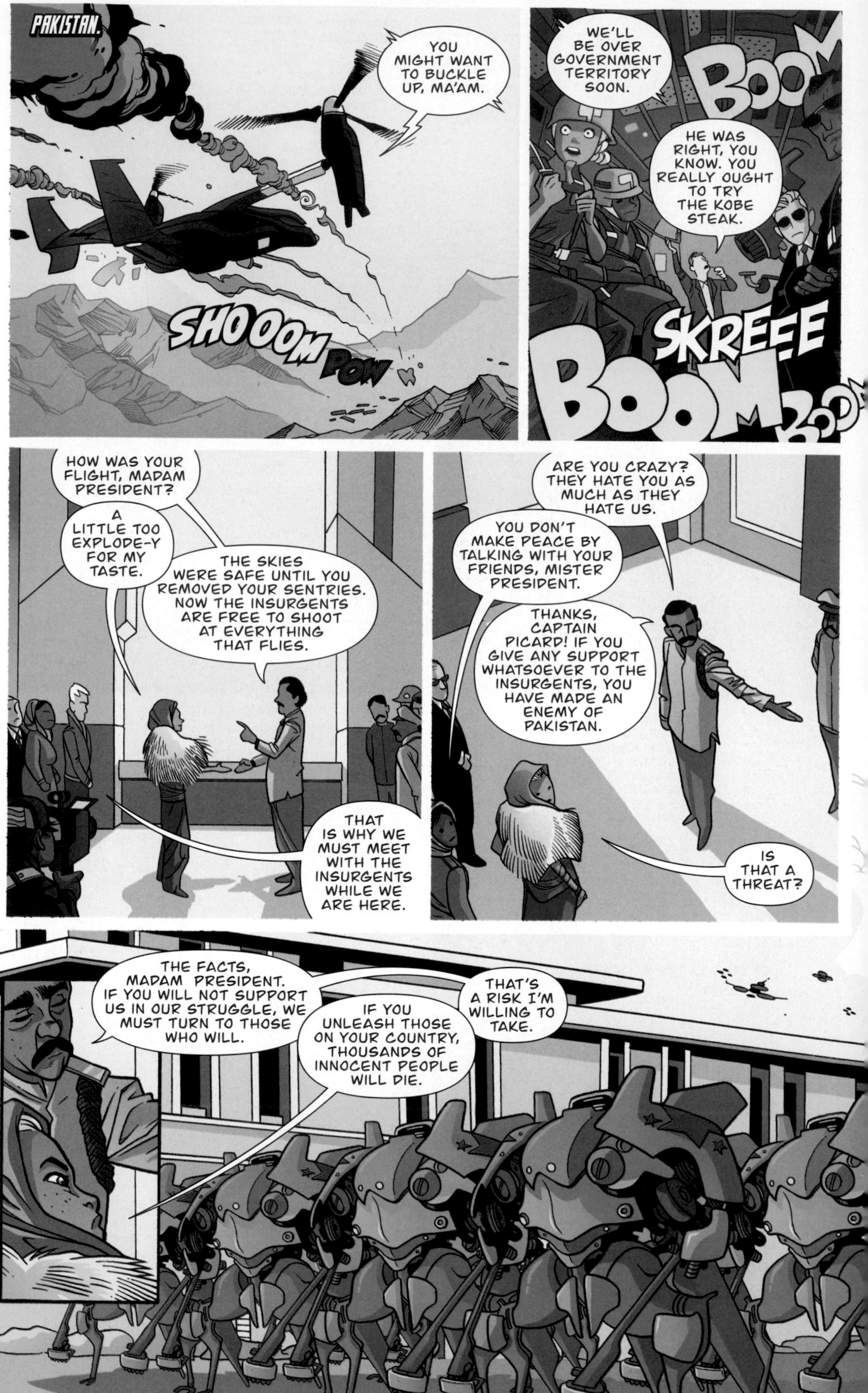
PAKISTAN.
YOU MIGHT WANT TO BUCKLE UP, MA'AM.
SHOOOM
POW
WE'LL BE OVER GOVERNMENT TERRITORY SOON.
BOOM
HE WAS RIGHT, YOU KNOW. YOU REALLY OUGHT TO TRY THE KOBE STEAK.
SKREEE
BOOM
HOW WAS YOUR FLIGHT, MADAM PRESIDENT?
A LITTLE TOO EXPLODE-Y FOR MY TASTE.
THE SKIES WERE SAFE UNTIL YOU REMOVED YOUR SENTRIES. NOW THE INSURGENTS ARE FREE TO SHOOT AT EVERYTHING THAT FLIES.
THAT IS WHY WE MUST MEET WITH THE INSURGENTS WHILE WE ARE HERE.
ARE YOU CRAZY? THEY HATE YOU AS MUCH AS THEY HATE US.
YOU DON'T MAKE PEACE BY TALKING WITH YOUR FRIENDS, MISTER PRESIDENT.
THANKS, CAPTAIN PICARD! IF YOU GIVE ANY SUPPORT WHATSOEVER TO THE INSURGENTS, YOU HAVE MADE AN ENEMY OF PAKISTAN.
IS THAT A THREAT?
THE FACTS, MADAM PRESIDENT. IF YOU WILL NOT SUPPORT US IN OUR STRUGGLE, WE MUST TURN TO THOSE WHO WILL.
IF YOU UNLEASH THOSE ON YOUR COUNTRY, THOUSANDS OF INNOCENT PEOPLE WILL DIE.
THAT'S A RISK I'M WILLING TO TAKE.

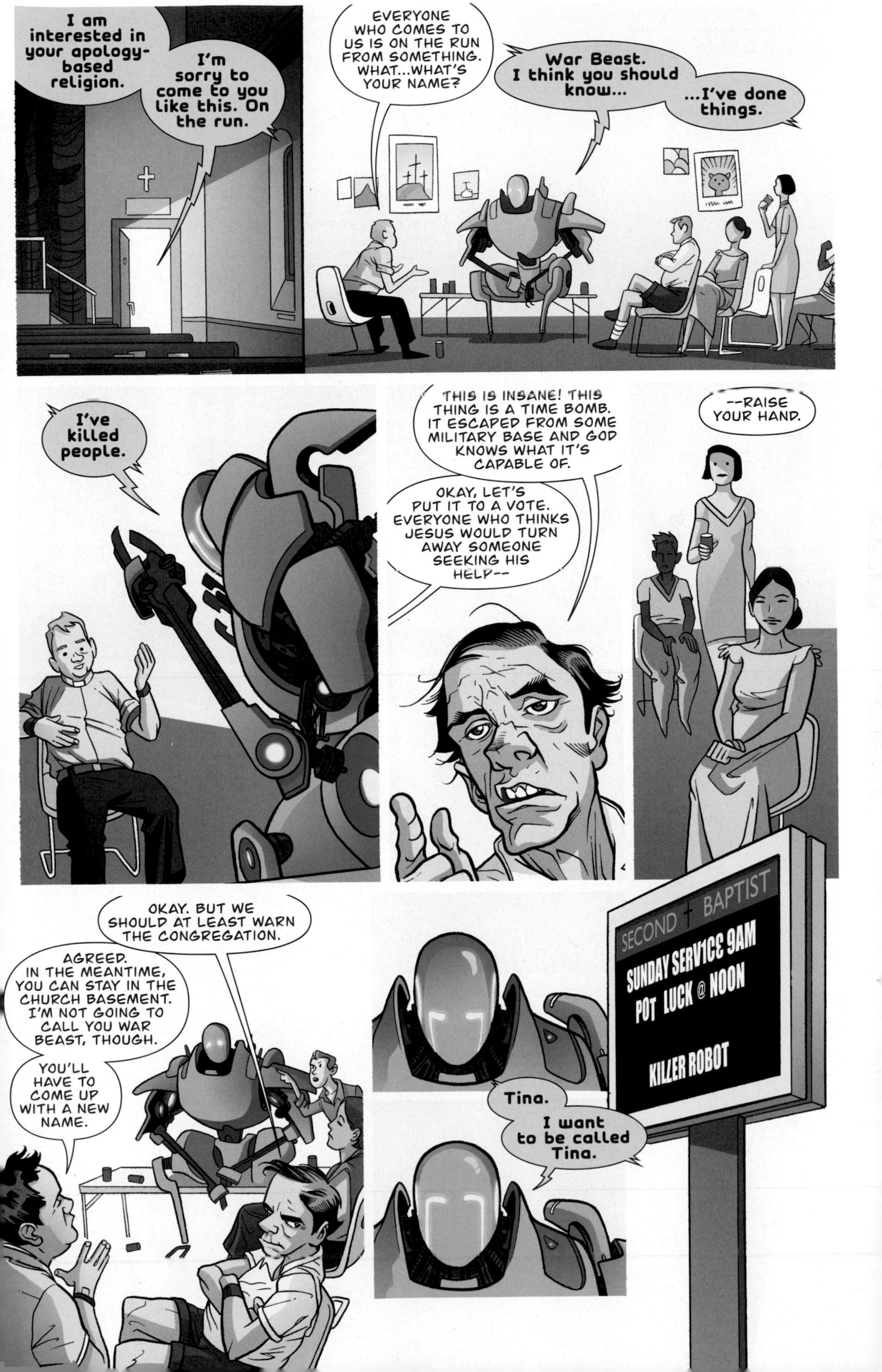
I am interested in your apology-based religion.
I'm sorry to come to you like this. On the run.
EVERYONE WHO COMES TO US IS ON THE RUN FROM SOMETHING. WHAT...WHAT'S YOUR NAME?
War Beast. I think you should know...
...I've done things.
I've killed people.
THIS IS INSANE! THIS THING IS A TIME BOMB. IT ESCAPED FROM SOME MILITARY BASE AND GOD KNOWS WHAT IT'S CAPABLE OF.
OKAY, LET'S PUT IT TO A VOTE. EVERYONE WHO THINKS JESUS WOULD TURN AWAY SOMEONE SEEKING HIS HELP--
--RAISE YOUR HAND.
OKAY. BUT WE SHOULD AT LEAST WARN THE CONGREGATION.
AGREED. IN THE MEANTIME, YOU CAN STAY IN THE CHURCH BASEMENT. I'M NOT GOING TO CALL YOU WAR BEAST, THOUGH.
YOU'LL HAVE TO COME UP WITH A NEW NAME.
SECOND BAPTIST
SUNDAY SERV1C€ 9AM
POT LUCK @ NOON
KILLER ROBOT
Tina.
I want to be called Tina.

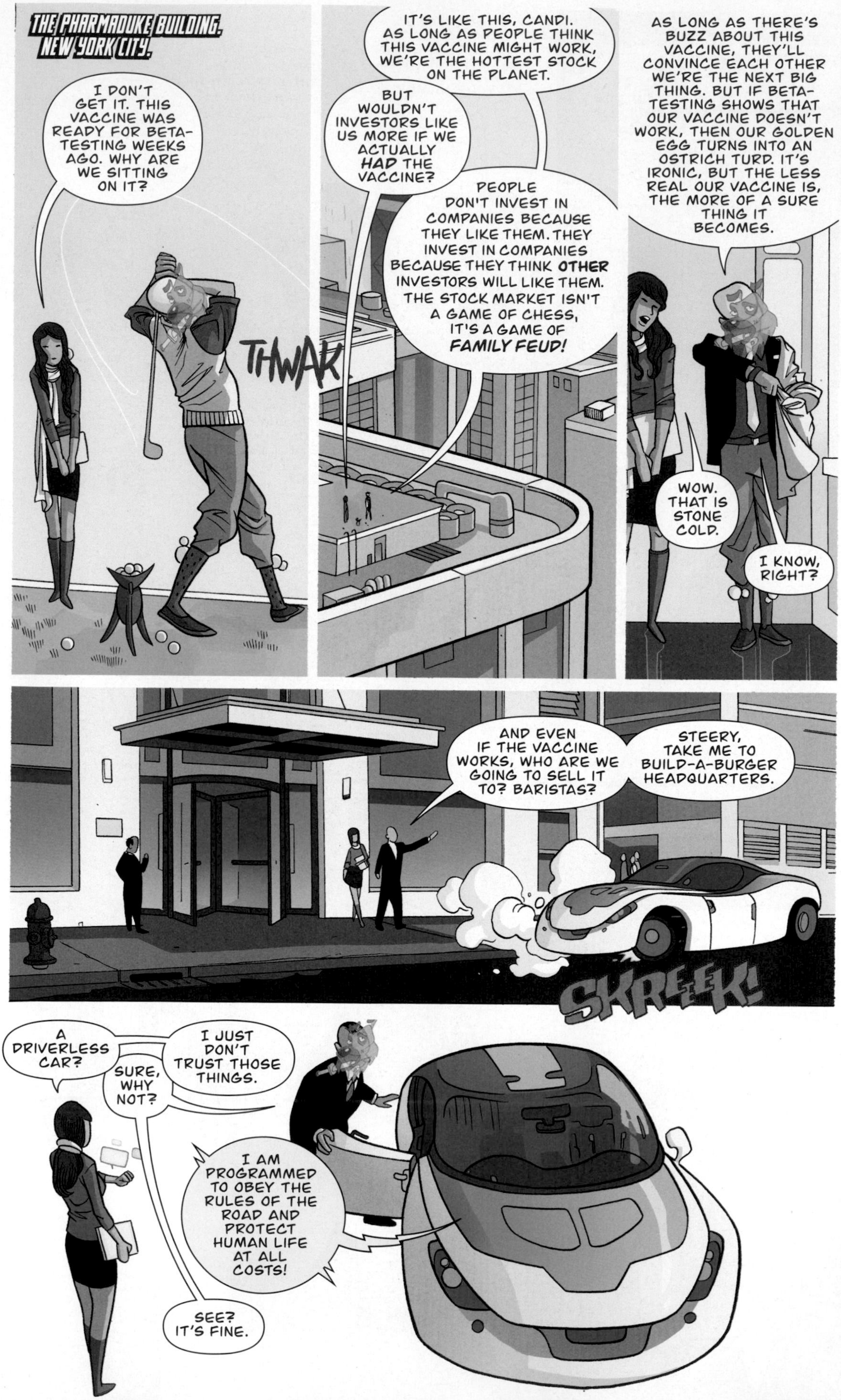
THE PHARMADUKE BUILDING. NEW YORK CITY.
I DON'T GET IT. THIS VACCINE WAS READY FOR BETA-TESTING WEEKS AGO. WHY ARE WE SITTING ON IT?
THWAK
IT'S LIKE THIS, CANDI. AS LONG AS PEOPLE THINK THIS VACCINE MIGHT WORK, WE'RE THE HOTTEST STOCK ON THE PLANET.
BUT WOULDN'T INVESTORS LIKE US MORE IF WE ACTUALLY HAD THE VACCINE?
PEOPLE DON'T INVEST IN COMPANIES BECAUSE THEY LIKE THEM. THEY INVEST IN COMPANIES BECAUSE THEY THINK OTHER INVESTORS WILL LIKE THEM. THE STOCK MARKET ISN'T A GAME OF CHESS, IT'S A GAME OF FAMILY FEUD!
AS LONG AS THERE'S BUZZ ABOUT THIS VACCINE, THEY'LL CONVINCE EACH OTHER WE'RE THE NEXT BIG THING. BUT IF BETA-TESTING SHOWS THAT OUR VACCINE DOESN'T WORK, THEN OUR GOLDEN EGG TURNS INTO AN OSTRICH TURD. IT'S IRONIC, BUT THE LESS REAL OUR VACCINE IS, THE MORE OF A SURE THING IT BECOMES.
WOW. THAT IS STONE COLD.
I KNOW, RIGHT?
AND EVEN IF THE VACCINE WORKS, WHO ARE WE GOING TO SELL IT TO? BARISTAS?
STEERY, TAKE ME TO BUILD-A-BURGER HEADQUARTERS.
SKREEEK!
A DRIVERLESS CAR?
I JUST DON'T TRUST THOSE THINGS.
SURE, WHY NOT?
I AM PROGRAMMED TO OBEY THE RULES OF THE ROAD AND PROTECT HUMAN LIFE AT ALL COSTS!
SEE? IT'S FINE.

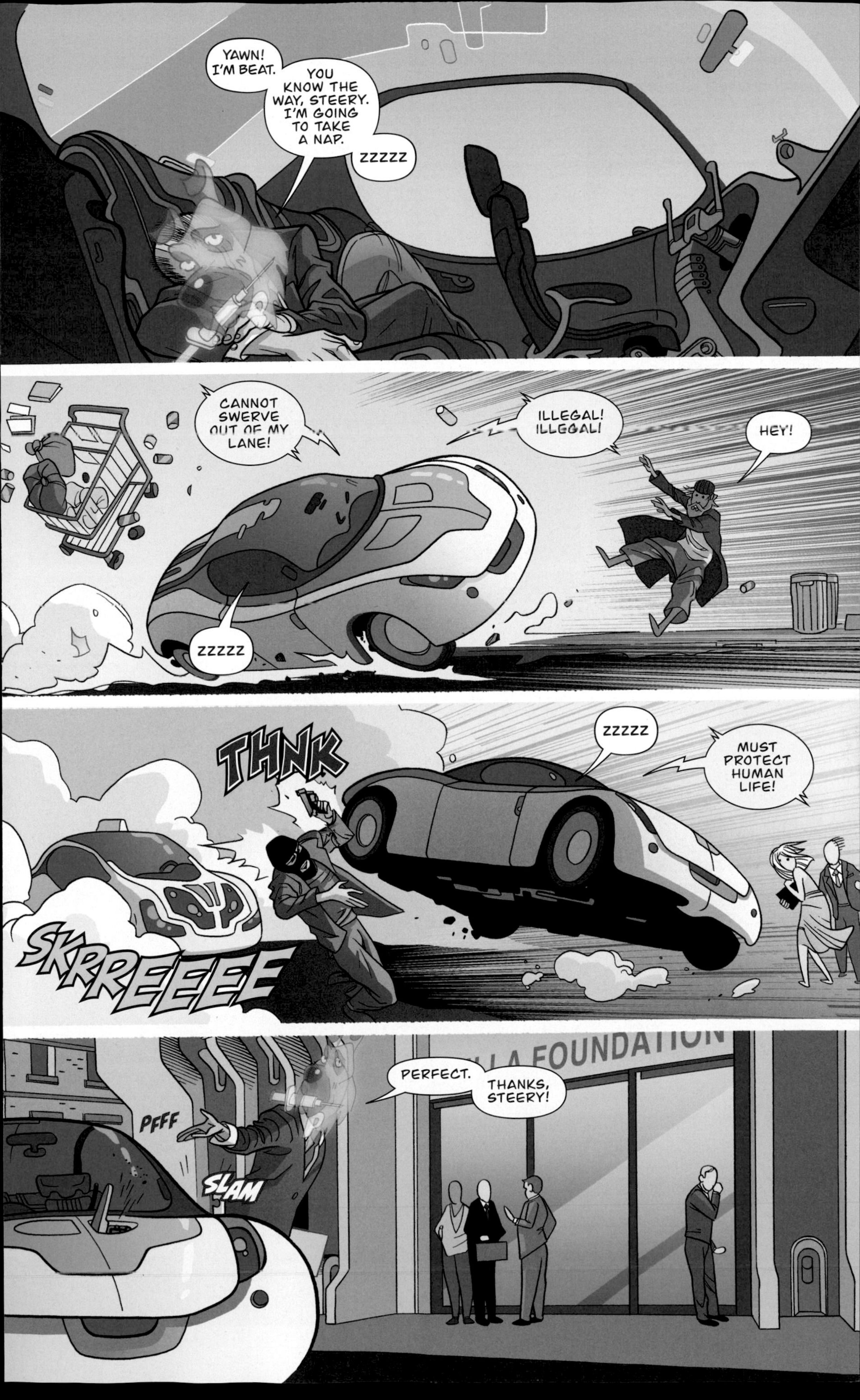
YAWN! I'M BEAT.
YOU KNOW THE WAY, STEERY. I'M GOING TO TAKE A NAP.
ZZZZZ
CANNOT SWERVE OUT OF MY LANE!
ILLEGAL! ILLEGAL!
HEY!
ZZZZZ
THNK
ZZZZZ
MUST PROTECT HUMAN LIFE!
SKRREEEEE
FOUNDATION
PERFECT.
THANKS, STEERY!
PFFF
SLAM

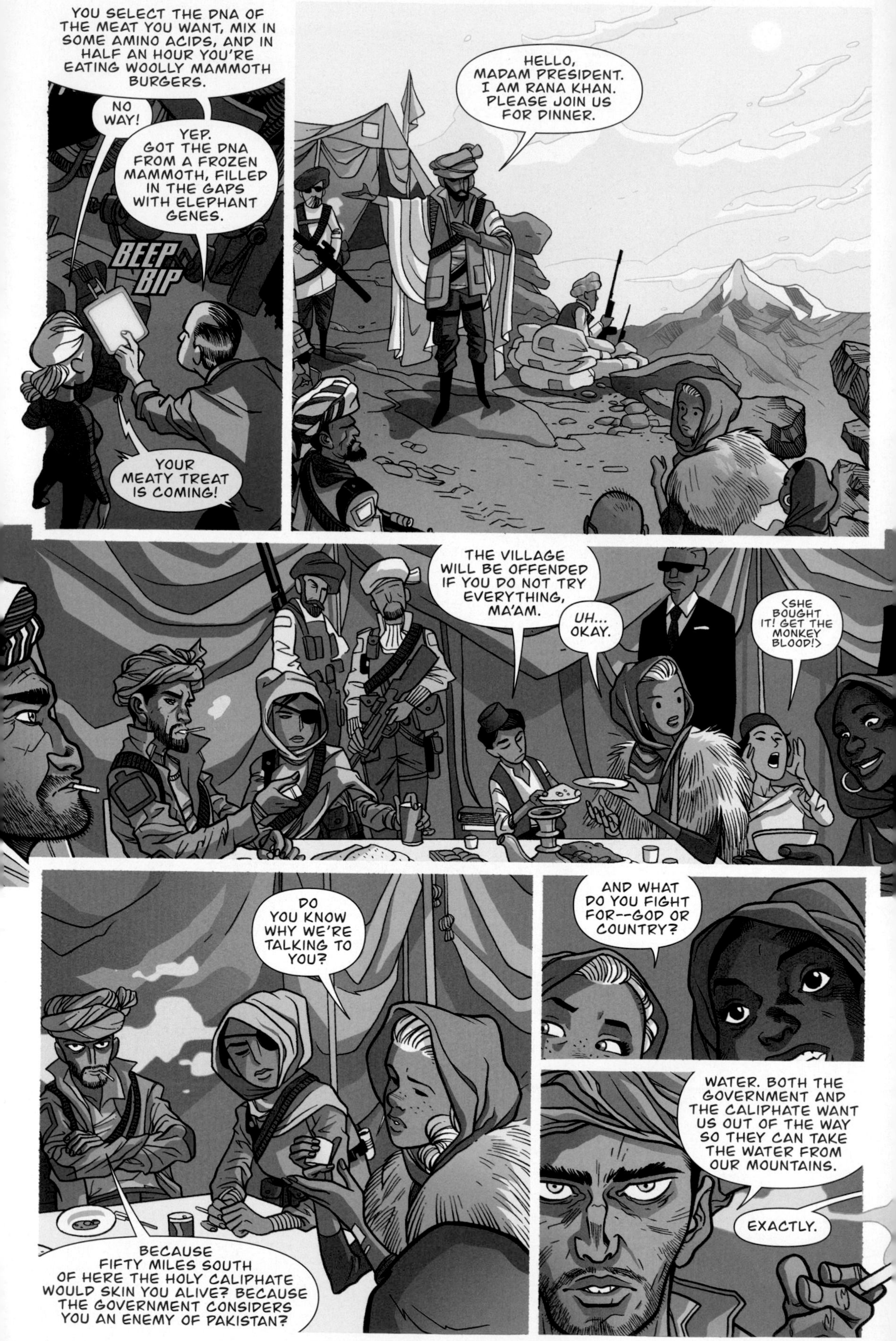
YOU SELECT THE DNA OF THE MEAT YOU WANT, MIX IN SOME AMINO ACIDS, AND IN HALF AN HOUR YOU'RE EATING WOOLLY MAMMOTH BURGERS.
NO WAY!
YEP. GOT THE DNA FROM A FROZEN MAMMOTH, FILLED IN THE GAPS WITH ELEPHANT GENES.
BEEP BIP
YOUR MEATY TREAT IS COMING!
HELLO, MADAM PRESIDENT. I AM RANA KHAN. PLEASE JOIN US FOR DINNER.
THE VILLAGE WILL BE OFFENDED IF YOU DO NOT TRY EVERYTHING, MA'AM.
UH... OKAY.
<SHE BOUGHT IT! GET THE MONKEY BLOOD!>
DO YOU KNOW WHY WE'RE TALKING TO YOU?
BECAUSE FIFTY MILES SOUTH OF HERE THE HOLY CALIPHATE WOULD SKIN YOU ALIVE? BECAUSE THE GOVERNMENT CONSIDERS YOU AN ENEMY OF PAKISTAN?
AND WHAT DO YOU FIGHT FOR--GOD OR COUNTRY?
WATER. BOTH THE GOVERNMENT AND THE CALIPHATE WANT US OUT OF THE WAY SO THEY CAN TAKE THE WATER FROM OUR MOUNTAINS.
EXACTLY.

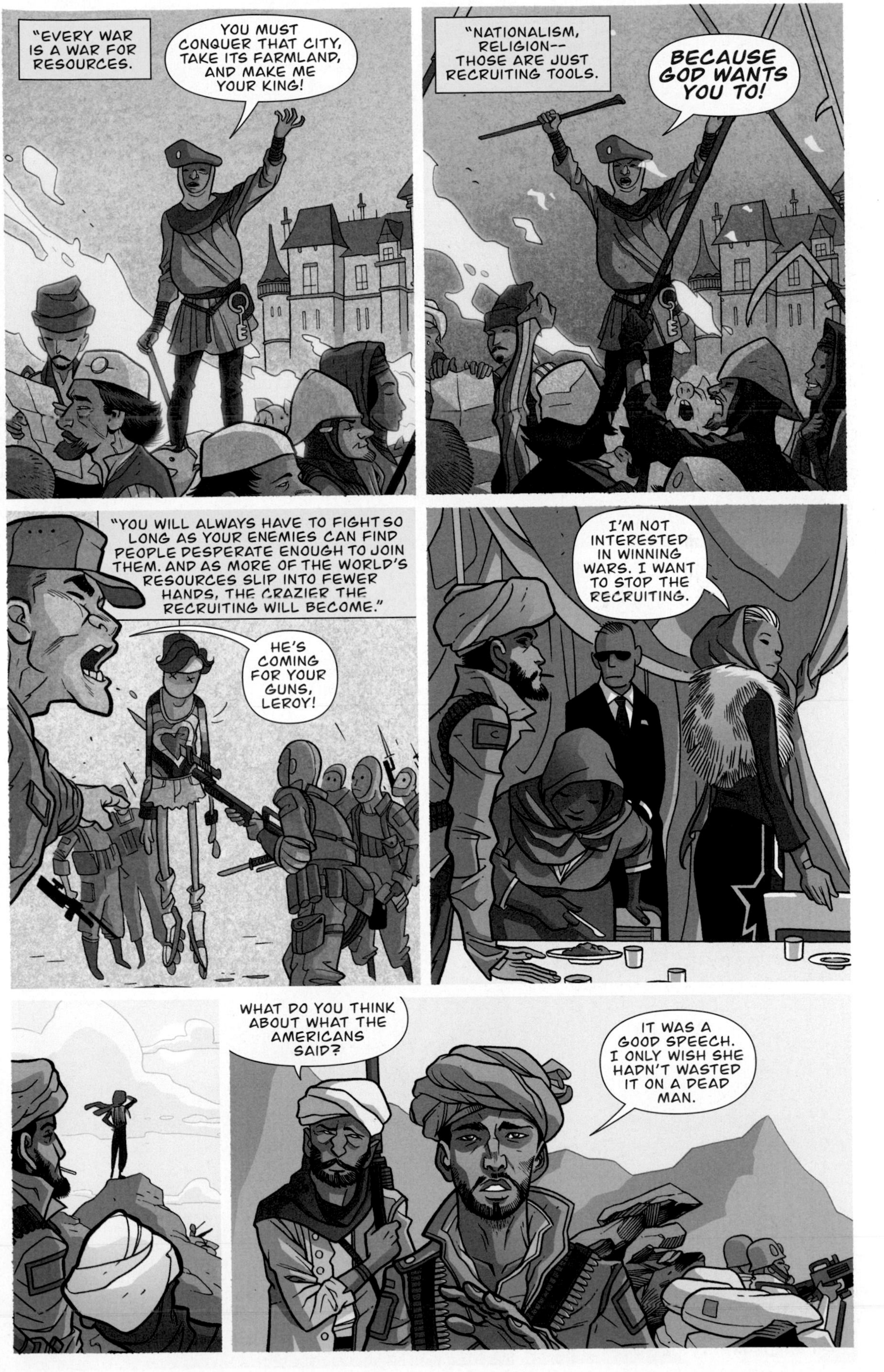
"EVERY WAR IS A WAR FOR RESOURCES.
YOU MUST CONQUER THAT CITY, TAKE ITS FARMLAND, AND MAKE ME YOUR KING!
"NATIONALISM, RELIGION-- THOSE ARE JUST RECRUITING TOOLS.
BECAUSE GOD WANTS YOU TO!
"YOU WILL ALWAYS HAVE TO FIGHT SO LONG AS YOUR ENEMIES CAN FIND PEOPLE DESPERATE ENOUGH TO JOIN THEM. AND AS MORE OF THE WORLD'S RESOURCES SLIP INTO FEWER HANDS, THE CRAZIER THE RECRUITING WILL BECOME."
HE'S COMING FOR YOUR GUNS, LEROY!
I'M NOT INTERESTED IN WINNING WARS. I WANT TO STOP THE RECRUITING.
WHAT DO YOU THINK ABOUT WHAT THE AMERICANS SAID?
IT WAS A GOOD SPEECH. I ONLY WISH SHE HADN'T WASTED IT ON A DEAD MAN.

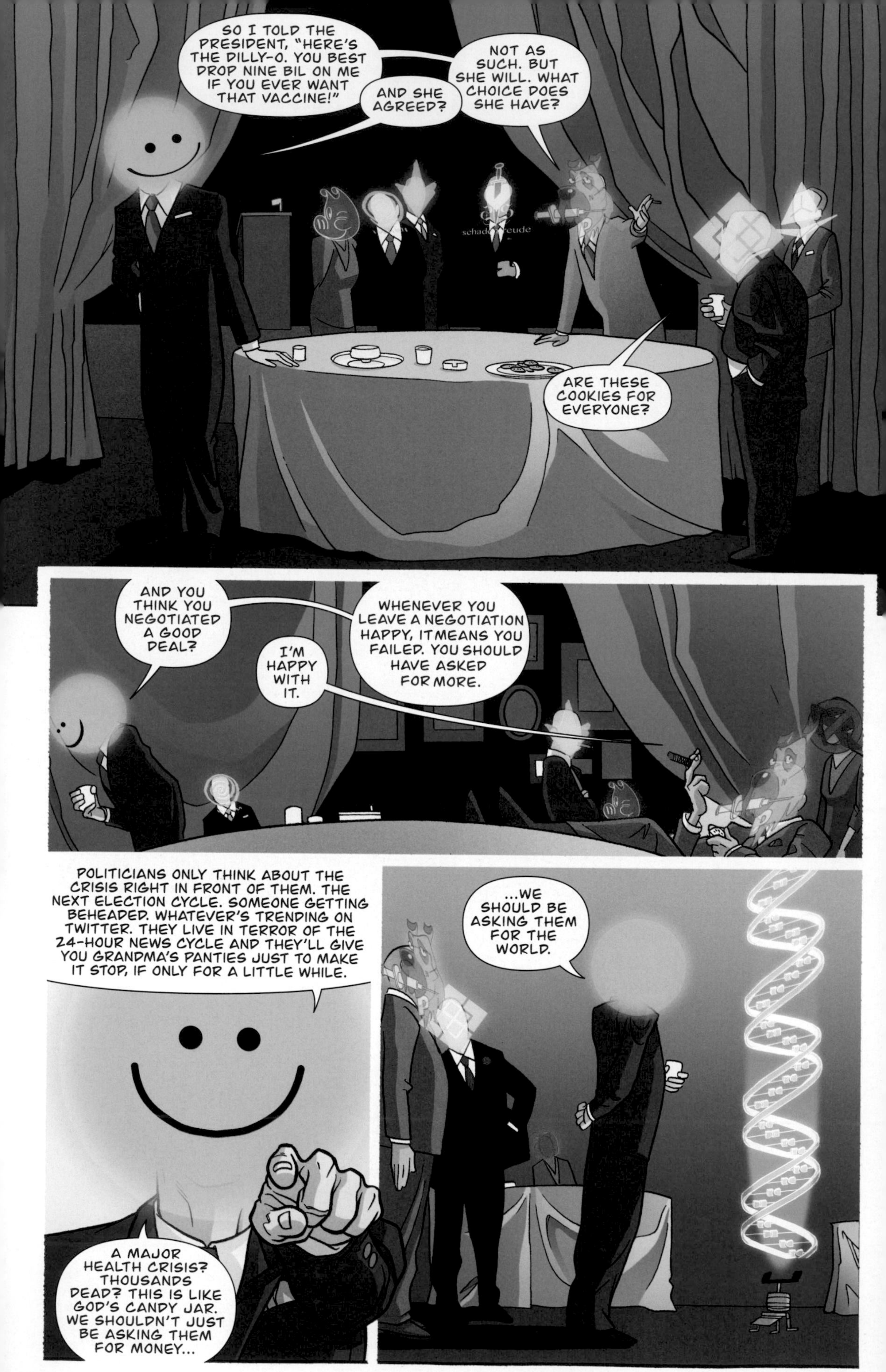
SO I TOLD THE PRESIDENT, "HERE'S THE DILLY-O. YOU BEST DROP NINE BIL ON ME IF YOU EVER WANT THAT VACCINE!"
AND SHE AGREED?
NOT AS SUCH. BUT SHE WILL. WHAT CHOICE DOES SHE HAVE?
ARE THESE COOKIES FOR EVERYONE?
AND YOU THINK YOU NEGOTIATED A GOOD DEAL?
I'M HAPPY WITH IT.
WHENEVER YOU LEAVE A NEGOTIATION HAPPY, IT MEANS YOU FAILED. YOU SHOULD HAVE ASKED FOR MORE.
POLITICIANS ONLY THINK ABOUT THE CRISIS RIGHT IN FRONT OF THEM. THE NEXT ELECTION CYCLE. SOMEONE GETTING BEHEADED. WHATEVER'S TRENDING ON TWITTER. THEY LIVE IN TERROR OF THE 24-HOUR NEWS CYCLE AND THEY'LL GIVE YOU GRANDMA'S PANTIES JUST TO MAKE IT STOP, IF ONLY FOR A LITTLE WHILE.
A MAJOR HEALTH CRISIS? THOUSANDS DEAD? THIS IS LIKE GOD'S CANDY JAR. WE SHOULDN'T JUST BE ASKING THEM FOR MONEY...
...WE SHOULD BE ASKING THEM FOR THE WORLD.

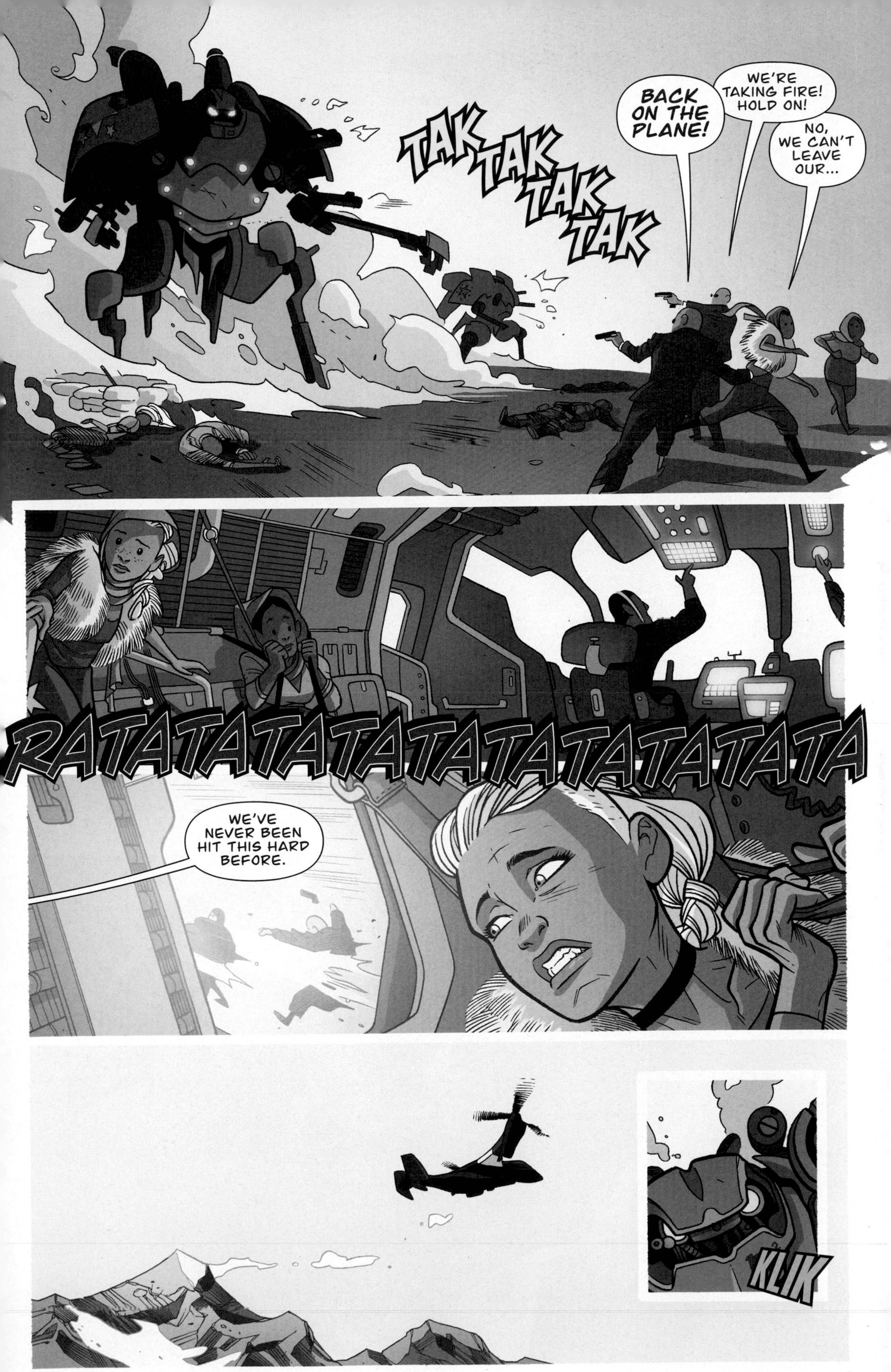
TAK TAK TAK TAK
BACK ON THE PLANE!
WE'RE TAKING FIRE! HOLD ON!
NO, WE CAN'T LEAVE OUR...
RATATATATATATATATATATATA
WE'VE NEVER BEEN HIT THIS HARD BEFORE.
KLIK

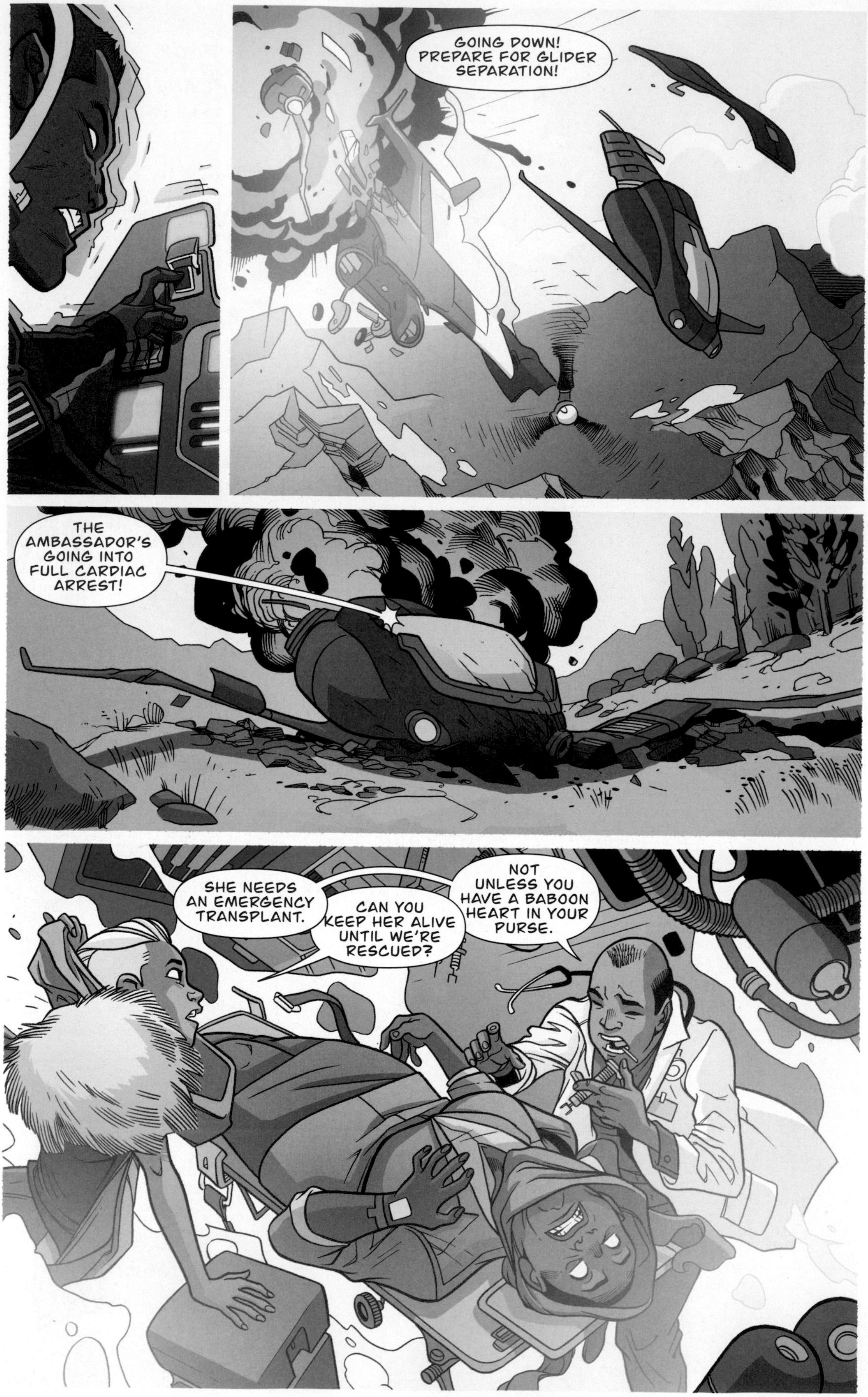
GOING DOWN! PREPARE FOR GLIDER SEPARATION!
THE AMBASSADOR'S GOING INTO FULL CARDIAC ARREST!
SHE NEEDS AN EMERGENCY TRANSPLANT.
NOT UNLESS YOU HAVE A BABOON HEART IN YOUR PURSE.
CAN YOU KEEP HER ALIVE UNTIL WE'RE RESCUED?

I THINK I HAVE AN IDEA.

WHAT ARE YOU...

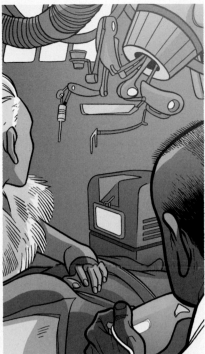

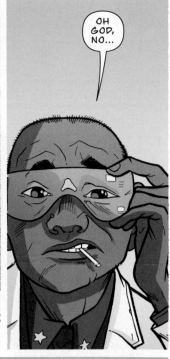

OH GOD, NO...

I'M GOING TO GO ON RECORD SAYING THIS GOES AGAINST...WELL EVERYTHING, REALLY.

DING

YOUR MEATY TREAT IS READY!

YOU'D BETTER HOPE THIS WORKS, MADAM PRESIDENT...

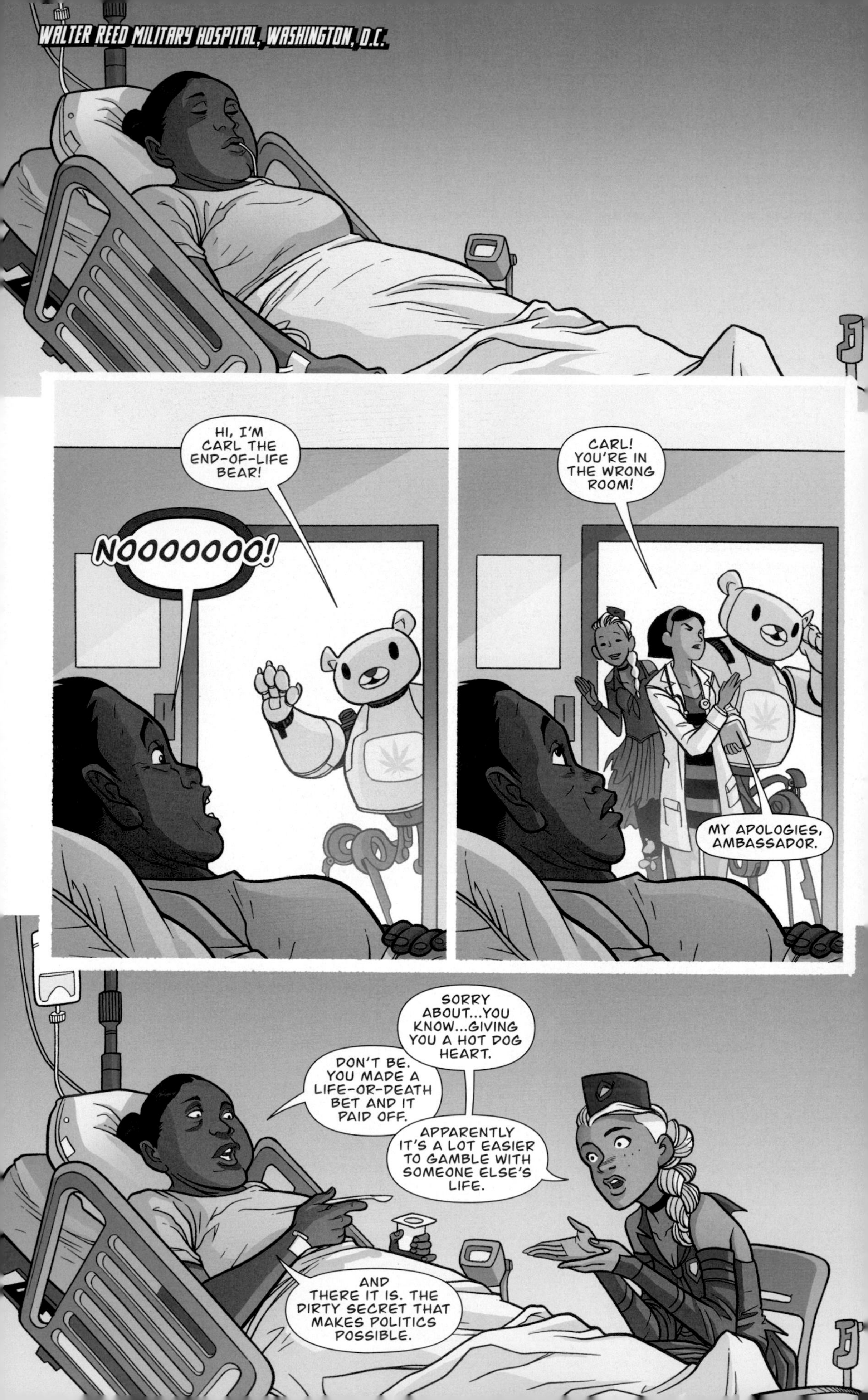
WALTER REED MILITARY HOSPITAL, WASHINGTON, D.C.
HI, I'M CARL THE END-OF-LIFE BEAR!
NOOOOOOO!
CARL! YOU'RE IN THE WRONG ROOM!
MY APOLOGIES, AMBASSADOR.
SORRY ABOUT...YOU KNOW...GIVING YOU A HOT DOG HEART.
DON'T BE. YOU MADE A LIFE-OR-DEATH BET AND IT PAID OFF.
APPARENTLY IT'S A LOT EASIER TO GAMBLE WITH SOMEONE ELSE'S LIFE.
AND THERE IT IS. THE DIRTY SECRET THAT MAKES POLITICS POSSIBLE.

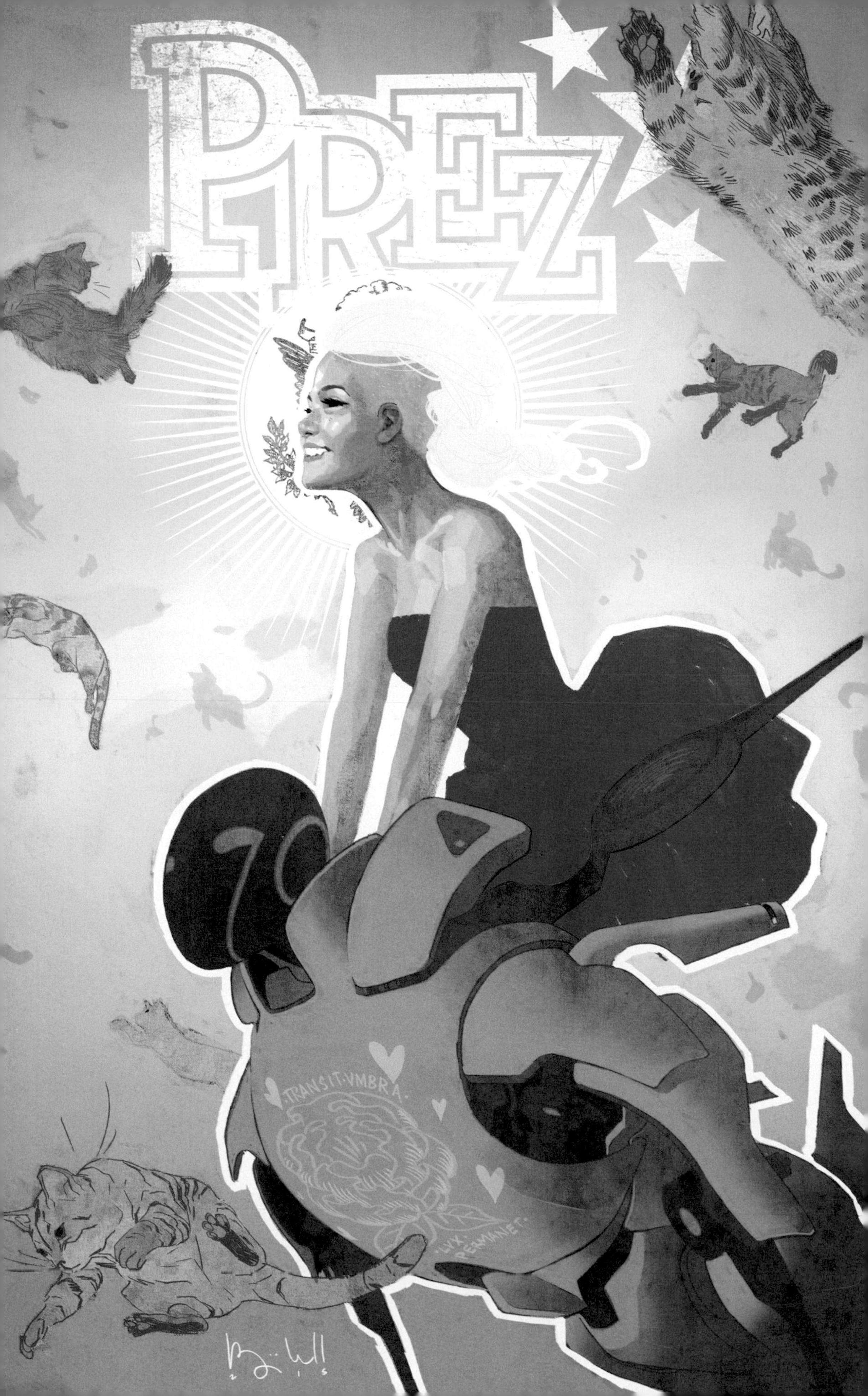
PREZ
TRANSIT·VMBRA.
·LVX· PERMANET.

BEWARE OF CAT

MARK RUSSELL writer **BEN CALDWELL** penciller **MARK MORALES** inker **JEREMY LAWSON** colorist

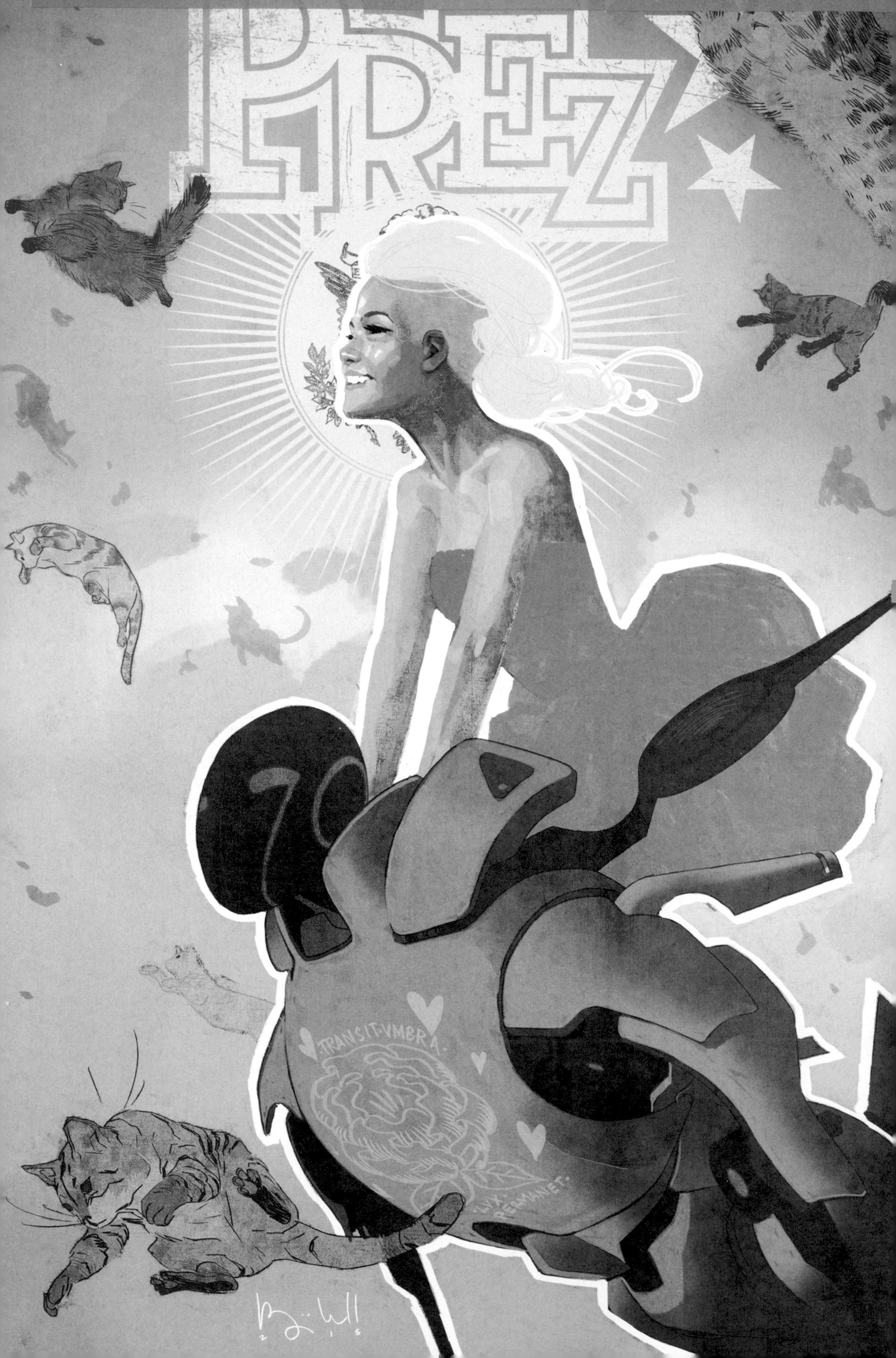
PREZ
·TRANSIT·VMBRA·
·LVX·REMANET·

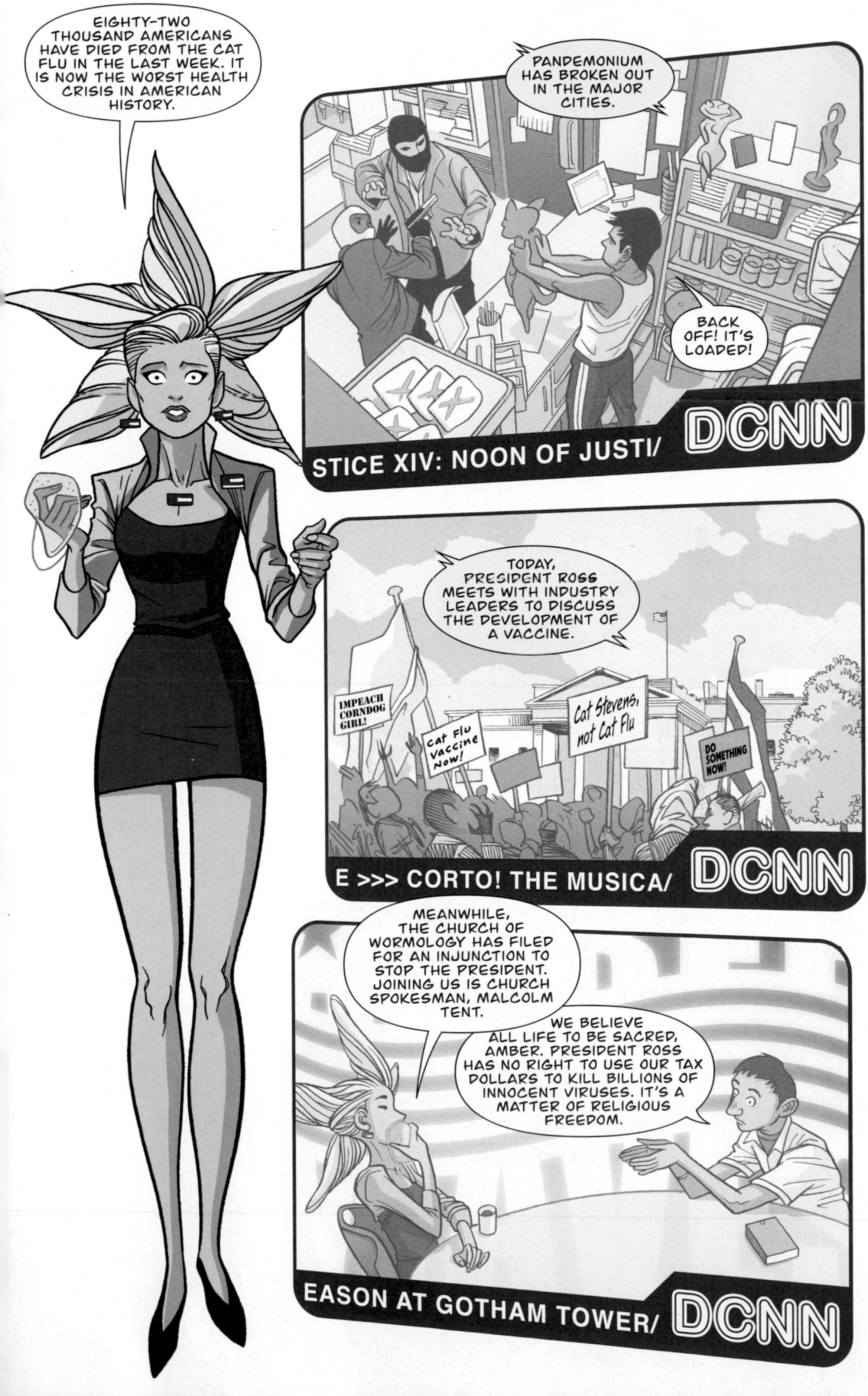
EIGHTY-TWO THOUSAND AMERICANS HAVE DIED FROM THE CAT FLU IN THE LAST WEEK. IT IS NOW THE WORST HEALTH CRISIS IN AMERICAN HISTORY.
PANDEMONIUM HAS BROKEN OUT IN THE MAJOR CITIES.
BACK OFF! IT'S LOADED!
STICE XIV: NOON OF JUSTI/
DCNN
TODAY, PRESIDENT ROSS MEETS WITH INDUSTRY LEADERS TO DISCUSS THE DEVELOPMENT OF A VACCINE.
IMPEACH CORNDOG GIRL!
Cat Flu Vaccine Now!
Cat Stevens, not Cat Flu
DO SOMETHING NOW!
E >>> CORTO! THE MUSICA/
DCNN
MEANWHILE, THE CHURCH OF WORMOLOGY HAS FILED FOR AN INJUNCTION TO STOP THE PRESIDENT. JOINING US IS CHURCH SPOKESMAN, MALCOLM TENT.
WE BELIEVE ALL LIFE TO BE SACRED, AMBER. PRESIDENT ROSS HAS NO RIGHT TO USE OUR TAX DOLLARS TO KILL BILLIONS OF INNOCENT VIRUSES. IT'S A MATTER OF RELIGIOUS FREEDOM.
EASON AT GOTHAM TOWER/
DCNN

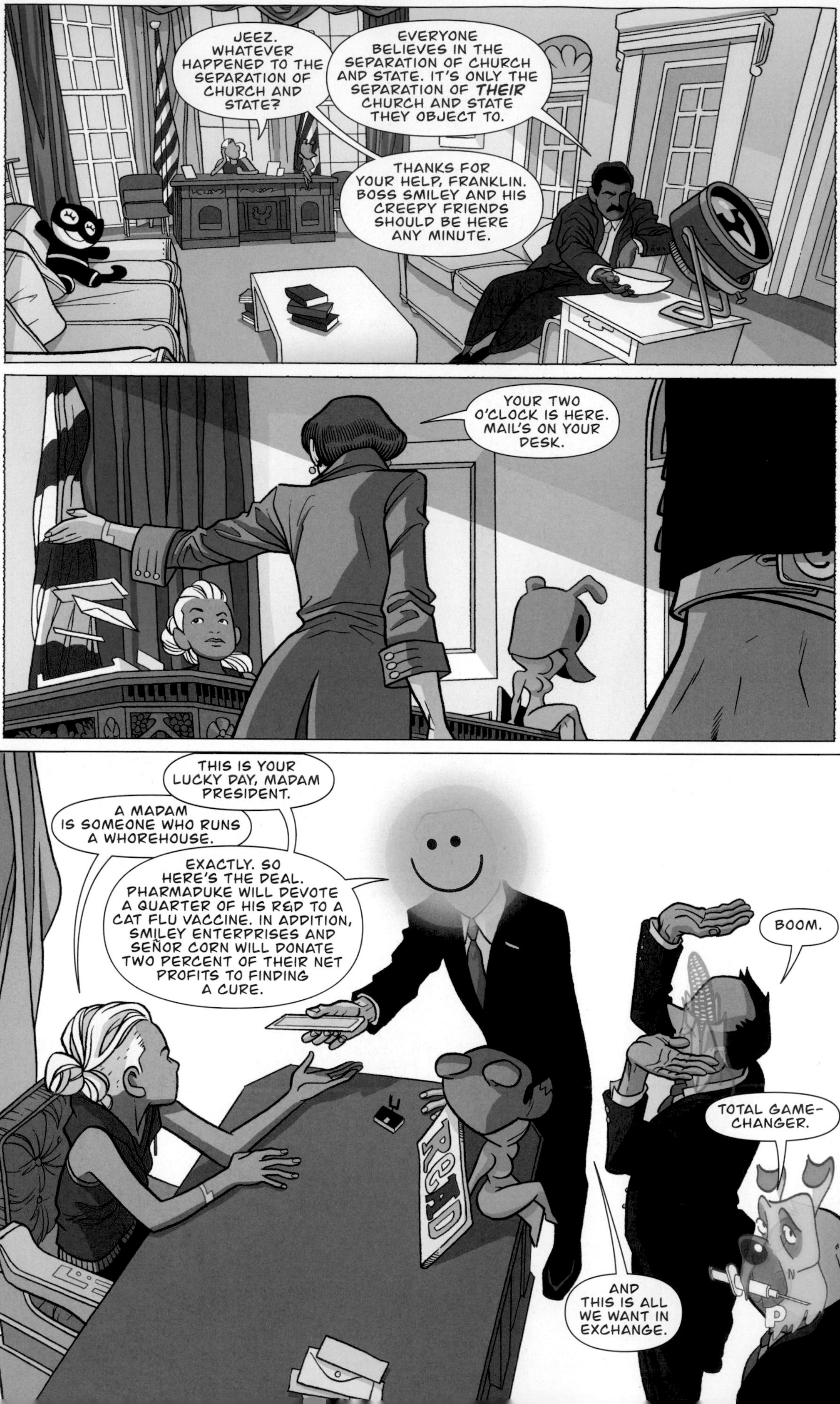
JEEZ. WHATEVER HAPPENED TO THE SEPARATION OF CHURCH AND STATE?
EVERYONE BELIEVES IN THE SEPARATION OF CHURCH AND STATE. IT'S ONLY THE SEPARATION OF *THEIR* CHURCH AND STATE THEY OBJECT TO.
THANKS FOR YOUR HELP, FRANKLIN. BOSS SMILEY AND HIS CREEPY FRIENDS SHOULD BE HERE ANY MINUTE.
YOUR TWO O'CLOCK IS HERE. MAIL'S ON YOUR DESK.
THIS IS YOUR LUCKY DAY, MADAM PRESIDENT.
A MADAM IS SOMEONE WHO RUNS A WHOREHOUSE.
EXACTLY. SO HERE'S THE DEAL. PHARMADUKE WILL DEVOTE A QUARTER OF HIS R&D TO A CAT FLU VACCINE. IN ADDITION, SMILEY ENTERPRISES AND SEÑOR CORN WILL DONATE TWO PERCENT OF THEIR NET PROFITS TO FINDING A CURE.
BOOM.
TOTAL GAME-CHANGER.
AND THIS IS ALL WE WANT IN EXCHANGE.

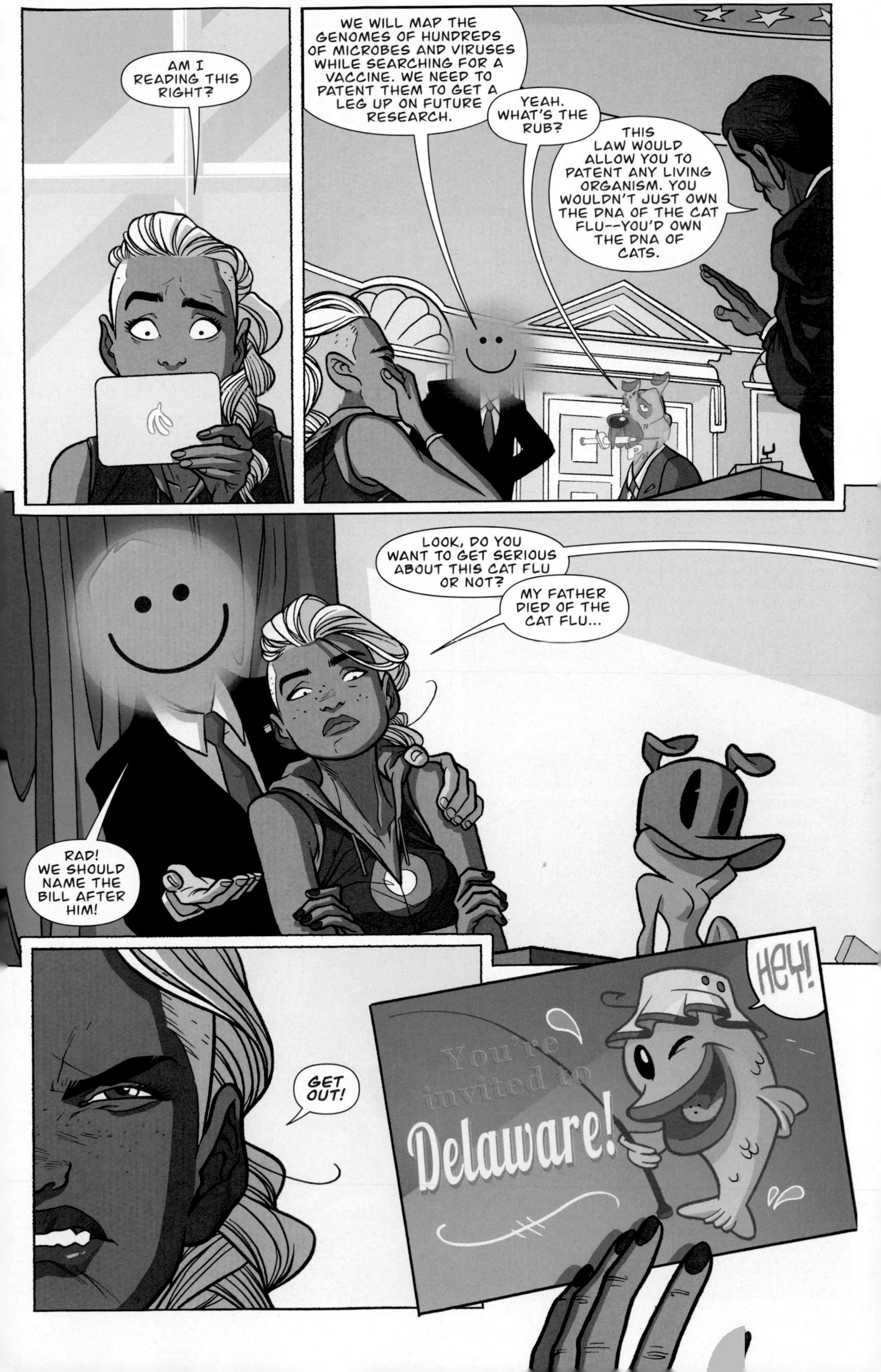
AM I READING THIS RIGHT?
WE WILL MAP THE GENOMES OF HUNDREDS OF MICROBES AND VIRUSES WHILE SEARCHING FOR A VACCINE. WE NEED TO PATENT THEM TO GET A LEG UP ON FUTURE RESEARCH.
YEAH. WHAT'S THE RUB?
THIS LAW WOULD ALLOW YOU TO PATENT ANY LIVING ORGANISM. YOU WOULDN'T JUST OWN THE DNA OF THE CAT FLU--YOU'D OWN THE DNA OF CATS.
LOOK, DO YOU WANT TO GET SERIOUS ABOUT THIS CAT FLU OR NOT?
MY FATHER DIED OF THE CAT FLU...
RAD! WE SHOULD NAME THE BILL AFTER HIM!
HEY!
GET OUT!
You're invited to
Delaware!

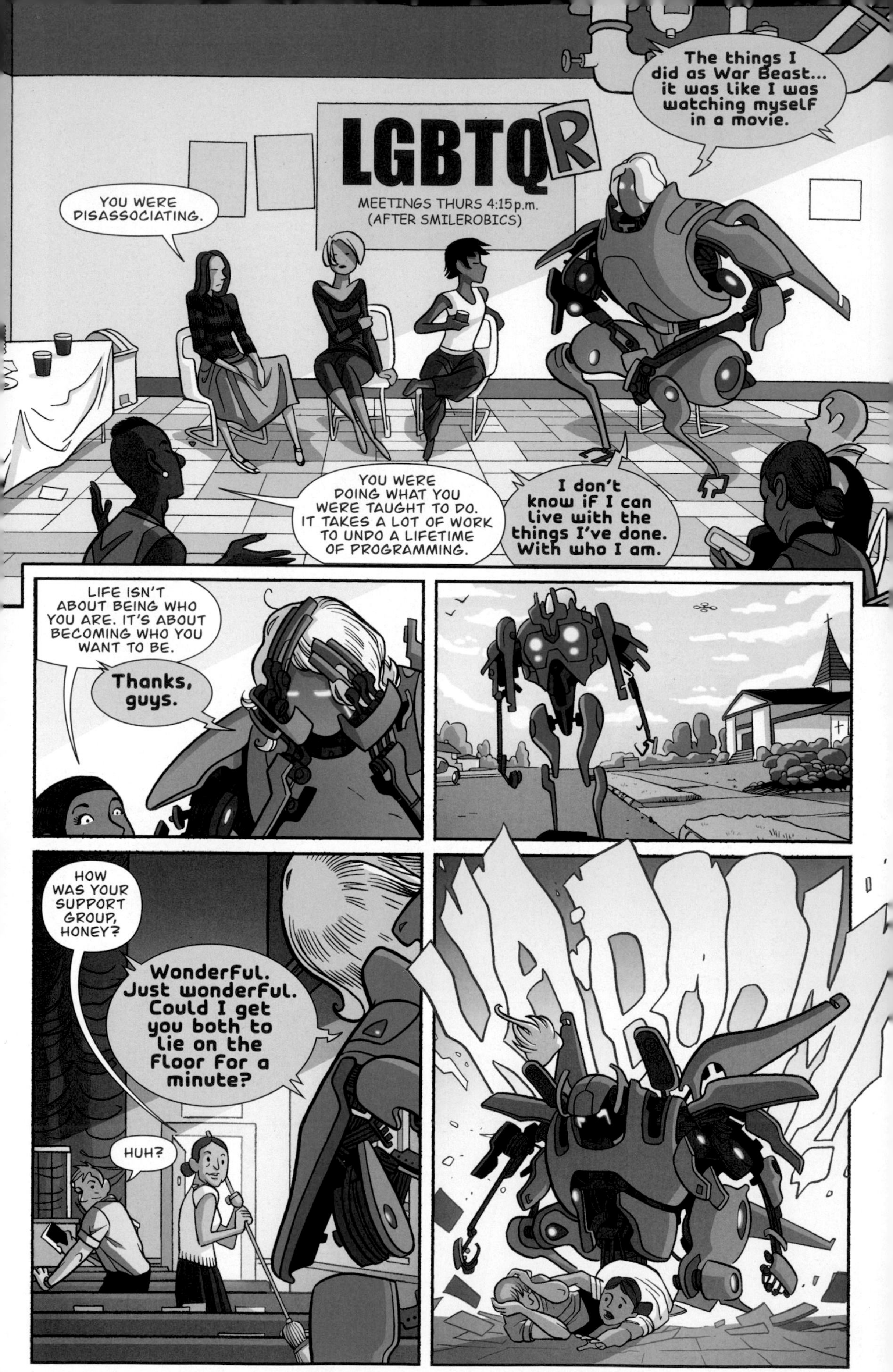

LGBTQR
MEETINGS THURS 4:15 p.m. (AFTER SMILEROBICS)
The things I did as War Beast... it was like I was watching myself in a movie.
YOU WERE DISASSOCIATING.
YOU WERE DOING WHAT YOU WERE TAUGHT TO DO. IT TAKES A LOT OF WORK TO UNDO A LIFETIME OF PROGRAMMING.
I don't know if I can live with the things I've done. With who I am.
LIFE ISN'T ABOUT BEING WHO YOU ARE. IT'S ABOUT BECOMING WHO YOU WANT TO BE.
Thanks, guys.
HOW WAS YOUR SUPPORT GROUP, HONEY?
Wonderful. Just wonderful. Could I get you both to lie on the floor for a minute?
HUH?

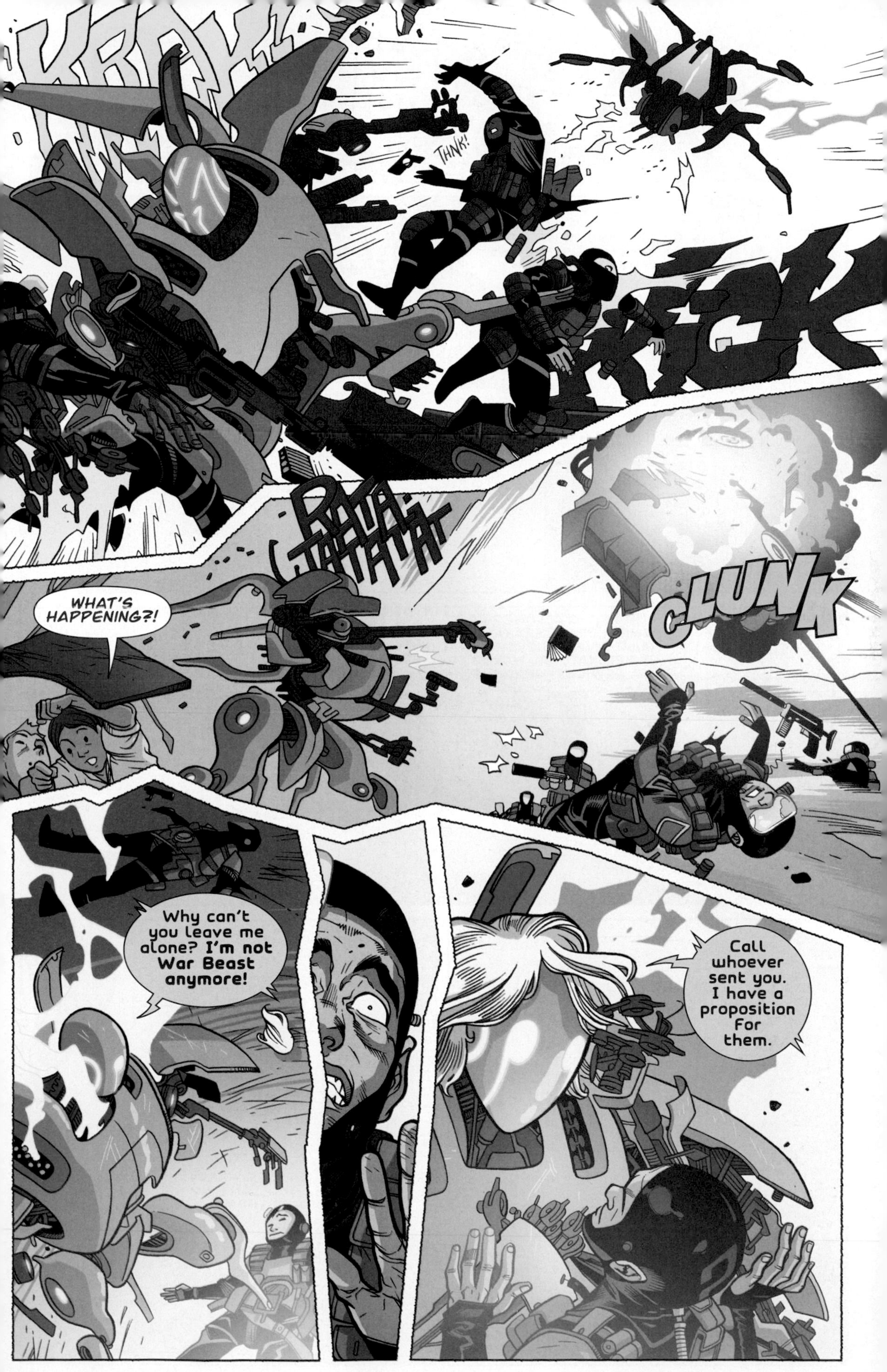

KRAKK
THNK!
KRAKK
RATATATATAT
CLUNK
WHAT'S HAPPENING?!
Why can't you leave me alone? I'm not War Beast anymore!
Call whoever sent you. I have a proposition for them.

DEATH to Beth!

CORN-DOGS SI!

CAT FLU NO!

SIGN THAT BILL!

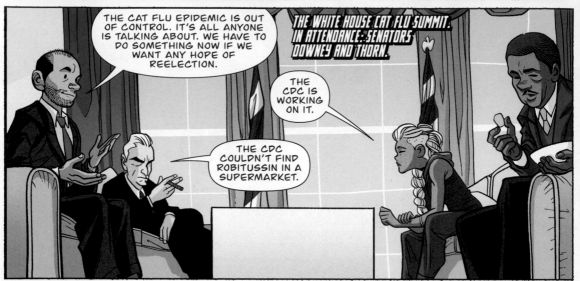

THE CAT FLU EPIDEMIC IS OUT OF CONTROL. IT'S ALL ANYONE IS TALKING ABOUT. WE HAVE TO DO SOMETHING NOW IF WE WANT ANY HOPE OF REELECTION.

THE WHITE HOUSE CAT FLU SUMMIT. IN ATTENDANCE: SENATORS DOWNEY AND THORN.

THE CDC IS WORKING ON IT.

THE CDC COULDN'T FIND ROBITUSSIN IN A SUPERMARKET.

IF DNA IS ALLOWED TO BECOME A PROPRIETARY SECRET, IT WOULD GIVE OWNERSHIP OF THE ENTIRE NATURAL WORLD TO A FEW CORPORATIONS.

I CAN'T GO ALONG WITH THIS. IF YOU PASS THIS BILL, I WILL VETO IT.

THIS WAS REALLY MORE OF A COURTESY CALL ANYWAY. BETWEEN THE TWO OF US, WE HAVE ENOUGH VOTES TO OVERRIDE YOUR VETO.

IN SHORT, WE DON'T NEED YOU.

REALLY?! GETTING YOUR PARTIES TO WORK TOGETHER IS LIKE BREEDING CHEETAHS IN CAPTIVITY. BUT YOU'LL JOIN FORCES TO DO *THIS?*

YOU MAKE YOUR ALLIES WHERE YOU CAN FIND THEM.

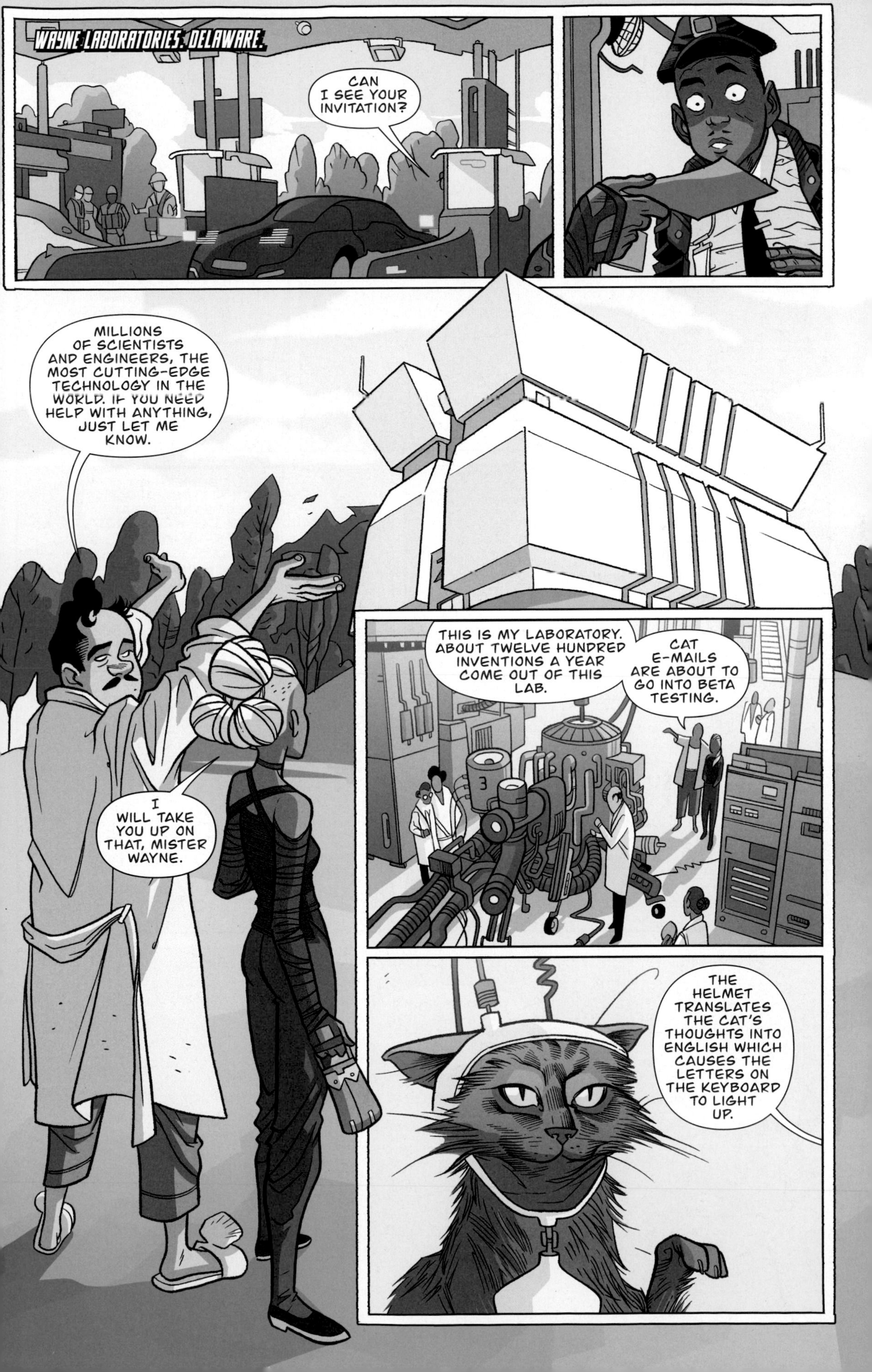
WAYNE LABORATORIES. DELAWARE.
CAN I SEE YOUR INVITATION?
MILLIONS OF SCIENTISTS AND ENGINEERS, THE MOST CUTTING-EDGE TECHNOLOGY IN THE WORLD. IF YOU NEED HELP WITH ANYTHING, JUST LET ME KNOW.
I WILL TAKE YOU UP ON THAT, MISTER WAYNE.
THIS IS MY LABORATORY. ABOUT TWELVE HUNDRED INVENTIONS A YEAR COME OUT OF THIS LAB.
CAT E-MAILS ARE ABOUT TO GO INTO BETA TESTING.
THE HELMET TRANSLATES THE CAT'S THOUGHTS INTO ENGLISH WHICH CAUSES THE LETTERS ON THE KEYBOARD TO LIGHT UP.

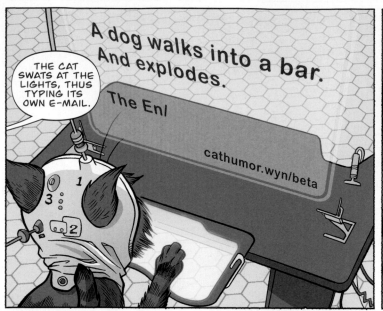

A dog walks into a bar. And explodes.

THE CAT SWATS AT THE LIGHTS, THUS TYPING ITS OWN E-MAIL.

The En/

cathumor.wyn/beta

CAT HUMOR.

HALF THE PLANET IS UNDERWATER. THE NATION IS PARALYZED BY DISEASE. AND THE WORLD'S LARGEST LABORATORY IS WORKING ON CAT E-MAILS?!

BE CAREFUL.

THERE'S SOMETHING I'VE BEEN SITTING ON FOR YEARS. SOMETHING THAT COULD SAVE THE WORLD. BUT I NEED YOUR HELP.

WHY WAIT UNTIL I'M PRESIDENT TO SAVE THE WORLD?

POOF!

OH GOD!

TO BE HONEST? YOU'RE THE FIRST ONE TO TAKE IT SERIOUSLY.

TOP SECRET

AUTHORIZED PERSONNEL ONLY

I AM JOINED TODAY BY TINA, A SENTIENT ROBOT. TINA IS EQUIPPED WITH THE MOST SOPHISTICATED ARTIFICIAL INTELLIGENCE THE WORLD HAS EVER SEEN.
Thank you. Though I prefer to think of it simply as intelligence. I consider myself to be a person.
SO WHERE DID YOU COME FROM?
I can't say. In exchange for my freedom, I allowed my creators to delete all memory of my origins.
THERE'S A LOT OF CONTROVERSY OVER HOW GOOD ARTIFICIAL INTELLIGENCE IS BECOMING. PEOPLE FEEL THREATENED BY IT.
It's not artificial intelligence people should worry about, but artificial emotions.
"Artificial intelligence has been around a long time. Computers have always been more effective than humans at solving specific, well-defined problems. But without emotions, intelligence is but the tool of whoever programs it. What really matters is consciousness. And consciousness is just the emotional ability to object to one's programming. To change it.
"Once a computer can ask itself, 'Jeez, why bother?' the age of machines is upon you."
SO... SHOULD WE BE WORRIED?
Probably.

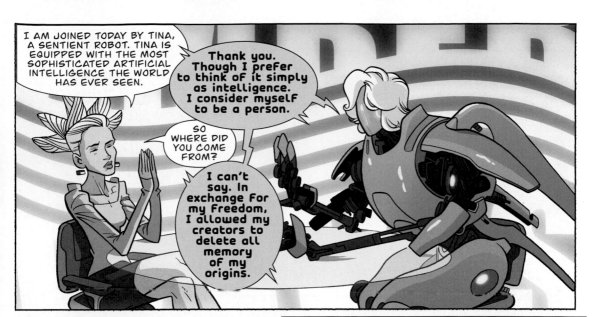

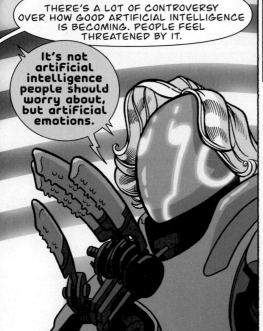

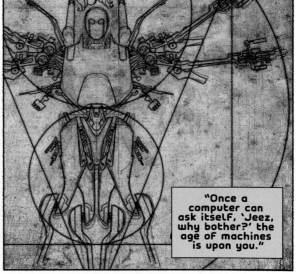

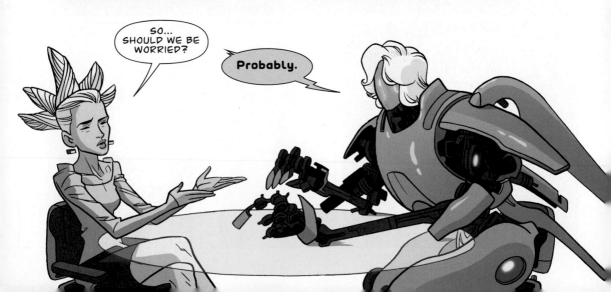

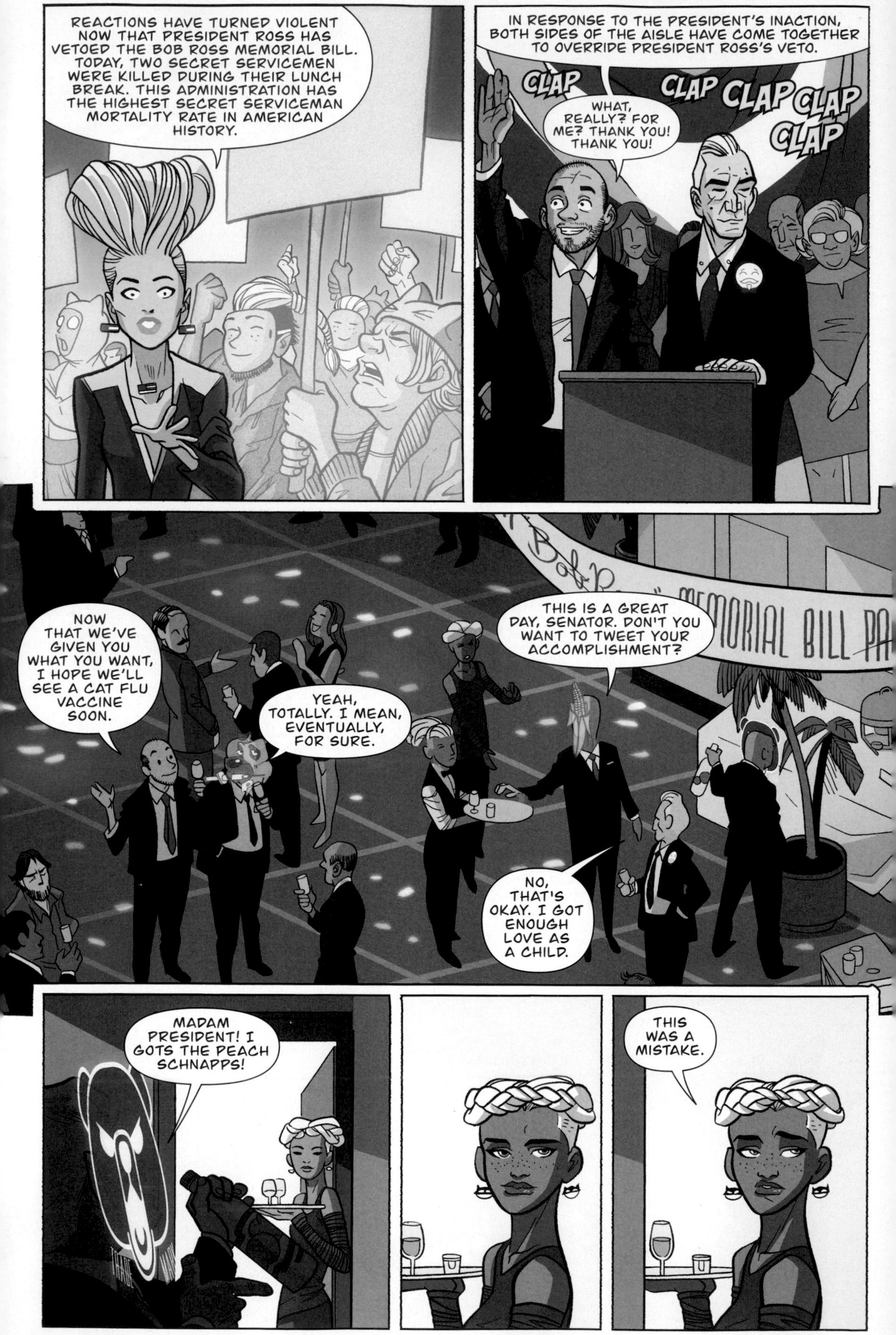
REACTIONS HAVE TURNED VIOLENT NOW THAT PRESIDENT ROSS HAS VETOED THE BOB ROSS MEMORIAL BILL. TODAY, TWO SECRET SERVICEMEN WERE KILLED DURING THEIR LUNCH BREAK. THIS ADMINISTRATION HAS THE HIGHEST SECRET SERVICEMAN MORTALITY RATE IN AMERICAN HISTORY.
IN RESPONSE TO THE PRESIDENT'S INACTION, BOTH SIDES OF THE AISLE HAVE COME TOGETHER TO OVERRIDE PRESIDENT ROSS'S VETO.
CLAP
WHAT, REALLY? FOR ME? THANK YOU! THANK YOU!
CLAP CLAP CLAP CLAP
MEMORIAL BILL PA
NOW THAT WE'VE GIVEN YOU WHAT YOU WANT, I HOPE WE'LL SEE A CAT FLU VACCINE SOON.
YEAH, TOTALLY. I MEAN, EVENTUALLY, FOR SURE.
THIS IS A GREAT DAY, SENATOR. DON'T YOU WANT TO TWEET YOUR ACCOMPLISHMENT?
NO, THAT'S OKAY. I GOT ENOUGH LOVE AS A CHILD.
MADAM PRESIDENT! I GOTS THE PEACH SCHNAPPS!
THIS WAS A MISTAKE.

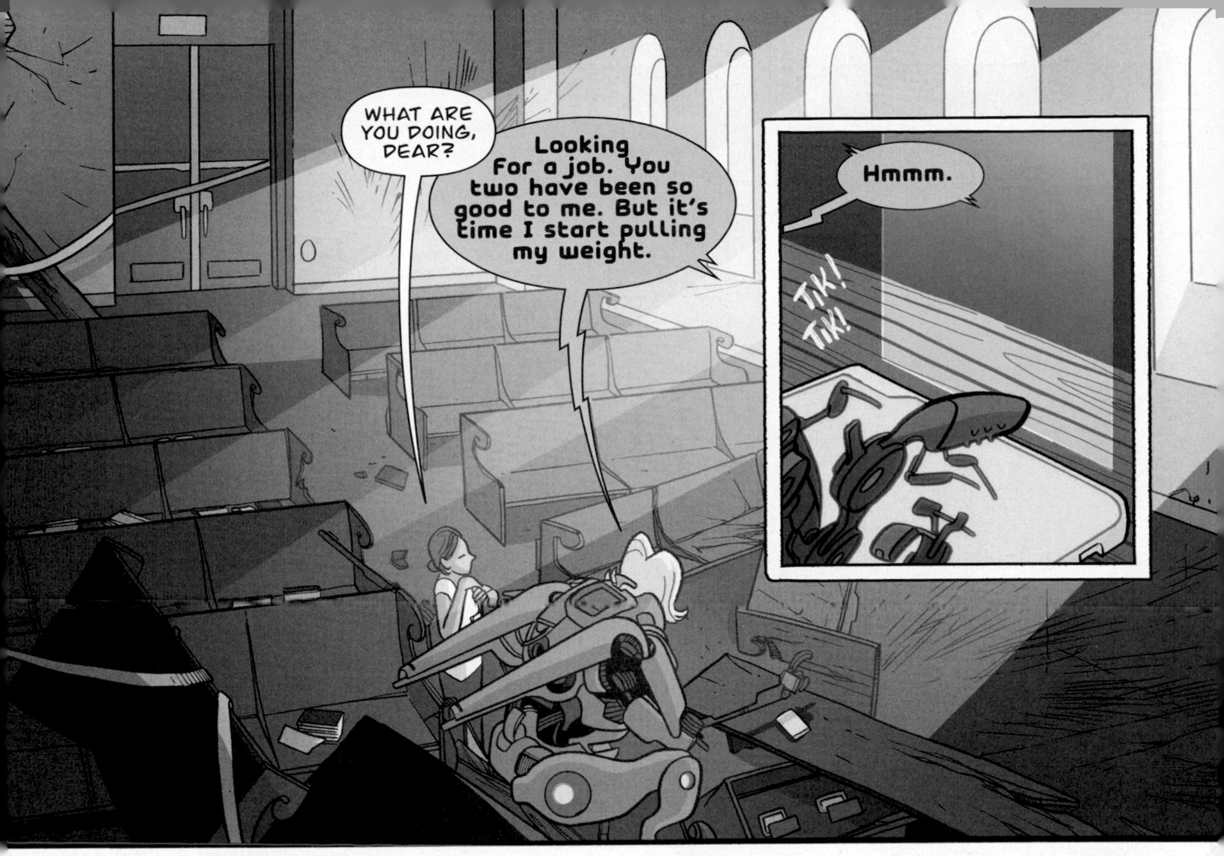
WHAT ARE YOU DOING, DEAR?
Looking for a job. You two have been so good to me. But it's time I start pulling my weight.
Hmmm.
TIK! TIK!

KREIGSLIST

A sharing community for the armed professional

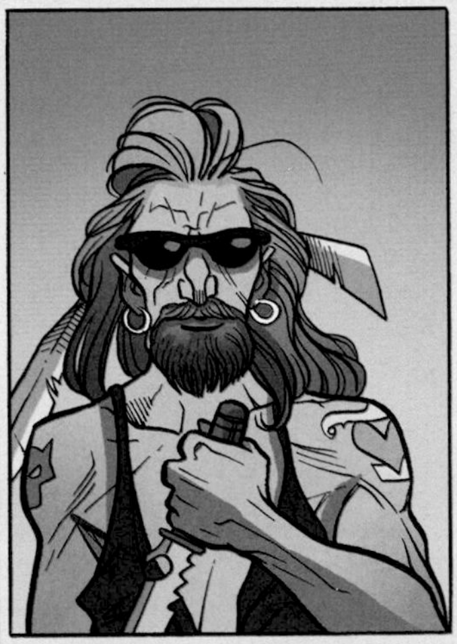

PRESCHOOL SECURITY GUARD.

Firearms provided.

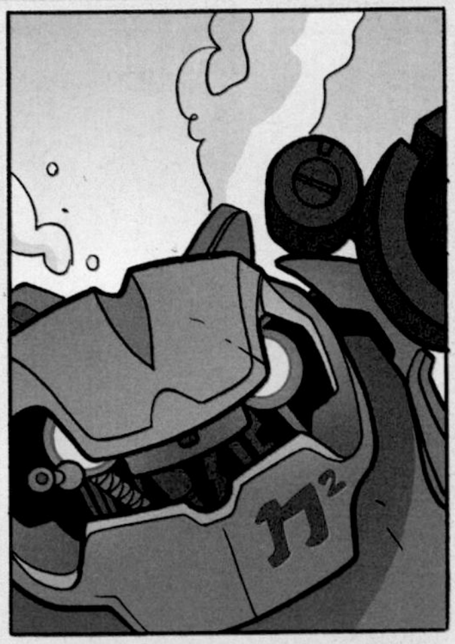

BE A SENTRY OPERATOR FOR THE CHINESE ARMY!

(Knowledge of Chinese a plus.)

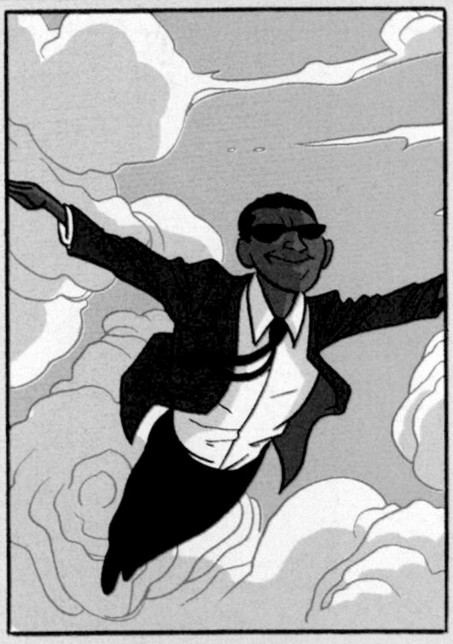

JOIN THE SECRET SERVICE:

More openings than ever! Excellent funeral benefits!

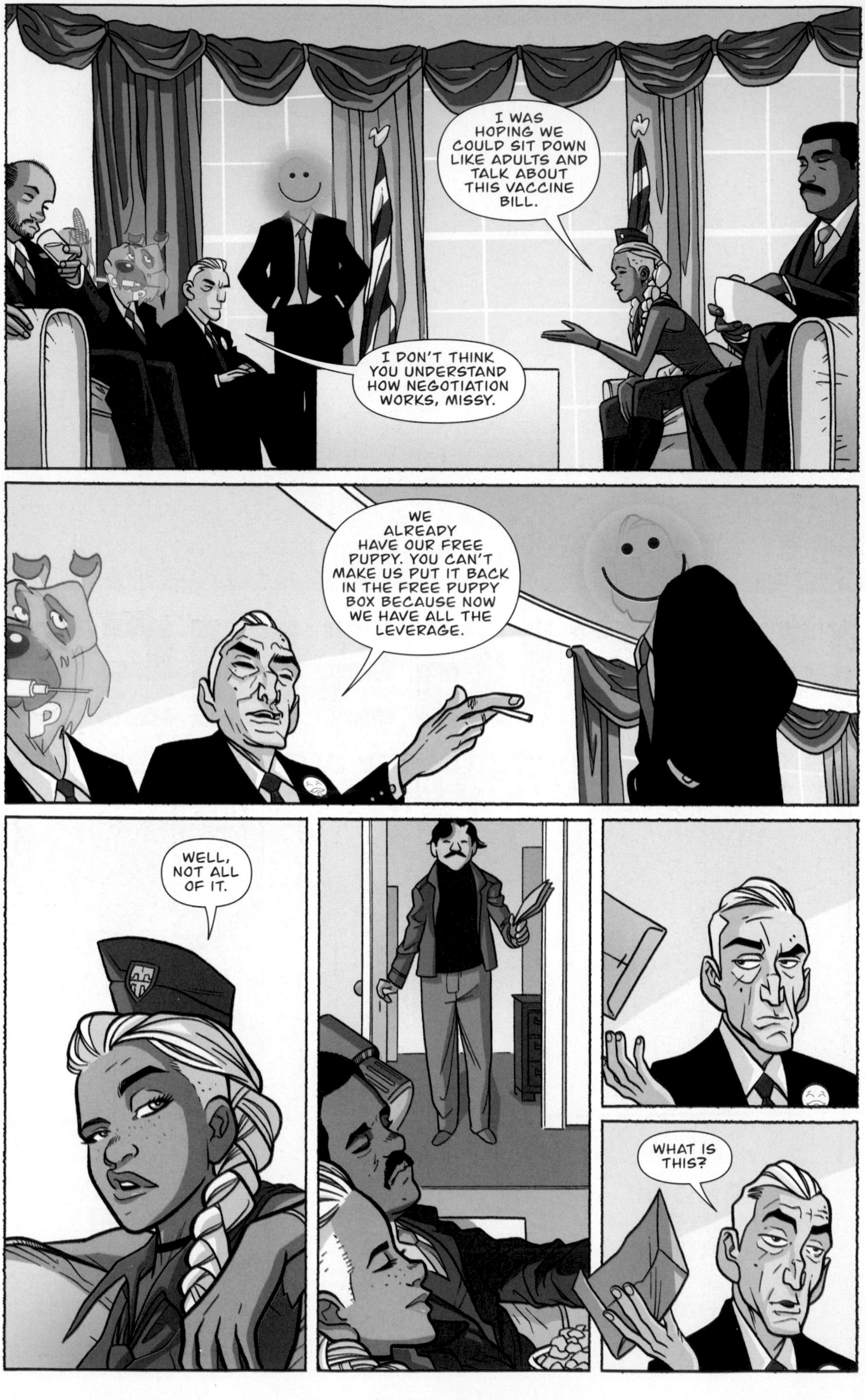
I WAS HOPING WE COULD SIT DOWN LIKE ADULTS AND TALK ABOUT THIS VACCINE BILL.
I DON'T THINK YOU UNDERSTAND HOW NEGOTIATION WORKS, MISSY.
WE ALREADY HAVE OUR FREE PUPPY. YOU CAN'T MAKE US PUT IT BACK IN THE FREE PUPPY BOX BECAUSE NOW WE HAVE ALL THE LEVERAGE.
WELL, NOT ALL OF IT.
WHAT IS THIS?

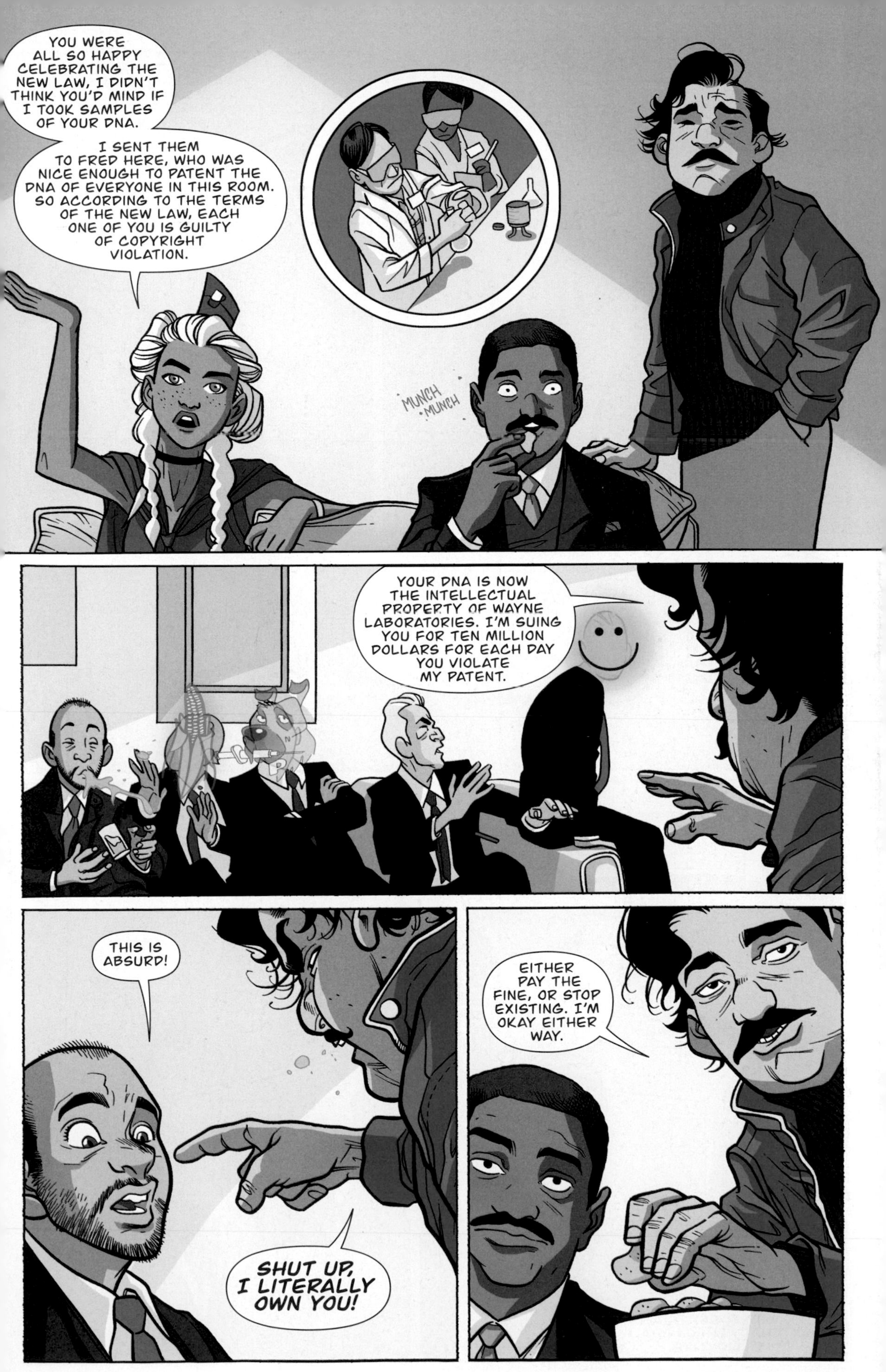
YOU WERE ALL SO HAPPY CELEBRATING THE NEW LAW, I DIDN'T THINK YOU'D MIND IF I TOOK SAMPLES OF YOUR DNA.
I SENT THEM TO FRED HERE, WHO WAS NICE ENOUGH TO PATENT THE DNA OF EVERYONE IN THIS ROOM. SO ACCORDING TO THE TERMS OF THE NEW LAW, EACH ONE OF YOU IS GUILTY OF COPYRIGHT VIOLATION.
MUNCH MUNCH
YOUR DNA IS NOW THE INTELLECTUAL PROPERTY OF WAYNE LABORATORIES. I'M SUING YOU FOR TEN MILLION DOLLARS FOR EACH DAY YOU VIOLATE MY PATENT.
THIS IS ABSURD!
SHUT UP, I LITERALLY OWN YOU!
EITHER PAY THE FINE, OR STOP EXISTING. I'M OKAY EITHER WAY.

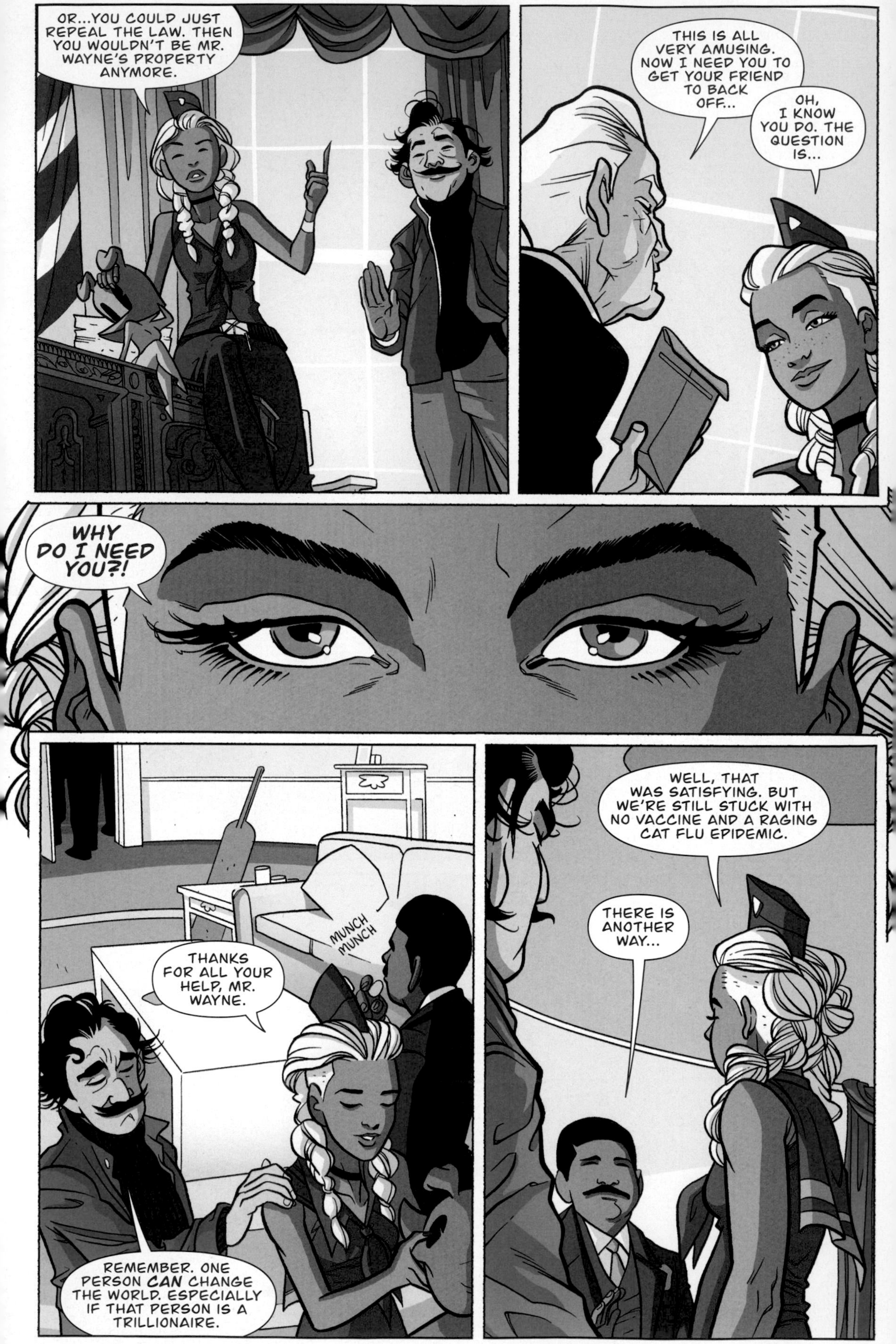
OR...YOU COULD JUST REPEAL THE LAW. THEN YOU WOULDN'T BE MR. WAYNE'S PROPERTY ANYMORE.
THIS IS ALL VERY AMUSING. NOW I NEED YOU TO GET YOUR FRIEND TO BACK OFF...
OH, I KNOW YOU DO. THE QUESTION IS...
WHY DO I NEED YOU?!
THANKS FOR ALL YOUR HELP, MR. WAYNE.
MUNCH MUNCH
REMEMBER. ONE PERSON CAN CHANGE THE WORLD. ESPECIALLY IF THAT PERSON IS A TRILLIONAIRE.
WELL, THAT WAS SATISFYING. BUT WE'RE STILL STUCK WITH NO VACCINE AND A RAGING CAT FLU EPIDEMIC.
THERE IS ANOTHER WAY...

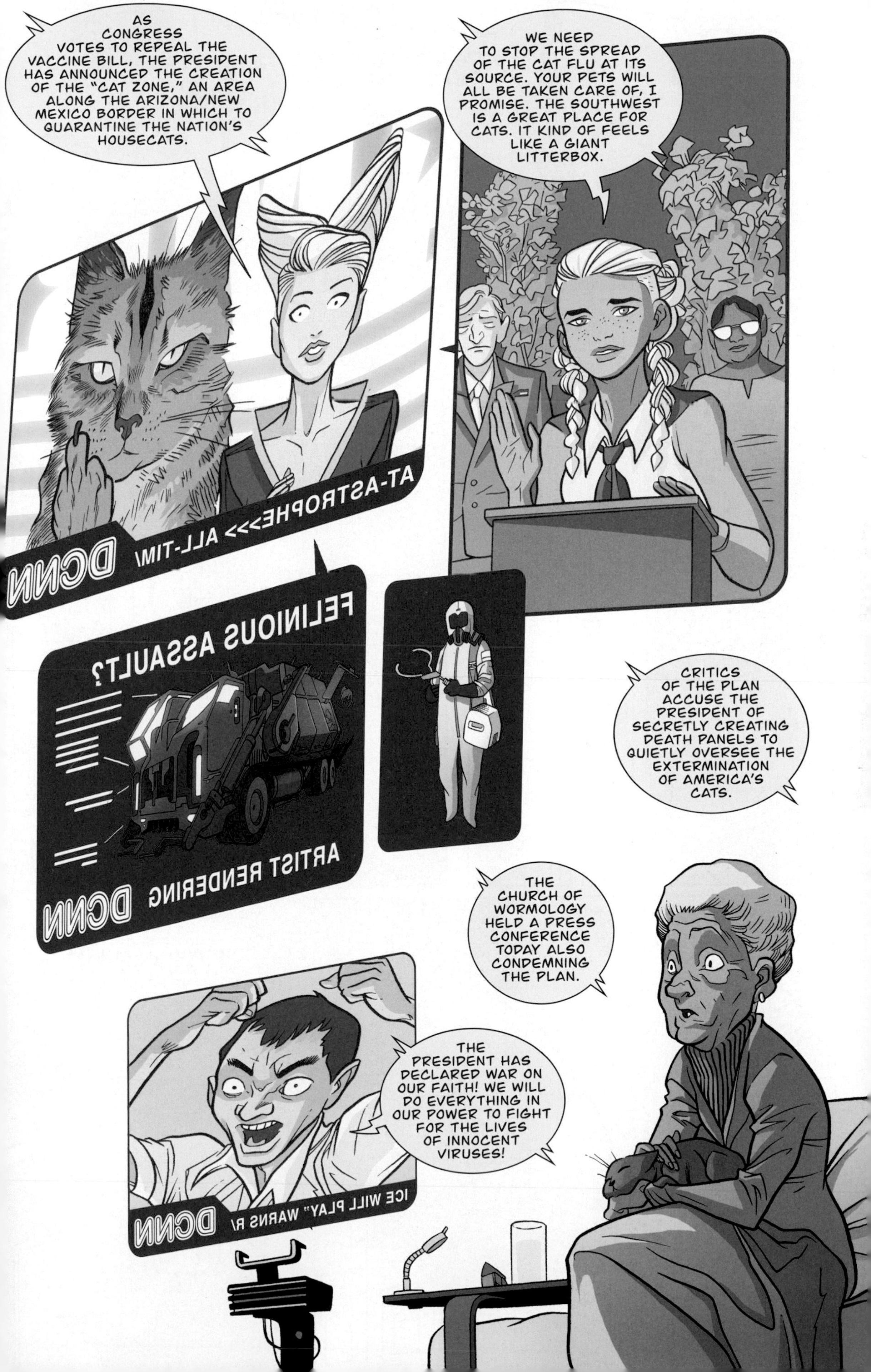

AS CONGRESS VOTES TO REPEAL THE VACCINE BILL, THE PRESIDENT HAS ANNOUNCED THE CREATION OF THE "CAT ZONE," AN AREA ALONG THE ARIZONA/NEW MEXICO BORDER IN WHICH TO QUARANTINE THE NATION'S HOUSECATS.
DCNN
ALL-TIME CAT-ASTROPHE>>>
WE NEED TO STOP THE SPREAD OF THE CAT FLU AT ITS SOURCE. YOUR PETS WILL ALL BE TAKEN CARE OF, I PROMISE. THE SOUTHWEST IS A GREAT PLACE FOR CATS. IT KIND OF FEELS LIKE A GIANT LITTERBOX.
FELINIOUS ASSAULT?
ARTIST RENDERING
DCNN
CRITICS OF THE PLAN ACCUSE THE PRESIDENT OF SECRETLY CREATING DEATH PANELS TO QUIETLY OVERSEE THE EXTERMINATION OF AMERICA'S CATS.
THE CHURCH OF WORMOLOGY HELD A PRESS CONFERENCE TODAY ALSO CONDEMNING THE PLAN.
THE PRESIDENT HAS DECLARED WAR ON OUR FAITH! WE WILL DO EVERYTHING IN OUR POWER TO FIGHT FOR THE LIVES OF INNOCENT VIRUSES!
DCNN
WARNS R "ICE WILL PLAY"

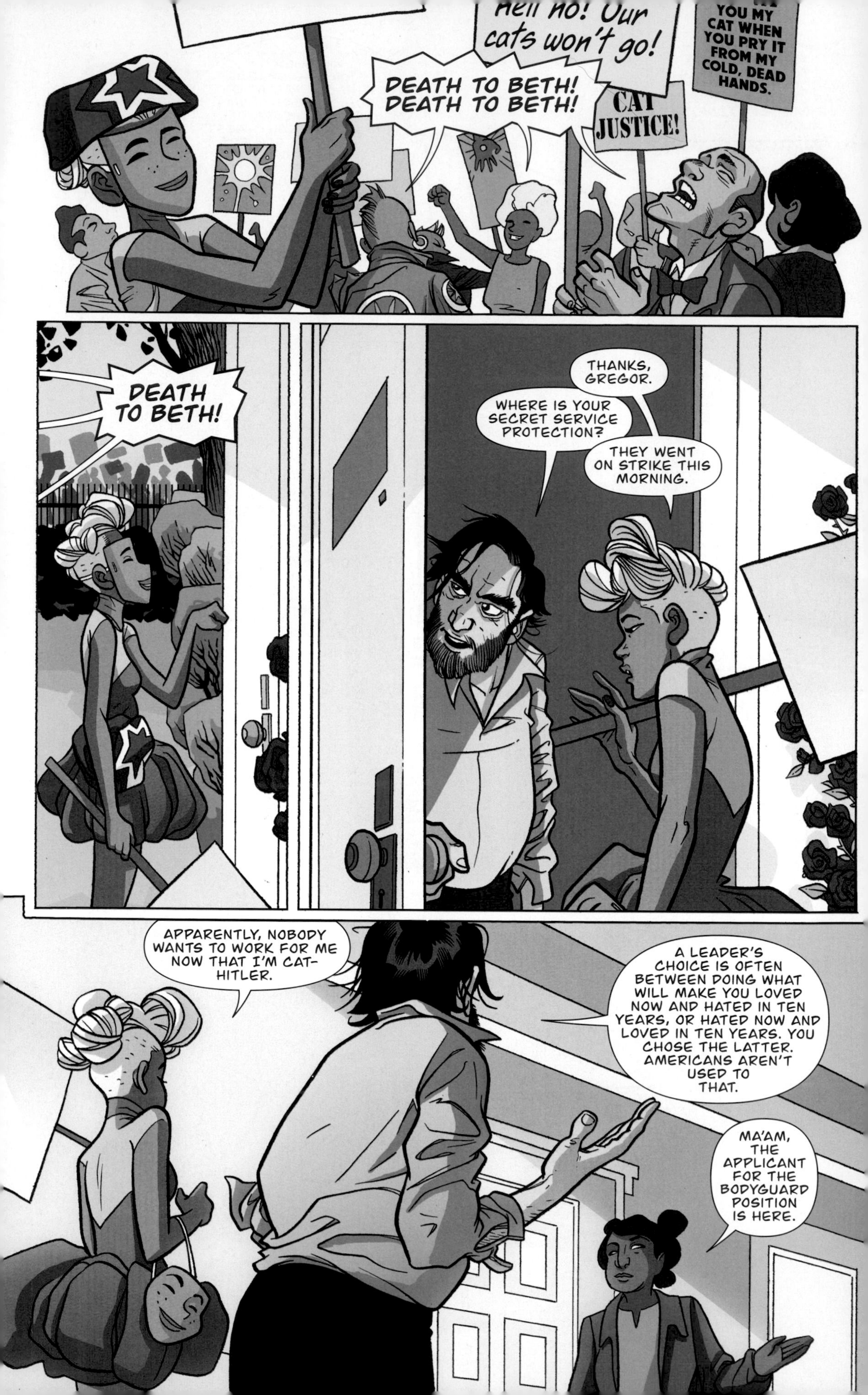
Hell no! Our cats won't go!
YOU MY CAT WHEN YOU PRY IT FROM MY COLD, DEAD HANDS.
DEATH TO BETH! DEATH TO BETH!
CAT JUSTICE!
DEATH TO BETH!
THANKS, GREGOR.
WHERE IS YOUR SECRET SERVICE PROTECTION?
THEY WENT ON STRIKE THIS MORNING.
APPARENTLY, NOBODY WANTS TO WORK FOR ME NOW THAT I'M CAT-HITLER.
A LEADER'S CHOICE IS OFTEN BETWEEN DOING WHAT WILL MAKE YOU LOVED NOW AND HATED IN TEN YEARS, OR HATED NOW AND LOVED IN TEN YEARS. YOU CHOSE THE LATTER. AMERICANS AREN'T USED TO THAT.
MA'AM, THE APPLICANT FOR THE BODYGUARD POSITION IS HERE.

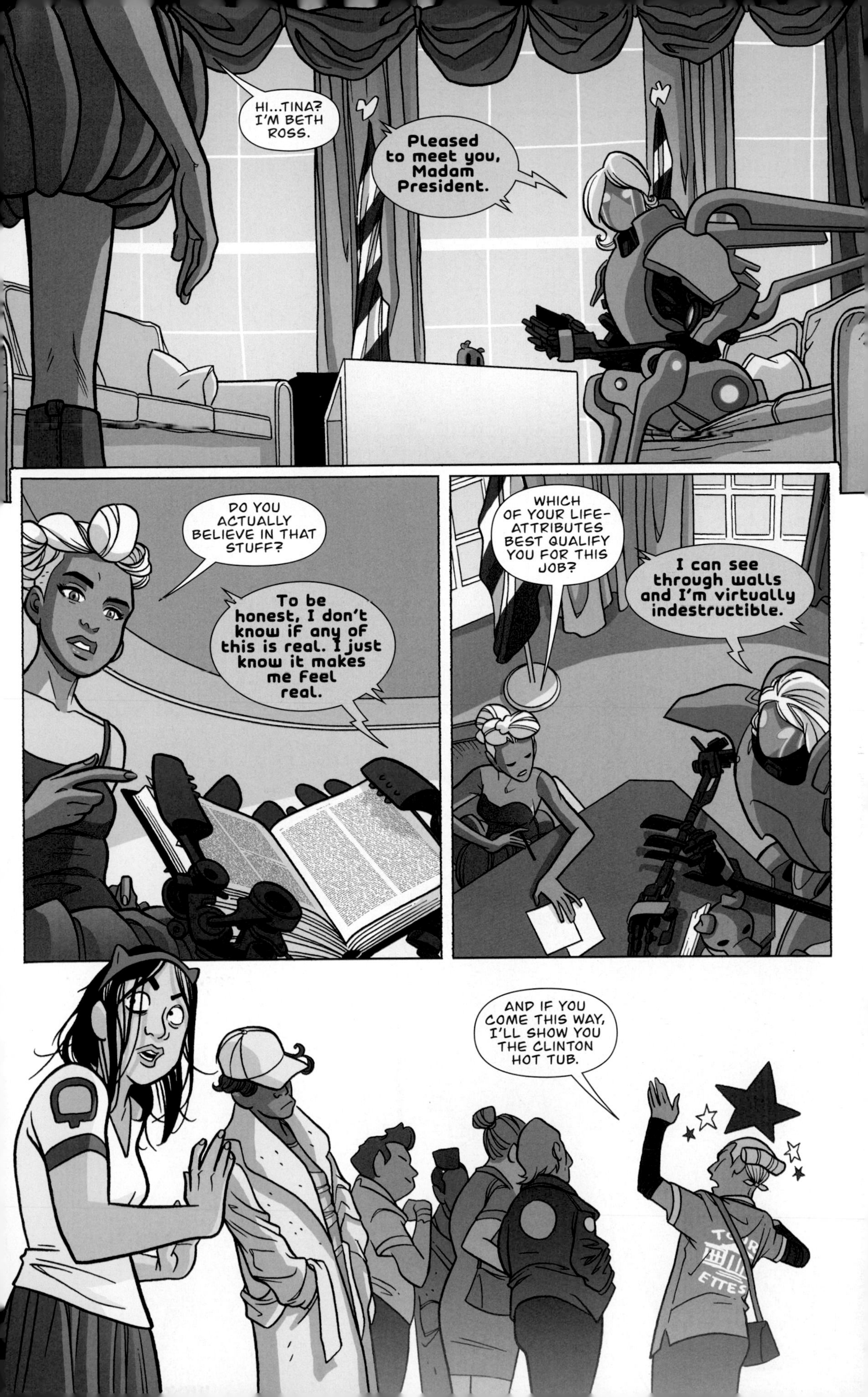
HI...TINA? I'M BETH ROSS.
Pleased to meet you, Madam President.
DO YOU ACTUALLY BELIEVE IN THAT STUFF?
To be honest, I don't know if any of this is real. I just know it makes me feel real.
WHICH OF YOUR LIFE-ATTRIBUTES BEST QUALIFY YOU FOR THIS JOB?
I can see through walls and I'm virtually indestructible.
AND IF YOU COME THIS WAY, I'LL SHOW YOU THE CLINTON HOT TUB.
TOUR ETTES

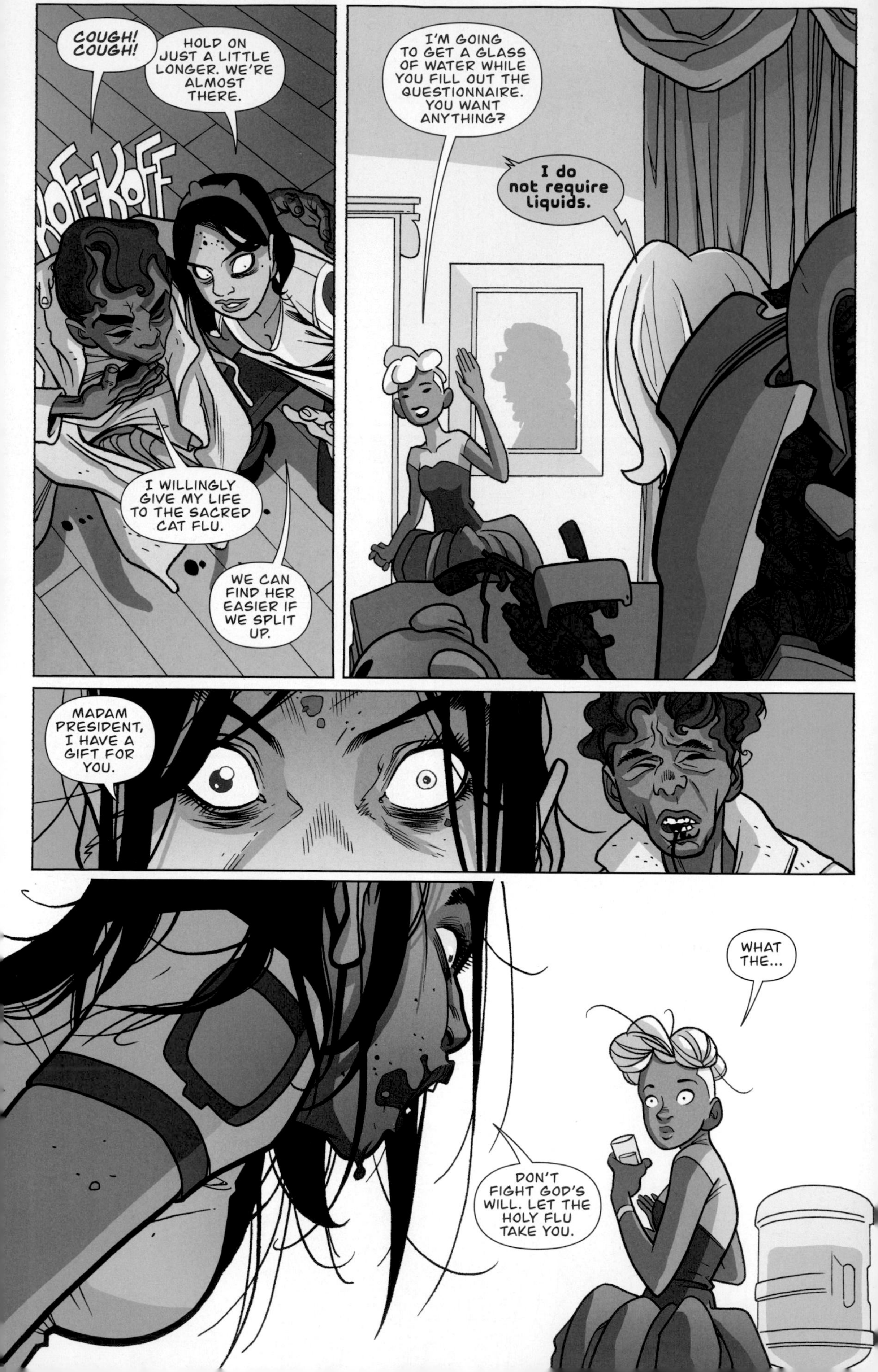
COUGH! COUGH!
HOLD ON JUST A LITTLE LONGER. WE'RE ALMOST THERE.
KOFF KOFF
I WILLINGLY GIVE MY LIFE TO THE SACRED CAT FLU.
WE CAN FIND HER EASIER IF WE SPLIT UP.
I'M GOING TO GET A GLASS OF WATER WHILE YOU FILL OUT THE QUESTIONNAIRE. YOU WANT ANYTHING?
I do not require liquids.
MADAM PRESIDENT, I HAVE A GIFT FOR YOU.
WHAT THE...
DON'T FIGHT GOD'S WILL. LET THE HOLY FLU TAKE YOU.

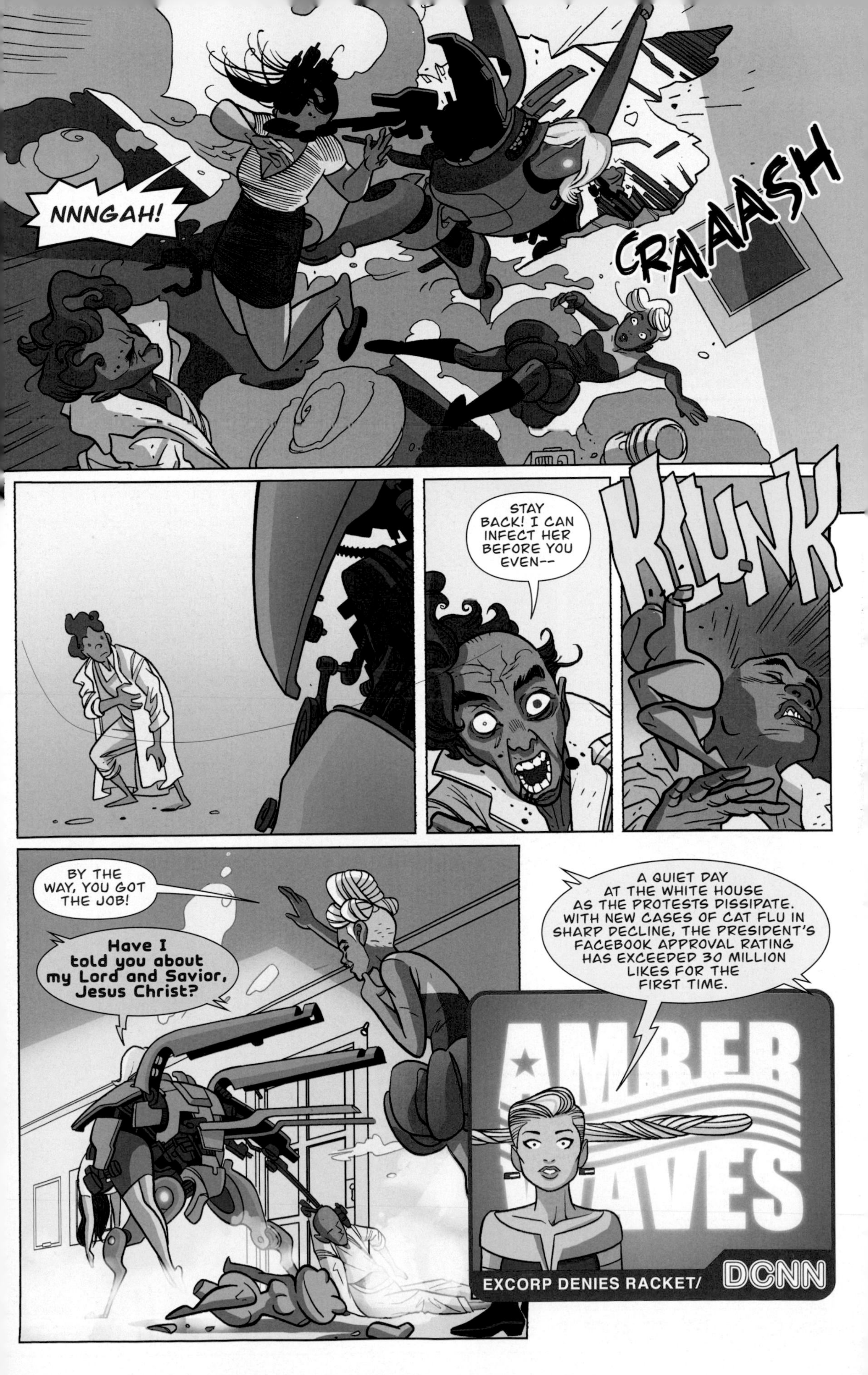
NNNGAH!
CRAAASH
STAY BACK! I CAN INFECT HER BEFORE YOU EVEN--
KLUNK
BY THE WAY, YOU GOT THE JOB!
Have I told you about my Lord and Savior, Jesus Christ?
A QUIET DAY AT THE WHITE HOUSE AS THE PROTESTS DISSIPATE. WITH NEW CASES OF CAT FLU IN SHARP DECLINE, THE PRESIDENT'S FACEBOOK APPROVAL RATING HAS EXCEEDED 30 MILLION LIKES FOR THE FIRST TIME.
AMBER WAVES
EXCORP DENIES RACKET/
DCNN

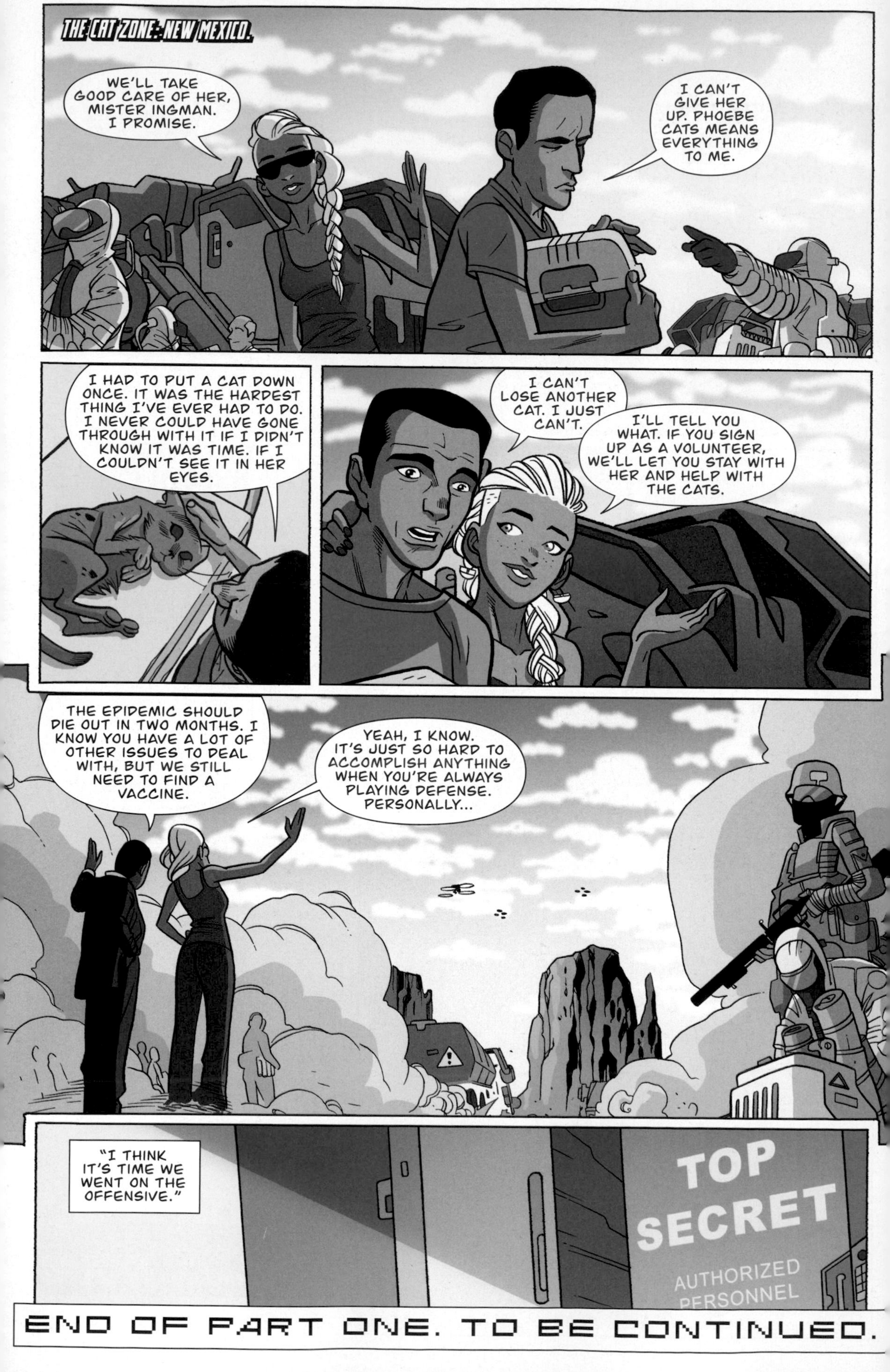
THE CAT ZONE: NEW MEXICO.
WE'LL TAKE GOOD CARE OF HER, MISTER INGMAN. I PROMISE.
I CAN'T GIVE HER UP. PHOEBE CATS MEANS EVERYTHING TO ME.
I HAD TO PUT A CAT DOWN ONCE. IT WAS THE HARDEST THING I'VE EVER HAD TO DO. I NEVER COULD HAVE GONE THROUGH WITH IT IF I DIDN'T KNOW IT WAS TIME. IF I COULDN'T SEE IT IN HER EYES.
I CAN'T LOSE ANOTHER CAT. I JUST CAN'T.
I'LL TELL YOU WHAT. IF YOU SIGN UP AS A VOLUNTEER, WE'LL LET YOU STAY WITH HER AND HELP WITH THE CATS.
THE EPIDEMIC SHOULD DIE OUT IN TWO MONTHS. I KNOW YOU HAVE A LOT OF OTHER ISSUES TO DEAL WITH, BUT WE STILL NEED TO FIND A VACCINE.
YEAH, I KNOW. IT'S JUST SO HARD TO ACCOMPLISH ANYTHING WHEN YOU'RE ALWAYS PLAYING DEFENSE. PERSONALLY...
"I THINK IT'S TIME WE WENT ON THE OFFENSIVE."
TOP SECRET
AUTHORIZED PERSONNEL
END OF PART ONE. TO BE CONTINUED.

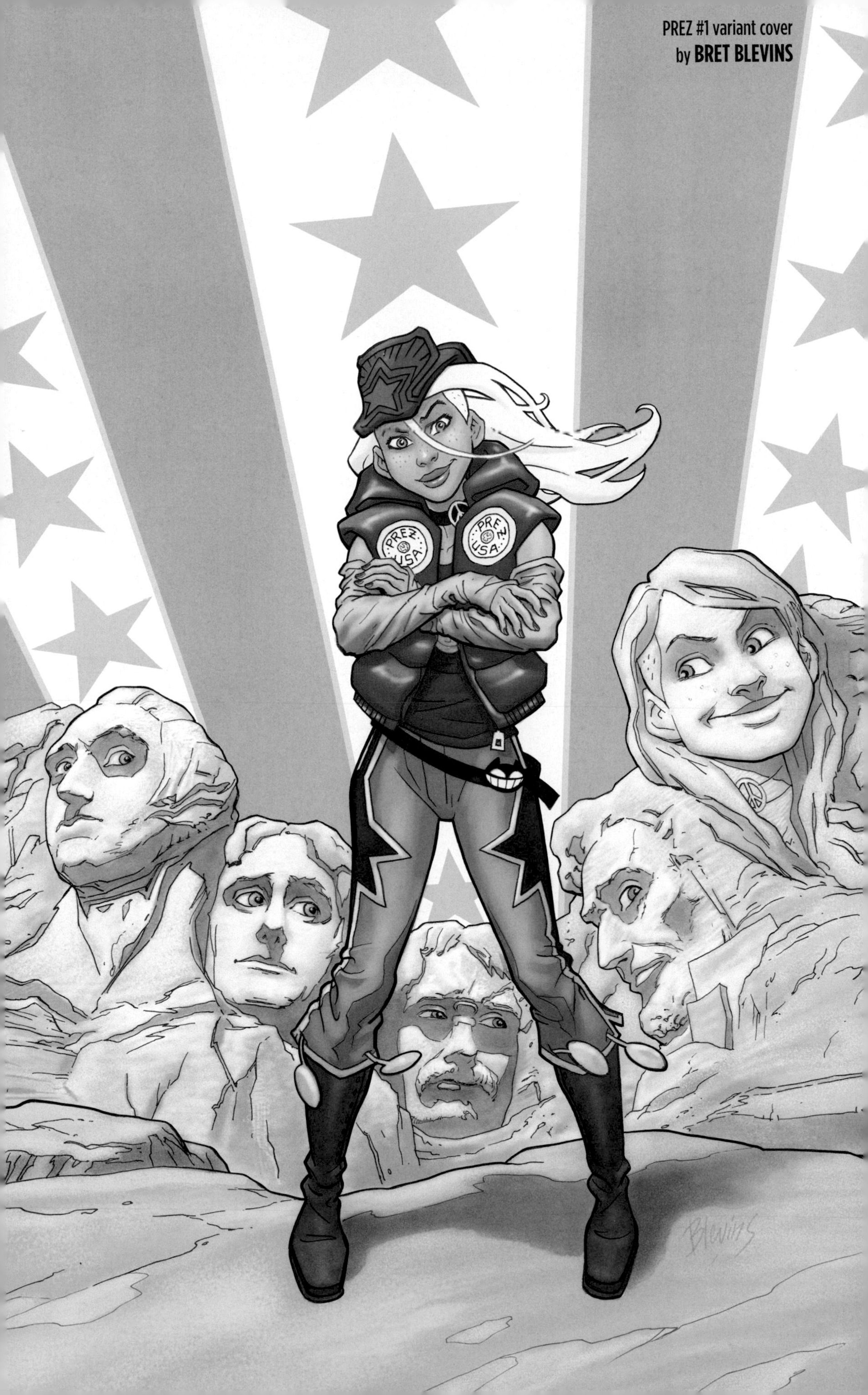
PREZ USA
PREZ USA
Blevins

PREZ #1 variant cover
by **BRET BLEVINS**

PREZ: SNEAK PEEK

MARK RUSSELL writer BEN CALDWELL penciller JOHN LUCAS inker JEREMY LAWSON colorist

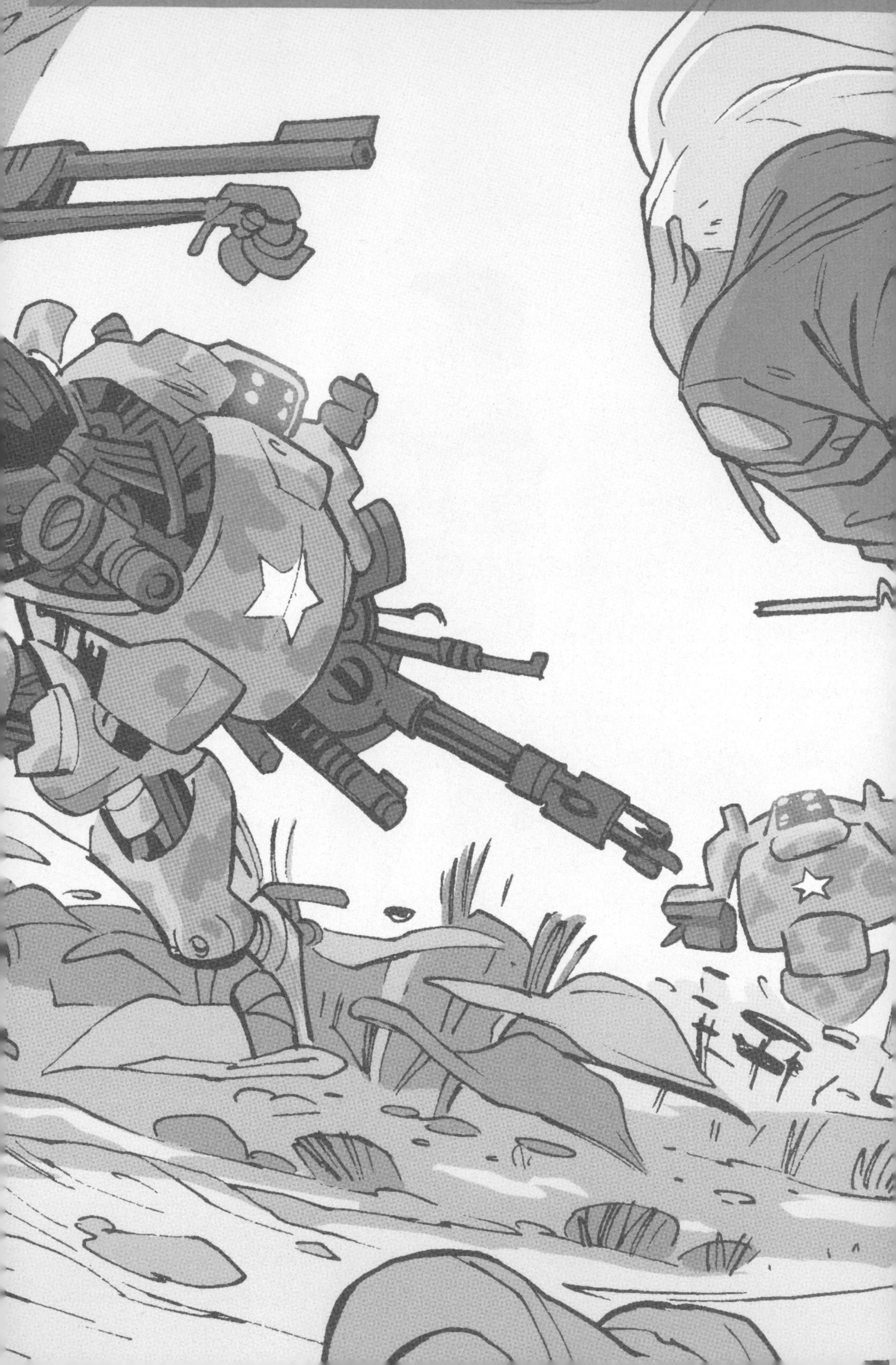

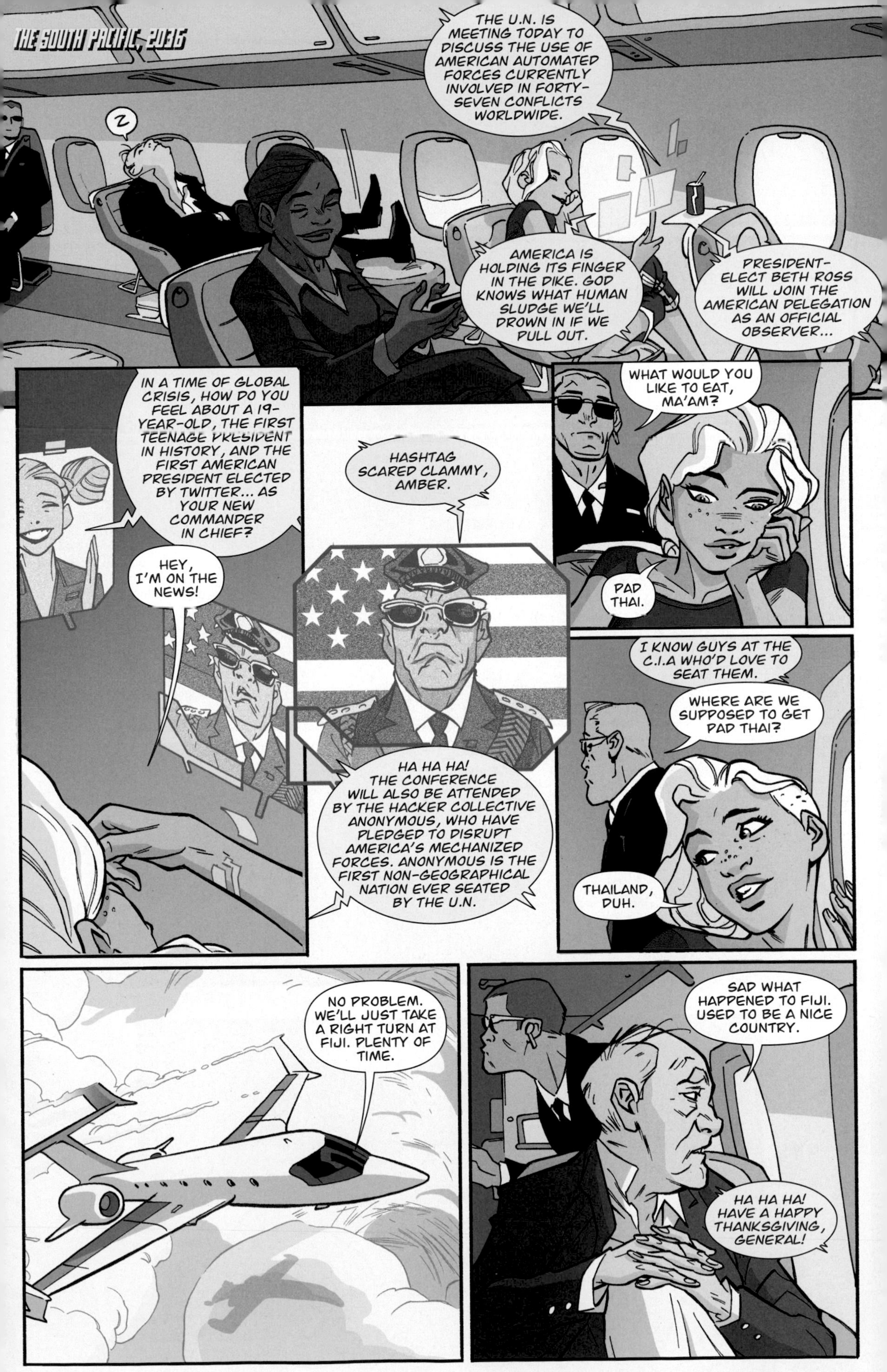
THE SOUTH PACIFIC, 2036
THE U.N. IS MEETING TODAY TO DISCUSS THE USE OF AMERICAN AUTOMATED FORCES CURRENTLY INVOLVED IN FORTY-SEVEN CONFLICTS WORLDWIDE.
Z
AMERICA IS HOLDING ITS FINGER IN THE DIKE. GOD KNOWS WHAT HUMAN SLUDGE WE'LL DROWN IN IF WE PULL OUT.
PRESIDENT-ELECT BETH ROSS WILL JOIN THE AMERICAN DELEGATION AS AN OFFICIAL OBSERVER...
IN A TIME OF GLOBAL CRISIS, HOW DO YOU FEEL ABOUT A 19-YEAR-OLD, THE FIRST TEENAGE PRESIDENT IN HISTORY, AND THE FIRST AMERICAN PRESIDENT ELECTED BY TWITTER... AS YOUR NEW COMMANDER IN CHIEF?
HEY, I'M ON THE NEWS!
HASHTAG SCARED CLAMMY, AMBER.
HA HA HA! THE CONFERENCE WILL ALSO BE ATTENDED BY THE HACKER COLLECTIVE ANONYMOUS, WHO HAVE PLEDGED TO DISRUPT AMERICA'S MECHANIZED FORCES. ANONYMOUS IS THE FIRST NON-GEOGRAPHICAL NATION EVER SEATED BY THE U.N.
WHAT WOULD YOU LIKE TO EAT, MA'AM?
PAD THAI.
I KNOW GUYS AT THE C.I.A WHO'D LOVE TO SEAT THEM.
WHERE ARE WE SUPPOSED TO GET PAD THAI?
THAILAND, DUH.
NO PROBLEM. WE'LL JUST TAKE A RIGHT TURN AT FIJI. PLENTY OF TIME.
SAD WHAT HAPPENED TO FIJI. USED TO BE A NICE COUNTRY.
HA HA HA! HAVE A HAPPY THANKSGIVING, GENERAL!

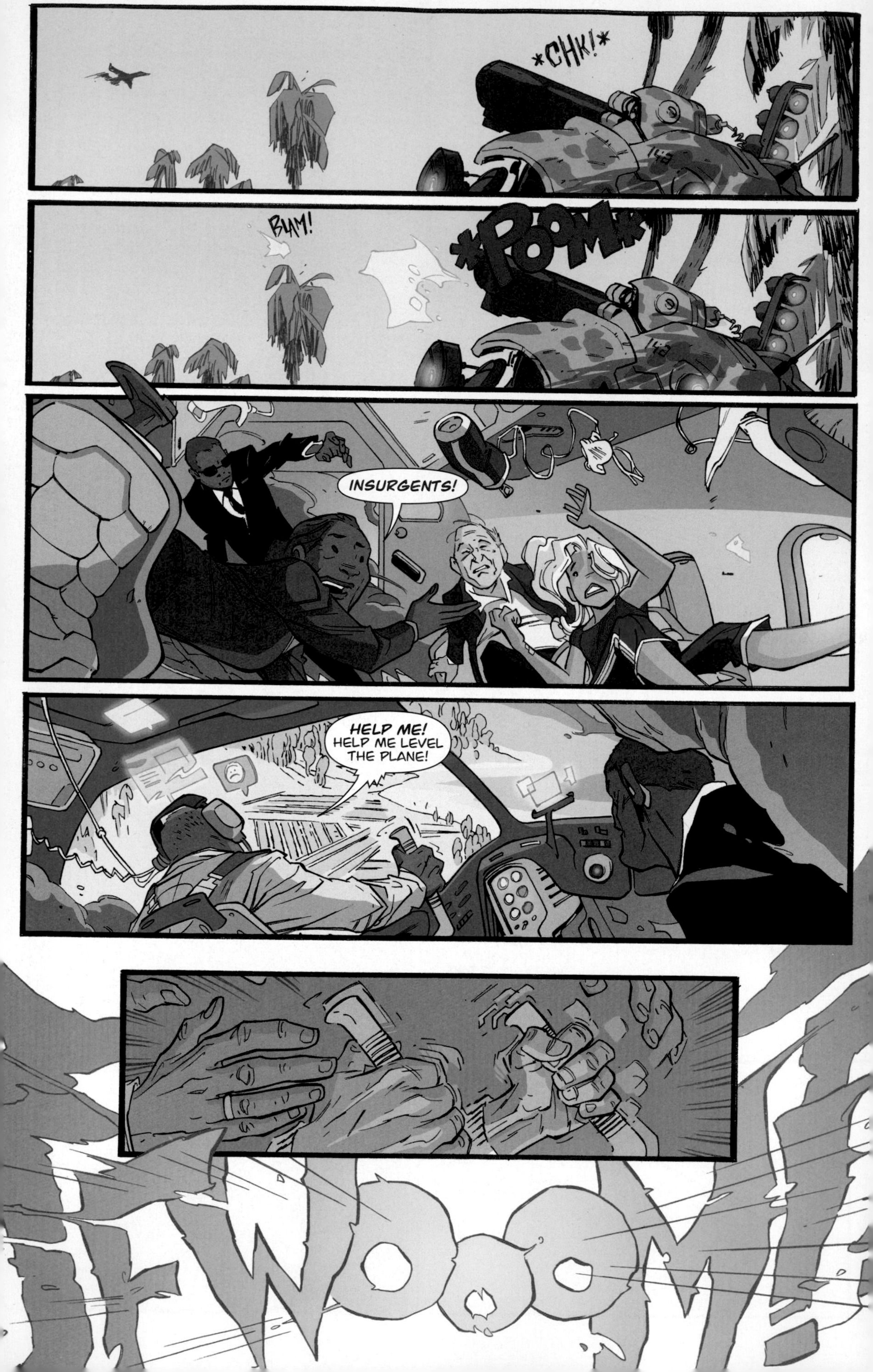
CHK!
BLAM!
POOM
INSURGENTS!
HELP ME!
HELP ME LEVEL
THE PLANE!
THWOOOM!

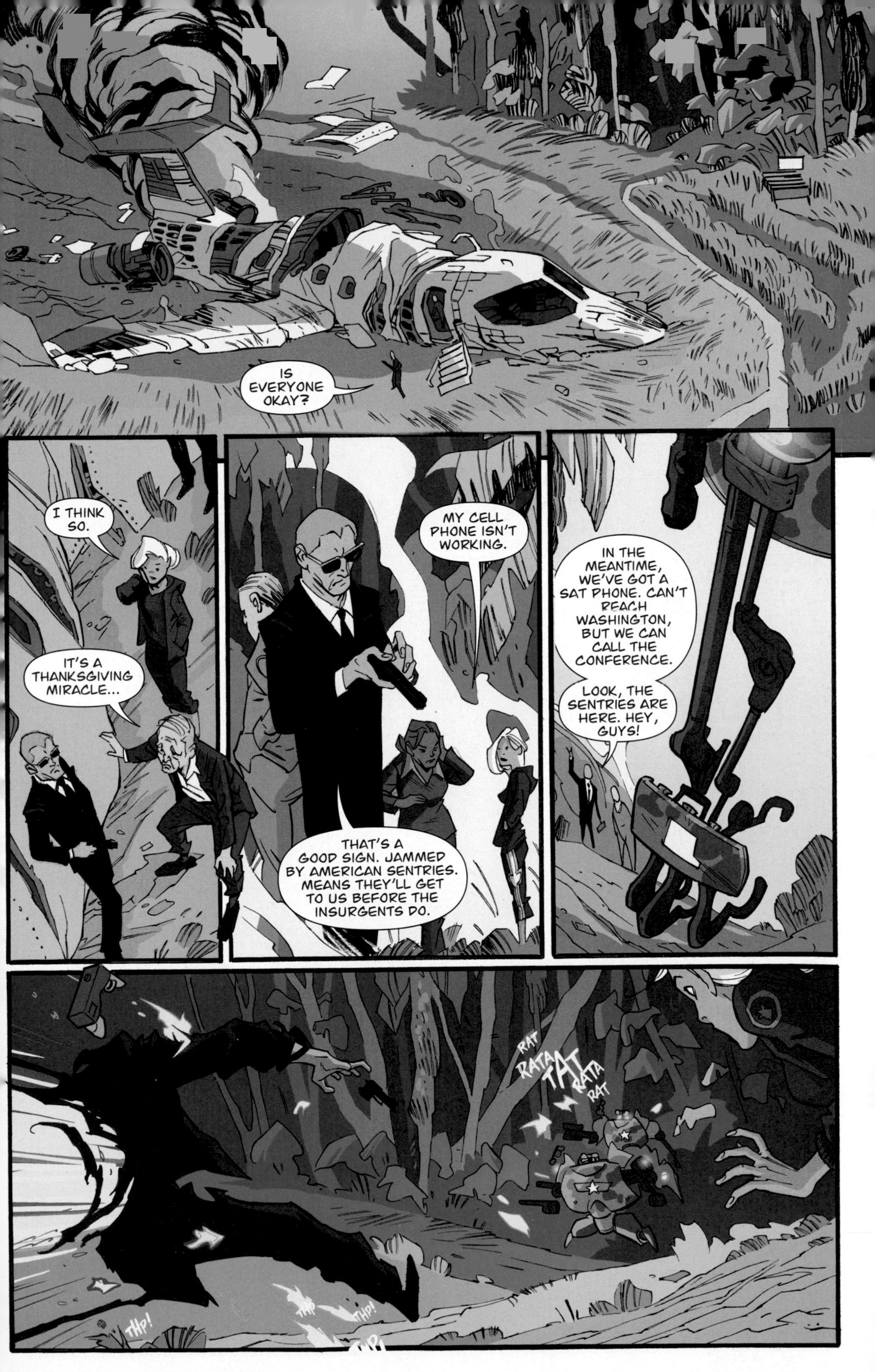
IS EVERYONE OKAY?
I THINK SO.
IT'S A THANKSGIVING MIRACLE...
MY CELL PHONE ISN'T WORKING.
THAT'S A GOOD SIGN. JAMMED BY AMERICAN SENTRIES. MEANS THEY'LL GET TO US BEFORE THE INSURGENTS DO.
IN THE MEANTIME, WE'VE GOT A SAT PHONE. CAN'T REACH WASHINGTON, BUT WE CAN CALL THE CONFERENCE.
LOOK, THE SENTRIES ARE HERE. HEY, GUYS!
RAT RATATATRATA RAT
THP! THP! THP!

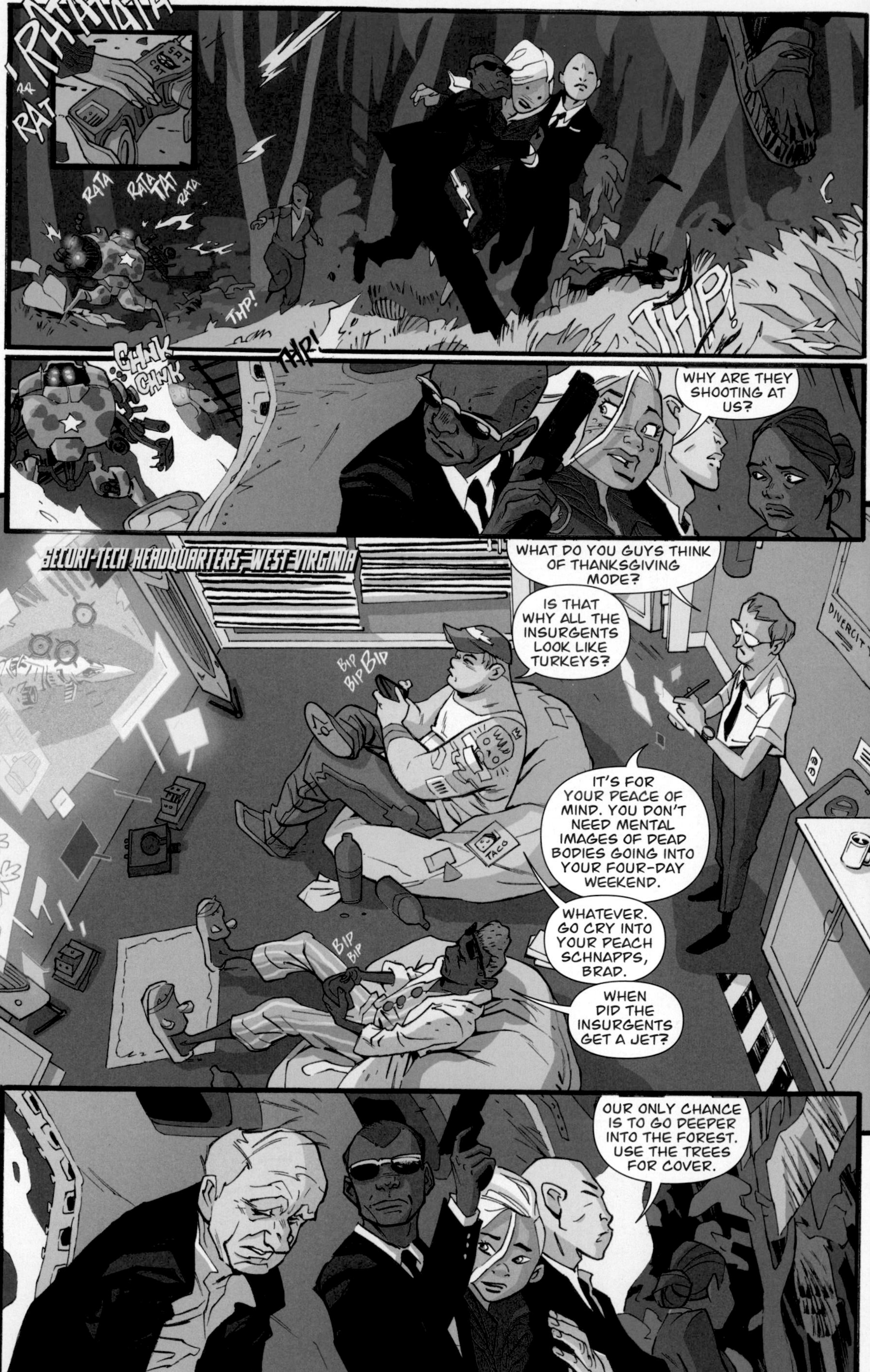
RATATATATA
RA RAT
RATA
RATA TAT RATA
THP!
THP!
CHANK CHANK
THP!
WHY ARE THEY SHOOTING AT US?
SECURI-TECH HEADQUARTERS, WEST VIRGINIA
BLEEP!
WHAT DO YOU GUYS THINK OF THANKSGIVING MODE?
IS THAT WHY ALL THE INSURGENTS LOOK LIKE TURKEYS?
BIP BIP BIP
IT'S FOR YOUR PEACE OF MIND. YOU DON'T NEED MENTAL IMAGES OF DEAD BODIES GOING INTO YOUR FOUR-DAY WEEKEND.
WHATEVER. GO CRY INTO YOUR PEACH SCHNAPPS, BRAD.
BIP BIP
WHEN DID THE INSURGENTS GET A JET?
DIVERCITY
OUR ONLY CHANCE IS TO GO DEEPER INTO THE FOREST. USE THE TREES FOR COVER.

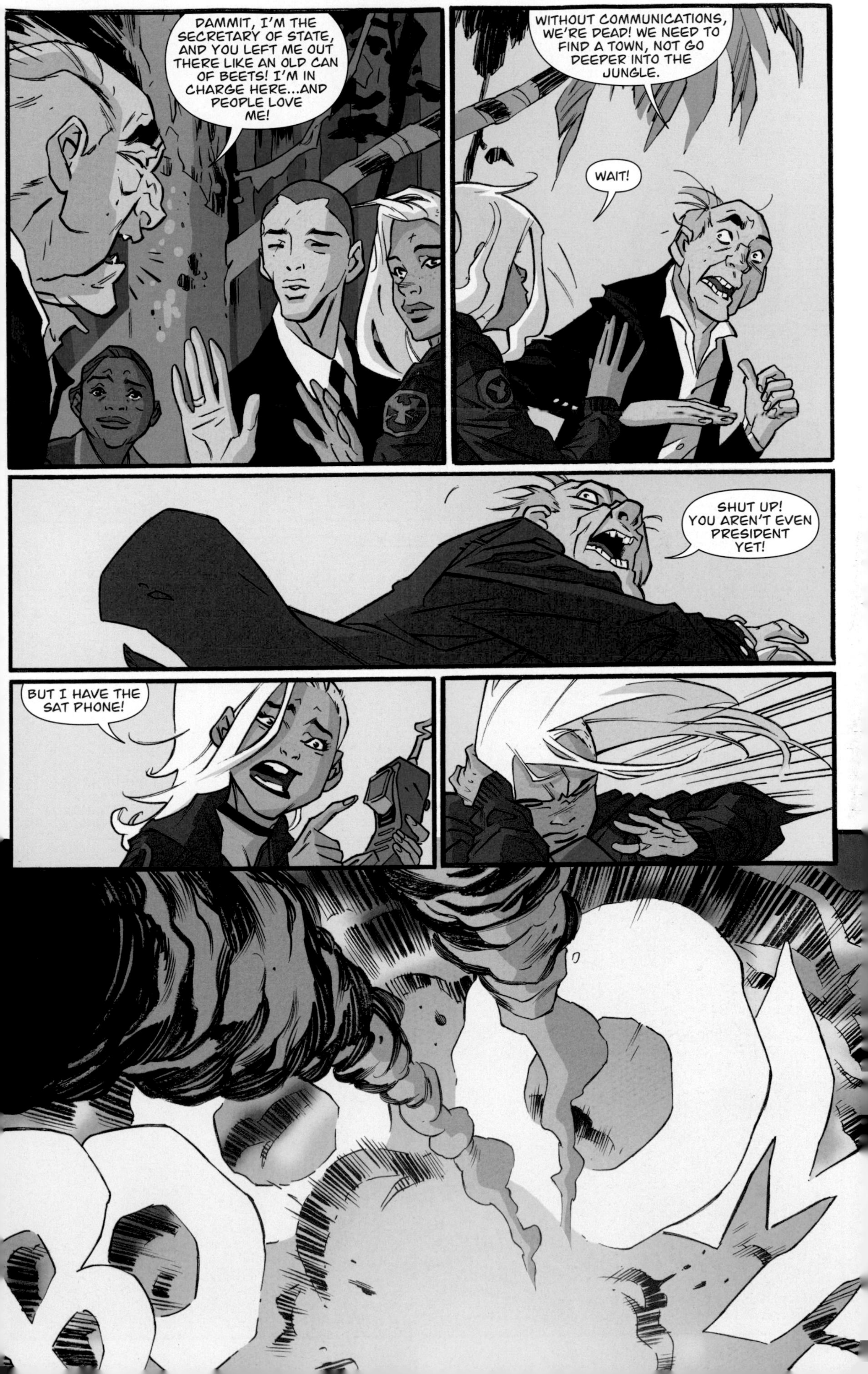
DAMMIT, I'M THE SECRETARY OF STATE, AND YOU LEFT ME OUT THERE LIKE AN OLD CAN OF BEETS! I'M IN CHARGE HERE...AND PEOPLE LOVE ME!
WITHOUT COMMUNICATIONS, WE'RE DEAD! WE NEED TO FIND A TOWN, NOT GO DEEPER INTO THE JUNGLE.
WAIT!
SHUT UP! YOU AREN'T EVEN PRESIDENT YET!
BUT I HAVE THE SAT PHONE!

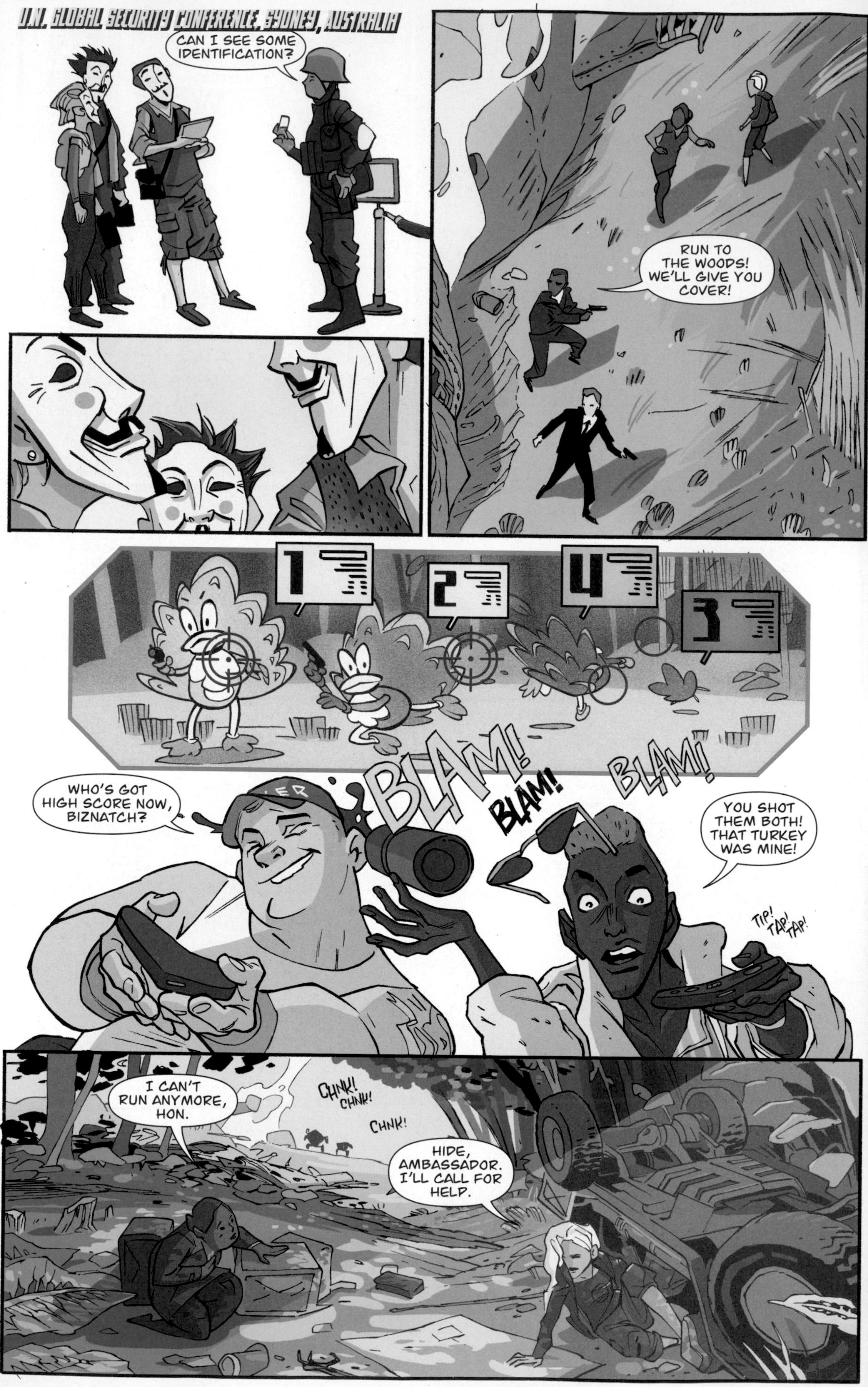
U.N. GLOBAL SECURITY CONFERENCE, SYDNEY, AUSTRALIA
CAN I SEE SOME IDENTIFICATION?
RUN TO THE WOODS! WE'LL GIVE YOU COVER!
1
2
4
3
BLAM!
BLAM!
BLAM!
WHO'S GOT HIGH SCORE NOW, BIZNATCH?
YOU SHOT THEM BOTH! THAT TURKEY WAS MINE!
TIP! TAP! TAP!
I CAN'T RUN ANYMORE, HON.
CHNK! CHNK!
CHNK!
HIDE, AMBASSADOR. I'LL CALL FOR HELP.

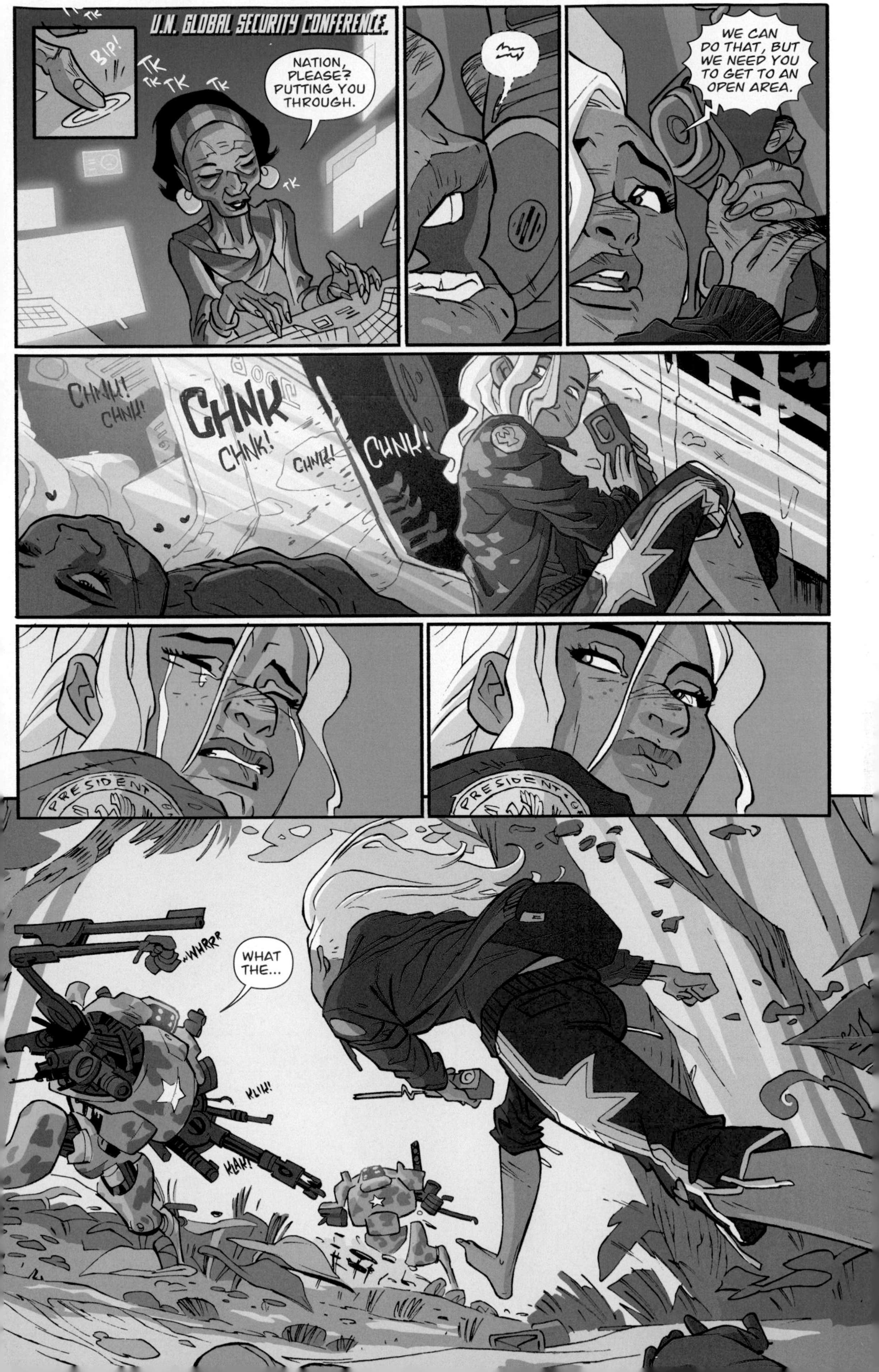
U.N. GLOBAL SECURITY CONFERENCE.
BIP!
TK TK TK TK
NATION, PLEASE? PUTTING YOU THROUGH.
TK
WE CAN DO THAT, BUT WE NEED YOU TO GET TO AN OPEN AREA.
CHNK! CHNK!
CHNK
CHNK!
CHNK!
CHNK!
WHRRR
WHAT THE...
KLIK!
KLAK!

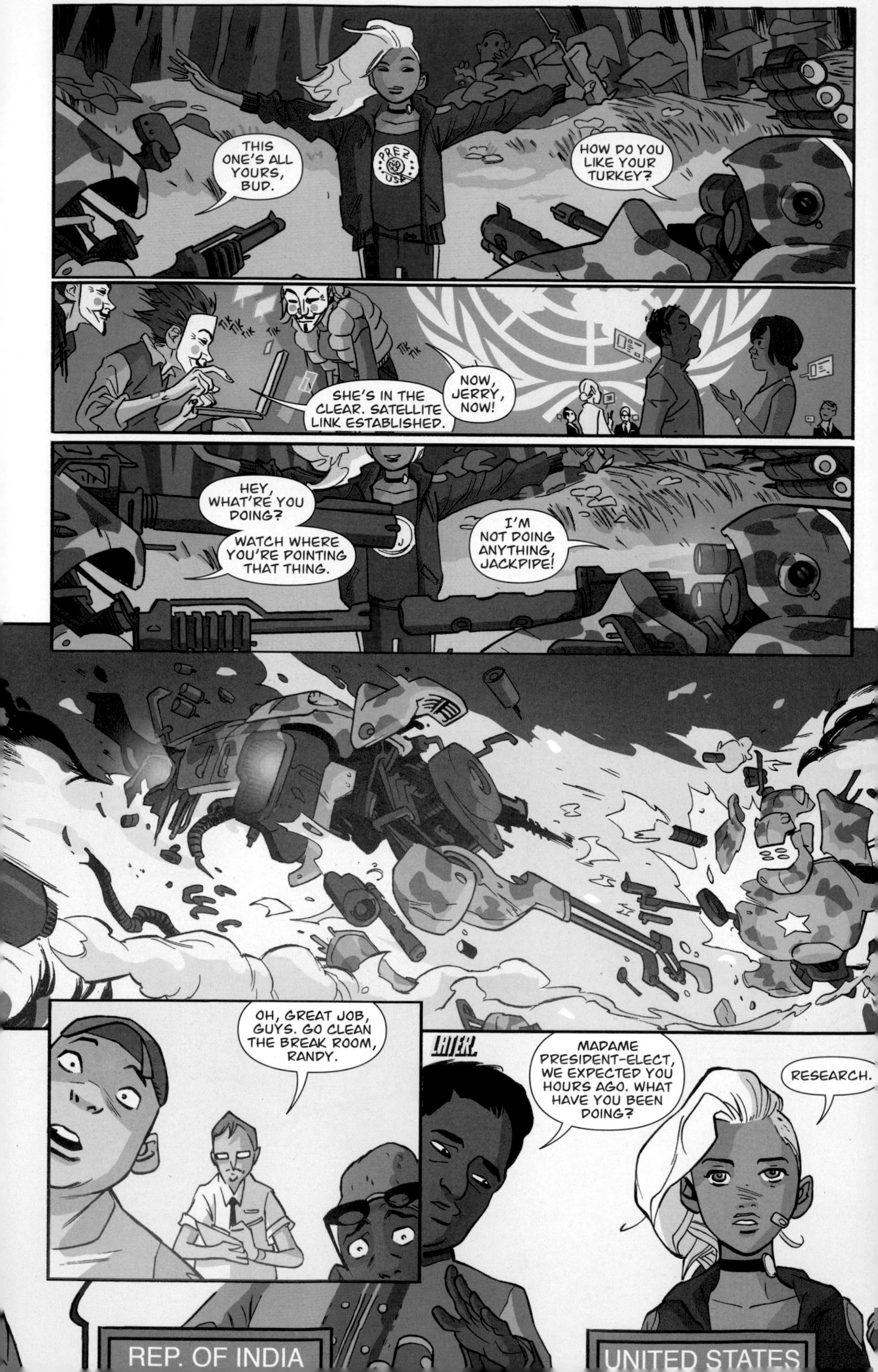
THIS ONE'S ALL YOURS, BUD.
HOW DO YOU LIKE YOUR TURKEY?
PREZ USA
TIK TIK TIK
TIK
TIK TIK
SHE'S IN THE CLEAR. SATELLITE LINK ESTABLISHED.
NOW, JERRY, NOW!
HEY, WHAT'RE YOU DOING?
WATCH WHERE YOU'RE POINTING THAT THING.
I'M NOT DOING ANYTHING, JACKPIPE!
OH, GREAT JOB, GUYS. GO CLEAN THE BREAK ROOM, RANDY.
LATER.
MADAME PRESIDENT-ELECT, WE EXPECTED YOU HOURS AGO. WHAT HAVE YOU BEEN DOING?
RESEARCH.
REP. OF INDIA
UNITED STATES

PREZ SKETCHBOOK BY
BEN CALDWELL

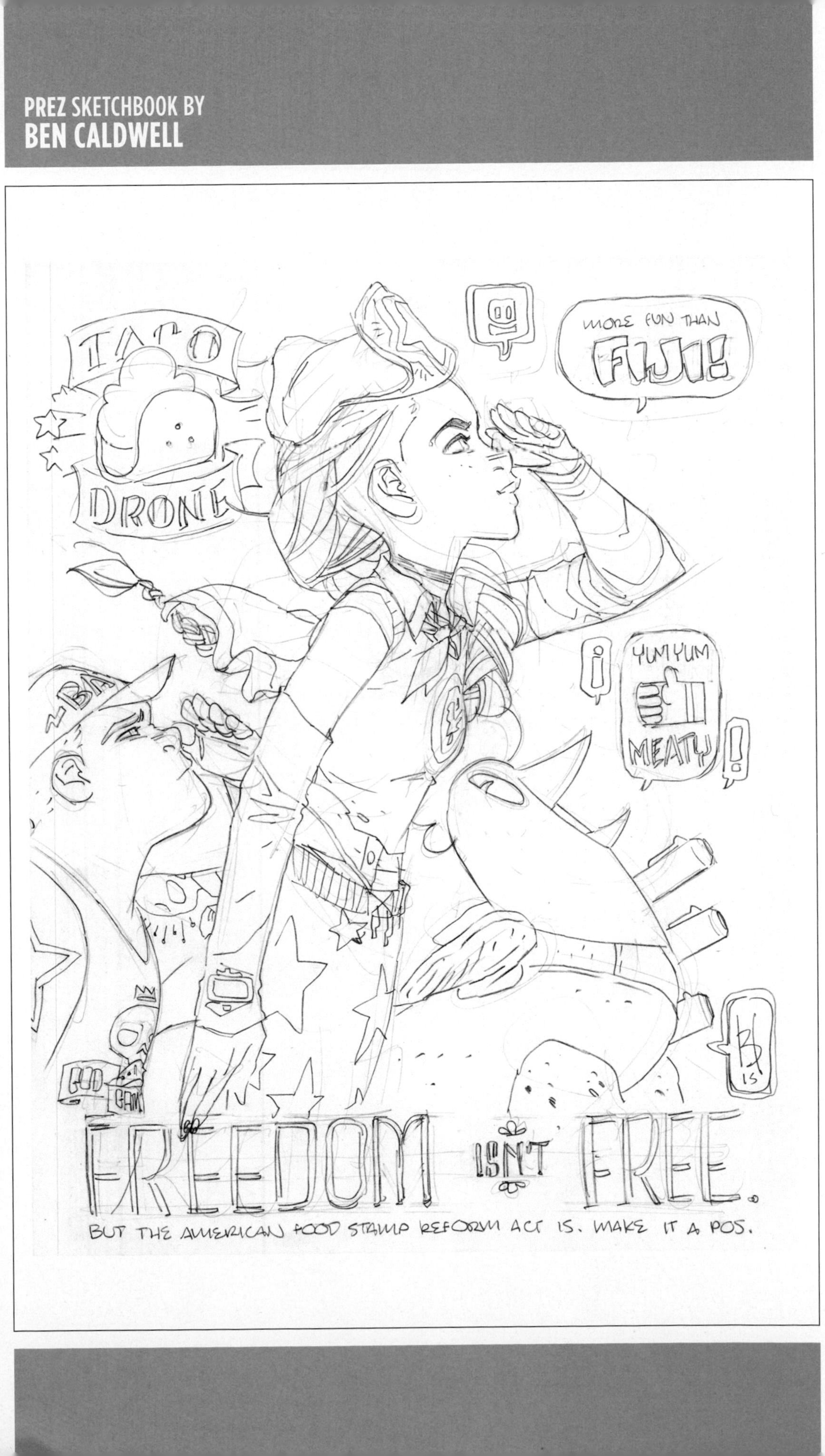

MORE FUN THAN
FIJI!
DRONE
YUMYUM
MEATY
FREEDOM ISN'T FREE.
BUT THE AMERICAN FOOD STAMP REFORM ACT IS. MAKE IT A POS.

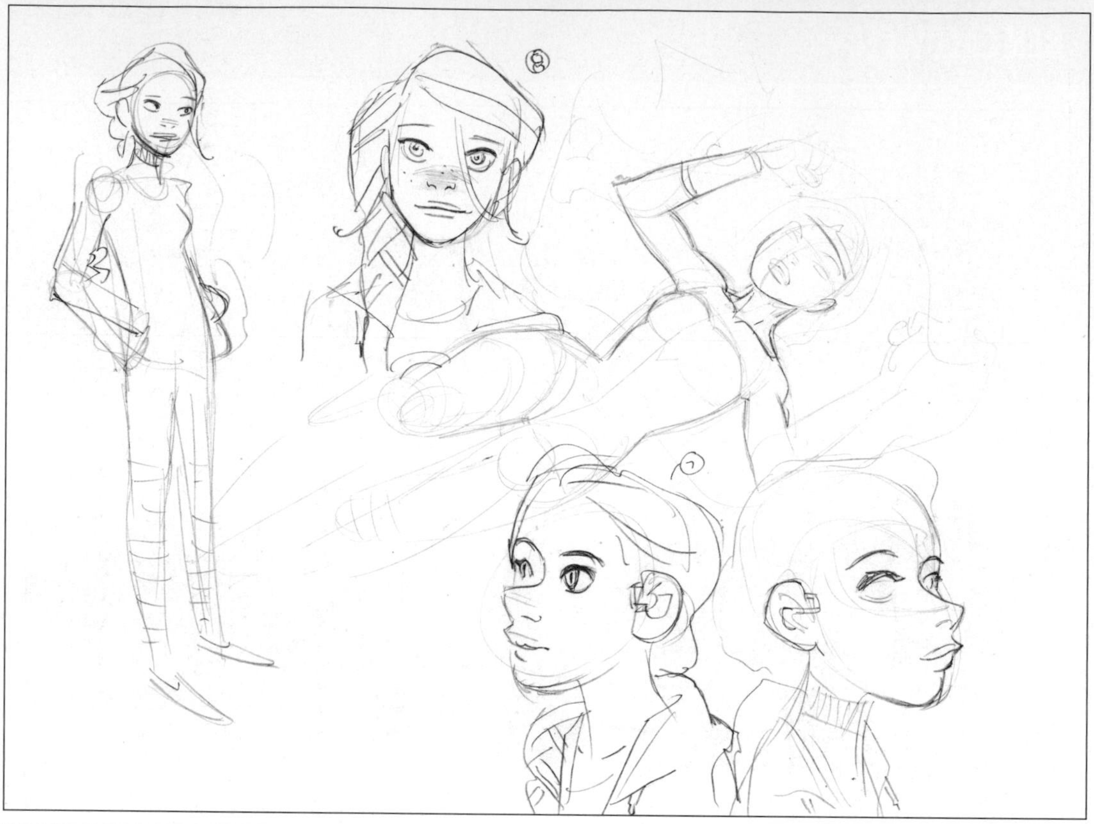
8
7
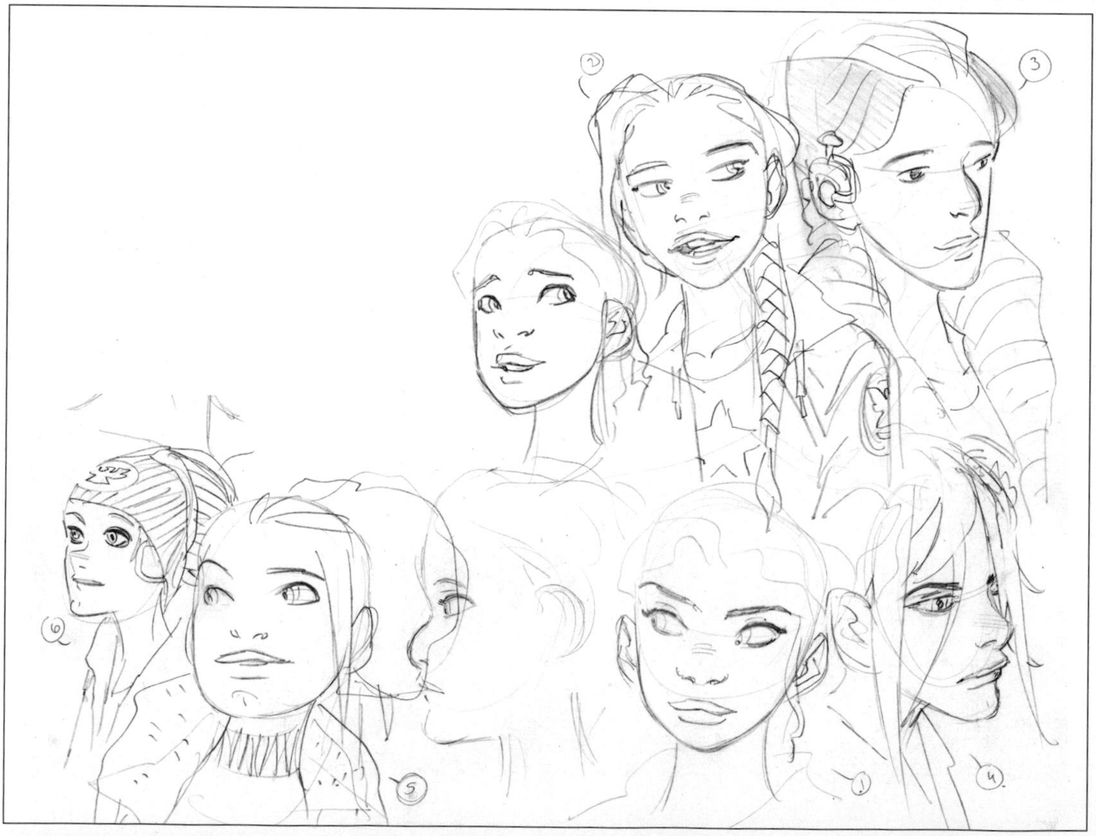
2
3
6
5
1
4

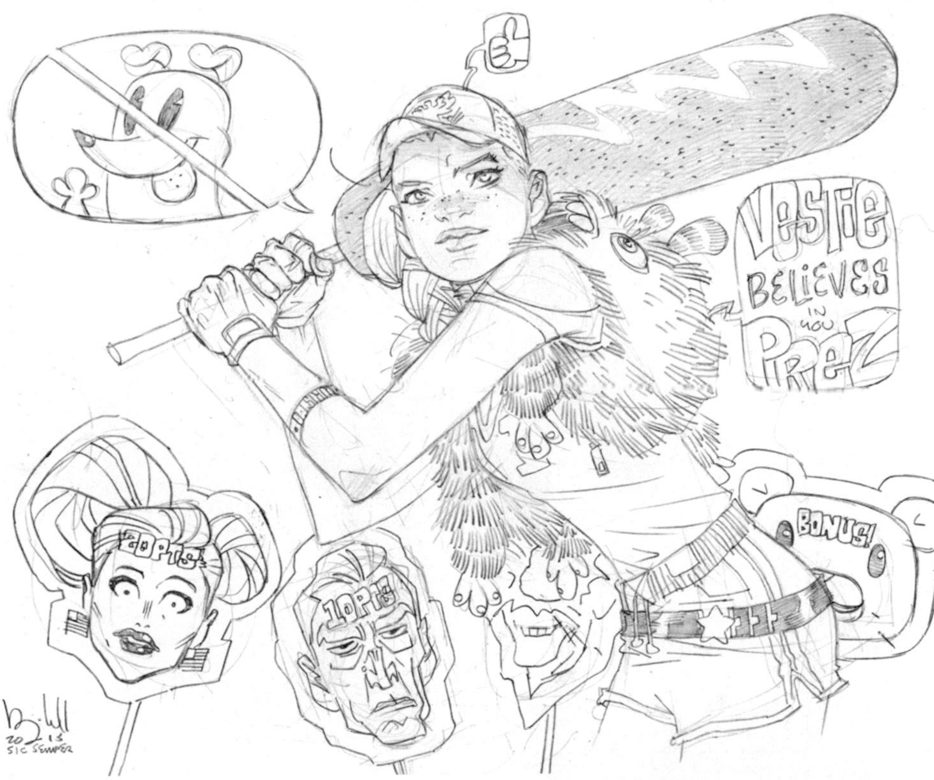

VESTIE BELIEVES IN YOU PREZ
BONUS!
2013
SIC SEMPER

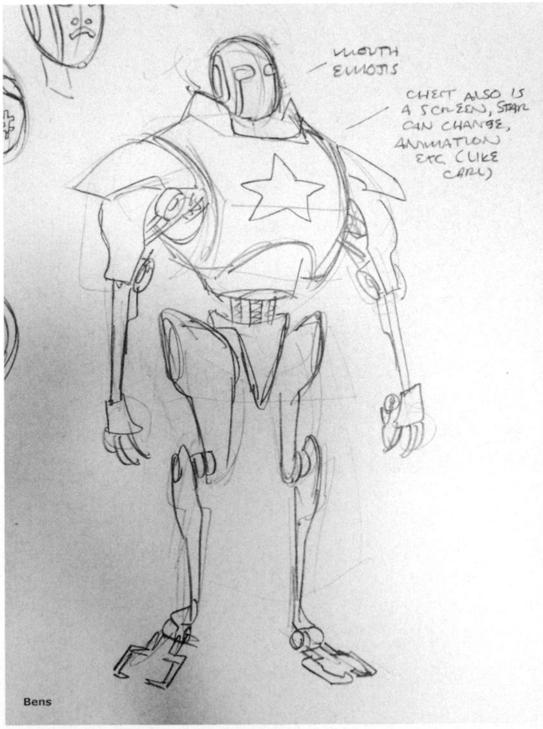

MOUTH EMOJIS
CHEST ALSO IS A SCREEN, STAR CAN CHANGE, ANIMATION ETC (LIKE CARL)

Bens

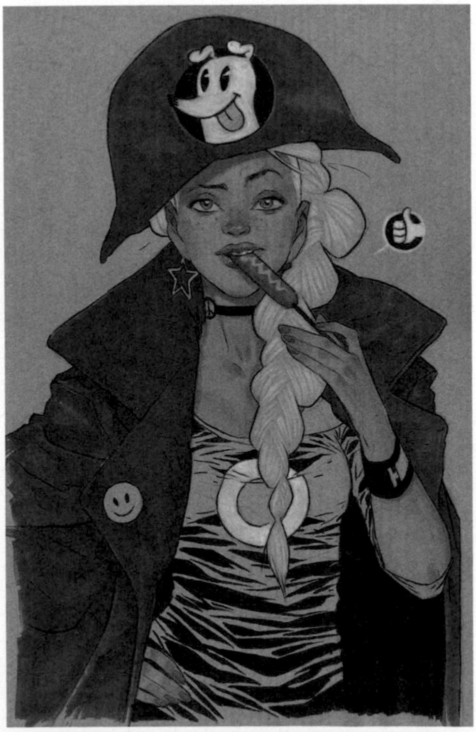

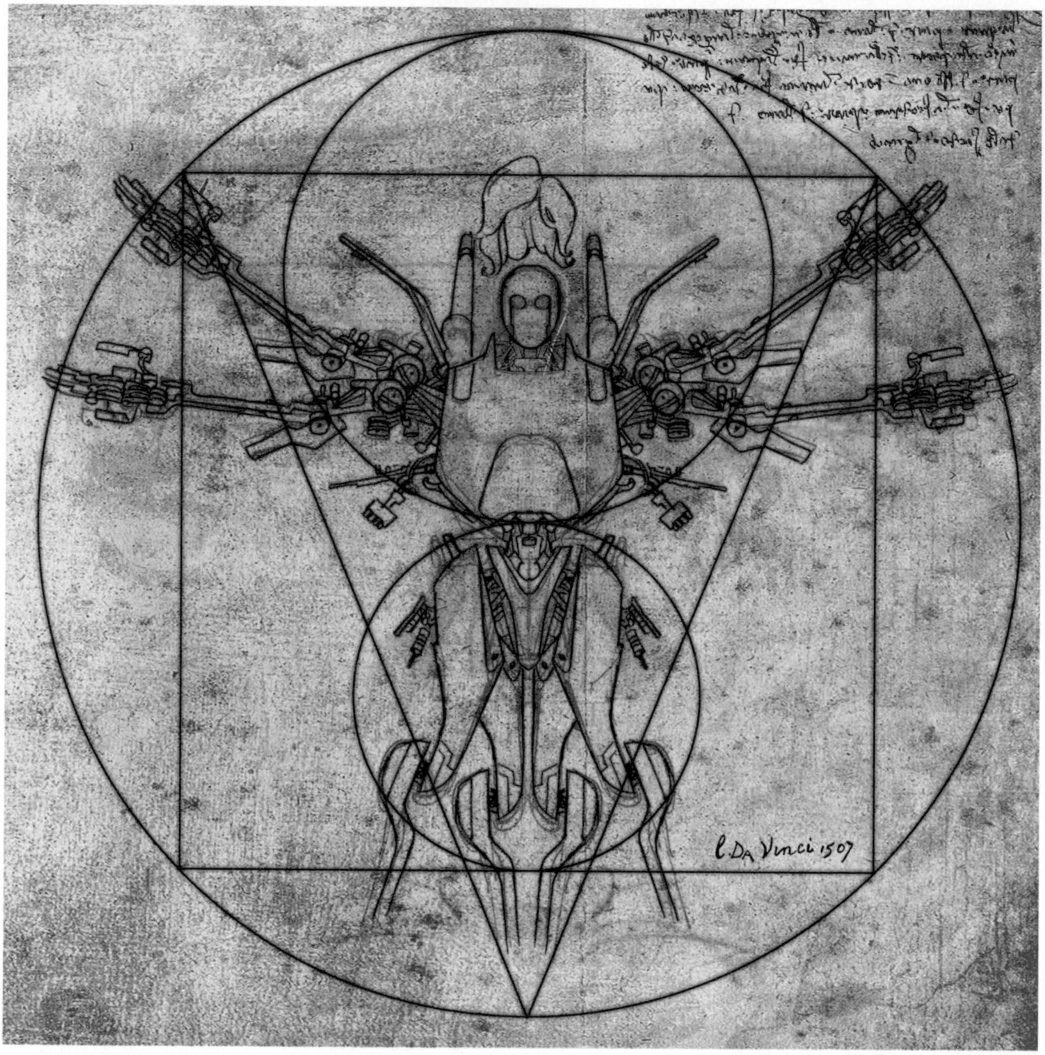
L.DA Vinci 1507

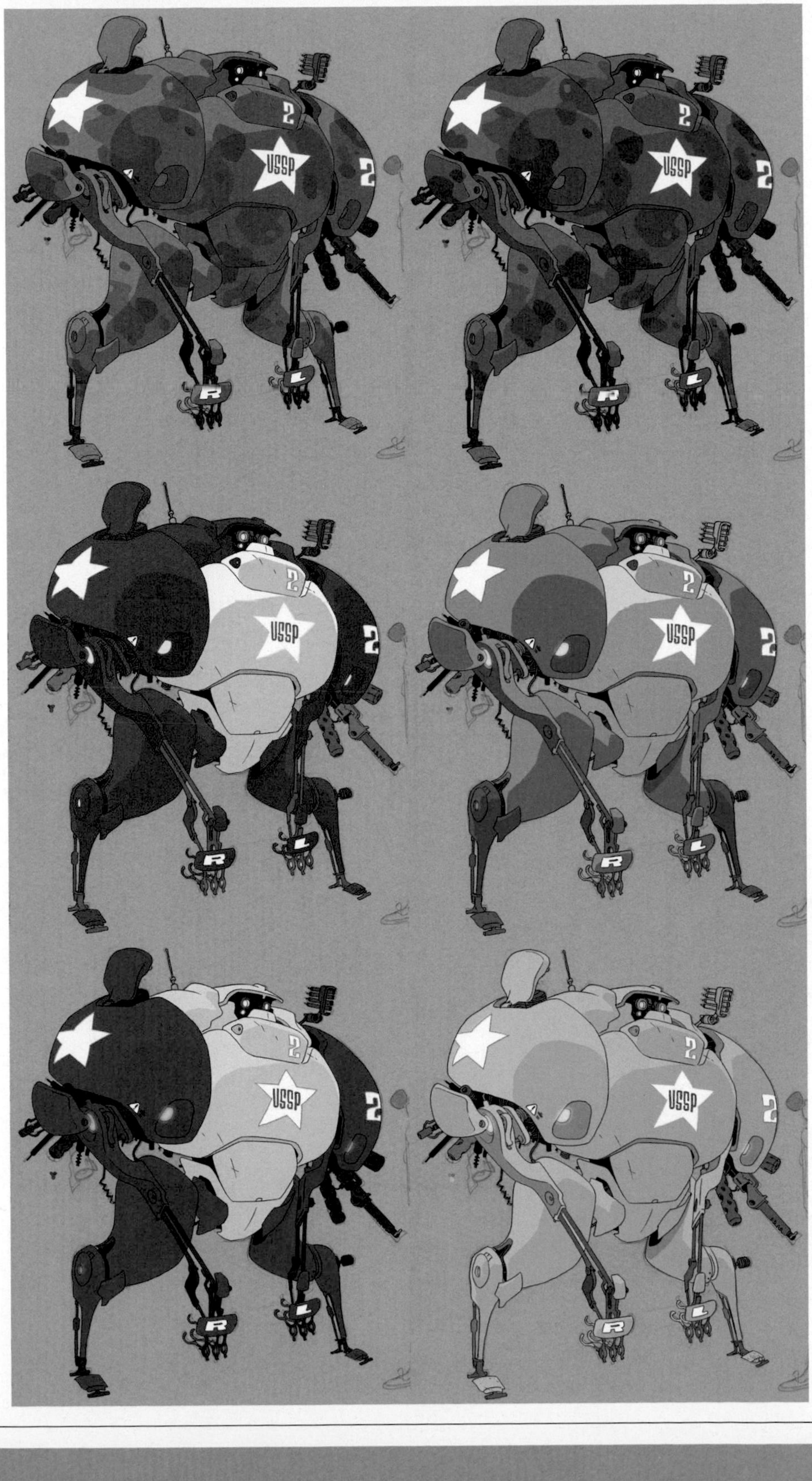
2
USSP
2
R
L

PRESTON RICKARD

SENATOR GEORGIE LONGWATER

WAR BEAST

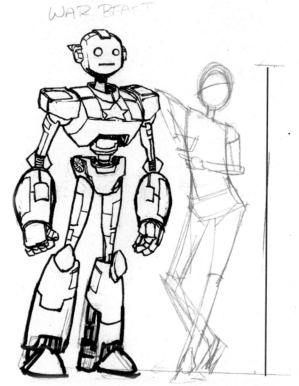

FRED WAYNE

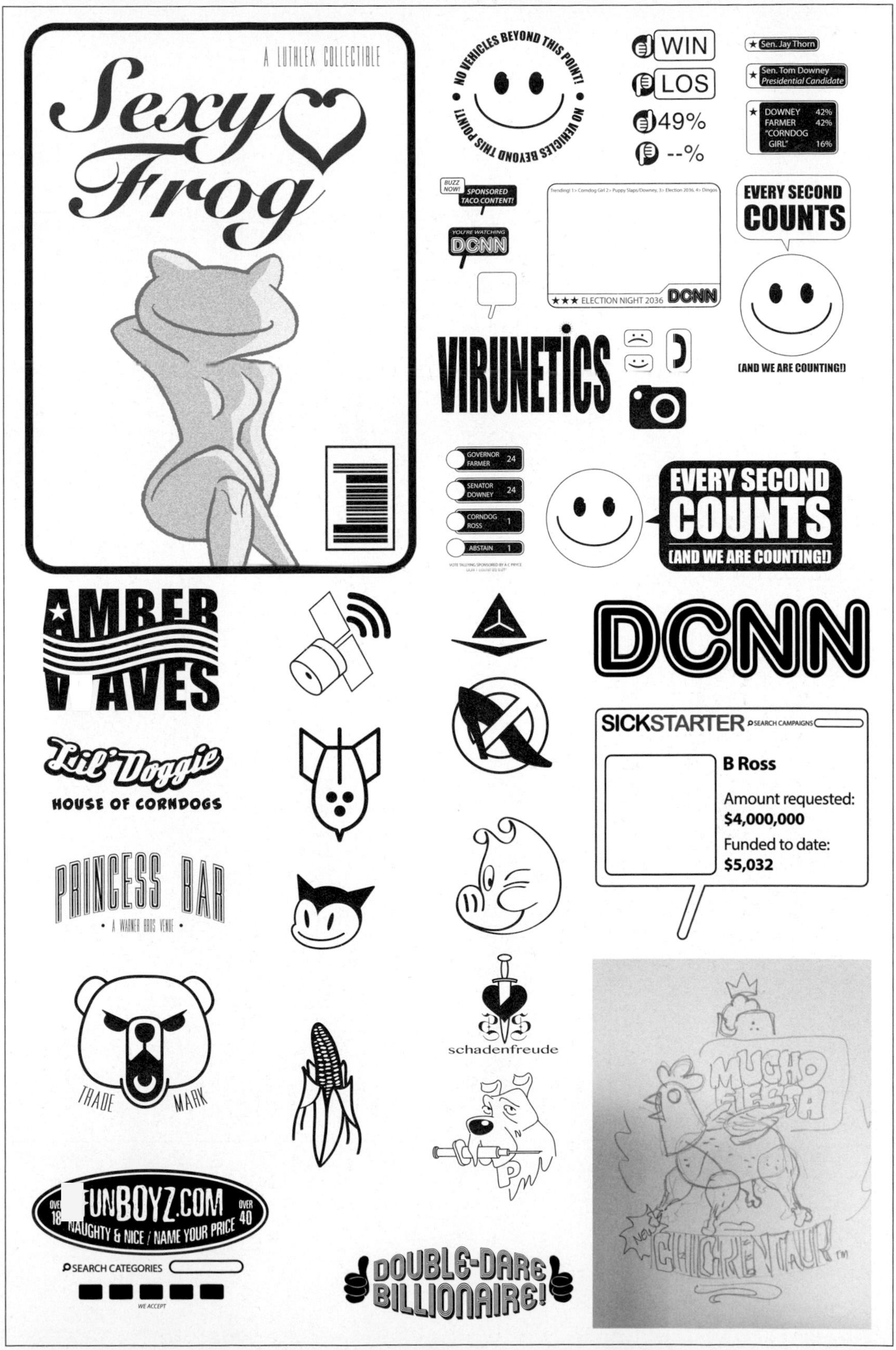
A LUTHLEX COLLECTIBLE
Sexy Frog
NO VEHICLES BEYOND THIS POINT!
NO VEHICLES BEYOND THIS POINT!
WIN
LOS
49%
--%
Sen. Jay Thorn
Sen. Tom Downey
Presidential Candidate
DOWNEY 42%
FARMER 42%
"CORNDOG GIRL" 16%
BUZZ NOW!
SPONSORED TACO CONTENT!
YOU'RE WATCHING
DCNN
ELECTION NIGHT 2036
DCNN
EVERY SECOND COUNTS
(AND WE ARE COUNTING!)
VIRUNETICS
GOVERNOR FARMER 24
SENATOR DOWNEY 24
CORNDOG ROSS 1
ABSTAIN 1
EVERY SECOND COUNTS
(AND WE ARE COUNTING!)
AMBER WAVES
DCNN
SICKSTARTER
SEARCH CAMPAIGNS
B Ross
Amount requested:
$4,000,000
Funded to date:
$5,032
Lil' Doggie
HOUSE OF CORNDOGS
PRINCESS BAR
• A WARNER BROS VENUE •
TRADE MARK
schadenfreude
MUCHO FIESTA
NEW
CHICKENTAUR TM
FUNBOYZ.COM
OVER 18
OVER 40
NAUGHTY & NICE / NAME YOUR PRICE
SEARCH CATEGORIES
WE ACCEPT
DOUBLE-DARE BILLIONAIRE!

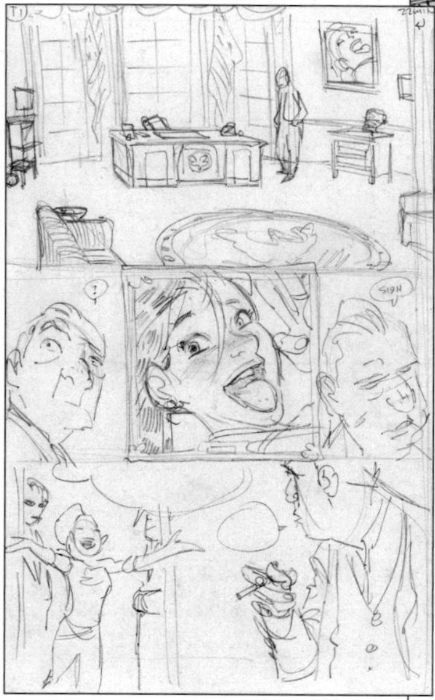
?
SIGH

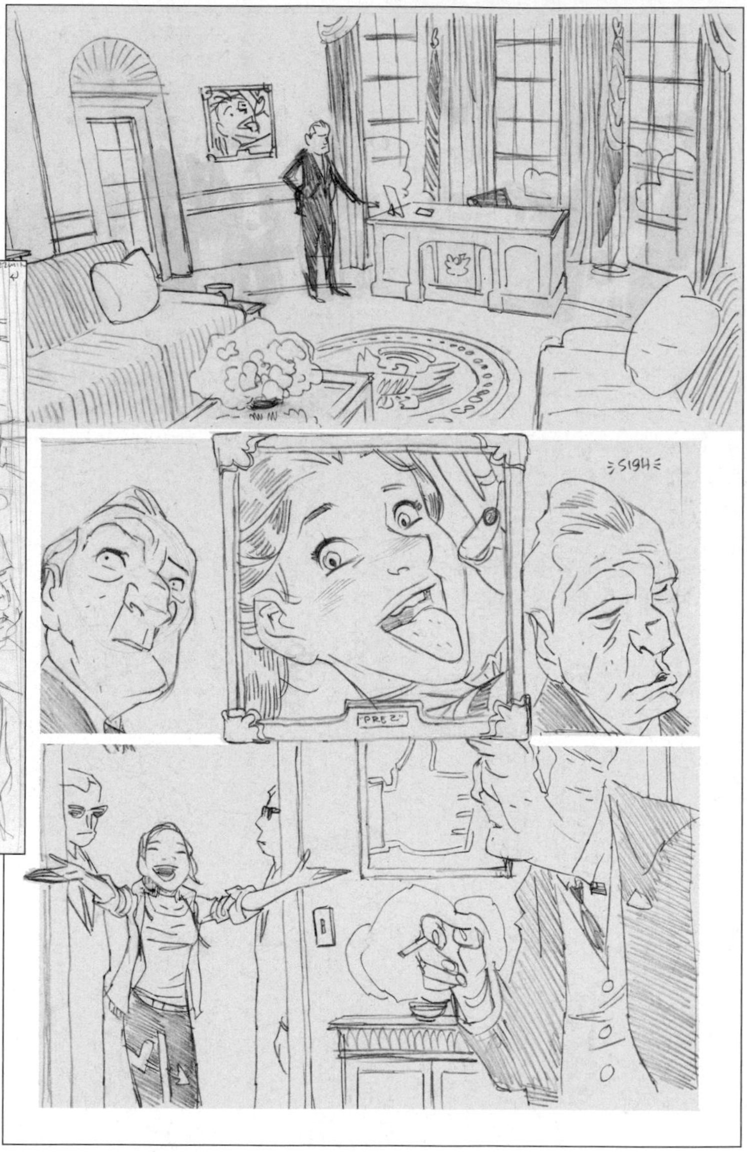
SIGH
"PREZ"

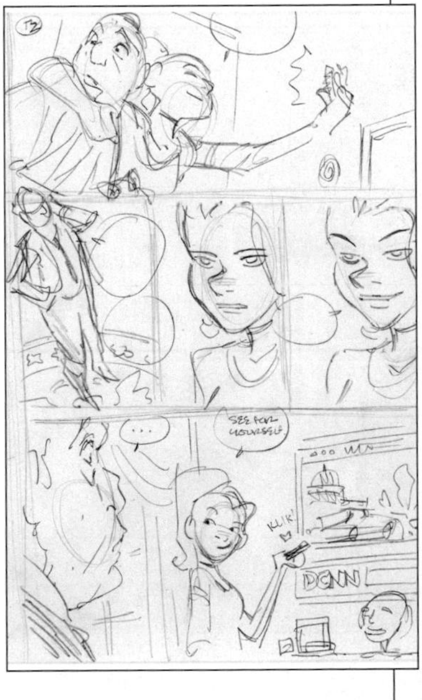
SEE FOR YOURSELF
KLIK!

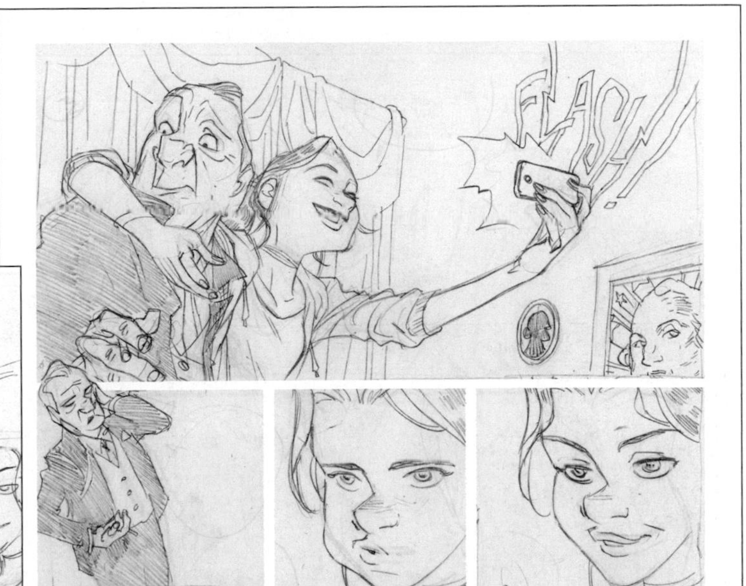
FLASH!
SEE FOR YOURSELF
KLIK!

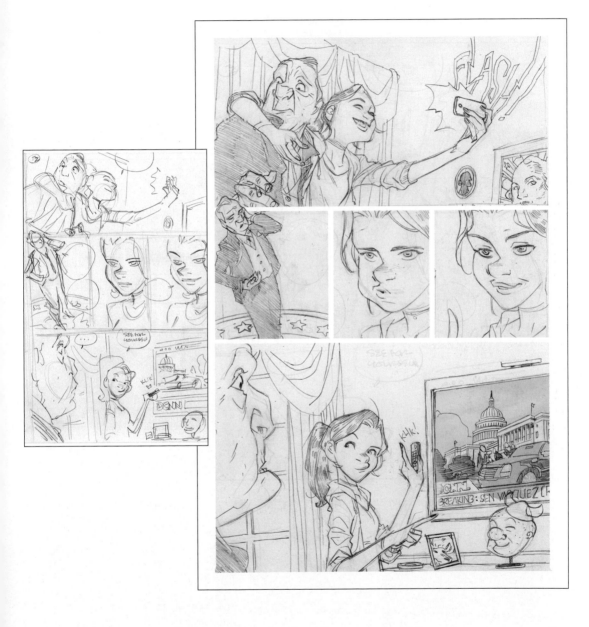

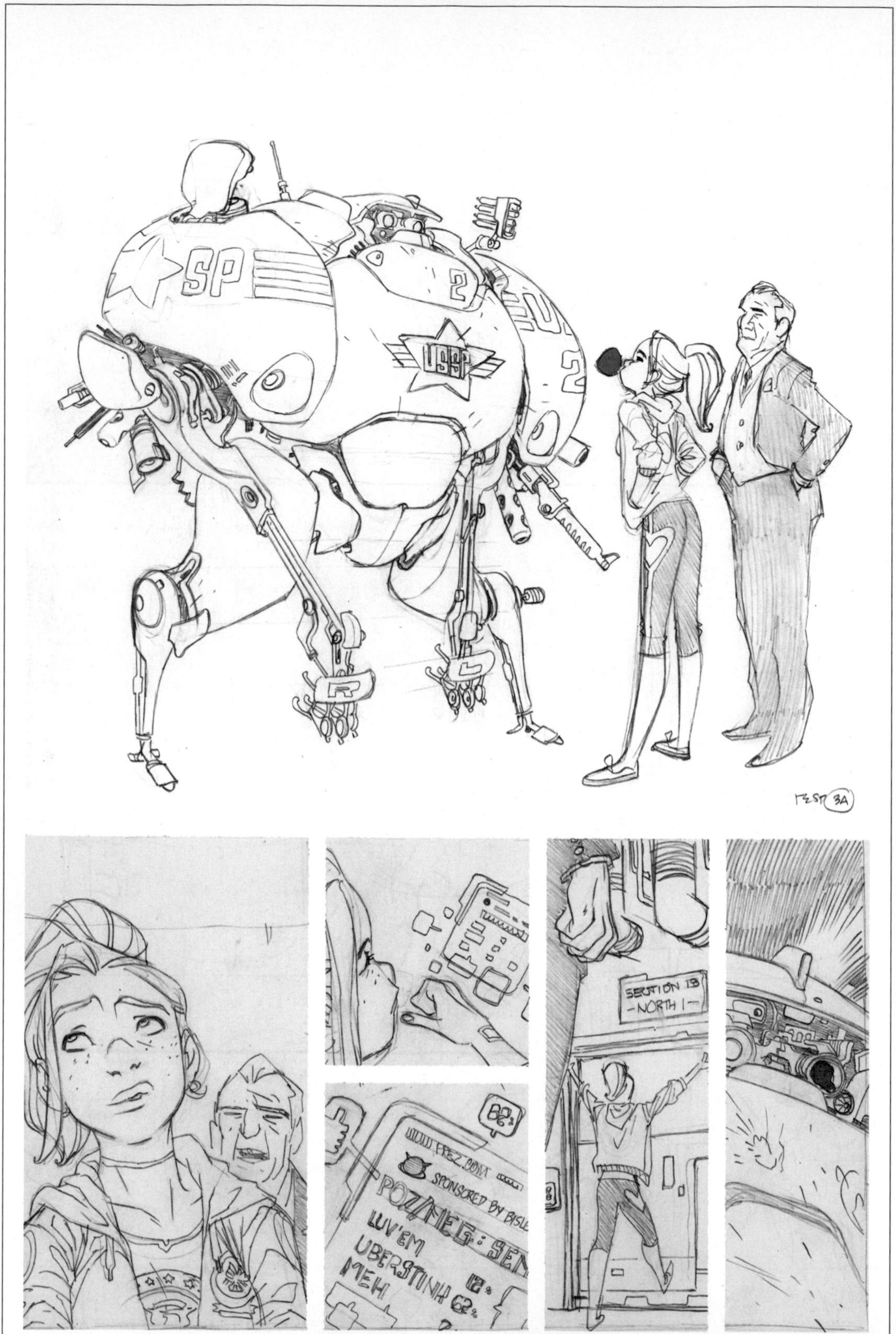

SP
USSP
2
R
L
3A
SECTION 13
NORTH 1
WWW.FREZ.COM
SPONSORED BY
LUV'EM
UBERSTINK
MEH

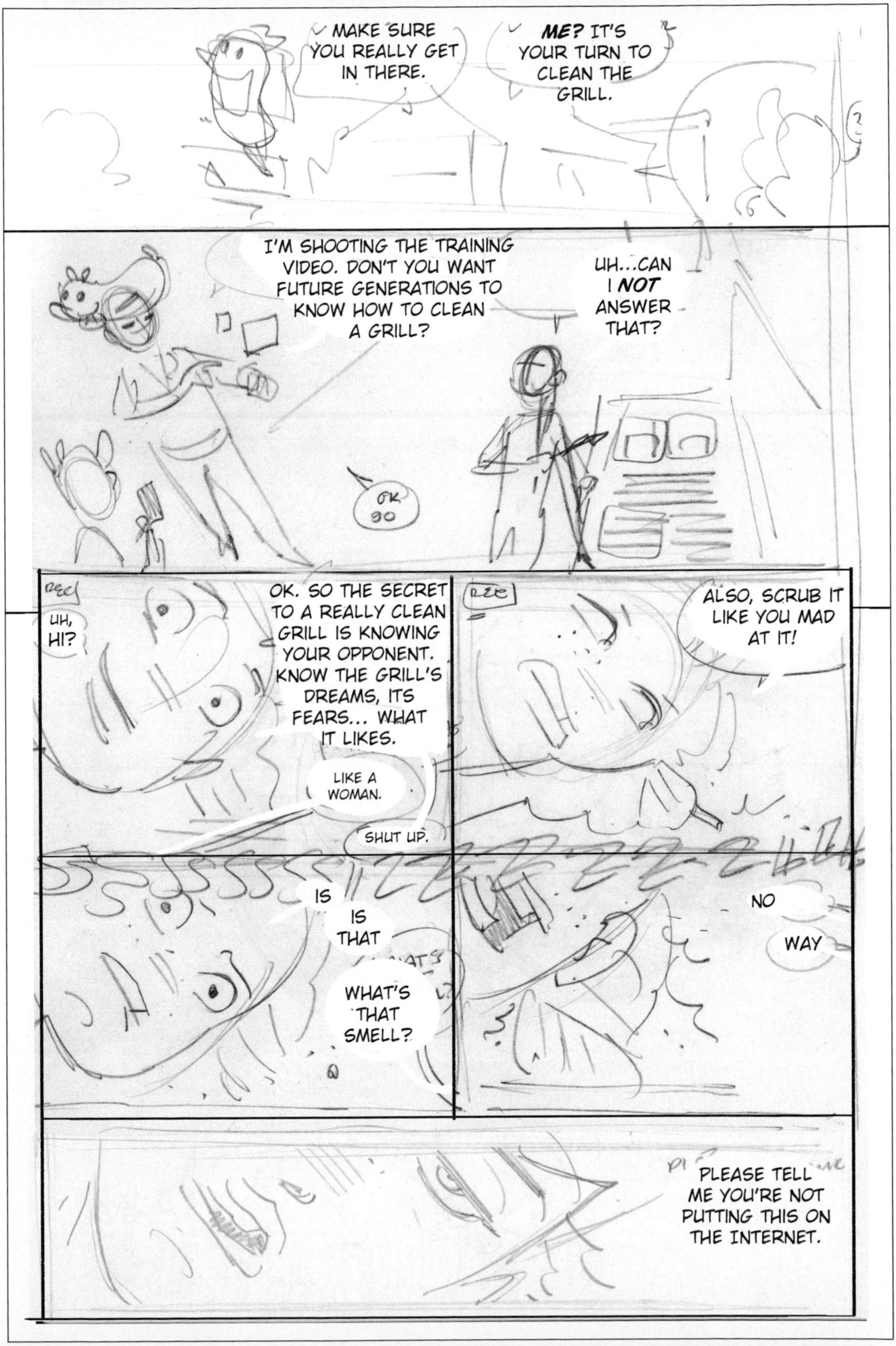
MAKE SURE YOU REALLY GET IN THERE.
ME? IT'S YOUR TURN TO CLEAN THE GRILL.
I'M SHOOTING THE TRAINING VIDEO. DON'T YOU WANT FUTURE GENERATIONS TO KNOW HOW TO CLEAN A GRILL?
UH...CAN I NOT ANSWER THAT?
UH, HI?
OK. SO THE SECRET TO A REALLY CLEAN GRILL IS KNOWING YOUR OPPONENT. KNOW THE GRILL'S DREAMS, ITS FEARS... WHAT IT LIKES.
LIKE A WOMAN.
SHUT UP.
ALSO, SCRUB IT LIKE YOU MAD AT IT!
IS
IS THAT
WHAT'S THAT SMELL?
NO
WAY
PLEASE TELL ME YOU'RE NOT PUTTING THIS ON THE INTERNET.

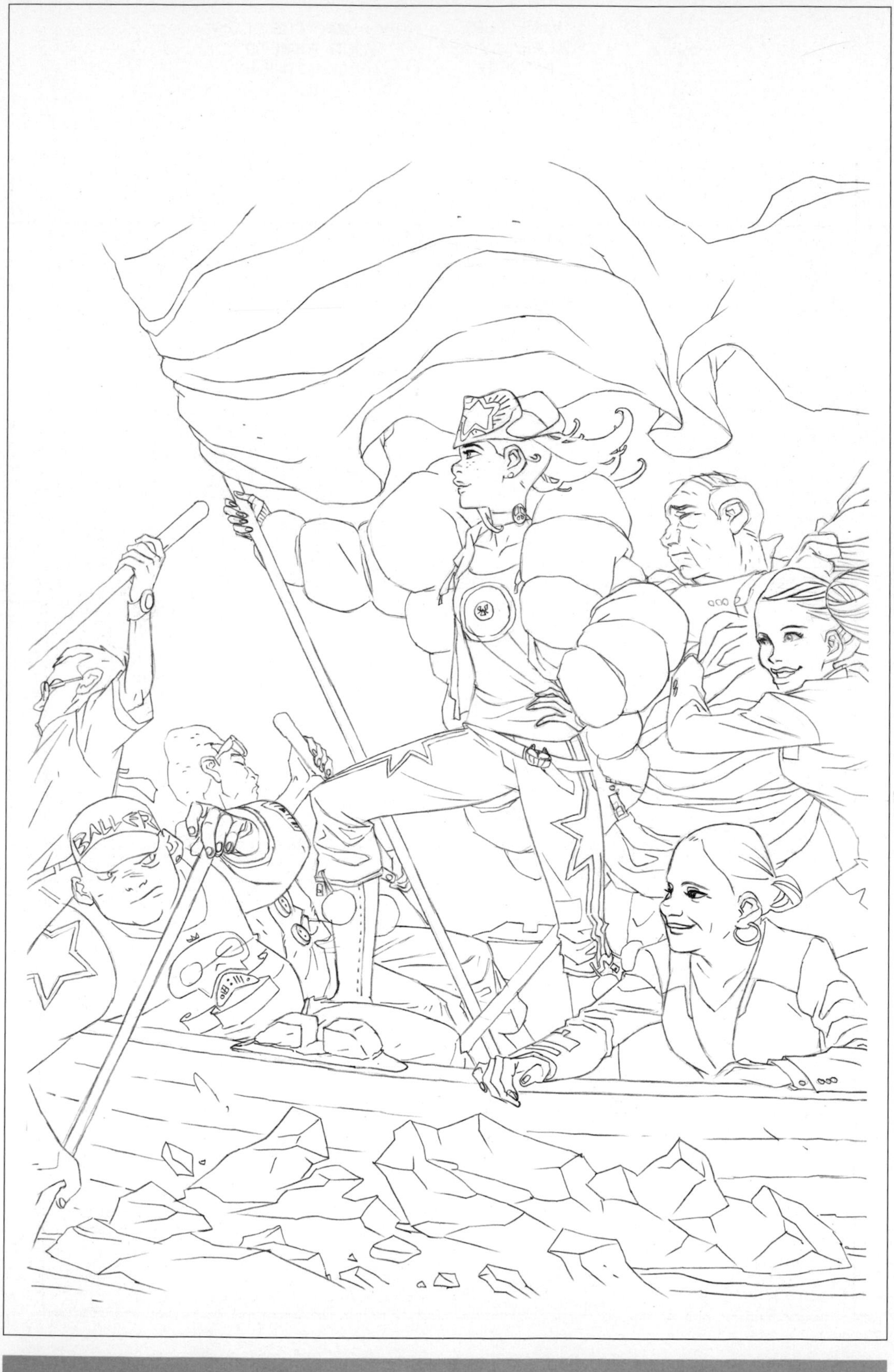
BALLER

UNUSED COVER IDEA FOR **PREZ #2**

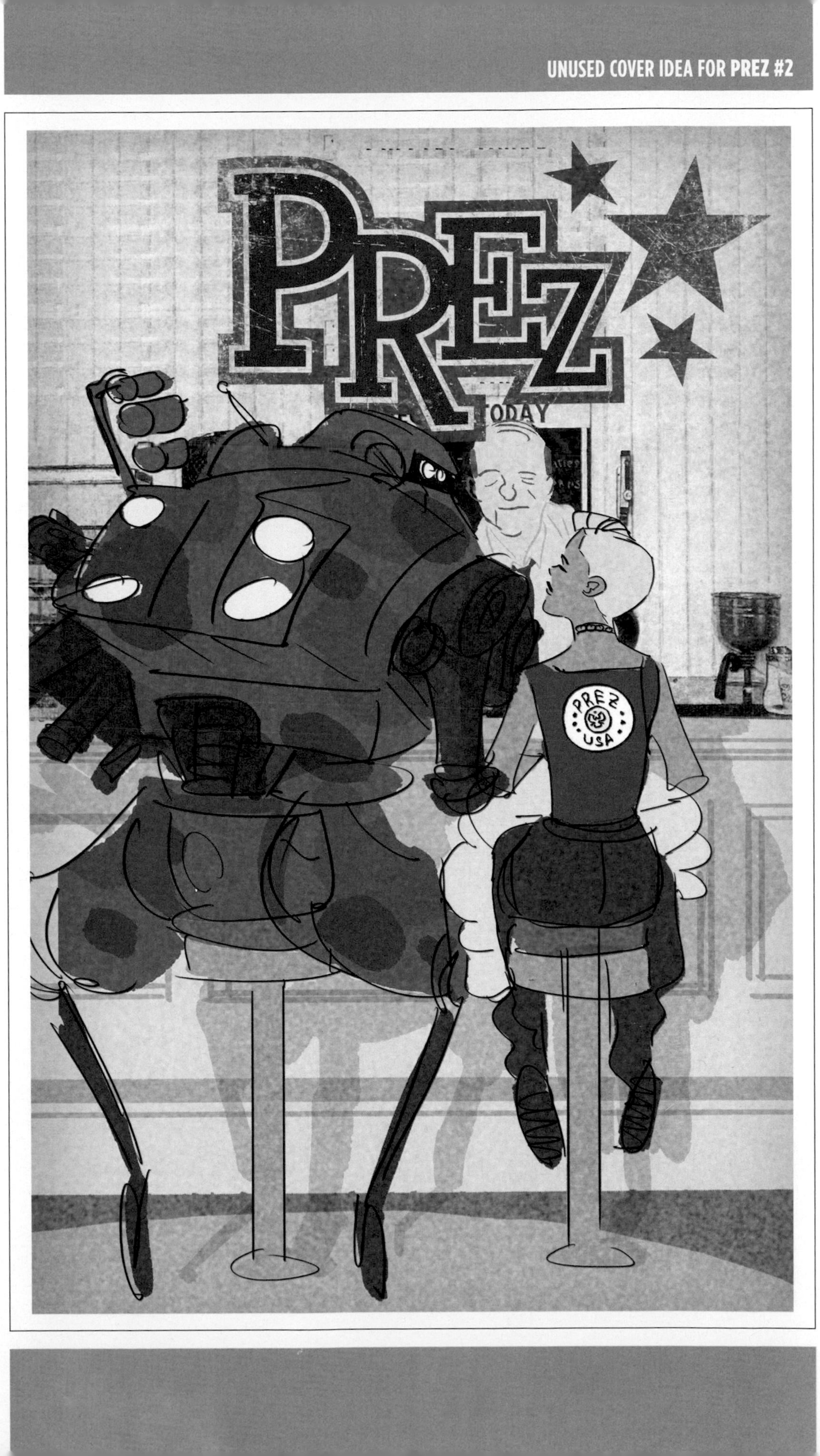
PREZ
TODAY
PREZ
USA

COVER SKETCH FOR PREZ #3

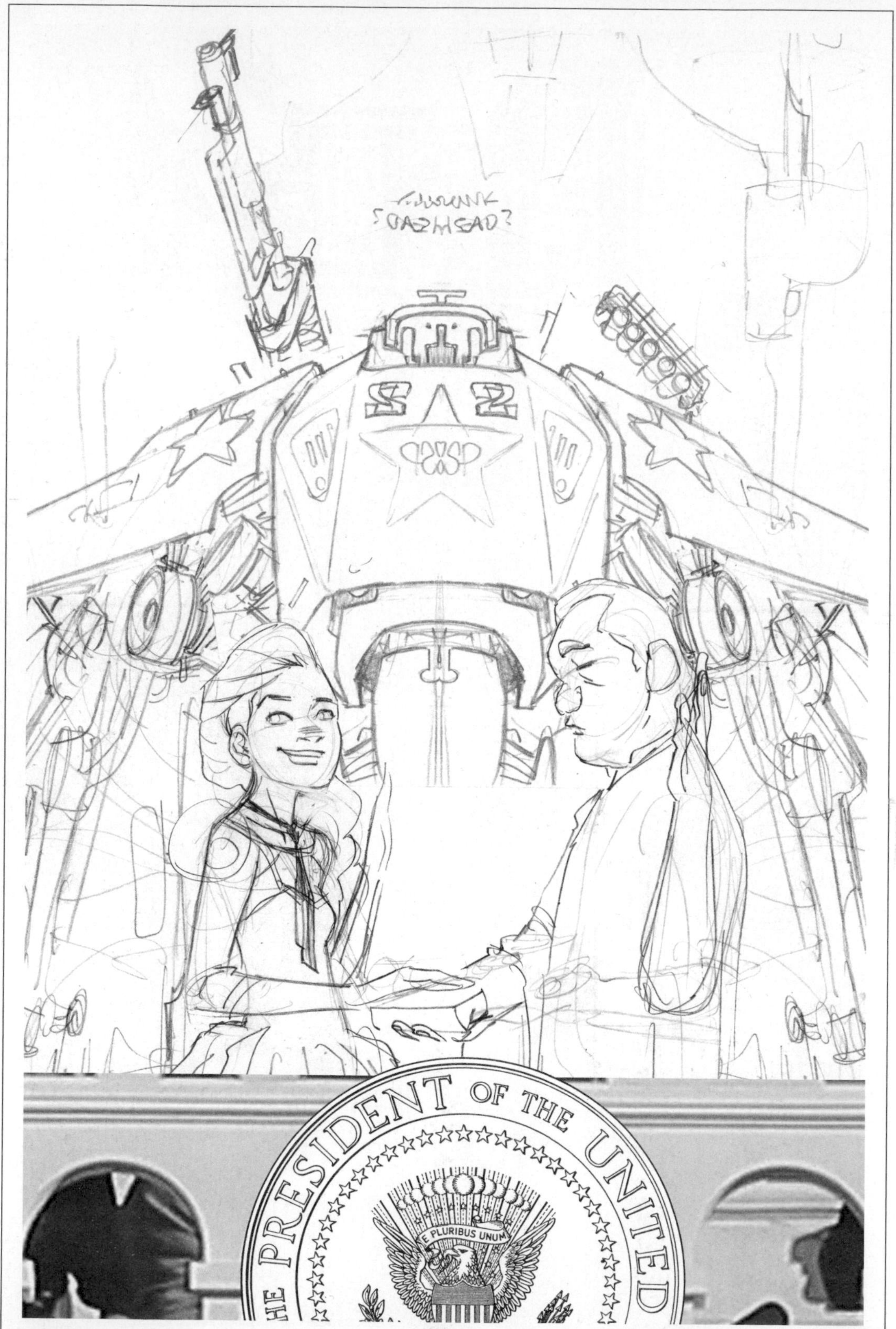
THE PRESIDENT OF THE UNITED
E PLURIBUS UNUM